The M & E Higher Business Education Series

Advanced Management Accountancy

General Editor

Dr Edwin Kerr
*Chief Officer, Council for National
Academic Awards*

Advisory Editors

K. W. Aitken
*Vice-Principal, South East
London College*

P. W. Holmes
*Director, Regional Management
Studies Centre, Bristol Polytechnic*

Other titles in the same series:
Economics for Business Decisions
Financial Accounting
Human Behaviour in Organisations
Personal Management
Practical Business Law
Quantitative Approaches in Business Studies

The M & E Higher Business Education Series

Advanced Management Accountancy

G.D. Donleavy
MA, FCCA, MICA(USA)
*Associate Member
of the Institute of Management Consultants
Senior Lecturer
School of Accountancy
National University of Singapore*

Macdonald and Evans

Macdonald & Evans Ltd
Estover, Plymouth PL6 7PZ

First published 1984

© Macdonald & Evans Ltd 1984

British Library Cataloguing in Publication Data

Donleavy, G.D.
   Advanced management accountancy—(The
M & E higher business education series)
   1. Managerial accounting
   I. Title
   658.1'511   HF5635

ISBN 0-7121-0181-0

Typeset 10/12 Times by
Mathematical Composition Setters Ltd,
Ivy Street, Salisbury, Wilts, England
Printed in Great Britain by
J. W. Arrowsmith Ltd, Bristol

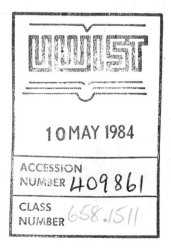

Foreword

In recent years business practice has been undergoing major and fundamental changes for a variety of economic, social and technological reasons. In parallel with these changes the developments of education for business at all levels have also been extensive and far-reaching. In particular this is true at the advanced levels for courses leading to (*a*) the first degrees of the Council for National Academic Awards and of the universities, (*b*) the higher awards of the Business Education Council and its Scottish equivalent, and (*c*) examinations of the relevant professional bodies. Many such courses are now offered in educational institutions which include the polytechnics, the universities, the colleges and institutes of higher education, the further education colleges and the Scottish central institutions. In addition to these developments in curricular design there have also been important advances in educational and teaching methods.

Macdonald & Evans already has a large involvement in meeting the needs of students and staff in business education through its BECBOOK and HANDBOOK series. It has now decided to complement these with its Higher Business Education series.

The series is intended to be one of major educational significance which will cover all important aspects of higher business education. It will be designed for students and staff use with all of the advanced courses at all of the educational institutions mentioned above. Each book will have both a planned part in the series and be complete in itself and, in it, a thematic and problem-solving approach will be adopted, thus bringing a body of theory to bear on business problems—a major feature of the whole series.

The editorial team have chosen authors who are experienced people from technological institutions and from professional practice and will collaborate with them to ensure that the books are authoritative and are written in a style which will make them easy to use and will assist the students to learn effectively from such use.

The editorial team will welcome criticisms on each of the books so that improvements may be made at the reprint stages to ensure a closer achievement of the objectives of the books and the entire series.

Edwin Kerr
General Editor

Preface

In the field of management accountancy, many of the textbooks that dominate the market currently are written in the United States, with American students and practitioners in mind. American terminology differs significantly from British. British stocks are American inventory, British shares are American stock, British debtors are American receivables and British gearing is American leverage. Such differences in usage can be confusing.

The American approach to examinations is also rather different from that of the British. In American examinations high priority is given to the criterion of objective verifiability. This results in a focus on practical calculation problems and multiple choice tests. British colleges, universities and professional bodies, however, have been less concerned with objective verifiability hitherto than with conceptual understanding of underlying principles and issues. Discussion questions are common and the belief in uniquely correct answers rare. This difference of approach is important and a chief objective of the present book is to help students to achieve the required grasp of underlying issues and principles. Readers are asked to think about the meaning of what they read, not merely to apply accounting rules. Very few previous textbooks on the subject in question have had this focus.

Accounting texts are apt to be filled with procedure, arithmetic and even algebra, to the detriment of the student who is verbally rather than numerically oriented. In the present volume, such students are borne in mind throughout and there is on the one hand less emphasis on calculation and, on the other, much more on interpretation than in most other books. It is obvious that an accountant must be able to handle numbers, yet most books take such ability for granted rather than assisting its development. The present book aims to make numbers serve principles, especially principles expressed in words rather than vice versa.

While the title of this book is *Advanced Management Accountancy*, it can be used as a first text. No previous costing knowledge is assumed. However, it is an *advanced* book. It goes deeply into key concepts such as opportunity costs, performance evaluation, control techniques and risk methods. It explores thoroughly areas of student difficulty such as process costing, variance analysis and risk in capital expenditure appraisals. Its ten chapters are carefully divided into sections in order to be compatible with a one-year, eighteen-month or two-year course. Two teaching weeks are the absolute minimum period necessary for most college or professional students to master the material in one chapter.

A subtitle for the book might be "a conceptual approach," since experience shows that students respond to being asked to consider the kinds of topics raised in the discussion questions sections that follow each chapter on the roots and implications of the subject. Only when they can visualise or verbalise a topic are such students ready to crunch numbers. In my experience, the proportion of such British and Commonwealth students in accounting classes has since 1975 been steadily rising—a side-effect perhaps of the economic recession, which possibly has led more and more non-mathematically gifted students into the real or supposed security of an accounting career. This book is targeted particularly at such students.

I regard management accountancy as an art rather than a science, and this view suffuses the entire book. The misleading impression of accuracy that numbers convey is periodically stressed and the reader's attention is drawn to the qualitative aspects of judgment and evaluation. The centre of management accountancy is, it is argued, (in Chapters 1 and 10), the art of evaluation, whereas most current textbooks state or assume that the subject's centre is *providing data to assist in management decision-making*. Such a focus on decision-making lays the new accountant open to being required to produce figures and data in order to support a decision already taken by the boss. A focus on evaluation, however, has a better chance of developing the prospective management accountant's intellectual integrity. The accountant in industry and commerce needs a sense of independent judgment no less than does his colleague in a professional office. Such a sense is hampered rather than helped by undue focusing on the assisting of decisions, although decision accounting will always be a key activity of any foreseeable management accountant. This book is the only one whose explicit focus is on evaluation rather than decision-making, but decision-making is certainly given its due and very considerable place.

Management accountancy is a subject with the most elastic of boundaries. By the widest definition it includes not only costing, budgeting and decision accounting but operational research, systems analysis, applied economics and financial management, plus behavioural aspects of accounting and social accounting too. This book addresses itself to all of these areas, but only in so far as they are closely and directly relevant to those questions of evaluation that are indisputably the province of the management accountant. The attention given any one of these areas may need to be modified in any future editions of the book in order to reflect a changing consensus as to their significance in management accountancy.

A book with the word "Advanced" in the title might be expected to be replete with footnotes and citations of leading contributors to the field. The choice is whether explicitly to acknowledge leading contributions by name or to incorporate such work implicitly. Since the present volume will be used in some quarters as a first textbook on management accountancy,

I decided to eschew explicit citations in the interests of greater student comprehension, although this was not an easy decision to make.

The aim throughout has been to take an average student from the basic rules of costing to the most advanced aspects of decision accounting and evaluation, so that he or she may emerge with a deep and thorough comprehension of the current art of management accountancy.

Thanks are due to the Association of Certified Accountants and the Institute of Cost and Management Accountants for permission to reproduce (in Appendixes IV and V) a wide selection of the questions set in their examinations up to the end of 1982.

I should like also to acknowledge my gratitude to my history teacher at school, Mr C.H.C. Blount, for his example in indexing and organising material, and to my colleague, Dr H.L. Jensen, for discussing and clarifying various difficult and ambiguous areas.

My principal debt, however, is to Mrs G.F. Levy who typed, sub-edited and generally assisted in the production of the typescript against demanding deadlines and from not always legible handwritten copy.

This book is dedicated to my wife Lilian.

1984   GDL

Contents

List of Illustrations

CHAPTER ONE

Fundamental Issues and the Manufacturing Account

We think in generalities but we live in detail.
Whitehead

OBJECTIVES

(*a*) To demonstrate the relevance of first-year studies of bookkeeping and financial acounting to costing and management accountancy.

(*b*) To explore the costing use and management accounting qualities of the final accounts in general, and the Manufacturing Account in particular.

(*c*) To introduce and convey an understanding of the most fundamental costing terms.

THE CATEGORIES OF ACCOUNTING

Financial accounting

Financial accounting is the collection, review and adjustment of data in the books for the purpose of presenting final accounts to particular types of user, including the Board of Directors, the Annual General Meeting of the shareholders and the Inspector of Taxes. The final accounts consist of the Income Statements, the Sources and Applications of Funds Statements and the Balance Sheet. For a company engaged in making and selling articles, the Income Statements are the Manufacturing, Trading and Profit & Loss Accounts. Financial accounting's objective is to present a true and fair view of company income, funds and financial position at regular intervals of no longer than a year. This objective does not imply that those who consult final accounts put the true and fair view they are given to any specific use. There is in particular no implication that the user is going to read the accounts to help him/her decide whether to buy or sell shares in the firm. Many users of final accounts will in fact be contemplating just such a decision, but assisting such users is not the chief aim of financial accounting in such accounts. The document that financial accounting helps produce and that does have this aim is the prospectus which is issued when a company invites investors to subscribe to its shares. The prospectus will quote extensively from recent years' final accounts and include a forecast of future income. However, forecasting is not the business of financial accounting. Moreover, the final accounts required in a prospectus will not be amended from their pristine "true and fair view" even if such amendment might assist investors to decide whether or not to buy shares in the company. Financial accounting is purely a reporting activity that has to conform to the rules of statute law, the standards of the accounting profession and, in many countries, also to stock exchange regulations.

Costing and cost accounting

Cost accounting is another reporting activity with the objective of establishing a true and fair view of past, present and expected future costs of products made, services supplied and departments organised by the firm's management team. Financial accounting is concerned largely with past activity; cost accounting is not so restricted. Cost accounting data may be derived directly from the books or may instead be built up from cost-books kept in parallel with the traditional books, depending on the system employed (*see* pages 4ff.). Data are required to identify the costs of running particular areas of the firm's activity such as the accounts office. These would involve ascertaining such things as the electricity costs incurred by the accounts office. The traditional books would have a single electricity account in the nominal ledger for the whole firm. The cost-books would tell us how much of the total electricity cost is attributable respectively to the accounts office, to the sales office and to each of the other user departments. Other costs would be similarly analysed and apportioned to departments. We would then be able to work out how much it costs to run each department. Any statement that informs us how much something costs is a costing statement.

Costing is the activity of finding out (and clearly presenting) how much something costs. Cost accounting is costing which uses double-entry book-keeping as the basis for drawing up schedules showing the cost of any part of the firm's activities.

Management accounting

A broad definition of management accounting is all accounting activity not clearly within the definitions of financial or cost accounting. Accounting activity is defined for the purposes of this book as: the collection, arrangement and presentation of information about monetary flows and values to enable a *judgment* to be made about such flows and values.

Still widely accepted among accountants is a far narrower definition of management accounting as: the production and presentation of information to business managers in such a way as to enable them to make *decisions* about the optimum allocation of the firm's resources among competing potential user departments, activities or products.

The narrower definition stresses decision-making, the broader one making judgments. Decision-making involves choosing between alternative courses of action and acting on that choice. Making judgments means evaluation—taking a view about the picture a report gives of the items depicted; and while such evaluation may cause decision-making, it need not always do so. For example, a report may show that product X is making slightly better profits than had been forecast. The report is merely attention directing. It necessitates no decision. The manager reading the report may "decide" to take no action, but he is not required to make any decision at all. In this book we adopt the broader definition. When the narrow definition is to be highlighted, we shall use the term "decision accounting" to emphasise the fact that the accounting activity concerned is aimed at enabling a decision to be made. We use the term "management accountancy" to mean *all* the arts involved in accounting activity, whereas by management account*ing* we mean the relatively mundane actions of collection, arrangement and presentation of the relevant data. The distinction between the two is comparable with the distinction between authorship and writing—the former involves a range of talents, the latter only a small number of mechanical skills. This book aims to help produce management accountancy talent in the reader. It employs management accounting skills in a range of techniques as a prime means of achieving that aim.

FINAL ACCOUNTS AS MANAGEMENT ACCOUNTING

The end-products of financial accounting are the final accounts, which should give a true and fair view of the firm's income flow, funds flow and state of affairs. Management accounting has been said above to produce information enabling a judgment to be made. If the final accounts already give a true and fair view, what further judgment can be made? Judgments on the following is the answer.

(*a*) Does the firm seem to be controlling its costs in relation to its income?

(*b*) Has the firm sold more than in previous years?

(*c*) Are net profits rising in proportion to the rise in sales income?

(*d*) Is the firm becoming more indebted to lenders?

(*e*) Is the firm pursuing profit at the expense of solvency?

(*f*) Are funds largely generated from profits?

(*g*) Are dividends to shareholders keeping pace with profit growth?

(*h*) Is the firm investing adequately in fixed assets for future production?

(*i*) Is the firm's production improving?

(*j*) Is the firm satisfactorily handling the effects of inflation on its operations?

These questions, which all involve accountancy judgments, are questions of performance evaluation, the topic examined in Chapter 7. Performance evaluation is management accountancy rather than management accounting. It involves the analysis and interpretation of figures and the clear presentation of qualitative conclusions in verbal reports. Management accountancy is, in essence, the art of evaluating numerical data and presenting them in such a way as to convey a clear and deliberate message.

THE MANUFACTURING ACCOUNT

Introduction
The reader is assumed to possess a grounding in financial accounting. We therefore begin our exposition of management accountancy by focusing on one of the products of financial accounting—the Manufacturing Account. This focus is appropriate for the following reasons.

(*a*) The Manufacturing Account is the first of the final accounts prepared at the period end.

(*b*) That account is a prototype of all other costing statements.

(*c*) It exemplifies all the three types of accounting described above.

(*d*) It is often given insufficient attention in financial accounting courses.

(*e*) It provides an excellent foundation for conveying basic principles of management accountancy but is seldom so used in previous textbooks.

Interpreting the manufacturing account
The table below shows a summary of the AB Company's manufacturing account. A detailed manufacturing account would list all the types of materials purchased, all the grades and skills of labour employed and all the categories of factory overheads incurred during the year. A summary is more useful for our purposes, especially for the particular purpose of interpreting the significance of the information given in the account.

In financial accounting terms, all the entries in the left of the two columns in the account come from the ordinary books and the account is itself in the nominal ledger. All the entries are debits to the Manufacturing Account except those marked *, which are credits. The other side of the entries is in the accounts named by their entries: stock, purchases, direct labour, factory overheads and work-in-progress. Each of those accounts is built up by debits through the year (creating cash-book or bought ledger as appropriate), and at the end of the year the total net debits are transferred to the Manufacturing Account.

In costing terms, the Manufacturing Account shows the reader the total net cost of the goods produced by the company in the year. The cost of goods produced is shown to be £1,096,000. If the total number of articles produced in the year was 54,800 we can work out the *average* production

AB CO. LTD: SUMMARY MANUFACTURING ACCOUNT
FOR THE YEAR ENDED 31ST DECEMBER

	£000	£000
Materials		
Opening stock of raw materials	44	
Purchases of raw materials	600	
Materials available in the year	644	
Less closing stock of raw materials*	(60)	
Raw materials used		584
Conversion		
Direct labour	240	
Factory overheads	288	
Conversion costs		528
Total manufacturing cost		1,112
Opening work-in-progress	80	
Less closing work-in-progress*	(96)	
(Increase) Decrease in work-in-progress		(16)
Net cost of goods produced		1,096
(carried down to Trading Account)		

cost per article as:

$$\frac{\text{Total cost of goods produced}}{\text{Total number of goods produced}} = \frac{£1,096,000}{54,800} = £20$$

The total cost of goods produced is different from the total manufacturing cost by the amount of increase in the value of work-in-progress (semi-finished goods) over the year. Opening work-in-progress is added to manufacturing cost because it represents the cost of materials and work done *last* year on goods which are finished for sale this year. Last year's cost is relevant to this year because we want to know the cost of *all* the goods we finish producing this year including those on which work began last year. Conversely, we deduct the value of closing work-in-progress from total manufacturing cost because the semi-finished goods in stock at the year end will not be finished and sold until next year. The total materials, labour and overheads we used in finding the total manufacturing cost includes the materials and work done which has been absorbed by articles we shall not finish making until next year, and therefore the cost incurred this year for those articles should be excluded from the cost of goods manufactured this year. The cost of goods manufactured therefore can be seen to mean the total cost of goods the company *finishes making* this year.

The total manufacturing cost consists of two parts: the materials and the work done with those materials. The cost of materials used in producing finished goods is our opening stock plus purchases in the year less materials in stock at the year end (which we shall not be using until next year, so they must be excluded from *this* year's materials cost). Raw materials include not only the basic ingredients put through the production process but any materials or components added during assembly, such as batteries during car assembly, glaze during pottery making, or polythene wrapping at the end of baking bread in factory conditions. Any material or component that forms part of the product eventually sold to the customer is a raw material, irrespective of the stage it enters the production process. In particular, wrapping for food, bottles for liquids, and cases for such goods as typewriters are raw materials and should always therefore be charged to the materials section of the Manufacturing Account. Materials such as packaging boxes and crates are usually overheads because they are either returnable, or reusable by the manufacturer or not part of what is actually sold to the customer.

Work done to the raw materials consists of converting the raw materials into finished goods. The cost of the work is therefore called "conversion cost" and it includes processing, assembling, baking, wrapping and all the other means whereby raw materials become saleable finished goods. The conversion cost is not confined to the wages and related costs of the labour force directly employed in manufacturing and includes such overheads as electricity, factory rent and machine repairs that are necessary for the conversion work to be done. Among the overheads will be indirect materials, such as cleaning materials, which do not form part of the product but are necessary in manufacturing it. Indirect labour, such as the cost of employing people to maintain and repair the machines, is also an overhead. Only factory overheads are charged to the Manufacturing Account.

Office costs, costs of selling and delivering the final product, advertising and all the other costs of running a company which do not *directly* spring from the manufacturing process in the factory are charged in Trading, Profit & Loss Accounts, not in the Manufacturing Account. Such costs will be considered when the company is deciding on the price it should charge for its product, as it wants to be sure that the price covers *all* its costs, but the Manufacturing Account is *not* meant to give a total cost of running the company, only a factory cost of manufacturing its products. Thus the final figure in the Manufacturing Account should not be thought of as the total cost to be recovered from the customer for each article sold but only as the total production part of the cost—and this will always be considerably less than the full total cost to be recovered because of office and other non-factory costs.

All costing statements resemble the Manufacturing Account in the following respects.

(*a*) They identify the materials and conversion elements of total costs.
(*b*) Overheads are separately identified within conversion costs.
(*c*) Costs attributable to future periods are excluded.

(*d*) The final figure is the purpose of the statement—the cost of the products made, in the case of the Manufacturing Account.

Management accountancy impinges on the Manufacturing Account in both its presentation and its interpretation. In financial accounting textbooks the Manufacturing Account is often shown as a long list of items subtotalled for materials used, then for so-called prime cost of production, and finally for total manufacturing cost. The presentation adopted in this book differs:

(*a*) in being a summary rather than a list;
(*b*) in subtotalling conversion costs but not prime costs; and
(*c*) in distinguishing between manufacturing costs and cost of goods manufactured quite clearly.

The presentation used in the table above exemplifies an essential part of management accountancy—namely, the need to present data succinctly (i.e. without unnecessary details—additional information can be given in appendixes if desired), clearly (avoiding terms such as "prime cost", which are somewhat ambiguous and archaic) and logically (so that the data lead neatly and naturally to the final figure which should be the key figure the reader wishes to know). Bookkeeping is a matter of accurate and thorough recording, financial accounting a matter of conforming to statutory and professional disclosure requirements first and conveying meaningful information second; whereas management accountancy is centrally concerned with conveying useful and meaningful statements to its readership, so that clear, succinct and logical presentation is of the first importance. The reader must be able to read and understand a management accountancy statement without needing a glossary of accounting jargon. Hence it is important to group items under easily understood headings in order to minimise the number of items actually presented and, as far as possible, to ensure that the statement speaks for itself.

The Manufacturing Account in the table on p. 5 speaks for itself in the following ways.

(*a*) It clearly shows the total costs of goods produced.
(*b*) It shows the relative insignificance of movements of work-in-progress levels (only £16,000 out of a net total cost of £1,096,000).
(*c*) It shows the importance of raw materials in the final cost, representing over 50 per cent of the final total.
(*d*) It shows that factory overheads cost rather more than direct factory labour, which raises the question of whether the overheads are capable of being reduced.
(*e*) It conveys all the above four pieces of information at the first reading and without the need for further interpretation. In this respect, the

Manufacturing Account could be said to interpret itself, as should any principal statement in management accountancy.

BOOKS FOR COSTING PURPOSES

Costing data
All costing statements are built from four types of costing data.

Cost elements
These consist of materials, labour and expenses, depending on the intrinsic nature of the cost. Thus:

(*a*) materials are anything that can be stacked, stockpiled or stored. Examples are food ingredients, metals, component parts, paper, stationery and liquids;

(*b*) labour refers to the cost of employing and paying any human being in any period. Labour consists of directors, managers, full-time and part-time employees of the company. The company is responsible for the welfare, safety and income tax of its employees. Employees are paid under employment contracts and never invoice the company for their salary and wages; and

(*c*) expenses are all costs not clearly labour or materials. The symptom of an expense is an invoice. All expenses are traceable to an invoice. Plumbers are an expense if they are outsiders who invoice the firm but are labour if they are employees of the firm who submit time-sheets internally rather than invoices as the basis of their remuneration. Expenses are like materials in that both are invoiced but unlike materials in that the supply in question, such as electricity, cannot be physically stacked or stored.

Costing records must clearly distinguish cost elements.

Capital and revenue costs
Cost elements can be of either a capital or revenue nature.

(*a*) Revenue costs are running costs and relate to the normal operations of the firm. Revenue costs are debited to Manufacturing, Trading, Profit & Loss Accounts at the year end, while stockpiles of materials of a revenue cost nature are entered in the Balance Sheet as the Current Asset—Stocks & Work-in-Progress. An item is a revenue cost if it is consumed during the year in the process of making goods sold or running the office. Raw materials, factory and office labour costs and expenses, such as rent, transporting articles for sale and electricity, are all revenue costs.

(*b*) Capital costs are costs of acquiring and improving productive assets. The costs of buying land, buildings, machinery and furniture are capital costs. These assets are all a type of material in that they can be physically stockpiled. What distinguishes them from revenue cost materials is that they are not consumed or sold as part of the articles or services offered by the company to its customers. Furniture is a capital cost to most businesses, but to a shop selling beds, desks, tables, chairs, etc., furniture is a revenue cost because furniture is what is sold to customers.

Many firms treat materials like nuts, bolts, furniture coverings, cleaning materials and stationery items as revenue costs forming part of the Current Asset of Stocks, although these items are not part of the product sold to customers. Strictly speaking, these items are capital costs. However, since their economic life may not be greater than a year and their value is relatively small, it is considered acceptable to treat the items as revenue items. This means their cost is debited to Manufacturing, Trading, Profit & Loss Accounts rather than to Fixed Asset Accounts. If they were debited to Fixed Asset Accounts at the date of purchase, then depreciation of 100 per cent would be charged to the Manufacturing or Profit & Loss Acount at the year end, as the items have such a short life. Charging the initial costs directly to the final revenue accounts has the same effect as charging 100 per cent depreciation and wastes less time and space. For most practical purposes we may consider short-lived capital costs as indistinguishable from revenue costs.

The costing records must clearly distinguish revenue from capital items. However, the same applies to the financial accounting records because of the provisions of statute law. In this case then, no extra records are needed for costing purposes beyond those provided by the ordinary ledgers kept by financial accounting staff.

Cost centres
The Manufacturing Account is drawn up for the company as a whole. If a firm has three factories, it could draw up manufacturing accounts for each one, then aggregate the data in preparing the company-wide account. In this case the company would be making each of its three factories a separate cost centre subsidiary to the chief cost centre, which is the company itself. The factories could be further analysed into departments, the departments into sections and the sections into teams—each with its own operating costs. The team as a cost centre is part of the larger cost centre section. The section is part of the still larger cost centre, department, and so forth up to company level.

A cost centre is any part of the company *authorised* to incur costs on behalf of the company. The sales function is a cost centre consisting of smaller centres such as regions. Regions may consist of areas and areas of sales teams. If the sales representatives are authorised individually to incur a given amount of entertaining, travel and subsistence expense, each sales representative is a cost centre.

The financial accounting books may well be kept on a company-wide basis. Costing may well require the identification of costs incurred at cost centre level inside the company. This requirement means records must be kept at cost centre level. If such records are built into the financial books, the system is said to be "integrated". If the records are outside the financial books, but reconciled regularly to them, the system is called "interlocking". With interlocking systems double entry occurs on both in the financial books and independently in the cost-books. For example, a purchase of raw materials is entered in the financial books as a debit to the purchases account in the nominal ledger and a credit to the cash-book or the supplier's account in the bought ledger. The same transaction is independently written into the cost-books as a debit to the cost centre (or centres) receiving the material and a credit to a cost control account. With an integrated system the transaction is debited to the cost centre(s) and credited to the cash-book or supplier's account.

Costing records must clearly identify cost centre costs. This is especially important for budgeting, which is always done on a cost centre basis.

Cost units

A cost unit is the item sold to customers appropriately measured. Cans of baked beans, car batteries, bottles of beer, aeroplanes and houses are all examples of cost units easily identified, since it is obvious that the product is being sold to the public in units —by the can, bottle, etc. Other products are sold by the tonne, metre, litre, square metre, cubic centimetre, gallon, kilogram, troy ounce, etc. In such cases the cost unit is tonne, metre, litre, etc.

The service industries also have cost units, but their identification is slightly more difficult. The basis of invoicing in many cases is the man-hour. Car repairs, auditors' fees, doctors' fees, and plumbers' and electricians' charges are usually based on the man-hours spent on the job concerned. Different grades of skill or responsibility give rise to different man-hour cost units. Thus an hour of an audit firm's partner's time is charged at a higher rate than an hour of a junior clerk's time, reflecting the difference in pay rate. Transport is bought and sold by means of tickets of some sort, but the ticket is not the cost unit because its only value is as a certificate of entitlement to transport. What the customer is really buying is passage from origin to destination. Measures of distance such as miles or kilometres form part of the cost unit. Measures of usage form the other part, such measures usually being per passenger. Thus a bus company's cost unit is the passenger-mile. Miles alone would not enable the company to form an intelligent pricing policy. If it costs a bus £5 per mile (after including and apportioning all the running costs of the company, as we shall learn to do in Chapter 2), the bus tickets must be priced to cover this cost. If one route has an average of two passengers, another an average of fifty, the first route has to obtain £2.50 from each passenger to cover its costs but the second need charge only 10p. Thus cost units have to be based on usage as well as distance.

Electricity is invoiced on the kilowatt-hour, a combined measure of usage and electrical power. The reader should try to take a number of products and services with which he or she is familiar and identify the cost units involved.

Arguably the chief objective of a costing system in a company is to identify the cost of the cost unit. For a company producing only one manufactured product, such identification is achieved in the Manufacturing Account. Multiproduct companies will need as many manufacturing account-style statements as there are products. Service industries have to use a rather different procedure, which we shall cover in Chapter 3. Clearly cost records must enable cost units to be clearly identified. Indeed, we can state that just as the physical product is the end-result of the manufacturing process, so the cost unit is the end-result of the costing process.

A physical analogy
Cost elements are comparable to the physical division of matter into animal, vegetable and mineral. Matter consists of these three states, often mixed in any single article. Similarly most products and services reflect a mix of cost elements.

The distinction between capital and revenue is rather similar to the physical distinction between solids and liquids. Solid objects are like capital in that they are separate, independent substances just as capital costs are separately represented by each machine, each item of furniture, each expansion project, etc. Revenue costs are like liquids in that they all mix together in two lakes, one being the Manufacturing Account, the other being the Profit & Loss Account. No such mixing at the year end occurs with capital costs, which are listed instead by type on the Balance Sheet as Fixed Assets.

Cost centres are comparable to the specialised organs of the body. The office is the brain, the factory the digestive system, the accounts function is the nervous system, money is like blood and enters all the cost centre systems with the board as the heart; while the marketing function is rather like the respiratory system—inhaling consumer needs and exhaling marketable products to satisfy the needs. Just as the bodily systems can be subdivided into their component subsystems, so larger cost centres can be subanalysed into smaller cost centres.

Finally, just as the systems of the body produce both waste products and useful ones (the work of the hands or the mouth), so the combined effort of the cost centres produces cost units and some waste matter.

Cost accounting systems

Interlocking accounts
Interlocking accounts involve the complete separation of the financial books and ledgers from the cost-books and ledgers. The financial books

follow the double-entry procedures the reader has learnt from his previous financial accounting studies. The cost-books and ledgers are also maintained under double-entry rules. To illustrate their operation we shall assume only one cost centre, which means our imaginary firm must be a small one with a little workshop and no separate office—probably a one-person business. Transactions are illustrated below by way of journal entries.

		Dr(£)	Cr(£)
1.	Stores	4,000	
	to Cost Control		4,000

Purchase of materials received into store.

		Dr(£)	Cr(£)
2.	Wages	5,000	
	to Cost Control		5,000

Gross wages and employers' social security burden paid in the period.

		Dr(£)	Cr(£)
3.	Expenses	3,000	
	to Cost Control		3,000

Electricity and other expenses incurred in the period.

		Dr(£)	Cr(£)
4.	Overheads	3,000	
	to Stores		500
	Wages		1,500
	Expenses		1,000
		3,000	3,000

Identification and transfer to overheads account of all costs not wholly and exclusively attributable to the production process (see Chapter 2 for a full explanation).

		Dr(£)	Cr(£)
5.	Work-in-progress	10,000	
	to Stores		3,500
	Wages		3,500
	Expenses		2,000
	Overheads		1,000
		10,000	10,000

Clearance of balances to work-in-progress in order to indicate value of work done on materials and the materials themselves.

		Dr(£)	Cr(£)
6.	Finished goods	5,000	
	to Work-in-progress		5,000
	Transfer of completed work to finished goods, at manufacturing cost.		
7.	Cost Profit & Loss Account	4,000	
	to Finished goods		4,000
	Transfer of cost of goods manufactured and sold to Cost Ledger's Profit and Loss Account.		
8.	Cost Profit & Loss Account	2,000	
	to Overheads		2,000
	Overheads not directly associated with production, such as selling costs transferred to Cost P.& L.		
9.	Cost Control	8,000	
	to Sales		8,000
	Sales income arising during the year.		
10.	*Sales*	8,000	
	to Cost Profit & Loss Account		8,000
	Clearance of sales account at the year end		
11.	*Cost Control*	2,000	
	to Cost Profit & Loss Account		2,000
	Clearance of cost-books' net profit to Cost Control to balance.		

The Cost Control Account is merely a receptacle for completing double entry rather like a suspense account and is not remotely comparable with such true control accounts in the financial books as the Bought Ledger Control. The Cost Profit & Loss Account has the same function as the financial books' Profit & Loss Account—that is, to disclose the net profits earned by the firm in the year. Financial expenses such as bank charges and such professional fees as audit fees may not be entered in the overheads account in the cost-books. This will cause the net profit shown in the Cost Profit & Loss Account to exceed that shown in the financial Profit & Loss Account. Reconciliation then would be effected by entering such expenses into the overheads account in the cost-books.

Interlocking accounts are seldom seen nowadays, as most firms large enough to employ both financial accounting bookkeepers and cost clerks are able to employ mechanised or computerised accounting systems which can easily handle integral accounting. There is rarely, if ever, a situation where costing records are wholly separated from the ordinary books. Instead, the books are kept on an integral basis which generates special costing records above and beyond those provided by the double-entry system. The time cannot be far in the future when costing syllabuses no longer require candidates to understand how interlocking systems work, but unfortunately that time has not yet arrived.

Integral systems

In exemplifying the workings of an integral system we shall imagine we are dealing with a firm possessing three cost centres: office, factory A and factory B. All purchase invoices are received and sales invoices issued from the office which also controls and handles all cash. Each cost centre will have its own nominal ledger, while the personal ledgers and cash-book are kept centrally. In each of the nominal ledgers there will be accounts for materials, labour (wages) and expenses. The two factories' nominal ledger will also have work-in-progress accounts to record the materials and conversion costs of semi-finished goods as they pass through to the finished goods state. Finished goods will be cleared to the Cost of Sales Account kept by the office. Final accounts are prepared in the office's nominal ledger. Office expenses are not directly associated with either factory's production but may be charged to the factories as overheads in the overheads account in each factory nominal ledger. The balances on the accounts in a factory nominal ledger can be listed at any time to make a cost centre manufacturing account. In such a case we must remember to exclude finished goods, as they belong in the Trading Account, which would be kept centrally.

Computerised accounting has made possible very sophisticated integral systems. All the things one might like to know can be coded into the accounts code. For example, when entering into the computer an invoice for materials purchased from a supplier, the accounts code for the invoice can be used to identify:

(*a*) all the cost centres (from the smallest to the largest) incurring the cost;

(*b*) the exact type of cost element, subanalysed by quality, grade, yield rate, etc.;

(*c*) (*i*) the cost centre for which the material is destined after being fully processed; or

(*ii*) the cost unit for which the material is ultimately destined;

(*d*) the official designation of the person authorising acceptance of the invoice; and

(*e*) the supplier of the goods and many other factors.

A simple sort program can be used to interrogate the computer to list all items entered in any given period with the same material quality code, or going to the same cost centre, or authorised by the same official, and so on. Sorting can be executed on any of the input code digits. Especially useful for costing is the facility to sort and list by cost centre. This is only possible, however, if a clear and orderly coding system is in operation and the computer operator codes input data correctly. Cost coding systems are discussed in more detail in Chapter 6, when we consider modern control systems.

SUMMARY

(*a*) There are three types of accounting: financial, cost and management. All are concerned with presenting data in order to enable the reader to evaluate them, but management accounting is more concerned with reader evaluation than are the other types of accounting. Management *accountancy* is like authorship, whereas management *accounting* is like the lower level skill of writing. Accountancy involves a depth of understanding simply not required in accounting.

(*b*) The final accounts are management accounts in that they enable a series of judgments to be made about performance. Evaluation of performance is accountancy rather than accounting.

(*c*) The Manufacturing Account is a product of financial accounting but shows many of the most important features of a management accounting statement and virtually all the key requirements of a costing statement. Particular attention was directed to the derivation of unit cost from the Manufacturing Account.

(*d*) Costing records need to identify cost elements, cost centres, cost units and to separate capital from revenue costs. These terms have been defined and exemplified. Cost records can be kept either on an interlocking or integral basis. Interlocking systems are wasteful and outdated in an age of computerised accounting. The more sophisticated the cost code, the greater the variety of costing information that can be extracted from the cost accounting system.

QUESTIONS

1. Contrast financial accounting with cost accounting and with management accounting.
2. Explain the difference between accounting and accountancy.
3. What do you understand by the word "evaluation"?
4. What is "accounting activity"?
5. What costing principles are shown in the Manufacturing Account?
6. Why are the financial accounting records not necessarily appropriate for costing purposes?

7. Which four cost characteristics must be identified by costing records?

8. Why is a salesman more likely to be a cost centre than is a book-keeping clerk?

9. What purpose is served by the Cost Control Account in an interlocking accounts system?

10. Explain why manufacturing cost, cost of goods produced and cost of goods sold will not usually be the same.

For calculation questions, see number 1 in Appendix V.

CHAPTER TWO

Cost Categories

With a knowledge of the name comes a distincter recognition and knowledge of the thing.

Thoreau

OBJECTIVES

(*a*) To realise clearly the nature and scope of direct costs.

(*b*) To acquire the ability to measure cost elements.

(*c*) To comprehend the difference between period costs and product costs.

(*d*) To appreciate the conceptual and practical frontiers between expenses and overheads.

(*e*) To understand how invoices billed to the firm are apportioned to its cost centres.

(*f*) To apprehend the treatment of service cost centres in product costing.

(*g*) To realise the importance of overhead recovery from the cost unit.

(*h*) To perceive the extent to which production losses are handled as expenses.

(*i*) To appreciate the importance of operating leverage.

DIRECT MATERIALS

Nature of direct materials

Materials we have defined already as anything that can be stored, stacked or stockpiled. Direct materials are those that form part of the finished product which is sold to customers. Direct materials include not only the raw materials entering into the start of the production process but all of the following.

(*a*) Any materials entering into production after the initial stage, e.g. glazing in the manufacture of pottery and crockery.

(*b*) Any fully finished components assembled into the firm's product, e.g. car batteries and radios assembled into the completed car.

(*c*) Any material used in production but wholly consumed or lost in the production process, e.g. fertiliser used in growing plants—the cost of pot plants sold should include the cost of fertiliser consumed by the plant.

(*d*) Any container sold with the final product, e.g. bottles for beer, cans for tinned food and drink, polythene for prepacked fruit, boxes for chocolates.

All other materials are indirect materials.

Levels of material and the product cost idea

Direct materials enter the company's premises, are inspected for quality and correct quantity, then put into store. In the Balance Sheet all direct materials in store, including finished components bought from outside suppliers, are aggregately described as "raw materials". "Raw" in this context signifies that the company has not yet begun any conversion work on the materials.

Materials are issued from the stores to the factory's production lines. Many manufacturing systems involve a sequence of several processes of conversion of raw materials into finished goods. Once materials pass from store to production, their costing state has changed from raw material to work-in-progress. Work-in-progress thus includes material whose conversion is just beginning and all materials on the production line whose conversion to finished goods is not yet complete. In costing terms the further on a material is in the production process, the greater is the proportion of conversion costs to basic direct material costs. The cost of a work-in-progress unit is composed of its material ingredients and also the cost of labour and expenses absorbed by the unit in the production process it has undergone so far. The costing technique applicable is explained in Chapter 3 when we examine process costing. Work-in-progress at the period end is represented in the Balance Sheet as a form of materials stock. It is important to realise that as materials emerge from a raw state to fully completed products, their cost will reflect a rising burden of labour and expenses. Thus, although work-in-progress is grouped as materials in financial accounting, it is composed of all three cost elements and not just the element of materials. The application of labour to raw materials "adds value" to the materials. Such added value is reflected in the price eventually charged for the finished product.

Materials fully converted by production are transferred from the factory into the finished goods store. At the point of transfer the stocks in question become finished goods, to be recorded as such on the Balance Sheet. Finished goods are completed cost units that have received their full complement of conversion costs. Being capable of being stacked, stockpiled or stored, finished goods are still materials; but they are materials whose cost reflects the importance of the labour and expenses absorbed throughout production.

We have said that direct materials include the containers sold with the product. In the case of finished goods put into store without such packaging, the finished goods in store are theoretically still at work-in-progress stage. In practice, however, such goods are treated as finished for financial accounting purposes, and any container stocks are included with finished goods in the Balance Sheet. For costing purposes the cost unit is not completed until the product it represents is in exactly the state in which it is to be sold. Packaging is not a selling or distribution cost to be charged to the Trading Account but a direct material to be charged to the Manufacturing Account, so long as the packaging forms part of the product sold. If packaging is for the convenience of the seller and is retained or destroyed by him before sale, such packaging is an indirect material to be classified with selling expenses and usually excluded from the Manufacturing Account. The test of the directness of a material is whether it usually forms part of what the firm sells to the customer.

Any cost forming part of the cost unit at its fully finished stage is termed a "product cost". Direct materials and conversion costs are product costs. Other costs, more exactly other revenue costs, are termed "period costs". In the United States product costs are said to be "inventoried" (put into stock costs) and period costs are said to be "expensed" (written off as a charge in the Income Statements). Product costs store added value, period costs reduce profits (but are necessary in earning the profits, as we shall see later in the present chapter).

A detailed discussion of materials records and accounting systems is deferred to Chapter 4, where we shall deal with all aspects of stock.

Materials yield

Causes of materials loss
Production consists of converting raw materials into finished goods. It is one of the laws of physics that in physical and chemical processes matter is neither created nor destroyed—only converted—unless the process involves nuclear energy, which converts matter into energy. Factory production involves physical and chemical processes and so is under the physical law just stated. However, part of the materials consumed in production may not find its way into the finished product for one or more of the following reasons.

(a) Evaporation of liquid materials.

(b) Extraction of unwanted waste products during conversion.

(c) Loss of raw materials caused by "breaking bulk" as when a block of salt is broken down into usable pieces and some is inevitably spilt on to the floor.

(d) Off-cuts of such materials as cotton used in mass production of clothes and soft furnishings—such off-cuts are usually thrown away, as they are too small to be used.

(e) Deterioration in store as caused by rust or food ingredients going stale. This normally occurs prior to production, but could occur during production itself if, for example, material is left exposed too long because of machine breakdown, strikes or even week-ends.

(f) Operator carelessness involving excessive spillage, excessive use of catalysts in chemical processes or any other avoidable cause.

It is readily observed that such losses as the above do not involve any exceptions to the law of conservation of matter.

Types of loss
Costing identifies three types of materials loss: scrap, waste and spoilage.

Scrap is the physically tangible residue of the production process and usually (but not necessarily) signifies metals. Scrap can be sold. Residue which has no market and must therefore be thrown away is classified as waste.

Waste is material lost or incapable of either being used or sold. All of the losses listed above are waste. Waste differs for costing purposes from scrap and spoilage in that it has zero value.

Spoilage is material in a partly or fully finished state that could not pass existing quality-control tests but is too far converted to be considered as scrap and sufficiently well put together to be capable of being repaired and then made into normal finished goods. The process of repair and restoration to the main production process is termed "rectification".

All the above losses can be further classified as normal or abnormal. Normal losses are losses unexpected by the firm to occur because of unavoidable spillage and evaporation, through operator carelessness and machine breakdown rates. *It is a basic principle of costing that normal losses are borne by the cost unit as product costs, while abnormal losses are written off as period costs.*

Normal losses

If every 12 kg of material input are expected to produce after conversion 10 kg of finished output, we have a normal loss of 2 kg. We can express this in costing terms in any one of the following ways.

(*a*) A normal loss of 2 kg for every 12 kg input.
(*b*) A normal loss rate of $16\frac{2}{3}$ per cent ($\frac{2}{12}$ as a percentage).
(*c*) A normal usage of 12 kg per kilogram of output.
(*d*) A standard yield of 10 kg per 12 kg of input.
(*e*) A standard yield of $83\frac{1}{3}$ per cent (100 per cent $- 16\frac{2}{3}$ in (*b*) above).

If the input costs £5 per kilogram and every 10 kg of output involves £20 conversion costs, the cost unit of 10 kg output must cost £$(5 \times 12) + 20 =$ £80. This cost includes not only the 10 kg input that emerged as output, but also the 2 kg production loss. Since this loss is a normal one, we know we shall have to buy and use 20 per cent more kilograms of input than we expect to produce as output. It is therefore sensible to treat the *whole* of the purchased material as part of our finished product cost. As far as costing is concerned, not only is such a procedure sensible, it is obligatory.

The materials element in the final cost unit consists *both* of materials forming part of the final product *and* of materials normally used up and lost in production. Production losses are considered in some quarters as an expense rather than as materials, since such losses are not physically represented in the final product, whereas true materials are. The reader is cautioned against this view, since the invoice to which the expense is traceable is the materials purchase invoice and expenses imply that the item cannot pass the test for materials. Scrap, spoilage and physical waste can pass the test, of course, as they can all be stacked, stored or stockpiled. However, whether materials lost in production are seen as materials or as expenses has absolutely no effect on the need to ensure that the cost of materials normally lost is fully reflected in the finished cost unit.

Abnormal losses never form part of the cost unit but are charged to the Profit & Loss Account as exceptional items. However, the custom is to treat all losses as abnormal when no normal loss rate is specified; but when this happens, most financial accounting authorities would think it appropriate to charge losses to the Manufacturing Account and thereby charge the cost unit. In the cost accounts, especially the process accounts, abnormal losses are never charged to the cost unit even if all production losses are regarded as abnormal. This is discussed further in Chapter 3.

DIRECT CONVERSION COSTS

Direct labour

Direct labour is the work-force wholly and exclusively employed by the firm to produce the cost unit. Direct labour costs consist of gross wages for time actually worked. Foremen and factory managers do not produce, they supervise the production of the work-force. Since they are not actually producing directly, they are indirect labour even though they spend their whole time involved with production.

Direct labour is paid as direct wages. Idle time, holiday pay, sick-leave with pay, employers' contribution to social security and pensions are all classified as indirect labour costs. Bonus payments are also counted as indirect, and even overtime is widely costed as indirect. However, if overtime hours are wholly and exclusively attributable to a particular product, job or special service for a customer, it would be more logical to charge the relevant gross overtime pay to the cost unit concerned as direct labour cost.

Direct expenses

Direct expenses are expenses wholly and exclusively arising from production of the cost unit. Freight of incoming materials, subcontractors' pay for working on the cost unit and hire of equipment exclusively to produce the cost unit are examples of direct expenses. In manufacturing most expenses will be indirect, since most will not be wholly and exclusively traceable to the production of any one product. However, in service and construction industries where the cost unit is the job done for a given customer, there will usually be expenses exclusively arising from the job and these will be clearly identifiable as direct expenses. Minor direct expenses of little value are treated as indirect for convenience in virtually all firms.

A major item of direct expense in the factory is electricity. However, it is usually treated as indirect because to trace the exact amount of electricity used by every product would necessitate metering every machine in the factory, the cost and inconvenience of which outweigh the benefits of knowing the precise amount of electricity used in converting material into each of the completed units.

Thus, although there is a sharp distinction between expenses and overheads in strict costing theory, in practice the distinction is rather blurred. This does not matter too much if we keep in mind the fact that direct expenses will increase as production volume increases, decrease as volume decreases, but that only certain overheads termed "variable overheads" will display the same tendency. This is amplified below.

Variable costs

All direct production costs are variable. This means that the more we produce, the more variable costs we incur. It is obvious that the more products we make, the more materials we shall use, so materials must be direct and variable. Labour is commonly employed to work a set number of hours a day. If we want to produce more than we can with the available labour, we shall have to hire more operators. This makes direct labour a variable cost. More labour means either more machines or using the same machines for longer hours (as when a night-shift is taken on). The machines use the direct expense of electricity and, the more machines are used, the more direct expenses we shall incur. Thus direct expenses rise or fall with production volume, so they too are variable.

In manufacturing, all direct costs are variable, but in service industries and building it is possible for direct costs to be fixed. The cost unit in these industries is often the job (e.g. the contract to build, say, a hospital). If cranes are hired for a fixed period, the hire charges must be paid whether work is being done on the building site at the time or not. The hire charge does not vary with the amount of work done but is contractually fixed at the outset of the hire period. Thus the hire charge is a fixed cost, not a variable one. Equally, if the crane is used wholly and exclusively on one site for one contract during the hire period, the charge is a direct expense, for only one cost unit is involved. This is an example of a direct cost that is also fixed.

Some very important expenses are indirect but variable. We have already seen that although machine electricity is a direct expense in theory, in practice it is costed as indirect. Transportation costs similarly have aspects about them which are direct in that they can often be attributed solely to one product, but they tend to be classified as indirect as well. It is, however, obvious that transport and electricity costs will rise as production rises, and fall as production falls. They are both variable costs. Indirect costs both in theory and practice that are classified as variable include selling costs (sales commissions, carriage outwards and packaging which is not part of the product), telephone and postal charges (which are assumed to vary in direct proportion to *expected sale* volume) and machine repair and maintenance (which vary with machine use and machine use is *expected* to vary with production volume). Because variable indirect costs do vary with production volume, it is relatively straight forward to allocate them to cost units. This means that variable costs as a whole, rather than just direct variable costs, can be treated as product costs. If we can say that every unit of output increases variable indirect costs by £1, we can attribute to the finished cost unit £1 of variable indirect costs on top of the direct costs already charged to it. Our ability to do this makes the distinction between direct and indirect costs less important than it otherwise would be and explains why the blurring of the boundary between direct expenses and variable indirect costs is not as serious as strict theory might suggest.

In pricing, the boundary between fixed and variable is much more important than the boundary between direct and indirect. This is because in pricing we want to be sure to set a price that covers all our costs; and while we can be confident that the allocation of variable costs to a cost unit is objectively quite accurate, the allocation of fixed costs to the cost unit is more arbitrary and fraught with the possibility of error. In control accounting, however, the boundary between direct and indirect is an important one. That is because in control accounting we are concerned to assess whether a cost centre has been managed more or less efficiently than expected. Direct costs tend to be regarded as controllable by the head of the cost centre, whereas indirect costs are not. It is management of direct costs that forms the basis of assessment of cost centre managerial performance, as these costs are under the cost centre head's control while indirect costs, by definition, are not wholly and exclusively attributable to the item in question; in this case the cost centre rather than the cost unit.

INDIRECT COSTS

Functional classification

It is common, especially in control accounting, to classify indirect costs by function. Such classification is similar to the textbook presentation of Profit & Loss Account categories of selling expenses, administration expenses, financial expenses, etc. In costing, however, functional classification is by managerial function in a far stricter sense than occurs with the Profit & Loss Account. Indirect costs are grouped by the following managerial functions: production, marketing, administration and research. Indirect production costs include: small pieces of equipment and consumable materials such as lubricating oil; gross pay of foremen, inspection staff, stores staff, repair-men and overtime, bonuses and employers' contributions attributable to direct labour employees; factory rent, factory heating and lighting bills, depreciation of factory buildings and plant and insurance on any of the preceding items. All the production

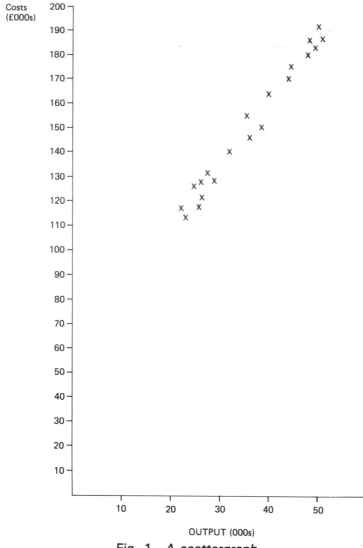

Fig. 1. *A scattergraph.*

overheads just listed are for items that are actually located in the factory area. That is, *they are "direct" costs to the factory as a cost centre but are considered to be indirect to the production process itself.*

Indirect marketing costs include delivery costs from finished goods store to customer (petrol, vehicle depreciation, truck-drivers' gross pay, etc.), packing materials not part of the product, pay and commission paid to sales staff, bad debts, market research, merchandising and usually also advertising (although this is not exclusively a revenue cost as advertising for a new product is a development cost which is capital in nature).

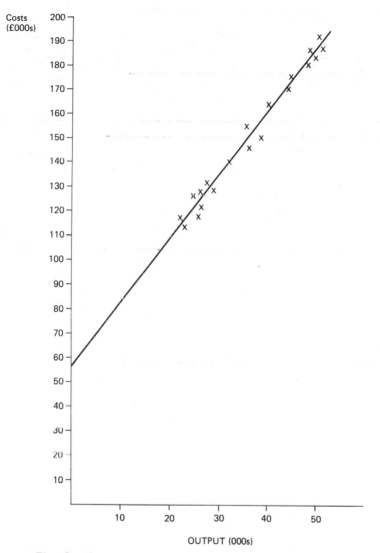

Fig. 2. *A scattergraph with line of best fit added.*

Administration overheads include the costs of operating all the office cost centres, and accounts—personnel, secretarial, legal, buying, planning, etc. This category can be divided into its functional components—accounts, personnel, etc.—as we must do for control accounting purposes. However, for broad costing purposes, administration is a catch-all category that takes in all the office staff and expenses.

Indirect research costs include computer time-based costs, gross pay of research workers, depreciation of test equipment and product development expenditure of a revenue rather than capital nature.

The word "overheads"

In the previous section we used the word "overheads" and the phrase "indirect costs" interchangeably. This is correct. Overheads are synonymous for all purposes with indirect costs. It follows that there can be no such thing as a direct overhead—it would be a contradiction in terms.

For most purposes overheads are defined as costs not wholly and exclusively attributable to the process of production. Hence foremen's pay is an indirect cost, as we have seen. Overheads generally signify costs of doing all the other things besides actual production, including supervising production. *For control accounting purposes,* however, the direct–indirect boundary is not between production activity and other activity but between one cost centre and the others. In control accounting, a direct cost is one wholly and exclusively attributable to one cost centre. Factory overheads in control accounting signify costs shared with other cost centres such as directors' fees (or which *all* cost centres bear the burden). The word "overhead" used in connection with control accounting meant any cost that went over the head of the cost centre. Foremen's pay, for example, goes "over the head" of the individual assembly line cost centres, so is an overhead to each one.

We shall use "overhead " in the wider sense to mean cost not associated wholly and exclusively with production, and use the phrase "cost centre overhead" to mean costs indirect to a specific cost centre.

COST BEHAVIOUR

Derivation of cost lines

Figure 1 shows a scattergraph of the various total direct labour costs a firm incurs at various levels of production output. The scattergraph is drawn from a table showing the cost applicable for different levels of output. Each little cross is a point whose vertical distance from the X-axis represents its £ cost and whose horizontal distance from the Y-axis represents the volume of output incurring that cost. The figure has twenty such crosses.

To obtain a cost line from a scattergraph we have to find the "line of best fit" through the crosses. We can do this arithmetically by employing the least squares method. This method will provide us with the line that minimises the total distances, horizontally and vertically, of all the crosses from the line. Hence it will be the line of best fit.

The line of best fit will follow the general formula for a linear equation: $y = a + bx$. This tells us that the vertical distance of any point on the line (its y value) is the sum of a constant (a, where the line intercepts the y-axis) and the result of multiplying the point's horizontal distance (its x value) by another constant—b. The aim of least squares method is to find the value of the two constants a and b.

We can take five crosses from our scattergraph and tabulate them as under. All figures are in thousands—for example, 40 in column $x = 40,000$, etc.

Output (x)	Cost (y)	xy	x^2
40	164	6,560	1,600
32	140	4,480	1,024
48	180	8,640	2,304
44	170	7,480	1,936
36	146	5,256	1,296
Totals Σx 200	Σy 800	Σxy 32,416	Σx^2 8,160

The total number of pairs used above is five and in the formulae below 5 is therefore the value of n.

The least squares method says:

$$b = \frac{n\Sigma xy - \Sigma x \Sigma y}{n\Sigma x^2 - (\Sigma x)^2}$$

Applying this formula to our table:

$$b = \frac{(5 \times 32,416) - (200 \times 800)}{(5 \times 8,160) - (200)^2} = \frac{162,080 - 160,000}{40,800 - 40,000} = \frac{2,080}{800} = 2.6$$

The formula for finding a is:

$$a - \frac{\Sigma y}{n} - \frac{b\Sigma x}{n} \text{ which in our case } - \frac{800}{5} - \frac{2.6 \times 200}{5} - 160 \quad 104 - 56$$

We now have the equation necessary to draw our line of best fit

$$y = 56 + 2.6x$$

Figure 2 shows the scattergraph with the line of best fit drawn in.

We should really have used all twenty crosses' x and y values to compute the values of a and b, but in this case there is almost perfect correlation between cost and output (y and x), so the end-result would have been the same.

Least squares method will give us cost lines which enable us to predict the particular cost (direct labour in the case of our current example) of any desired level of output. For example, if we wish to know the direct labour cost of 50,000 units we can look at Fig. 2 and find the y value for $x = 50,000$ and the answer is 186,000.

Whenever we believe the cost line is straight rather than curved, the least squares method applied to a scattergraph table of actual costs for stated outputs will enable us to find the cost line of best fit. We cannot use this method for costs that rise irregularly or in accordance with a quadratic equation. Cost curves, cost zigzags and cost steps, in other words, cannot be found by least squares.

Cost behaviour patterns

Equations of variation

Figure 3 shows nine different ways in which costs of particular items can vary with output. Each cost pattern shown can be expressed as an equation of y (for cost) on x (for output volume). The equations are given under each individual graph, together with the cost item best exemplified by the cost pattern shown.

Only rent in Fig. 3(a) is completely fixed with an equation $y = a$, and only direct materials cost in Fig. 3(b) is wholly variable in a linear fashion with an equation of $y = bx$. Direct labour in Fig. 3 (c) with its equation of $y = a + bx$ is the simplest example of a general truth; most cost items are neither wholly fixed nor wholly variable. The a value in the cost equation is the fixed component and the bx value is the variable component.

To handle the complex diversity of cost behaviour patterns in control accounting and in costing for pricing purposes, it is necessary to treat all

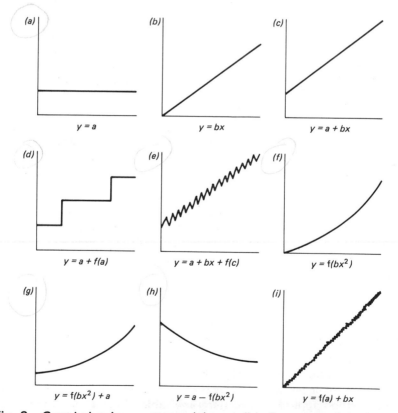

Fig. 3. *Cost behaviour patterns:*(a) *rent,* (b) *direct materials,* (c) *direct labour,* (d) *foremen,* (e) *telephones,* (f) *photocopying,* (g) *repairs and maintenance,* (h) *recruitment and training, and* (i) *sales commissions.*

cost items as if they had one of the three equations listed in the previous paragraph. We must isolate the fixed component and treat it as a pure fixed cost analogous to rent. We must deal with the variable component by finding the line of best fit through its zigzag, steps or curves.

Costs with stepped behaviour, such as happens with foremen in Fig. 3(d), are sometimes classified as "semifixed costs". Costs such as labour (Fig. 3(c)), telephones (Fig. 3(e)) or photocopying (Fig. 3(f)) are sometimes classified as "semivariable". Semifixed costs are fixed for specific ranges of output and rise in discrete jumps. As production increases, the ability of existing foremen to supervise operations becomes overstretched and a new one has to be recruited to share the work. Foremen are paid a fixed salary, usually irrespective of the volume of production supervised, so their cost is fixed; but of course more volume means more foremen, so we have the stepped pattern. Telephone bills consist partly of a fixed rental (the fixed element) and partly of metered charges (the variable element). Direct labour has to be paid if it turns up for work even if, say, the electricity breaks down, so even labour has a fixed element not dependent on production volume.

Figure 4 shows the labour cost line from Fig. 3(c) decomposed into its fixed and variable components. Figure 5(a) shows a linear approximation of the sales commission cost pattern taken from Fig. 3(i), and Fig. 5(b) shows a linear approximation of the photocopying cost taken from Fig. 3(f).

Costing and, to date, management accounting assume all costs to be fixed or variable. Any which are irregular are decomposed as in Fig. 4 into fixed and variable components and linearly approximated as in Fig. 5. In the rest of this book we shall adhere to the same assumption, although we note in passing that the advent of computer-based simulation means actual cost patterns can now in practice be handled without the need for simplification that there has been hitherto. However, treatment of such patterns by simulation is outside the scope of the present book. Henceforth we shall assume that all cost patterns have been simplified into $y = a$ (fixed) or $y = bx$ (variable) for all purposes.

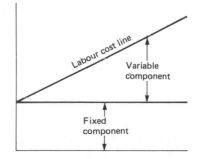

Fig. 4. *Decomposition of labour cost.*

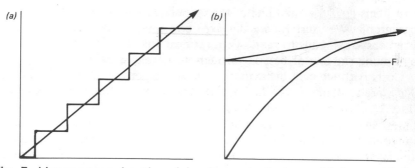

Fig. 5. *Linear approximation: (a) sales commission—this is a straight-forward line of best fit; and (b) photocopying—note the super-imposition of a fixed cost line, marked F, to ensure that the approximation rises at the slope closest to those slopes of the original curve that apply to the volumes actually experienced by the firm.*

The basis of variation and sales

All direct costs are charged to cost units; overheads tend to be written off to the Income Statements as period costs. Variable overheads may for convenience include some direct costs such as electricity, and these are also quite easily distributed to cost units in the cost-books regardless of how they are treated in the financial accounts.

Variable costs include some items that do not vary with production volume at all, but do vary with sales volume. For example, sales commissions and transport to customers vary with sales not production. Sales commissions are treated in some quarters not only as variable but as direct, since they arise directly from selling the product. This is bad practice, because selling is not producing. If sales commissions are direct because they arise from selling the product, foremen's salary must be direct, as it arises directly from supervising the product. It is advisable to keep production as the direct—indirect boundary for most purposes.

Costs which vary with sales volume rather than production volume are still regarded as variable. The justification for this is that sales volume and production volume are mutually dependent. No firm will continue to produce what it cannot sell and no sales force can sell what has not been produced.

OVERHEAD DISTRIBUTION

Overview

For control accounting purposes we need to know if a cost centre has performed better or worse than expected. This involves comparing its actual costs against the costs expected. To do this we must debit to the cost centre as fairly as possible the costs, both direct and indirect, that it has incurred. This is done by directly charging it with its direct costs and by allocating to it the overheads for which it is responsible and also apportioning to it a fairly judged proportion of the firm's overheads. (Allocation of overhead is described below, as is apportionment.)

For pricing purposes we must know the full cost of producing a cost unit. This is not only the direct cost plus factory overhead shown in the Manufacturing Account, but a fair share of all the other overheads. The overheads are distributed to the cost unit by apportionment and by absorption (both described below). By apportionment and absorption of overheads, the cost unit recovers the firm's indirect costs in its sales price. The sales price is based on the total unit cost inclusive of overhead recovery. The name for the methods of ensuring that unit cost fully recovers all overheads as well as direct costs is "absorption costing". Absorption costing is discussed in the pages following.

see
p 38!

see
p 33!

Allocation of overhead

Allocation charges to a cost centre the overheads which arise solely from the operations of that centre. Allocation of overhead is dependent on two necessary conditions. These are that:

(*a*) the cost centre must have been the sole cause of the overhead (so overheads that would have occurred anyway cannot be allocated); and

(*b*) the exact amount of the overhead caused by the cost centre must be unambiguously known.

Indirect materials and indirect labour, including employers' contributions and bonuses, can usually be allocated. Sometimes machine-linked expenses such as repairs and depreciation can be allocated, so long as the machine is exclusively used by one cost centre.

Overheads which can be allocated are costs which are direct to the cost centre but indirect to the production process.

Apportionment

The basis of apportionment

Overheads that cannot be allocated must be apportioned. This involves choosing a basis of apportionment that most fairly distributes the overhead. The choice of basis always involves a subjective factor, convenience weighing more than strict fairness in the choice. If this were not so, overheads such as electricity would be apportioned by metering every user centre (at great inconvenience and expense); similarly with telephones, postage, stationery and cleaning. The fairest basis of apportionment is that which identifies the factor most likely to cause a rise in the level of the relevant overhead. Floor area, for example, is far more important than the number of employees in causing a rise in the amount of rent and rates paid, so that it is a fairer basis on which to apportion rent than is the number of employees.

Apportionment bases usually used.
The table below sets out the principal overheads in a firm and the basis
on which they are usually apportioned.

Overhead	*Basis of apportionment*
Rent and rates	Floor area occupied by the cost centre.
Office electricity	As above, but can be room volume or number of electric installations.
Factory electricity	Floor area, but can be number of electric installations.
Other heating fuels	Floor area, sometimes volume or number of radiators.
Building depreciation	Floor area.
Building repair and maintenance	Floor area, but repair costs could sometimes be *allocated*.
Insurance of tangible assets	Book value of assets insured.
Telephones and telex	Number of telephones and telex operator records of users.
Postage	Number of employees in cost centre authorised to write on behalf of the firm.
Stationery	Number of employees.
Administration cost centres' running costs	Number of employees.
Canteen, Welfare & Social functional costs	Number of employees.

Where more than one basis is mentioned, the first named is the one most
used in practice, but the others are sometimes used and may in theory be
fairer. For example, the heating use of electricity is more affected by the
number of radiators than by floor area, but this does not apply to the
lighting use.

Consider a firm with four cost centres—A, B, C and D. Its monthly rent
is £2,000 and its outlay on stationery is £500. To apportion these we make
use of the table below.

COST CENTRES

	A	*B*	*C*	*D*	*Total*
Floor area (sq ft)	20,000	16,000	18,000	18,000	72,000
Number of employees	100	10	30	60	200

The rent of £2,000 is apportioned pro rata to floor area. Thus, if £2,000
is the cost of the 72,000 total area, the apportionment to C is
$18,000/72,000 = \frac{1}{4}$ of the total rent = £500.

The stationery is apportioned pro rata to the number of employees, so A has half the total number and is accordingly apportioned half the total stationery cost of £500/2 = £250.

The completed apportionments are shown below (all figures are in £).

	A	B	C	D	Total
Rent	556	444	500	500	2,000
Stationery cost	250	25	75	150	500

The rent apportioned to A and B is rounded to the nearest whole £.

Service cost centres

In the previous subsection rent and stationery were apportioned to all four cost centres, A,B,C and D. After all the overheads are apportioned to all cost centres, we know the full cost of running each cost centre. This satisfies the requirements of control accounting, for we shall now be able to compare expected cost centre costs in total and in detail with costs actually incurred. For pricing purposes, however, we shall have to go futher than this, since in pricing we want to ensure that all costs are absorbed by the cost unit.

No cost units pass through service cost centres—that is, cost centres not directly involved in producing the product. Service centre costs are allocated and apportioned to productive centres in absorption costing, not to place an unfair overhead burden on production centres but to ensure that all costs reach the cost unit—and only production centres handle cost units.

Allocation and apportionment of service centre costs to production centres proceeds in the same way as distribution of the basic overheads previously described. Administration cost centres are usually apportioned on the number of employees in the factory cost centres receiving the overhead, but this is because such a basis is most convenient rather than because it is fairest in every case. Other service cost centres and their basis of apportionment include the following.

Service cost centre	Basis of apportionment
Cleaning staff	Floor area.
Factory stores	Number of material requisition slips from each centre.
Maintenance staff	Allocation *or* pro rata to repair time.
Security staff	Number of employees.
Quality control and inspection	Allocation *or* production volume.
Field sales staff labour costs	Numerical equality or production volume.

When service cost centres are allocated and apportioned to production centres as overheads, it is the *full running costs* of the service centres that are distributed, not just the service centres' own "overheads".

In examinations on overhead distribution, questions tend to list a series of overhead costs followed by a table of cost centres with their floor areas, numbers of employees, etc. The candidate is required to allocate and apportion each overhead to the cost centres, choosing in each case the most appropriate basis of apportionment. If two bases seem equally appropriate, the student is advised to select the one that apportions in round figures (without causing recurring decimals or odd numbers in the answer). If there is any doubt which basis the examiners intend the student to select and the rounding test is of no help, the student should choose the bases that he or she feels best able to justify in a brief note of explanation. No candidate ever lost marks by explaining his assumptions or decisions, but many have gained marks thereby that would be otherwise lost.

Reciprocal service costs

It is easy enough to apportion service centre costs to production centres if the service centres work only for the production centres, but not so easy when they work also for each other—as they usually do in practice. Canteen costs are apportioned to security staff centre, for example, but security costs are also apportioned to canteen. We cannot apportion service centre costs until we have a final total for the running costs of each one, and if cross-apportionment is involved we need a method of preventing a vicious circle. If 5 per cent of canteen costs are apportioned to security and 10 per cent of security's costs to canteen, the problem arises whether to say the canteen total should be found excluding security or the other way round. Either way round will mean that one of the centres avoids being burdened with the other's costs. The technique known as "specified order of closing" faces this problem by ignoring it. The technique requires decisions to be made about which centre's costs will be closed first, which next, etc. Once the costs are closed, the total is apportioned to the production centres and to the other service centres not yet closed. This prevents a vicious circle of cross-apportionment but relieves the first closed centre of its fair share of service overheads and burdens the last closed with more than its fair share.

Again, we have an example here of convenience taking precedence over precision or fairness. This is not very serious in practice, however, as the cost unit will still end up absorbing total costs. Nevertheless, if there are several products made in several different production cost centres, some using far more of a given service than others, the specified order of closing method might exaggerate the costs of some cost units and understate those of others. So for multiproduct firms whose production lines show greatly different use of services, one of the two methods outlined below must be used to apportion reciprocal services.

(1) The method of repeated distribution apportions service costs to all other centres including other service centres repeatedly. One service centre's cost is apportioned to all other centres, then the next centre on the list is apportioned to all others including the first one, then the next and so on to the end of the list. Then the process using the results of the first sequence is repeated right through the list and is repeated again and again until two successive sequences are giving the same apportionments in round £ (or a higher cut-off such as £000 if the management so desire). This is a fair method but rather tedious.

(2) The fairest method is the algebraic one. This involves modelling the reciprocal use of services by simultaneous equations. It is easiest understood through an example. Suppose security costs are £16,000, excluding other service centre apportionments, and if the only other service centre is the canteen and it costs £20,000 excluding security costs, but the canteen is to be apportioned with 10 per cent of security costs and security with 5 per cent of canteen costs. Let S stand for total security costs after apportionment of canteen costs, and let C stand for total canteen costs after apportionment of security costs.

$$S = £16,000 + 5\% \text{ of } C = 16,000 + 0.05C$$
$$C = £20,000 + 10\% \text{ of } S = 20,000 + 0.1S$$

Therefore	$S - 0.05C = 16,000$	(equation A)
	$C - 0.1S = 20,000$	(equation B)
A × 20 gives	$20S - C = 320,000$	(equation C)
B × 10 gives	$10C - S = 200,000$	(equation D)
C × 10 gives	$200S - 10C = 3,200,000$	(equation E)

D + E gives $10C + (-10C) + 200S + (-S) = 3,400,000 = 199S$

$$\therefore \quad S = 3,400,000 \div 199 = 17,085 \text{ (to the nearest £)}$$

Substituting in equation D gives:

$$10C - 17,085 = 200,000$$
$$10C = 217,085$$
$$C = 21,709 \text{ (rounded up to nearest £;}$$

NOTE: round 5 up and not down)

The full security costs to be apportioned to production centres is S, which equals £17,085, and the full canteen cost is £21,709. The algebraic method is not confined to two service centres but can handle any number. It is very unlikely that the student will be asked to solve a reciprocal service apportionment involving more than three centres in any foreseeable cost-and-management accounting examinations.

Overhead absorption

Purpose and definition
Once all reciprocal service centre costs are apportioned, the full service centre costs are allocated and apportioned to production cost centres. Finally, the production cost centre's overhead (consisting of its own allocation and its full apportionment of the service centres' costs) is allotted to the cost units passing through the production centres. The whole procedure is entitled "absorption costing" and its effect on the cost unit is to load it with all the firm's costs, both product and period, direct and indirect, fixed and variable. The purpose of such loading is to establish a total unit cost for each product, job or service sold by the firm so that a price may be charged which covers the total unit cost—that is, a profitable price. The final stage in absorption costing as far as overheads are concerned is the allotment of overhead using an absorption rate.

The basis of absorption
Just as it was necessary to select a basis of apportionment, so it is necessary to select a basis of absorption most appropriate to the production process of each production cost centre. The table below gives the bases of absorption, their calculation method and the production processes to which they are most appropriate.

Basis	Calculation method	Suitable processes
Direct labour-hour rate	Total cost centre overhead ÷ total direct hours *worked*	All service industries and any manufacturing process not specified below.
Machine-hour rate	Total cost centre overhead ÷ total hours of machine use	Processes where the machine's contribution is more important than that of any human operative.
Direct materials rate	(Total cost centre overhead × 100) ÷ total direct materials cost	Processes using very high value materials or where the cost of materials affects overhead use more than labour.
Direct wages rate	(Total cost centre overhead × 100) ÷ direct labour cost	Processes and servives where labour is paid different wages and salaries *and* hours worked are not usually recorded.

Direct cost rate	(Total cost centre overhead × 100) ÷ cost centre's direct costs	Processes where machinery and manpower contribute equally to production can be suitable for construction contracts.
Unit rate	Total cost centre overhead ÷ cost units produced by centre	Processes involving the mass production of large numbers of units per hour or if the centre produces only one product'.

To illustrate the application of the above rates, let us use a total cost centre overhead of £100,000. Using the direct labour-hour rate and assuming 10,000 labour-hours *worked*, overhead is absorbed at £10 per hour. Using machine-hour rate and 5,000 machine-hours, the absorption rate would be £20 per hour. With a direct materials cost of £1 million, the absorption rate would be 10 per cent of cost of direct materials used. Using direct wages of £$\frac{1}{2}$ million, the rate would be 20 per cent of direct wage costs. Using direct costs (still called prime costs also in some quarters) of £2 million, the rate would be 5 per cent of direct costs. Finally if 1 million units are normally produced by the cost centre, the unit absorption rate is 10p per unit. In practice, the first mentioned, direct labour-hours, is the most frequently used rate and the last mentioned, product units, is the next most used.

Application of overhead rate
Overheads are charged to cost units thus:

Overheads per cost unit = overhead rate × units of hours, materials in the cost unit.

For example, a unit of product A uses half an hour of labour, one machine-hour, £4 of wages cost and £10 of materials, and its total direct costs are £20. Using the overhead rates given above would result in the following.

Basis	Rate	Base units	Overhead absorbed
Unit	10p	1 (by definition)	10p
Labour-hrs	£10 per hr	$\frac{1}{2}$	£5
Machine-hrs	£20 per hr	1	£20
Wage %	20%	£4	80p
Materials %	10%	£10	£1
Direct cost %	5%	£20	£1

Very different amounts are absorbed by the different bases, so the total costs absorbed by the cost unit will depend quite significantly on the choice of base. Nevertheless, any base will ensure that all overheads are absorbed by the cost units produced. It is because the total cost of a cost unit is so much affected by the relatively subjective decision as to the most appropriate base that absorption costing has fallen into disrepute in some quarters. Another approach, marginal costing, is an alternative procedure for pricing purposes which does not involve overhead apportionment or absorption. In Chapter 4 we shall compare the two methods and their effects on stock valuation and period profits. In Chapter 8 we shall compare the advantages and disadvantages of the two methods in a pricing context.

Predetermined absorption
It was not specified above whether either overheads or units of base for absorption were actual (past) or expected (future). In practice, for control accounting purposes, both expected and actual must be calculated. The basis used for expected must also be used for actual so that we can compare like with like. In pricing based on the absorption costing method, expected overheads and expected units of base (labour-hours, units produced, etc.) must be used, as we cannot wait until we have precise data recorded on overheads and volumes before pricing. Our expected overhead costs and expected units of base will be calculated on the basis of the figures of previous periods being adjusted for expected inflation and other foreseeable charges. However, our expectations could be wrong. Either we could wrongly estimate total overhead costs or the total units of base.

Let us suppose we base our control accounting and our pricing on a forecast overhead cost of £100,000 and a forecast volume of units produced of 50,000. Our predetermined overhead rate is therefore £2 a unit. If our overheads turn out to be only £80,000 but we still sell 50,000 units, overhead recovered in sales = £100,000. This is £20,000 more than we turned out needing to recover—such a situation is a favourable expenditure variance in control accounting terms. Alternatively, suppose our expenditure guess was right at £100,000 but, instead of producing and selling 50,000 units, in fact we produce only 40,000. This means our sales recover only 40,000 × £2 = £80,000 of the £100,000 we actually spent. Such a situation is generally termed an "under-recovery" or "under-absorption" of overhead. In control accounting it is termed an "adverse volume variance". It will be appreciated that for pricing based on absorption costing methods, wrong forecasts of total overhead or of total volume (whether measured in units, labour-hours or any other base) can have very serious results on profits. This applies with especial severity to firms with a high burden of overhead. Outlined below are the special problems facing such firms.

OPERATING LEVERAGE

Operating leverage is the ratio of fixed costs to total costs. The higher this is, the more sensitive is overhead recovery to volume forecasting errors. In other words, under- or over-recovery is more likely to have a more severe effect on the profits of a firm with high operating leverage than on those of other firms. This means that firms with high operating leverage are riskier undertakings than other firms. This is clarified by an example.

Say two firms both make a similar product retailing for £100 each, but one has to meet fixed costs of £800,000 a year, and the other only £80,000. If variable costs are £20 a unit, each sale brings in a contribution of £100 − 20 = £80 to cover fixed costs. The firm with the higher operating leverage has to sell 80,000 units before it breaks even, while the other firm needs to sell only 8,000. In times of recession the firm with high operating leverage is in far greater danger of making losses and going out of business than is the other firm.

SUMMARY

(*a*) Direct costs are costs of materials, labour and expenses wholly and exclusively arising from production. Other costs are overheads.

(*b*) Direct costs and those overheads which are charged to the finished cost unit are product costs. Other costs are period costs. Costs that vary with volume are variable costs; costs that do not are fixed costs. Actual cost patterns must be decomposed and linearly approximated to wholly fixed and wholly variable components before costing can handle them.

(*c*) Overheads must be allotted to cost centres for control accounting. General overheads must be apportioned to productive cost centres and absorbed by the cost unit for pricing purposes, and both these distributions are done after selecting a suitable basis.

(*d*) The larger the burden of fixed costs borne by a firm relative to its total costs, the higher is its operating leverage said to be. High operating leverage means that high volumes of sales are necessary to ensure profits, and this puts the firm at risk in a period of recession.

QUESTIONS

1. For a firm which manufactures furniture in several small workshops, which of the following items are overheads?

(*a*) Wood.

(*b*) Nails.

(*c*) Sandpaper.

(*d*) Carpenters' pay.

(*e*) Production managers' pay.

(*f*) Central heating bills.

(*g*) Factory rents.

(*h*) Subsidy to the workshop canteens.

(*i*) Discounts given to customers.

(*j*) Office furniture.

2. How far do you consider factory electricity to be a direct expense and how far an overhead?

3. To what cost centres could the following items be directly allotted?

(*a*) Gross pay of maintenance staff servicing accounting machines.

(*b*) Salesmen's entertaining expense claims.

(*c*) Foreman's pay for supervising product line N.

4. Match the overheads in column A with the most appropriate basis of apportionment in column B.

A	*B*
(*i*) Heating bills.	(*a*) Man-hours.
(*ii*) Personnel office costs.	(*b*) Number of employees.
(*iii*) Rent and rates.	(*c*) Wage costs.
(*iv*) Maintenance staff pay.	(*d*) Floor area.
(*v*) Postage.	(*e*) Direct allocation.
(*vi*) Audit fees.	(*f*) Room volume.

5. What is the importance of operating leverage to the business risk of a firm?

6. Why are normal losses treated as product costs?

For calculation questions, see numbers 3 and 5 in Appendix V.

CHAPTER THREE

Cost Accounting

The test of a vocation is the love of the drudgery it involves.

L.P. Smith

OBJECTIVES

(*a*) To understand the basic principles of costing and to be able to apply them in order to ascertain the cost of any product, service or department.

(*b*) To appreciate the similarities and the distinctions between Income Statements for the enterprise as a whole and costing statements for cost units.

(*c*) To recognise the situations where a cost unit is also a cost centre.

(*d*) To be able to write up the cost accounts for any manufacturing or service industry.

(*e*) To comprehend the special treatment of profit in uncompleted contracts.

(*f*) To understand the usual treatment of all types of process loss and all types of partly processed units.

(*g*) To appreciate the principles involved in accounting for by-products and joint products.

GENERAL PRINCIPLES

Fundamentals of cost accounting

Introduction

The purpose of the text below is to list and explain the ground rules of costing and cost accounting. Costing means finding out the cost of something, and cost accounting means costing using double-entry book-keeping methods. This chapter as a whole is concerned with costing any product, any service or any department.

Below are listed and explained five basic rules that apply throughout all costing. These rules should be learnt and borne in mind in any situation requiring the use of cost information. They are not narrowly limited to pure costing but apply also to any area of management accountancy involving cost data.

The student, having learnt the necessary basic vocabulary of costing from Chapters 1 and 2, can now truly begin developing management accountancy skills.

The Causative Rule (CR)

Costs should be attributed to their causes. This rule states that cost centres and units should be charged only with the costs to which they give rise. Maintenance overhead, for example should be allocated to those centres using maintenance in the period and not to any others. Only overheads such as interest on borrowed funds which apply to the firm as a whole should be regarded as "general" overheads to be apportioned to every single cost centre. Machine depreciation is a factory overhead, but not one to be absorbed into all cost units—only into those cost units produced by or passing through the machine in question. If office staff eat in public restaurants while factory staff generally eat in the firm's canteen, canteen running costs should not be apportioned to office cost centres. If the Causative Rule is breached, the total period cost of a cost centre and the total production cost of a cost unit will be wrongly or inequitably stated. This will make effective control accounting, decision accounting and, in some cases, costing for pricing, very difficult to achieve. It follows from the Causative Rule that direct allocation is to be preferred to apportionment whenever this is practicable.

The Rule Against Anticipating (RAA)

A cost should be charged to a centre or unit only once it has been incurred and not in any circumstances before then. Thus finished goods cannot be charged with selling and distribution costs while they are still in the factory awaiting packing, transport and sale. Estimates of costs to be incurred are necessary for control accounting and pricing, but such estimates must never enter the cost accounts in the guise of actuals. Normal losses may seem an exception to this rule but in fact they are not so. Normal loss rates are established on the basis of past experience and cost units are charged not only with them but, as we shall see below, are effectively credited with any abnormal gain (the difference between normal loss and actual but smaller loss).

Predetermined overhead rates may also seem an exception to the Rule Against Anticipating, since actual overhead expenditure or the volume of production against which overhead is recovered may both turn out to be different from that which is forecast. This being the case, it may seem as if apportioning and absorbing overhead on predetermined estimates breaches the rule. Here we must be careful to distinguish between the *fact* of incurring overhead and the *uncertainty* as to the actual amount incurred. We know for example that machines, radiators and lights all use electricity as soon as they are switched on, but we cannot tell how much until we receive the electricity bill (and the bills arrive only at quarterly intervals). In other words, we know we have incurred the expense/overhead of electricity and so we must charge the cost centre and cost units therewith. The charge must necessarily remain an estimate until we receive and apportion the actual bill at some considerable time after we incur the expense. However, if we find our estimate to have been wrong, we charge (or credit as the case may be) the centre and unit with the variance between estimate and actual. The rule is similar to the financial accounting year end procedure of accruals and provisions—both of which relate to liabilities that have already been incurred but whose precise amount has yet to be clearly identified.

The Rule Against Anticipating applies to the cost accounts. But it does not prevent us from forecasting costs for decision accounting, capital costing or any other reason, so long as we do not enter any such forecast costs into the cost accounting books for these must be confined strictly to costs actually incurred to date.

The Rule Against Deferrals (RAD)

Future periods must never be charged with sunk costs. Sunk costs are those costs that arose in the past but from which no future direct benefit can be expected. Thus losses made in 1982 may not be carried forward as an overhead to be recovered from cost units produced in 1983. This would be like debiting the 1983 Profit & Loss Account with the 1982 loss so that reported profit in 1983 were accordingly reduced. In fact, of course, the 1982 loss is brought forward in the Appropriation Account *after* ascertainment of the net profit for 1983.

The practice of charging depreciation is not an exception to the Rule Against Deferrals. Moreover, the capital expenditure to purchase the fixed asset arose in the past, the asset is used for the whole of its economic life and such usage must be charged. Depreciation is a principal means of charging such usage. Charging the cost of opening stocks against profits means charging against current profits some costs that arose in the previous year rather than in the current one. This does not breach the Rule Against Deferrals either, because it is the current period that receives the benefit of those costs (in the form of sales income), not the previous period. The year of sale is the criterion for whether or not a cost is being deferred, not the year of production. This is closely analogous to the matching principle in financial accounting which postulates that costs should be matched with the income to which they give rise.

The Rule Against Abnormal and Exceptional Items (RAE)

Abnormal and exceptional costs are excluded from product costs and separately identified in lists of period costs. Abnormal and exceptional items such as fire damage or losses consequent on power failures are beyond managerial control, so they should be routinely charged to the cost centres and units affected. This rule, however, has to be applied in a way that is consistent with the Causative Rule. If an abnormal materials loss is due to human error in Cost Centre X, then that loss should be charged to Cost Centre X. However, the cost units produced or services provided by Centre X should *not* be inflated by the loss in question because this would *breach* the Causative Rule, since user departments and customers would bear a burden then for which they were in no sense responsible.

The reader will observe that abnormal loss through human error is to be seen always as a period cost and never as a product cost. The special case of abnormal process gain is examined later in this chapter (*see* pages 71–2), where it is shown that even this case turns out to conform with the fundamental costing rules. Abnormal loss that is really exceptional and outside managerial control can be seen as giving rise to its own cost centre—a sort of cost centre to capture such misfortunes as the insurance industry terms "Acts of God".

The Realistic Value Rule (RVR)

In decision accounting it can be more important to know values than costs. For example, capital expenditure decisions involve matching acquisition costs with the value of assets acquired, so that the size of the "bargain" the purchase represents can be assessed. In Chapter 4 we shall see that value may be more important than cost in the fair attribution of amounts to finished stocks. Value here means that the asset is worth what it is shown to be by its use in capital costing or by its retail sales value in other contexts. Balance Sheets list assets at historic cost less depreciation, and current cost Balance Sheets list them at "current cost" less adjusted depreciation. In decision accounting we must identify the measure of value most appropriate to the problem and value the asset accordingly. The appropriate realistic value will very rarely be historical cost, which in a decision accounting context is usually a sunk cost.

A second aspect of the Realistic Value Rule is that the costs most relevant in decision accounting will be opportunity costs. These costs are the sacrificed net income that is incurred as a result of making one decision rather than another. We shall reopen this subject in Chapter 5 when we deal with the opportunity costs of current assets.

Summary of fundamental principles

(*a*) CR (the Causative Rule)—costs should be attributed to their cause.

(*b*) RAA (the Rule Against Anticipating)—costs should not be charged before they are incurred.

(*c*) RAD (the Rule Against Deferrals)—future periods should not be charged with sunk costs.

(*d*) RAE (the Rule Against Abnormal and Exceptional Items)—cost units should not bear abnormal or exceptional costs.

(*e*) RVR (the Realistic Value Rule)—in decision accounting realistic values of assets are to be used and matched with opportunity costs.

Henceforth, these rules will usually be cited by their abbreviations unless a full discussion of the rule is merited in a particular context.

The general absorption formula

It will be recalled from Chapter 2 that, under absorption costing, the unit cost of a product or service is found after allocating all overhead to production and after recovering all overhead from units produced. In Chapter 1 it was stated that unit production cost could be found by taking from the Manufacturing Account the total cost of goods produced and dividing it by the number of units produced in the period. Both of these techniques are particular applications of the GAF, the General Absorption Formula.

The General Absorption Formula is:

$$\text{Total cost per unit} = \frac{\text{Total costs incurred in the period}}{\text{Total number of units produced}} = \frac{Ci}{Np}$$

The GAF is the essence of absorption costing, the technique whereby the cost unit is made to recover all the normal costs of the firm, inclusive of all normal overheads

The GAF can be applied in its simple form to firms producing one standardised product or selling one standard service. Thus a dairy producing 1-litre bottles of milk would compute costs incurred per bottle of milk as total costs of the firm (excluding abnormals) divided by the total number of bottles produced. A car-wash whose sole service was providing an automated car-wash would compute the cost per wash as total costs divided by the number of washes provided in the period. Both these situations are examples of uniform costing, so called because the cost unit is uniform. Uniform costing simply requires the direct application of the GAF in order to find the cost per unit provided.

Throughout this chapter absorption costing is applied, which means that all normal overheads have to find their way to the cost unit through allocation apportionment and absorption. In Chapter 4 we shall begin to look at alternatives to absorption costing.

Classification of costing methods

Operation costing
Operation costing is the general name for the costing methods appropriate to production for markets in general rather than for any specific customer order. Uniform costing of a standardised product and uniform costing of a standardised service (which is often termed "operating costing") are both examples of operation costing. When one *or more* standardised products are made from a sequence of production processes, each process has its own costs and those costs have to be accumulated in order to ascertain the total production cost of the final unit. In such sequential processes, production losses, by-products and more than one end-product are not unusual.

Process costing deals with sequential processes and the associated problems just described. Because the output is standardised, even though processes may manufacture two or more types of product, process costing is a type of operation costing.

Specific order costing

Specific order costing is the general name for the costing methods appropriate to production for, or service of, a specific customer order. The order may be actual or anticipated for the methods to apply. Each order is different from every other order, so the materials, labour, expense and capital mix will be different for each one. This is another way of saying that every cost unit is unique, and thus the methods of operation costing with their assumption of standardised cost units cannot apply.

Job costing is appropriate where:

(*a*) a service is rendered in keeping with customer specifications;

(*b*) a product is made to match exactly a customer's stated requirements; and

(*c*) work is done on customer's premises to achieve a given limited object.

The three situations just listed are exemplified respectively by:

(*a*) undertaking a market research survey in order to test acceptance of a client's product by a sample of the customers or public at large;

(*b*) made-to-measure tailoring; and

(*c*) any kind of domestic plumbing or electrical repair work.

Similar to the job-costing situation is the case of a factory producing batches of products to customer order (actual or anticipated). Each new batch requires retooling of machinery and familiarisation of the labour force. The batch consists of standard products, but no two batches are precisely alike. The batch is itself the cost unit, not the product units within the batch. Batch costing follows very similar procedures to job costing and is another example of specific order costing. The final example of specific order costing involves very large jobs often taking several years from start to finish, and instead of being initiated by customer order, the job is initiated by the signing of a binding legal contract under seal. Contract costing applies in this case and the industries involved are building, civil engineering, aircraft and arms manufacture. The contract for which contract costing is most suitable is not an ordinary contract to supply goods, far less a contract (properly called a "conveyance") to sell a building or land, but one for the construction of a major physical asset such as a house, factory or road. In contract costing the cost unit—the completed house, for example—is usually also a cost centre (the building site). It is only in contract costing that the physical identity of cost centre with cost unit occurs.

Pages 48–9 deal with uniform service costing. Pages 49–54 cover job and batch costing, the next easiest methods. Then comes contract costing (*see* pages 54–9). Finally the more difficult problems of process costing are tackled (*see* pages 60–76).

Treatment of scrap and by-products

Normal loss
The GAF can be elaborated upon in order to take explicit account of normal production loss either through its numerator, total costs, or its denominator, number of units produced. To illustrate this let us take a firm with a total cost excluding production losses of £1 million and total units produced (excluding any scrap or spoilage) of £$\frac{1}{2}$ million. Unit cost with no production loss is £2. Now, let us suppose the same firm encounters a normal loss rate of 20 per cent of *out*-put. This means its number of units produced in good condition is 500,000 − (20% of 500,000 − 100,000) − 100,000. Unit cost is now £1 million ÷ 0.4 million − £2.50. Alternatively, we could value the production loss at £2$\frac{1}{2}$ per cost unit to obtain a total cost of £1 million + (£2.50 × 100,000 = £250,000) = £1.25 million. This total of £1.25 million is divided by the $\frac{1}{2}$ million units of total production to obtain a unit cost of £2.50 again. However, the latter method works only if we value lost production at the revised unit cost computed by the former method and it adds nothing to that former method. The amendment to the GAF to account for normal loss is therefore:

$$\text{Unit cost} = \frac{\text{Total costs exclusive of scrap and spoilage}}{\text{Number of } \textit{saleable} \text{ units produced}} = \frac{Ctx}{Ng}$$

Scrap
Scrap has sales potential. Any income derived from sales of scrap is applied to reduce the production cost. For example, our firm above can realise 50p per unit of scrap. Let us assume that all the lost 100,000 units are lost as scrap. Then they realise in sales income £50,000 altogether. This is applied to the numerator of the GAF as a reduction in total cost. Thus:

$$\text{Unit cost} = \frac{\text{Total costs less scrap sales proceeds}}{\text{Number of saleable finished units}} = \frac{Ctx - Ss}{Ng}$$

$$= \frac{£1 \text{ million} - £50,000}{400,000} = \frac{£950,000}{400,000} = £2.37\frac{1}{2}$$

Unit cost of good finished units has fallen from £2.50 to £2.37$\frac{1}{2}$ as a result of scrap sales income. Note that this is the full scrap sales *proceeds* which are subtracted on the GAF numerator, *not scrap sales profits* of any kind.

By-products
By-products are products emerging incidentally and in relatively small quantities from the production process. They are treated in the same way as scrap, as far as the GAF is concerned. For process costing we shall

briefly outline some alternative treatments, but the general rule is to treat by-products for the purpose of costing the main product(s) in exactly the same way as scrap.

Work-in-progress (w-i-p)

Units not fully finished at the period end constitute work-in-progress. When we want to know total *period* costs, we are interested in the costs of *finishing* the manufacture of our *opening* w-i-p and the costs of *having started* the manufacture of our *closing* w-i-p. RAA and RAD have to be carefully observed here. However, when we want to know the *product* costs of *units sold* during a period, we are not concerned with closing w-i-p at all (as it has yet to be sold). However, we are interested in opening w-i-p, not only in the costs to complete it during this period *but* the costs it incurred in the previous period, as *both* of these together make up the total cost of the units eventually sold. This distinction between the period cost and the product cost approaches is especially important in process costing. Pages 62–5 take the period approach, and pages 65–70 take the product approach to w-i-p. Both will need to be fully understood.

UNIFORM SERVICE COSTING (OPERATING COSTING)

Service costing is used by road haulage firms, hospitals, schools, passenger transport firms and all other types of firm providing a service rather than a product to the general public. The GAF applies to ascertainment of unit cost, but the problem here is finding the most suitable cost unit. The key to this is identifying the independent variables that affect costs so that a composite cost unit can be used. In transport, for example, cost is affected by distance travelled and by weight carried, so the composite unit would be the ton-mile (or in metric the tonne-kilometre) for freight transport and the passenger mile for passenger transport. Schools and colleges costs are strongly affected by the number of staff employed, which is itself a function of the number of courses offered and the number enrolled. Part-time and evening tuition is costed by course-hours per student (and fees paid per course based on hours per course). Full-time tuition is costed per term per student (and we may note in passing that schools, colleges and universities exemplify high operating leverage so must ensure a minimum number of enrolments per course if the courses are to run). Private hospital costs are related to the treatment and facilities provided. These in turn are functions of time spent by each patient in hospital and the type of treatment/facilities provided. The composite cost unit in this situation is the treatment day. Types of treatment could be coded alphabetically, with type A representing the most expensive, type Z the least. The cost unit would be expressed as the A day, the B day and so forth. Patients would be charged so many days of type A treatment, so many days using type M facilities and so on.

Generally, services are costed on time rates, with the rate per hour being related to the level of skill and of pay of the labour providing the service. Car repairs are costed per fitter-hour; while psychologists' fees are based on a much higher rate per hour of consulting time and so on. Accountancy firms and lawyers base their costings on rates per hour, with junior clerical time having the lowest hourly rate and senior partners having the highest. All staff in service firms need to complete time-sheets indicating how time has been spent, so that the correct client can be charged with the rate and hours applicable. Time not spent on client matters will be chargeable as overhead and will not be directly claimable from any client because of the CR.

JOB AND BATCH COSTING

Introduction

The GAF does not apply to job costing, as jobs cannot be aggregated on the denominator to give a "total jobs done in the period" with any validity because no two jobs are identical. Of course, the GAF could be used to give management a figure for average cost per job done during the year, but such a figure could not be used as the basis for pricing, as no *actual* future job could be guaranteed to resemble the previous *average* cost profile. Each job must be separately costed because each job is a unique cost unit. A job is any work done to execute a customer's instructions per the customer's order. A customer may ask for several tasks to be performed—for example, change the car plugs, service the car generally, repair the rear bumper and, finally, clean the car. In such a case there is usually one customer order which sets forth the various tasks required, and so in costing terms there is only one job. The job is circumscribed by the originating order, not by discrete tasks within the order.

Batch costing

Instead of manufacturing one article to a customer's specification, some firms produce a batch of standardised articles, say 500 at a time. Cost per article will be less than under pure jobbing production. Overheads such as machine depreciation and electricity can be distributed among 500 units instead of being wholly absorbed by one. A firm will not produce in batches unless it has orders for batches or is confident of being able to sell all the articles in the batch. A production order is raised by the production manager, the production control department (in a large company) or by the customer for each batch. The costing method used is just like job costing, but the cost statements and cost accounts focus on the batch (rather than on the single article as happens in job costing). The batch is the cost unit, but the cost of each article within the batch can be found by applying the GAF. Thus:

$$\text{cost per article} = \frac{\text{total cost of batch per batch account}}{\text{Total number of } saleable \text{ units in the batch}}$$

Job cost bookkeeping

An account is opened for each job in the cost ledger with all entries being matched by control postings to the Cost Control Account. In an integral system of job cost accounting a frequently observed alternative is to keep the job accounts in a so-called work-in-progress ledger and to control that ledger by a work-in-progress control account with which the balance on the job accounts are regularly reconciled. Double entry is between material, labour, expense and overhead accounts on the one hand, and individual job accounts on the other (although some firms make the Control Account represent the other side of the double entry and keep the job accounts on a memorandum basis).

Each job is *debited* with the following as incurred.

(*a*) Materials issued from store—credit Stores Account.

(*b*) Materials purchased from suppliers—credit cash-book or bought ledger.

(*c*) Direct wages paid for time on this job—credit Gross Wages Account.

(*d*) Direct expenses—credit bought or nominal ledger account concerned.

(*e*) Overhead absorbed (usually on the basis of direct labour-hours)—credit overhead control in the nominal ledger.

(*f*) Any items transferred from another job—credit other job account.

Credited from the job accounts when appropriate are:

(*a*) materials returned to stores—debit Stores Account;

(*b*) items (not labour though!) transferred—debit the job account receiving the items; and

(*c*) cost of completed job (the balance on the account after all items have been entered)—debit the Cost of Sales Account (or, if job is a product, the Finished Goods Account is sometimes preferred).

In sum the job is charged (debited) with all the cost elements entering the job and an apportionment of overheads. It is credited with items left over or transferred, then finally *cleared* by a credit entry reflecting the total job cost. Any scrap sales arising from the job would have their proceeds credited to the Job Account, the corresponding debit being to the cash-book. All the entries listed above would also be made in the Control Account *except for* transfer of items between jobs, as such transfers do not affect the aggregate cost of work-in-progress.

Job cost cards

Each job is given a job number (sometimes called a "work number"), a job card being prepared at the outset of the job. The job card is used to collect all the cost data relating to the job. Direct materials and parts are listed, labour time and rates recorded, and direct expenses and production overheads are listed. Each of these items is totalled, then entered in a summary form on the card, thus giving the factory or production cost of the job. Thus far the job card is very similar to a manufacturing account, as both gather costs to reveal a total production cost. However, on the job card selling, distribution and other non-production overheads are apportioned to give a total job cost which should be identical to the cost shown in the Job Account.

The job card is kept in the factory or cost office, while the Job Account is usually kept in the accounts department. Regular audit should ensure that these match. The job card tends to be used to price the job, while the Job Account is used for period reports such as monthly reports against budgets. The cost office and the accounts department should both receive the same documentary data (such as copies of time-sheets, of materials issue notes and expense invoices) if the Job Account and job card are to stand a chance of matching. This is a matter of good systems design, which is outside the scope of this book, although some discussion of documentary system efficiency is necessary in Chapter 6 when control systems are examined.

An example of job costing

In July a firm was engaged in four jobs, all of which began in that month. The following details relate to the jobs' cost elements for July.

| | JOB NUMBERS | | | | |
	150	151	152	153	Totals
(All figures are in £)					
Purchases	2,000	2,100	1,400	500	6,000
Stores issues	240	—	700	80	1,020
Direct gross wages	900	600	700	500	2,700
Direct expenses	—	100		—	400	500
Materials returned to store	—	—	40	20	60
Materials transferred	(80) to 152	—	80 from 150	—	—

July's overhead expenditure was £3,600 and is absorbed on the basis of $1\frac{1}{3}$ of direct wages. Job 151 was completed in July and invoiced to the customer at £5,000. The other jobs remained in progress at the month end.

We shall use the above data to write up the job accounts, the Work-in-Progress Control Account, the Overhead Control Account and the March

Cost Ledger Profit & Loss Account. We begin with the Work-in-Progress Control Account, as most of the entries thereto are simply the row totals from the above table.

WORK-IN-PROGRESS CONTROL ACCOUNT

Dr	£	Cr	£
Purchases	6,000	Stores	60
Stores	1,020	Cost of sales—job 151	3,600
Direct gross wages	2,700	Balances c/d	10,160
Direct expenses	500		
Overheads (absorbed)	3,600		
	13,820		13,820
Balance b/d	10,160		

Note that the materials transfer does not appear in the Control Account and the cost of the complete job, No 151, is credited (after absorbing overhead at $1\frac{1}{3}$ of wages) to cost of sales. The closing balance of £10,160 is the cost to date of jobs not completed and represents the cost of month end work-in-progress. The job accounts now follow.

JOB 150 ACCOUNT

Dr	£	Cr	£
Purchases	2,000	Transfers to job 152	80
Stores	240	Balance c/d	4,260
Wages	900		
Overheads	1,200		
	4,340		4,340
Balance b/d	4,260		

JOB 151 ACCOUNT

Dr	£	Cr	£
Purchases	2,100	Cost of sales	3,600
Wages	600		
Direct expenses	100		
Overheads	800		
	3,600		3,600

JOB 152 ACCOUNT

Dr	£	Cr	£
Purchases	1,400	Returned to stores	70
Stores	700	Balance c/d	3,773
Wages	700		
Overheads	933		
Transfers			
from job 150	80		
	3,813		3,813
Balance b/d	3,773		

JOB 153 ACCOUNT

Dr	£	Cr	£
Purchases	500	Returned to stores	20
Stores	80	Balance c/d	2,127
Wages	500		
Direct expenses	400		
Overheads	667		
	2,147		2,147
Balance b/d	2,127		

The balances brought down on the job accounts should sum to the balance on the Work-in-Progress Control Account if our bookkeeping is right. The w-i-p balance was 10,160 and the job account balances of 4,260, 3,773 and 2,127 do add up to 10,160, so our bookkeeping seems to be correct.

OVERHEAD CONTROL ACCOUNT

Dr	£	Cr	£
Overhead expenditure	3,600	Overhead absorbed (w-i-p control)	3,600

COST PROFIT & LOSS ACCOUNT

	£		£
Cost of sale—job 151	3,600	Sale—job 151	5,000
Profit to			
P.& L. Account in			
nominal ledger	1,400		
	5,000		5,000

Had there been more than one completed job in July, the cost Profit & Loss Account would have shown a list of job costs of sale and a list of sales incomes, both subtotalled to reveal the period profit for the month. This would not allow us to ascertain the profit made on each job, so a better alternative layout which would achieve this objective is shown below.

COST PROFIT & LOSS ACCOUNT

Job no	Cost of sale	Sales income	Job profit	Total profit and adjustments
151	£3,600	£5,000	£1,400	£1,400

The final column in this revised layout enables us to total the profits from jobs completed in the month and then make such adjustments as subtracting under recovered overhead or adding over recovered overhead as well as any entering any other variances of a general nature that it is inequitable (or too late) to apply to any specific job. The final figure of profit after adjustments is transferred to the P. & L. Account in the nominal ledger and accumulated therein as profit from jobs done in the year.

CONTRACT COSTING

Nature of a contract

A contract is a legally binding agreement capable of being enforced in the civil courts by the party inconvenienced by the other party's breach of contract. Contract costing is particularly concerned with construction contracts where work continues for a long period, where the contract is a written document usually under seal and where the overall contract price is determinable. Before a client awards a construction contract, construction firms are invited to tender for the work. The client's architect will have prepared plans and the client's surveyor prepared a bill of quantities closely specifying the work to be done, and listing the materials and plant to be used in doing the work. A tender is submitted by filling in the bill of quantities so that the final total represents the price at which the contractor is prepared to do the work for the client. The client then selects a tender, not necessarily the one showing the lowest contract price, and awards the contract to the firm which submitted the tender selected. The contract is drawn up, then signed by client and contractor; from then on it is binding.

It is becoming general practice for contractors to protect themselves from the effects of cost inflation by including inflation adjustment clauses in the contract. Some clients will not allow such clauses and insist that tenders form the basis of a fixed contract price. Other clients, notably some government offices, insist that the contract be on a cost plus basis where the client approves the cost (per tender) and agrees in the contract to pay a percentage (say 5 per cent) above cost. Profit margins are thin in contract businesses, and bankruptcy rates noticeably high in the construction and allied industries partly in consequence of this.

Contract accounts are accounts in the contractor's books—not the client's—where costs are accumulated for each contract. They are similar to job accounts in essence but unlike them in one vital respect. Job accounts are (or should be) pure cost accounts with sales credited in the Cost P. & L. Account. Contract accounts are more like trading accounts than cost accounts, because credit is taken for the *sales value* of work done in the contract account itself. The account thus explicitly treats each contract not only as a cost centre only but as a profit centre—a cost centre generating directly its own income. It will be recalled that the cost centre (the building site) in contracting is also the cost unit (the building to be sold).

Contract costing terms

There are a small number of terms peculiar to contract costing. These are presented below with an explanation of each one.

(*a*) Prime cost—the direct costs charged to a contract. Virtually all materials and expenses are directly allocatable to a specific contract. Labour on site is direct, *inclusive* of site foremen, site clerks-of-works and night watchmen, because they are wholly and exclusively at the cost centre which is also the cost unit. Off-site costs will consist largely of head office running costs charged to the contract as overheads. These head office costs are associated with the paperwork arising from contracts. They therefore tend to vary with prime cost; overheads are apportioned to, and absorbed by, contracts on the prime cost percentage basis (e.g. 25 per cent of prime cost per period).

(*b*) Work certified—the sales value of work done on site. The client's architect regularly inspects the site and issues an architect's certificate stating how far the building has satisfactorily progressed. The certificate gives the value of work done, using the contract price as the measure of sales value. Take, for example, a fixed price contract to build four large houses for a total price of £1 million. The certificate issued after satisfactory completion of the second house might state "phase two fully complete—value of total work to date £500,000". The valuation is always cumulative. In the current example half the work has been done, so the work is certified at half the contract price. To calculate the value of work done since the last certificate was issued, we can easily deduct previous work certified from current work certified. The contractor uses the architect's certificates to confirm work done when he invoices the client. The value of work done since the previous certificate is the amount billed to the client, and the client's remittance in response to the invoice is termed a "progress payment". Contract accounts are not concerned with progress payments but do record the value of work certified.

(c) Subcontractors—firms or individual people doing such specialised work as plumbing on behalf of the main contractor. Labour only subcontractors may have to be treated for UK income tax purposes very similarly to direct labour. However, for costing purposes all subcontractors represent direct expenses. This is because all subcontractors should submit an invoice to the main contractor as a prerequisite of being paid. Fortunately, for contract costing purposes, the labour/expenses is not of major importance, as both are prime costs. If in any specific contracting firm overheads are recovered against direct wages or direct labour-hours, the distinction becomes important once more in order to safeguard against major overhead volume variances.

(d) Retention clauses—in the contract allow the client to hold back a specified percentage of the contract price for a specified period beyond the end of the contract. This is to insure the client against defective work. The contractor is paid the retention money only after any defects have been made good.

(e) Penalty clauses—in the contract allow the client to charge the contractor (using the retention monies to do so) for any work not completed within specified periods. The contractor is thus pulled in opposite directions. Penalty clauses induce him to work fast (or at least dissuade him from working slowly), while retention clauses preclude him from taking any time-saving short cuts that might result in the denial of an architect's certificate.

(f) Profit in suspense—profit carried down at the year end in the contract accounts from one year to the next. Because contracts face retentions and possible penalties, it is imprudent to credit the main Profit & Loss Account published for shareholders with *all* profit earned on contracts. Part of profits earned are "saved up" as contract profit in suspense, against which penalities and retentions can be charged. Any uncharged balance after full completion of the contract can be cleared to the main Profit & Loss Account.

Contract accounting
Contract accounts are debited with:

(a) materials delivered to site from stores, suppliers or other sites;
(b) the gross pay of direct labour on site;
(c) direct expenses including subcontractors;
(d) depreciation of any fixed assets owned by the firm and in use on the site. Many large firms now achieve this by running a plant division as a profit centre which hires out plant to sites for a hire charge to cover depreciation and related costs. The division will hire out plant surplus to site requirements to the contracting public at commercial daily, weekly or monthly rates;

(*e*) accruals under any of the previous headings;

(*f*) the profits to date on the contract, part being carried down as profit in suspense, the rest being credited to the Profit & Loss Account;

(*g*) stocks, work-in-progress and prepayments brought down from the credit side of the contract account in the previous period; and

(*h*) overheads apportioned.

The contract account is credited with:

(*a*) materials leaving the site to go back to store, to supplier or to other sites;

(*b*) prepayments (which are carried down to the debit of the subsequent period);

(*c*) period end stock on site (carried down) and work-in-progress (which means the cost of any work done but not yet certified—this is carried down to be certified in the subsequent period);

(*d*) the value of work certified in the period. This means the value certified on the last certificate issued in the year, less the value certified on the last certificate issued in the previous year (for which profit was taken in the published Profit & Loss Account of that previous year);

(*e*) accruals brought down from the previous year; and

(*f*) profit in suspense brought down from the previous year.

Computation of profit in suspense

The profit in suspense is the total of profit in suspense brought forward from the previous year plus the profit in suspense arising from work in the current year. Current year profit in suspense is computed on terms dependent on the content of the contract itself, but the general formulae now given applies to all situations.

Profit in suspense = Contract profit less profit credited to the main Profit & Loss Account

Contract profit = Value of work (certified) less cost of work, excluding closing w-i-p

Profit credited to main P. & L. = ($\frac{2}{3}$ of contract profit) $\times \dfrac{\text{value certified less retentions}}{\text{value certified}}$

Example: Retentions of 5 per cent are withheld from invoices and progress payments which are for work certified in the year as having a value of £100,000 and for which the contract account shows a cost of £70,000.

Contract profit = £(100,000 − 70,000) = £30,000

Profit credited to P. & L.

$$= £(30,000 \times \tfrac{2}{3}) \times \left(\frac{100,000 - 5,000}{100,000}\right) = £20,000 \times \frac{95}{100} = £19,000$$

Profit in suspense = £(30,000 − 19,000) = £11,000 which is added to any profit in suspense brought forward to give the profit in suspense carried forward.

The practice of crediting only main P. & L. with two-thirds of contract profit after accounting as above for retentions is general and has the effect of profit in suspense always being large enough at the contract end to meet penalty charges or legal claims. That any profit is credited to published P. & L. before a contract is finished reflects the fact that profits have been made from invoiced sales (the invoices following the architects' certificates) and have been largely realised (in the form of progress payments receivable).

An example of contract accounting

A contract account is shown below to reflect the following information. At the end of 1982, work amounting to 60 per cent of the full contract 311 had been certified. At the end of 1983, 75 per cent had been certified. The contract price is £5 million. The contract has a 10 per cent retention clause; this is applied in each invoice and progress payment.

At the end of 1982 the following items were carried forward: stocks of materials, £30,000; work done but not certified, £65,000; accrued expenses, £10,000; prepaid expenses, £15,000; and profit in suspense of £150,000.

At the end of 1983 the following items are to be carried forward; stocks, £70,000; work done but not certified, £120,000; accrued subcontract charges, £10,000; prepaid expenses, £10,000; and an appropriate amount of profit in suspense.

During 1983 materials costing £200,000 were issued from store to site. Materials costing £50,000 were returned from site to store. A total of £330,000 of materials was purchased, £100,000 was transferred from contract 308, and £50,000 was transferred to contract 314. Gross wages paid to site labour and staff totalled £300,000. Direct expenses billed to the site were £90,000 (inclusive of subcontractors' and architects' fees).

The book value of plant on site at 1st January 1983 was £490,000, and at the end of 1983 was £410,000, the difference being charged as plant usage by plant division. In addition, £20,000 of short-term plant hire charges were incurred, but these also were *not* included in direct expenses.

Overheads are recovered at one-ninth of prime cost.

A heavy storm destroyed materials costing £30,000 on 2nd July; these were replaced at cost on 10th July. Both deliveries are included in the yearly total of materials purchased. The insurance claim arising from this is not yet settled.

Workings

1. Work certified in the year = (75% − 50%) of £5 million = £1,250,000.

2. Materials purchased overstated by £30,000, which arose from the storm damage. The RAE applies to this cost, so £30,000 must be excluded.

3. Plant usage = opening plant value less closing = £80,000.

4. All items enter into the cost computation except the profit in suspense.

5. Prime cost = all costs brought down + costs in the year − costs carried down: (£000) = (110 − 10) + 990 − 190 = 900

6. Overheads = $\frac{1}{9}$ of 900 = 100 (£000)

7. Total costs = 900 + 100 = 1,000 (£000)

8. Contract profit = 1,250 − 1,000 = 250 (£000)

9. Profit to P. & L. = $\frac{2}{3} \times$ 90% of 250,000
$$= \frac{2}{3} \text{ of } 225,000$$
$$= 150,000$$

10. Profit in suspense = 250,000 − 150,000 = 100,000
$$\text{\textit{Add} PIS b/d} \quad \underline{150,000}$$
$$\text{PIS c/d} \quad \underline{250,000}$$

CONTRACT 311 ACCOUNT
1983

Dr	£000s	£000s	Cr		£000s
Stocks brought down	30		Profit in suspense b/d		150
W-i-p b/d	65		Stocks c/d	70	
Prepayment b/d	15		W-i-p (work done		
	110		but not certified)		
Less accruals b/d	10		c/d		
Costs b/d		100		120	
Materials in the year			Costs c/d		190
Store issues	200		Work certified		
Purchases	300		in the year		1,250
Transfer from 308	100				1,590
	600				
Less store returns	50				
	550				
Less transfers to 314	50				
Total		500			
Direct wages		300			
Direct expenses					
Plant usage	80				
Plant hire	20				
Other expenses	90				
Accrued subcontractors					
c/d	10				
	200				
Less prepayments c/d	10	190			
Overheads					
Profits					
Credited to P. & L. a/c	150				
Profit in suspense c/d	250	400			
		1,590			

PRINCIPLES OF PROCESS COST ACCOUNTING

Introduction
Process costing applies to the majority of factories because most manufacturing consists of a sequential series of processes. We shall use as our example a firm making only one end-product—loaves of bread. We shall simplify breadmaking into four sequential processes: milling, refining, baking and packaging. In pages 65–76 we shall introduce more complicated processes.

Each process is a cost centre and the cost unit is the end-product of the final process, in this case packaging. The GAF applies to process costing, but it is the GAF modified for normal losses and scrap sales which was:

$$\frac{\text{Total costs} - \text{scrap sales proceeds}}{\text{Units normally produced in saleable condition}}$$

We shall deal with further modifications necessary below.

The purpose of the process accounts is to accumulate costs from raw materials input stage to finished product stage so as to provide the numerator of the GAF. Following the CR properly, accounts should reflect the physical flow of units through the processes. This means that the major output of each process is a major input to the next process. The accounts reflect this by crediting a process account with its output and debiting it with input from the previous process. Outputs from one process to the next are semi-finished units so are work-in-progress. However, in process accounts it is better to call the output "output" and to reserve the term "work-in-progress" for units not fully processed by the process in question at the period end. Period end work-in-progress for Balance Sheet purposes will consist both of work-in-progress just defined *plus* output that has passed fully through any of the intermediate processes but is not yet in a fully finished condition.

Process accounts are not generally kept like other cost accounts but instead show two columns on the debit and on the credit side, one column for the physical quantities being processed, the other for costs in £s. Some firms also have a third column to show unit element costs, but this can be seriously misleading in certain cases and is not recommended.

Equivalent units
To compute work-in-progress as defined above we have to translate the units in mid-process to their equivalent in units which have completed the process. In the physical column we enter the w-i-p units at their physical quantity. For example, 500 units in mid-process are entered in the units column as 500 in all circumstances. The need to compute equivalent completed units is necessary for the cost column only, not for the physical units column. If our 500 units are 50 per cent complete (i.e. half-way through the process), their equivalent in completed units is 250. If the unit process cost is £2, w-i-p is valued at $250 \times £2 = £500$.

Units in mid-process may be complete in one cost element, say materials, but unfinished in the other elements (direct conversion costs and apportioned overheads). Suppose the 500 units in the previous paragraph were 100 per cent complete in materials but had only 10 per cent of their conversion complete. Suppose, further, that the £2 unit cost is decomposed into 50p unit material cost and £1.50 unit conversion and overhead cost. Then, 500 is still the right number for the physical units column but the entry in the cost column is computed thus:

	£
500 units 100% complete in materials at 50p per unit	
Equivalent material units $500 \times 100\% = 500$	
Materials cost of w-i-p = $500 \times 50p =$	250
500 units 10% complete in conversion and o/h at £1.50 per unit	
Equivalent conversion units $500 \times 10\% = 50$	
Conversion cost of w-i-p = $50 \times £1.50 =$	75
∴ Total cost *to date* of 500 units of w-i-p =	325

In the cost column £325 is entered as work-in-progress. This computation obeys the RAA. If anything other than 500 were entered in the physical units column the RVR would be broken, as it is 500 units in fact and *not* their completed equivalents which are actually in mid-process. The equivalent units figure is *never* entered in the process accounts.

Losses at the end of a process
Every process will have its own predetermined normal loss rate. Let us suppose this to be 10 per cent. For every 1,000 units entering a process, 100 are normally lost as scrap, waste or spoilage and 900 are transferred to the next process. In the process account both the 100 units lost and the 900 transferred on are credited. The 900 units are transferred at the full cost of production per the process account *inclusive of the cost of making the lost 100 units*. The 100 units are credited as normal loss with the entry 100 in the physical units column *but with a dash in the cost column* (except when scrap sales are involved, but we defer consideration of them until later in the chapter). The dash in the cost column is to signify that normal losses have no cost attributed directly to them but instead their cost is borne by good production transferred to the next process.

Actual production may be greater than the predetermined normal loss. The excess of actual over normal is termed "abnormal loss". Following the RAE, such abnormal losses cannot be carried by units of satisfactory output as we just saw happen with normal losses. The Process Account is credited with the full cost of abnormal losses. If we lost 600 units in a month against a normal loss of 500, we should credit the Process Account with abnormal loss, entering 100 in the units column and (given unit costs of £2) £200 in the cost column.

If actual loss is less than normal loss, the shortfall is termed "abnormal gain". The entries in the Process Account are just the same as for abnormal loss but they take place *on the debit side* of the account. The effects of this are discussed in pages 71–2.

Process account bookkeeping

The units column of the Process Account is debited *only* with the units incoming from the previous process. In the account for the first process in the sequence the units column debit is against materials. No other entries are made in the units column of the debit side unless there are any units of abnormal gain or opening work-in-progress. Except for the first process, materials are never debited with units. In no circumstances are conversion costs (labour and expenses) or overheads debited with physical units.

The cost column is debited with:

(*a*) input from previous process;
(*b*) opening w-i-p brought down;
(*c*) materials used by the process;
(*d*) direct conversion costs, either as a single figure or analysed into its direct wage and direct expense elements;
(*e*) overhead allocated and apportioned to the process; and
(*f*) abnormal gains.

The units column on the credit side will contain entries for:

(*a*) normal losses;
(*b*) units transferred to the next process, or in the final process to finished goods store;
(*c*) abnormal losses; and
(*d*) closing w-i-p carried down.

The cost column is credited with the same items as the units column, with the important exception of normal losses which receive only a dash in the cost column.

Example of process accounts

RHD plc produced 900,000 loaves of bread in August. Data for each process are tabulated below.

	Milling	Refining	Baking	Packaging
Normal loss rate	–	10%	5%	–
Actual loss rate	5%	5%	10%	–
Materials (£000s)	25	10	1	5
Conversion (£000s)	10	10	19	5
Opening w-i-p (£000s)	2	1	–	–
Opening w-i-p units	5,263	2,632	–	–

Total overhead of £25,000 is apportioned on the basis of direct labour hours and these were:

	Milling	Refining	Baking	Packaging
	250	750	1,000	500

Before we can write up the process accounts we have to work out the entries not obvious from the above data.

First, we have to compute the relevant physical units. The number of loaves output from packaging is 900,000. Since there are no losses or w-i-p, the same number must be input from the previous process, baking. Baking has an output of 900,000. An actual loss rate is suffered of 10 per cent. If the baking output is 900,000 after 10 per cent actual loss, then, since the loss rate is applied against *input*, this means output is $(100 - 10) = 90\%$ of input. To find the input we multiply output by $\frac{100}{90} = \frac{10}{9}$. $900,000 \times \frac{10}{9} = 1,000,000$ and this is the input from refining. Refining suffers actual loss of 5 per cent, so its input must be

$$\frac{100}{100 - 5}\% = \frac{100}{95}\%$$

of 1,000,000 which to the nearest whole number = 1,052,632. Part of this input is opening w-i-p of 2,632 units. The input from milling is $1,052,632 - 2,632 = 1,050,000$ units. Milling also suffers an actual loss rate of 5 per cent, so input is $\frac{100}{95}\%$ of 1,050,000 units = 1,105,263 to the nearest whole number. Of this, 5,263 comes from opening w-i-p, so the input in units (of loaf ingredient) to milling is 1,100,000 units as materials.

These results are tabulated below:

	Milling	Refining	Baking	Packaging
Input	1,100,000	1,050,000	1,000,000	900,000
Opening w-i-p	5,263	2,632	—	—
Output	1,050,000	1,000,000	900,000	900,000
Actual loss[1]	55,263	52,632	100,000	—
Normal loss[2]	—	105,263	50,000	—
Abnormal loss[3]	55,263	—	—	—
Gain		52,631	50,000	—

[1] Input + opening w-i-p − output
[2] 10 per cent and 5 per cent respectively of input + opening w-i-p
[3] Actual loss − normal loss.

Next, we have to apportion the £25,000 overhead pro rata to labour-hours. Total labour-hours are $250 + 750 + 1,000 + 500 = 2,500$. Applying the GAF overhead recovery rate per hour is £10, and overheads recovered from the process cost centres are simply $10 \times$ labour-hours.

Finally, we have to compute unit costs for each process so as to work out the entries in the cost columns for output and abnormal losses. This is done in the table overleaf.

£000s		Milling	Refining	Baking	Packaging
Materials		25	10	1	5
Conversion		10	10	19	5
Overheads		2.5	7.5	10	5
Opening w-i-p		2	1	–	–
Cost of input from previous process		–	39.5	68	–
Accumulated costs		39.5	68	98	113
Output units	1,050,000		1,000,000	900,000	900,000
+ Abnormal loss	55,263		–	5,000	–
or – Abnormal gain	–		(52,631)	–	–
Normal production units	1,105,263		947,369	952,500	900,000

GAF: $\dfrac{\text{Accumulated costs}}{\text{Normal production units}}$ – Unit costs

		= 3.57p	7.18p	10.29p	12.56p

We use the unit costs to value closing w-i-p and abnormal gains and losses thus:

	Milling	Refining	Baking	Packaging
1. Unit cost in pence	3.57	7.18	10.29	12.56
2. Units of abnormal loss (gain in brackets)	55,263	(52,631)	50,000	—
3. Cost of abnormal loss (gain)(row 1 × row 2)	£1,973	£(3,779)	£5,145	—

We may note in passing that the cost of opening w-i-p seems extraordinarily high for milling and refining, perhaps owing to special circumstances operating in the previous month! We are now ready to write up the process accounts for August.

MILLING PROCESS ACCOUNT

Dr	Units	£	Cr	Units	£
Opening w-i-p	5,263	2,000	Output to refining	1,050,000	37,527
Materials	1,100,000	25,000	Abnormal loss	55,263	1,973
Conversion	—	10,000			
Overheads	—	2,500			
	1,105,263	39,500		1,105,263	39,500

Note: The cost of output is the balancing item (total debits – abnormal loss).

REFINING PROCESS ACCOUNT

Dr	Units	£	Cr	Units	£
Opening w-i-p	2,632	1,000	Output to baking	1,000,000	69,806
Input from					
Milling	1,050,000	37,527	Normal loss	105,263	—
Materials	—	10,000			
Conversion	—	10,000			
Overhead	—	7,500			
Abnormal gain	52,631	3,779			
	1,105,263	69,806		1,105,263	69,806

Note: In this case units of normal loss are a balancing item but they do in fact equal 10 per cent of input plus opening w-i-p, as they should.

BAKING PROCESS ACCOUNT

Dr	Units	£	Cr	Units	£
Input from			Output to		
refining	1,000,000	69,806	packaging	900,000	94,661
Materials	—	1,000	Normal loss	50,000	—
Conversion	—	19,000	Abnormal loss	50,000	5,145
Overhead	—	10,000			
	1,000,000	99,806		1,000,000	99,806

PACKAGING PROCESS ACCOUNT

Dr	Units	£	Cr	Units	£
Input from					
baking	900,000	94,661	Finished goods	900,000	109,661
Materials	—	5,000			
Conversion	—	5,000			
Overheads	—	5,000			
	900,000	109,661		900,000	109,661

ADVANCED ASPECTS OF PROCESS COSTING

Process loss at process end and closing w-i-p

So far we have treated losses as all occurring at the end of a process. Following the RAA, we charge units with costs only as they are incurred. Units lost at the process end are thus chargeable with all cost elements debited to the process. Suppose a process has an input of 5,000 units, no w-i-p and a normal loss rate of 20 per cent. Total costs debited are £20,000. This cost is borne exclusively by the good units, which number 80 per cent of 5,000 = 4,000. Applying the GAF we have a unit cost of £5. Any closing w-i-p in this situation will not yet have suffered the process loss. If 1,000 units 50 per cent complete represented closing w-i-p in the previous example, 1,000 w-i-p of the 5,000 units input cannot suffer the losses, as they are not at the process end. This leaves relevant input of 4,000 to which the 20 per cent rate applies, so normal loss units would be 20 per cent of 4,000 = 800. Unit cost in this situation has to modify the GAF in order to reflect the existence of closing w-i-p as well as its effect on the amount of normal loss units. Thus:

$$\text{Unit cost} = \frac{\text{Total costs debited}}{\text{Units of satisfactory production + equivalent units of closing w-i-p}}$$

$$= \frac{£20,000}{(4,000 - 800) + (50\% \text{ of } 1,000)} = \frac{£20,000}{3,200 + 500}$$

$$= £5.41 \text{ (to the nearest penny)}$$

At first sight it seems odd that when we lose 800 units we have a unit cost of £5.41, whereas when we lose 1,000 units we have the lower unit cost of only £5. The difference is due to the existence of closing work-in-progress being only 50 per cent complete. If 1,000 units are only 50 per cent complete, that means we have lost in the current period the 500 equivalent units yet to be completed. Our effective loss in the period is then normal loss of 800 units plus equivalent units yet to be completed of 500 units, making a total effective loss of 1,300 units—a figure considerably higher than the 1,000 units lost when no closing w-i-p exists. Failure to complete conversion of all incoming units thus has the same effect on cost of completed units as have normal losses. Both reflect imperfections in the production process, although both may be impossible to avoid in practice.

Process losses at the start of a process and closing w-i-p
Again, let us suppose total costs are £20,000 for 5,000 input units, of which 1,000 are 50 per cent complete at the month end and a 20 per cent normal loss rate applies. This time process loss is suffered immediately the input from the previous process arrives. Clearly 4,000 units should be delivered to the next process, but of these 1,000 represent 50 per cent complete closing w-i-p. Applying the GAF to this situation:

$$\text{Unit cost} = \frac{\text{Total cost}}{\text{Satisfactorily completed units + equivalent units of closing w-i-p}}$$

$$= \frac{£20,000}{(4,000 - 1,000) + (50\% \text{ of } 1000)} = \frac{£20,000}{3,500} = 5.71$$

This unit cost is even higher than the £5.41 applicable when losses were at the process end. The reason for this is that our effective loss in the period is the full normal loss of 1,000 units plus 500 equivalent units yet to be completed, giving a total of 1,500 compared with the 1,300 applicable to end process losses with closing w-i-p.

Mid-process losses and closing w-i-p
Modifying our previous example we now have production losses occurring

when a unit is part way through the process. At the point where loss is incurred a unit is 50 per cent complete in added materials but only 25 per cent complete in conversion. Costs are still £20,000, normal loss rate still 20 per cent and closing w-i-p is still 1,000 units of an original 5,000 input units. The 50 per cent completion previously used still applies, but it consists of 1,500 units which are 40 per cent complete in materials and 20 per cent in conversion plus 500 units $93\frac{1}{3}$ per cent complete in materials and $46\frac{2}{3}$ per cent in conversion. The former we shall call the A units, the latter the B units. The A units are before the loss point, the B ones are after. We can treat the A units as we treated w-i-p with end process losses, and the B units as we treated start-of-process losses. We shall make the simplifying assumption that materials and conversion costs are exactly equal so that A's status as 40 per cent complete in materials and 20 per cent in conversion per cent has the effect of A units being:

$$\frac{40 + 20}{2} = 30\% \text{ complete overall while B units are}$$

$$\frac{93\frac{1}{3} + 46\frac{2}{3}}{2} = 70\% \text{ complete overall}$$

There are therefore 30 per cent of $500 = 150$ equivalent A units completed and 70 per cent of $500 = 350$ equivalent B units completed. The 500 A units are before the loss point, so are deducted from the input of 5,000 units to obtain the input to which the loss rate applies—4,500 units. The units of normal loss are 20 per cent of $4,500 = 900$ units, and the units of satisfactory production are $4,500 - 900 = 3,600$. However, of that 3,600 we have closing w-i-p beyond the loss point of 500 units and these increase our effective loss. The GAF is applied in its modified form thus:

$$\text{Unit cost} = \frac{\text{Total cost}}{\text{Satisfactory completed units} + \text{equivalent units of closing w-i-p}}$$

$$= \frac{£20,000}{(3,600 - 500) + 150 \text{ of A} + 350 \text{ of B}} = \frac{£20,000}{3,100 + 500}$$

= £5.56 a figure higher than the unit cost when all loss was end process but lower than the one when all loss was start-of-process; an unsurprising result.

Opening w-i-p and process losses
Retaining our example from the text above, but now making the 1,000 units opening w-i-p instead of closing, we shall see how unit costs are affected in each of the three alternative assumptions about loss points. The input of 5,000 units *includes* the w-i-p.

With end process losses, the opening w-i-p bears the losses in full as the units are completed and transferred out from the process before the period end. Five thousand units are input, but of these 1,000 units are 50 per cent complete at the start of the period. The normal loss rate of 20 per cent means an output of 4,000 satisfactorily completed units. The important point here is that 50 per cent of the work on the 1,000 units was done in the previous period. The £20,000 costs include the cost of opening w-i-p brought down, so is really the cost of fully converting the whole 5,000 units of input including the w-i-p. The £20,000 includes not just the cost of completing the w-i-p *but* the cost of creating it *in the previous period*— that is the effect of bringing down w-i-p from one period to the next. The unit cost is simply £20,000 ÷ 4,000 = £5. In this case the effect of opening w-i-p is identical to the effect of closing w-i-p and we have no need to consider equivalent units at all.

If the process were at the start of the process, then opening w-i-p of 1,000 units would have already borne the normal loss rate. The rate must therefore be applied to the other 4,000 units of input to give a normal loss of 800. In this case the number of satisfactorily completed units would be 4,000 − 800 = 3,200 plus the opening w-i-p of 1,000 units to give a total output of 4,200 units. Again, we assume the £20,000 total costs include the opening w-i-p brought down, so unit costs are £20,000 ÷ 4,200 = £4.76, the lowest unit cost so far. This is because we have the lowest level of effective loss so far—800 units only.

Finally, if our opening w-i-p consisted of the A units and B units described above with mid-process losses occurring as before, the 500 A units will suffer their loss in this period while the 500 B units suffered theirs in the previous period. The 5,000 input units include 500 B units which must be excluded from the computation of normal loss. This leaves 4,500 input units including A units w-i-p, and the loss suffered by these 4,500 units is 900 units. Units of satisfactory output will consist of 500 B units + (4,500 − 900 = 3,600), other units giving a total output of 4,100 units. Again, we assume the £20,000 total cost includes the cost of opening w-i-p brought forward. Unit costs are therefore £20,000 ÷ 4,100 = £4.88— higher than the previous cost of £4.76, but not as high as the first result of £5.

It can be seen that opening w-i-p is easier to handle than closing w-i-p in unit cost calculations, as it is unnecessary to compute equivalent units. Moreover, changing the assumption about when the process losses occur raised unit costs for closing w-i-p but lowered them for opening w-i-p. This, however, is due to our assumption that input units include opening w-i-p and that the total cost *included* the cost of w-i-p as well.

The calculation of w-i-p itself is the same, regardless of whether the w-i-p is opening or closing. What counts is work done to date in equivalent material and conversion units. The costs for valuing opening w-i-p, however, are the cost elements of the previous period, not the current one, since it was in the previous period that work was done to bring the w-i-p to its condition at the start of the current period.

Accounting for different types of loss

Scrap

The Process Account is credited with the physical units lost as normal scrap, but instead of a dash in the amounts column a figure is entered, following the RVR, that represents an accurate measure of the scrap's recoverable value. Scrap sales proceeds will often constitute the only measure available. Sometimes, however, scrap can be used in another process or another part of the firm altogether, so we must credit the amounts column with such "use value". The valuation of such value is part of the general problem of transfer pricing considered in Chapter 8. For the time being we shall assume the RVR to be satisfied if such scrap transfers are priced at an open market price, by which we mean the price that the user centre would have to pay to buy the scrap from an outside supplier. In sum, normal scrap is credited to the Process Account at its full physical measure in the units column and at its recoverable value in the cost column.

One final point should be noted. Suppose there are 100 units of normal scrap to be credited but only twenty have recoverable value (either as sales or transfers), amounting to £40 altogether. The 100 is credited to the units column and the £40 to the cost column, and the fact that only twenty units are responsible for the £40 is *irrelevant*, notwithstanding the CR. On a strict application of the CR we should enter eighty units and zero cost on one line as normal loss, then twenty units with a value of £40 also as normal loss on the next line. The effect is the same as entering 100 units and £40 on the same line. In any case, if the quantity and value of normal scrap is very large we should want to open a scrap trading account which would be credited with sales proceeds and transfer prices and debited both with normal scrap at zero cost and with abnormal scrap at full cost. Such a trading account would distinguish between incoming scrap with no recoverable value and other scrap as well as identifying the notional period profit made from scrap trading.

Normal scrap is always treated as having zero cost just like any other normal loss. Any entry in the cost column represents not cost but value. The effect of entering scrap value against normal scrap is to reduce the cost of satisfactory output. For example, 5,000 units input with process costs of £20,000 and a normal scrap rate of 20 per cent has a unit cost, as we saw above, of £5. If the 1,000 scrap units have a recoverable value of £2 each, their total value is £2,000. Applying the GAF, we have unit cost

$$= \frac{\text{Total costs} - \text{scrap sales values}}{\substack{\text{Units of satisfactorily completed} \\ \text{production}}} = \frac{£20,000 - 2,000}{4,000} = \frac{£18,000}{4,000} = £4.50$$

Abnormal scrap is credited in the Process Account at its full cost. Its full cost means its cost after absorption of its share of *normal* scrap losses less normal scrap recoverable values. Retaining our familiar example but now having actual scrap losses of 1,500 units, this means that 500 of the scrap units are abnormal scrap. The unit cost applicable is still £4.50, as this was found after accounting for *normal* loss. Abnormal scrap therefore costs $500 \times £4.50 = £2,250$, and that would be the entry against abnormal scrap in the cost column. However, if the abnormal scrap can obtain the same recoverable value as the normal scrap, £2, then its *net* unit cost is only £2.50 and the net cost to be entered against abnormal scrap loss is $(500 \times £2\frac{1}{2}) = £1,250$. The cost of satisfactorily completed output is not affected by abnormal scrap costs, gross or net of recoverable value; but the firm's overall period profit is affected—the smaller the *net* cost of abnormal scrap, the greater the period profit.

Wastage
This category is the easiest to deal with. If in pages 60–5 when we dealt with loss points, we replaced the word "loss" with the word "wastage", the costing and accounting treatment would be exactly as we outlined it then. Wastage is pure loss with no recoverable value, so no distinction between its gross and net costs is possible. When the word "loss" appears in a process costing question without any information as to the type of loss involved, it can be presumed to be wastage. Normal wastage is always credited at zero cost and abnormal wastage at full cost. No proceeds or transfers are possible.

Spoilage
Spoilage consists of products that have been through one or more processes but are defective and therefore unfit for sale. The distinction between spoilage and scrap is that the latter cannot be put through any rectifying process which will convert it into a satisfactory finished product. Spoilage can usually be rectified. All spoilage is credited to the Process Account yielding it and debited to the Spoilage Rectification Account. Costs of rectifying are debited to the Spoilage Rectification Account and the account is cleared by a credit transferring the rectified spoilage units to a normal process account or to finished goods. The Spoilage Rectification Account is itself a process account, but any normal spoilage is debited to it and credited in the Process Account at zero cost. Abnormal spoilage, like abnormal scrap, is written into the books at its full cost. Spoilage not fully rectified but sold as seconds is accounted for just as are scrap sales: proceeds are credited to the Process Account, directly for normal spoilage and indirectly as a deduction from gross cost for abnormal spoilage. Just as one can choose to keep a scrap trading account to ascertain profit on scrap sales, so one may keep a seconds trading account to ascertain profit on sales of spoilage.

Abnormal gains

Abnormal gains are debited in the Process Account at their full cost, the other side of the double entry being a credit in the Abnormal Loss Account. The Abnormal Account collects abnormal gains and losses through the year and is cleared at the year end to the Manufacturing Account. If at the year end the Abnormal Loss Account shows a debit balance, it is cleared by crediting it with the balance and debiting the Manufacturing Account. This has the effect of increasing the production cost for the year, but will not have affected product costs *during* the year because of the RAE. Conversely, if the Abnormal Loss Account shows a credit balance at the year end (because abnormal gains have exceeded abnormal losses), the effect of the transfer to the Manufacturing Account is to reduce the reported production cost for the year, but again product cost *during* the year will not reflect such reduction because of the RAE. Management may feel it sensible to change the predetermined normal loss rate if abnormal losses or gains have been regularly reported in any process.

Abnormal gain on scrap or spoilage rates is straightforward. The debit for these in the Process Account has the effect of increasing the debits in the account and hence of increasing the costs of process output (the main credit clearing the Process Account). This seems a strange result, as one would expect a gain to reduce costs, not increase them.

We have just seen how abnormal gains reduce the reported production cost at the year end in the Manufacturing Account. RAE means that abnormal items are to be excluded from costs, but now we are saying that abnormal gains increase process costs. The reason for this is that the result of abnormal gain is to increase the quantity of satisfactory units of output. Suppose that of 5,000 units of input with a 20 per cent normal loss rate, 4,500 units of output actually emerge. Given material conversion and overhead costs of £20,000 and no w-i-p, then unit cost is £5—as we have seen above. The £5 is the cost after accounting for a normal loss of 1,000 units, which implies only 4,000 satisfactory output units. The 500 units of abnormal gain are also valued at £5, to total £2,500. These are debited in the Process Account to give total debits of £22,500. These debits are borne by the sole credit—output to next process—which is costed at £22,500 as the result of the abnormal gain instead of at £20,000 which would have applied if no abnormal gain existed. There are 4,500 units of output, however, instead of the expected 4,000, so we would expect *total* output cost to be higher than normal. Unit cost of output is £22,500 ÷ 4,500 = £5 —confirmation that it is right to include the costs of abnormal gain in the cost of actual output. *Unit cost is unchanged by such inclusion*, so we have not, after all, breached the RAE.

Abnormal gains on scrap are debited at their *net* cost after sales proceeds, not at their gross cost before such proceeds. Thus the existence of such sales income will reduce the reported gain in the Process Account, and since gains are debited this will mean that costs of output will be that much less. This is common sense; one expects scrap income to reduce main product costs, and the accounting treatment just described ensures that this takes place.

Accounting for by-products

Definition
A by-product is any saleable product that emerges from a production process whose objective is to manufacture the main end-product. Scrap and saleable spoilage ("seconds") are thus types of by-product. The term is, however, usually reserved for products of sufficient sales value for it to be misleading to regard them as process losses in the way we regard scrap and spoilage. For example, if coal is heated without air, coke is obtained as a saleable by-product and so are such chemicals as benzene, creosote and bitumen. The difference between process losses and by-products is not a clear-cut one. It is a matter of the relative importance and value of the secondary products in the eyes of the management, not one of objective physical difference. However, the consequence of management's deeming a secondary product to be a by-product rather than to be scrap or spoilage is very important. The main end-product has to bear the cost of normal scrap and spoilage, but does not have the by-products' costs at all.

The RVR and by-products
Accounting for by-products involves a management decision as to how best to apportion process costs between the main end-product and the by-products. Decisions in accounting should automatically bring to mind the possible application of the Realistic Value Rule (RVR). Apportionment should be done on a basis that management believes to be most realistic for the circumstances of their particular business. The alternative bases to be considered are:

(*a*) standard value (credited to the Process Account);
(*b*) direct credit (to the Profit & Loss Account of sales income);
(*c*) realised value (credited to the Process Account);
(*d*) aggregation with main product; and
(*e*) joint product method (discussed below).

Explanation of by-product value bases

(*a*) *Standard value.* The by-product is given a standard value per unit representing a predetermined proportion (e.g. 75 per cent) of *average* expected sales income for each by-product. This value is credited in the Process Account and debited in a by-product trading account. The standard value is reviewed every year end but kept constant during the year.

This treatment isolates the reported costs of the main product from any price changes in the by-product. It is an easy method to operate but can involve breaches of the CR if major unanticipated process costs arise or if by-product sales income turns out to be widely different from the average expected.

(*b*) *Direct credit.* All by-product costs are treated as if they were normal losses in the process accounts. Process accounts are credited with units of by-product but at zero cost. The income arising from by-product sales is credited directly to the Profit & Loss Account as "other income". This is acceptable if the quantity and value of by-products is very small (say, less than 5 per cent), relative to the main product. In other circumstances this treatment would breach the CR by burdening the main product with costs of significant amounts of by-product. This could in turn involve main product customers paying more than really necessary, as a kind of subsidy to by-product customers.

(*c*) *Realised value* of by-products can be credited to process accounts either directly as per sales of normal scrap or indirectly as per abnormal scrap. If the output of by-products is significant, the abnormal scrap method should be used. This means by-products bear their full apportionment of costs incurred so far, but such costs are entered in the process accounts after subtracting sales proceeds. Now, since by-products will usually show a profit on costs to date (unlike scrap sales), we could be faced with reporting negative net costs. Suppose unit costs to date are £5 and by-products can be sold for £6, the abnormal scrap method would involve crediting the Process Account with £5 − £6 − − £1. Such a negative credit is bad accounting. One achieves the same effect in better accounting style by debiting the Process Account with profit on by-product sales (cf. abnormal gains). Conversely, losses on by-product sales would be credited to the Process Account. This treatment is the fairest if by-products are produced in significant quantities. Memoranda by-product trading accounts can be opened to show the profit or loss on sales of by-products.

(*d*) *Aggregation* of by-product sales with main product sales in the Trading Account involves a decision to treat by-products in the process accounts as indistinguishable from the main product. In other words, by-products never appear as such in the process accounts. This treatment is the simplest of all. However, it involves a direct breach of the CR no matter how insignificant the by-product may be. It cannot be justified except on the dubious grounds of administrative convenience.

(*e*) *Joint product method* treats by-products as if they were of comparable importance to the main product. This is justified in many instances and is recommended for any situation where the by-product accounts for over 10 per cent of physical output from a process or if its sales value exceeds 10 per cent of the main product's sales value. The treatment of joint products is detailed below.

Accounting for joint products

Definition of terms

Joint products are products of comparable importance that emerge from the production process at any point. As a rule of thumb, any product representing over 10 per cent by physical amount or by sales value of process output can be regarded as a joint product. While by-products may be the accidental result of a production process, joint products are planned. Many processes inevitably produce joint end-products rather than a single main product. For example, processing pig-meat involves producing the joint products bacon, ham, pork and sausage-meat as well as the probable by-product, lard. The more joint products a raw material can yield, the greater the productivity of the material.

Common costs, also called "joint costs", are costs incurred before the point that separates end-products can be identified. This point is called the "split-off point". After materials have passed the split-off point, the separated outputs go their separate ways through their individual finishing processes. Costs incurred after split-off are termed "subsequent costs".

Subsequent costs are debited to the Process Account as direct costs. Direct subsequent costs are easily allocatable to specific processes converting one specific product each. Overheads are recovered from post-split-off processes on the same basis as the firm uses for its other cost centres. The problem that arises with joint products is the valuation of input to the first of the post-split-off processes. Such input is the output of processes where separate end-products were not yet identifiable. The question is how to apply the RVR in apportioning common costs (incurred before split-off) to the separated joint products. This problem is discussed next.

Apportionment of common costs

There are two bases of apportionment found in practice to value output of the final pre-split-off process. One is the physical units basis; the other is the sales value basis.

Modifying the example we are now familiar with, let us suppose the incoming 5,000 units face a normal loss rate of 10 per cent and that one-ninth of normal output eventually becomes product A, one-third becomes product B and the rest (five-ninths) become product C. There is no w-i-p and process costs are £20,000. The split-off point and the loss point both occur at process end.

Of the 5,000 units of input, 500 are normally lost. The remaining 4,500 units are satisfactorily converted into output of A, B and C in the proportions 1, 3 and 5 respectively. Apportioning joint costs on the physical units basis involves dividing £20,000 by 9 to obtain the cost of A, multiplying A's cost by 3 to obtain B's cost and by 5 to obtain C's cost. A's output is thus valued at £2,222, B's at £6,667 and C's at £11,111 (all rounded to the nearest whole £). These are the values at which they will be credited from the process creating them and debited to their separate subsequent processes.

The physical basis is easy but it can be used only if outputs of joint product are commensurable—that is, if they are all expressed in the same units. Suppose in our example that the 5,000 units of input are actually 5,000 tonnes and that output of A is liquid and so measured in litres, while B is gaseous and so measured in cubic centimetres of a standard density, and only C emerges in solid form, so can be measured in tonnes. A, B and C are incommensurable, so that apportionment on a physical basis is very difficult and necessitates the use of production exchange ratios which translate the various measures of output back into tonnes of input. Even when such ratios are used, there is the further difficulty of deciding whether the normal pre-split-off loss is equitably apportioned on a physical output basis as the usual treatment of it implies. It might be that if we cut back on B type output our normal loss rate would be reduced to a far greater extent than if we cut back A or C. Using the CR we should then burden output B with a greater share of normal loss than A or C— this, however, will not reflect the physical output ratios. When the physical unit basis of apportionment is beset by the difficulties we have described, the sales value basis of apportionment should be used instead.

Apportionment on the sales value basis needs care. It is easy enough if the products are sold at the split-off point. Suppose A output is sold to realise £10,000 altogether, B to realise £20,000 and C to realise £20,000. Common costs are apportioned between A, B and C in the ratio 1:2:2. The resulting apportionments are £4,000 to A, £8,000 to B and £8,000 to C.

However, it is usually the case that products undergo further processing after split-off. Suppose the subsequent costs are £2,000 for A, £8,000 for B and £2,000 for C. These subsequent costs represent the work necessary to convert A, B and C from their raw state at the split-off point to a fully completed and saleable condition. Apportioning common costs on sales value in these circumstances has to reflect the Rule Against Anticipation (RAA). The sales proceeds that A, B and C eventually realise are partly the result of subsequent processing. Failure to take this subsequent processing into account breaches the RAE. If we apportion common costs on the basis of sales proceeds gross of subsequent costs, we are attributing to pre-split-off processes the work that is actually done post-split-off. In short, we are anticipating benefits before they arise. To prevent such a breach of the RAA, sales value is apportioned *net* of subsequent costs.

In our current example, instead of using the gross sales values of £(10,000:20,000:20,000) for A:B:C we use the net sales values, which are simply the gross values less the subsequent costs. Subsequent costs for A:B:C are £(2,000:8,000:2,000), so net sales values are £(8,000:12,000:18,000). These net values total £38,000. Common costs of £20,000 are apportioned $\frac{8}{38}$ to A, $\frac{12}{38}$ to B and $\frac{18}{38}$ to C. A, B and C are charged, in consequence, with £4,210, £6,316 and £9,474 respectively (all figures are to the nearest £). This apportionment should be compared with the one in the previous paragraph. The effect of taking subsequent costs into account is to increase A's share of common costs from £4,000 to £4,210, C's from £8,000 to £9,474, while B's are reduced from £8,000 to £6,316. This "redistribution" of common costs from B to C and A reflects the relatively small amount of C's subsequent costs (£2,000) relative to B (£8,000). A has the same subsequent costs as C, but these costs represent a greater proportion of A's sales income (£10,000) than they do of C's (£20,000). The net sales value method follows not only the RAA but the RVR as well. It is more *realistic* to apportion common costs on the basis of the sales value *at the split-off point* than at the point of sale. Here, obedience to the RAA automatically involves obedience to the RVR. Such harmony between the two rules is not always so readily obtained.

SUMMARY

The cost accounting rules

(*a*) CR (the Causative Rule)—costs should be charged only to those centres and units incurring them.

(*b*) RAA (the Rule Against Anticipating)—costs should not be charged before they are incurred.

(*c*) RAD (the Rule Against Deferrals)—future periods are not to be charged with sunk past costs.

(*d*) RAE (the Rule Against Abnormal and Exceptional Items)—only normal costs are to be treated as product costs.

(*e*) RVR (the Realistic Value Rule)—realistic values, often involving opportunity costs, are to be applied to assets in decision accounting.

The general absorption formula

The GAF states that unit cost is the result of dividing net total costs by the number of satisfactorily completed units (or their equivalents) in normal conditions. This can be expressed algebraically as

$$Cu = \frac{Ctn}{Nsp}$$

Uniform costing

The GAF can be directly applied to the mass production of one type of product or routine provision of one type of service.

Specific order costing

Job, batch and contract costs are collected in individual cost unit accounts. No two cost units are alike. Overheads are often recovered from cost units as a percentage of prime cost (but recovery against direct labour-hours is also quite widespread). Job accounts and batch accounts record only costs, sales income being credited to trading accounts. Contract accounts, however, record both costs and the sales value of work done, and, in addition, carry forward part of the profit made so far to future periods right up to the end of the contract. The contract is simultaneously both a cost unit and a cost centre.

Process costing

Process costing is a type of operation costing used when production involves a series of processes. Each process is a cost centre and is apportioned with its share of production overheads. Process losses are segregated between normal and abnormal; the former being costed at zero, the latter at their full net cost. Scrap sales proceeds are directly credited for normal scrap and applied to reduce the gross costs of abnormal scrap. W-i-p is costed after translating physical units into equivalent units of completed output. The point in the process where losses arise affects the cost of output, and the existence of w-i-p affects both the amount of normal loss and the total cost of process output. Spoilage rectification is costed just like any other process. By-products can be treated like normal scrap, abnormal scrap, joint products or even ignored altogether. Joint product common costs have to be apportioned between the joint products on the physical units basis where practicable and equitable, and the net sales value basis otherwise.

Cost accounting

In this chapter we have surveyed the methods of costing for all the operations, services and types of product found in business. We have used accounts employing double-entry bookkeeping to collect product cost unit costs. In other words, we have used cost accounting as our costing instrument. This is quite satisfactory in order to establish total unit costs on the absorption costing assumption. In the next chapter we shall see that cost accounting does not always offer the best means of achieving costing objectives. This will be further elaborated upon in Chapters 6, 8 and 9. As a foundation on which to build an understanding of costing and of management accountancy generally, cost accounting as outlined in the present chapter is indispensable. The chapter should be reread by the student, and he should bear in mind that the material in it is the vital foundation for the more advanced topics that follow.

QUESTIONS

1. Why is the GAF inapplicable to job costing?
2. Compare and contrast the information given in a contract account with that given in a manufacturing account.
3. What is the difference between operation costing and operating costing?

4. What happens to the amount of units normally lost when we change the assumption that process losses occur at process end to the assumption that they occur at the start of the process?

5. Why, when normal losses exist, does the effect of opening w-i-p go in the opposite direction from the effect of closing w-i-p on unit costs?

6. Explain the difference between work certified, progress payments and contract w-i-p.

7. How should cost units be identified in operating costing?

8. Contrast the accounting treatment of scrap sales proceeds for:

(*a*) normal losses;

(*b*) abnormal losses;

(*c*) abnormal gains; and

(*d*) spoilage sold as seconds.

9. Discuss the compliance of each of the methods of accounting for by-products with the fundamental costing rules.

10. How far is it true to say that the apportionment of common costs between joint products is a similar operation to the apportionment of overheads between cost centres?

For calculation questions, see Appendix V, questions 5–8.

CHAPTER FOUR

Stocks

I do not mind lying, but I hate inaccuracy.

Samuel Butler

OBJECTIVES

(*a*) To comprehend the nature and interrelationship of the most important factors in stock management.

(*b*) To be able to compute minimum stock level, reorder point level and economic order quantity.

(*c*) To be able to write up accurate stock accounts under FIFO, LIFO, weighted average cost or replacement cost assumptions.

(*d*) To apprehend the main arguments for and against the various methods of pricing stores issues to production.

(*e*) To understand the differences between, and the nature and effects of, absorption costing and marginal costing in the context of stock valuation.

(*f*) To appreciate the fundamentals of good stock management.

(*g*) To be able to calculate and interpret stock turnover periods.

(*h*) To be able to handle correctly make-or-buy decisions in the context of components held in materials stores.

(*i*) To grasp the fundamental concepts in decision accounting.

STOCK CONTROL

Introduction

Stocks of finished goods are held to minimise the effects of any differences between sales volume patterns and production volume patterns. When production volume exceeds sales, stockpiling occurs. When sales volume exceeds production levels, stock levels fall.

Stocks of raw materials are held because they are necessary to production. Control quantities are set for each type of raw material in order to control the costs associated with stocks. These are explained below.

Stocks of work-in-progress represent semi-finished articles and are held because they are inevitable concomitants of the production process. There is no virtue in holding w-i-p for its own sake and, in so far as possible, this level of stock should be minimised.

Overstocking causes the costs associated with stock to become unacceptably high. These costs are:

(*a*) storage (rent, heating, lighting, etc.);

(*b*) equipment (bins, pallets and handling machinery);

(*c*) personnel (stores staff, security staff and stock records clerks);

(*d*) insurance, deterioration and obsolescence of articles in store; and (*e*) opportunity costs of income lost through using funds to hold stocks rather than productive capital equipment.

Understocking leads to stockouts—that is, to being out of stock of a particular item. Consequences of stockouts include:

(*a*) loss of profit on lost sales;

(*b*) late deliveries leading to loss of goodwill and possibly penalty clauses;

(*c*) needing to buy substitutes on an emergency basis, usually at a price far above the normal; and

(*d*) dislocation of smooth production, causing labour and machine idle time to rise, both of which represent overhead costs that need not be incurred.

It is clear that a system is needed to prevent either overstocking or understocking. Overstocking is prevented by fixing for each item a maximum stock level. Understocking is avoided by fixing a minimum stock level (often called the "buffer stock"). Since suppliers take time to deliver materials, it is also necessary to fix the reorder point for each item, which is planned in such a way as to ensure that actual stock is not below the minimum level when the supplier eventually delivers the materials. Finally, for each item the amount to be ordered from the supplier at the reorder point is fixed so as to be at the optimum level below maximum and above minimum stocks. These four control quantities are calculated as shown below.

The control quantities

Maximum stock level
This level is set after evaluation of the risks of deterioration, the rate at which the stock item is issued to the production process and the storage costs. If it is set before the other levels, issue rate and storage costs will be the principal determinants. An item that is intensively used but has low storage costs will have a higher maximum set than an item with high storage costs and only infrequent issues to production.

Some writers on the subject state that maximum levels should be set after the reorder point and order quantity have been set. Since the reorder point cannot be set until the minimum level is set, this approach makes the maximum level a dependent variable, indirectly, of the minimum level. The calculation usually recommended for such dependent maxima is:

Maximum level = (reorder point level plus reorder quantity)
               Less (minimum average daily issues to production multiplied by minimum time taken from order to supplier delivery)
             = RPL + ROQ − (Min UD − Min LT) where UD is daily usage and LT is lead time.

The calculation of maximum stock level, given that it is not to be dependent on reorder point level and hence on minimum levels, involves probability calculations outside the scope of the present volume. This should not be interpreted to mean that it is better to set maximum levels last because it is easier to do so.

Minimum stock levels

The level of buffer stock (i.e. the minimum level) is a function of the costs of being out of stock, of the uncertainty about the lead time between order and delivery and of the uncertainty about the rate of daily issues to production. Suppose management estimates daily issues to be 200 units of stock item A and it estimates lead time to be twenty days. This means that $20 \times 200 = 4,000$ units will be issued between the date of order and the date of delivery. Suppose, further, that management regards it as wholly unacceptable for this item to be out of stock. So long as both the daily usage and the lead time are known with uncertainty, a minimum level of zero could be tolerated (so long as reorder point level is set at 4,000 units). However, suppose these two levels are thought to be accurate for 90 per cent of the time, but for the remaining 10 per cent daily usage is 250 units and lead time is twenty-seven days. If management ignores the 10 per cent figures, it will be out of stock 10 per cent of the time and incur the resulting costs. Instead, it must calculate the buffer stock as the difference between the exceptional usage and normal usage. Exceptional usage = $250 \times 27 = 6,750$. Normal usage was 4,000. Therefore safety or minimum stock to ensure that a stockout never occurs is as large as 2,750 units.

At this stage management may consider that this seems far too high for a minimum level. Snyder (1964) formulated a model which helps here. He postulates that the acceptability of a stock is inversely proportional (in the manner of a Poisson distribution) to usage. Figure 6 shows Snyder's

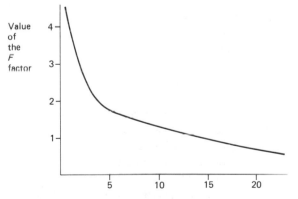

Acceptability of stockouts (as a percentage)

Source: A. Snyder, "Principles of Inventory Management", Financial Executive (Apr 1964)

Fig. 6. *Snyder's model of stockout acceptance factors.*

model. The x-axis gives the percentage acceptability of stockout and the y-axis gives the F value corresponding to that percentage. The F value is used to set the minimum stock level thus:

$$\text{Minimum stock level} = F \sqrt{ULQ}$$

Where U is daily usage, L is lead time in days and Q is quantity of units ordered on each order. If management now decides it will accept a 10 per cent possibility of being out of stock, then its F value from Fig. 6 is 1.29. Usage times lead time is a weighted average of 6,750 and 4,000. Thus:

$$\frac{(10 \times 6,750 + (90 \times 4,000)}{100} = 4,275 \text{ units} = UL$$

Let us assume Q, quantity ordered on each order, is ten units.

$$\text{Minimum stock} = F \sqrt{ULQ} = 1.29 \times \sqrt{4,275} \times 10 = 267$$

Reorder point level (RPL)

The reorder point is $UL + F \sqrt{UL}$. In our previous example, this equals $4,275 + 267 = 4,542$ units. The second term is the buffer stock. If management is prepared to accept a stockout because, for example, the item is of little importance, either it can specify $F = 0.5$ (or even $F = 0$, which means no minimum stock at all is thought necessary). With no minimum stock the reorder point level is simply daily usage times lead time. If either usage or lead time is subject to variation, management may take the average and risk a stockout when the average is exceeded, or take the maximum figures and cause average levels of stock carried to be well above the minimum. It should not take the minimum usage and lead times, as these will maximise the probability of a stockout.

It can be seen that the managerial judgments of stockout acceptability are as relevant to reorder point levels as they were to minimum levels. This is because the reorder point level is itself dependent on the minimum level. Even when no minimum is specified, management still has to take a definite view of stockout acceptability when either usage or lead time is not constant.

An alternative to setting RPL on stock levels is to set it on an interval basis. This involves checking actual stock levels at regular intervals— weekly for fast-moving stock, monthly for most stock and quarterly for slow-moving stock. After each inspection, orders are placed to bring the stocks to their maximum level. This method is risky, as the predetermined inspection intervals could turn out to be too long to stockouts result, and because replenishment to *maximum* levels may cause storage costs to be higher than really necessary. Finally, this method does not specify a reorder level at all, only a reorder interval.

A third alternative is easier to plan and handle than the previous two, and is therefore frequently used in practice. This is the two-bin system.

Here,the reorder level is planned as in the first alternative but, instead of all the stock being in one place, a quantity equal to the reorder level is sealed in an appropriate container and placed in a location away from the normal stock. When the normal stock is fully used up, the storeman has to open the sealed "bin", and this signals to him that it is time to requisition the firm's buying office to order fresh supplies. It is widely believed that the two-bin system is less likely to go wrong than the normal system whereby all four control quantities are on a "bin card" which the storeman is supposed to keep up to date. The normal system depends for its effectiveness on the storeman's noticing that actual stocks on hand have fallen to the reorder point level. This is more likely to happen under the two-bin system. However, this system does have the potentially serious drawback that storage costs are higher, as stocks are kept in two locations instead of the usual one.

The reorder quantity (ROQ)

The reorder quantity is the amount ordered from the supplier whenever actual stock falls to the RPL. The reorder quantity recommended in all texts on the subject is the economic order quantity (EOQ). This EOQ is the quantity which minimises total costs associated with stock. These costs consist of two components which have mutually opposing behaviour patterns, as Fig. 7 shows. Carrying costs, which are storage costs plus the interest on capital represented by stocks, increase as the quantity of stock

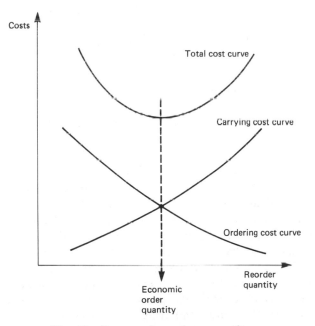

Fig. 7. *Economic order quantity.*

increases. Ordering costs, on the other hand, decrease as quantity of stock increases. Ordering costs include the variable costs—purchase price, inspection time, etc.—which do increase with stock size; but they are usually outweighed by fixed costs—paperwork and administration costs, delivery costs and buying office staff time. Variable costs cannot be reduced by bulk buying, but the unit fixed costs of ordering can be. The GAF applies and, the larger the volume of goods ordered, the lower the recovery rate per unit of fixed ordering costs needs to be. What EOQ tries to optimise, then, is the conflicting pressures of carrying costs (which imply minimised ROQ) and *fixed* ordering costs (which imply maximised ROQ). Figure 7 shows how EOQ represents such an optimum, as at the EOQ *total* stock costs are minimised.

The EOQ calculation is the most important of those described above, and exam questions on the subject are frequently set. The calculation is as follows:

$$EOQ = \sqrt{\frac{2FU}{C}}$$ where F = fixed costs per order
U = units issued to production (i.e. usage)
C = carrying costs per unit of stock

A mnemonic to assist the reader to memorise the formula is "Roo two fu on sea".

If we have carrying costs of £5, fixed order costs of £100, usage of 2,000 units:

$$EOQ = \sqrt{\frac{2 \times 100 \times 200}{5}} = 283 \text{ units}$$

To calculate the optimum replacement interval, the following formula applies:

$$ORI = \frac{U}{EOQ} \text{ which in our example} = \frac{2,000}{283} = 7.07$$

orders per year, and this means a replacement interval

of $\frac{365}{7,007} = 52.14$ rounded down to 52 days per year

EOQ questions sometimes include a supplementary part requiring the candidate to calculate whether a supplier's trade discount should be accepted. Since EOQ is by definition optimum, trade discounts for bulk buying should be accepted only if the savings exceed the costs.

Let us suppose we have an EOQ of 400,000 units at a purchase price of £2 and an ORI of twenty times a year. A supplier offers $\frac{1}{2}$ per cent trade discount if we buy 600,000 units. Total usage per year is 12 million units. We can decide whether to accept the discount by tabulating the costs per year under the EOQ and comparing them with costs if we adopt the discount.

	EOQ	Trade discount
Order quantity in units	400,000	600,000
Unit price	£2	£1.99
Annual Costs	£	£
Total purchase costs	24,000,000	23,880,000
Carrying costs (given)	60,000	89,550
Ordering costs (given)	60,000	40,000
Total stock costs	24,120,000	24,009,550

In this case, adoption of the discount reduced total annual costs below the level resulting from the EOQ without discount. A simple rule applies here.

(*a*) If the carrying cost (after adjusting for the bulk purchases) exceeds the ordering cost, the new EOQ is the quantity which attracts the trade discount.

(*b*) If ordering costs exceed the carrying cost, the discount should *still be taken* but a new EOQ should be calculated with carrying and ordering costs based on the minimum quantity which attracts the trade discount.

In other words, it is always worth taking trade discounts *so long as* the combined figures for ordering and carrying costs (after the discount) for a full year plus the purchase costs of the materials is below the total annual cost if the discount is refused and the old EOQ preserved.

The ABC approach

Stocks of raw materials conform to what is termed a "Pareto distribution". This means 80 per cent by value is represented by only 20 per cent of stock items by volume. In other words, of 1,000 different items of stock, only around 200 will account for most of the stock costs. Such items will include all the materials entering the production process and all other high value items. These stocks are classified as A stocks. B stocks account for 30 per cent of the total stock classes but only 15 per cent of total stock costs. C items account for only 5 per cent of stock costs but for 50 per cent of stock classes. Cost, here, includes the costs of any stockout. Any item whose absence could bring production to a halt is in the A class.

The point of classifying stock by ABC categories is to ensure that store management focuses on A items, which should be checked weekly or even daily. C items may not warrant the cost of installing sophisticated control systems, and their minimum levels will be set very low.

Annual stocktaking and perpetual inventory

Deliveries to store and issues from it are recorded on the bin cards kept on or in the container of each stock item. They should also be recorded on stock cards and/or in stock accounts in the stores ledger kept in the costing department or stores office. At the year end, stock items are counted and the bin cards and stock cards are adjusted to match the stocktake result. If the nominal ledger records purchases in purchases accounts rather than in stock accounts, the stocktake results form the basis of the year end debit to stock account for closing stocks. If purchases are debited to stock accounts as part of a cost ledger system on the integral basis, the balance in the stock accounts has to be adjusted to reflect the stocktake results, and differences are written off in the Manufacturing Account.

The annual stocktake is a tedious exercise and involves closing the factory for at least two days in most cases just to count the stocks in store and in progress through production. Continuous stocktaking (also called perpetual inventory) avoids this and has the added advantages of discovering discrepancies between actual and recorded stock far earlier, and also of building up stock-checking expertise on the part of the personnel who are given the job of inspecting stock records and the physical stocks at frequent intervals during the year. The presence of such personnel at frequent intervals in store and factory throughout the year but at unpredictable times acts as a deterrent to theft, fraud or carelessness. Under this system not only bin cards but stock cards and accounts can be kept up to date so that monthly final accounts can be prepared with accurate stock values being used. The checkers would naturally check A items most frequently and C items least.

Planning and control of finished goods stocks

All the remarks in pages 80–6 and immediately above applied mainly to stocks of raw materials, including components and C item indirect materials. Stocks of finished goods reflect rather different principles, as:

(a) there is no RPL or ROQ for finished goods;

(b) finished goods stock levels depend on the size of the discrepancy between production volume and sales volume in any period; and

(c) the distribution manager rather than the stores manager is responsible for finished goods stocks.

Sufficient stock of finished goods to satisfy orders on hand is the basic principle. The greater the uncertainty attaching to the future pattern of sales, the higher the level of buffer stock will be set. Snyder's F value applies, usage is measured in units sold (rather than issued) and lead time means time taken to deliver the goods to the customer.

Maximum levels should also be set where possible, since the interest cost of storage is much higher for finished goods than for raw materials, as finished goods have not only materials but conversion and overhead charges tied to them. The level is set after computing average levels of stock turnover to date and deciding whether these are likely to continue.

$$\text{Stock turnover} = \frac{\text{Cost of goods sold in a year}}{\text{Average stock held}}$$

For example, cost of sales in 1982 was £2,000,000, opening stock of finished goods was £150,000 and closing stock was £250,000.

$$\text{Average stock} = \frac{\text{Opening} + \text{closing stocks}}{2} = £200,000$$

$$\text{Stock turnover} = \frac{2,000,000}{200,000} = 10 \text{ times a year}$$

We can express stock turnover, alternatively, as the number of days' stock on hand. This is the reciprocal of stock turnover times 365. Thus with stock turnover of 10, stock on hand averages $\frac{1}{10}$ of a year $= \frac{365}{10} = 36\frac{1}{2}$ days.

Maximum stock could be set at previous average stock on hand plus an allowance for expected sales growth plus an allowance for uncertainty of growth. Thus, in our example:

Days max. stock = $36\frac{1}{2}$ + say 10% of $36\frac{1}{2}$ + say 5% of the previous sum
    = (36.5 + 3.65) + 5% of 40.15
    = 42.1575 days rounded down to 42 days

(Note that the cost of sales and average stock levels used to fit the 1983 maximum level are the 1982 figures, these being the latest available at the start of 1983.)

When important customers have orders on hand, the distribution manager may wish to reserve finished goods stocks coming in from production. Such reserve stocks are specified on the stock cards which will, in consequence, have four columns—namely, receipts, issues, reserves and free stocks. Free stock levels = receipts − (issues + reserves). Maxima and minima are applied only to the free stock, not to the total stock balance, which includes reserves. Reserved stock is a form of issue. It seems that the Rule Against Anticipating is being ignored here, since we are treating actually available stock as if it were already issued. We are doing so, however, only to identify the stock "not yet spoken for". Reserves are added to free stock to verify the total balance in hand for checking against a physical stock count.

Work-in-progress control

Since w-i-p arises only because some articles are unfinished at a period end, the control quantities applicable to raw materials and finished goods do not apply. W-i-p should nevertheless be minimised to the level just sufficient to satisfy finished goods stock levels not already filled by *free* stock on hand. Control of w-i-p is a matter of production control to ensure maximum materials yield, minimum process losses and the avoidance of abnormal losses as far as possible.

Contract w-i-p consists of work done but not yet certified. This means work has been done but not yet paid for. Naturally contract managers will try to minimise this item by trying to obtain certification of all work done at the year end.

Service industries have no stocks of finished goods and little or no stocks of raw materials, but they do have w-i-p. In their case, w-i-p is defined similarly to contract w-i-p—namely, as the cost of work begun (or completed) but not yet billed to the customer. Such work can be minimised by ensuring that all completed work is billed by the year end and that work on new jobs is begun only before the year end when this is unavoidable in the interests of sensible business practice. If a job takes three months and staff become free in mid-October, it is sensible to employ them in the three month job even though completion is in mid-January. It is better to have $2\frac{1}{2}$ months w-i-p at the year end than to have to carry the overhead of $2\frac{1}{2}$ months unproductive idle time.

STOCK VALUATION

Introduction

The three levels are valued differently.

(*a*) Raw materials are valued under the preferred assumptions about the physical flow of these materials and in accordance with management's view about what constitutes adherence to the Realistic Value Rule.

(*b*) W-i-p is valued at cost to date, with the materials element of w-i-p reflecting the choices made in (*a*) above. Only in contract accounting can profit be taken by w-i-p, and then only in the form of carried forward profit in suspense.

(*c*) Finished goods stocks are valued in the financial accounts at the lowest of sales value: replacement cost and historic cost. In the cost-books and the internal monthly accounts they are valued at historic cost and explicit adjustments should be made to such cost if management wants to know the sales value or replacement cost. Historic cost of finished goods will be computed either on the absorption costing or marginal costing assumption.

Raw materials valuation is covered from below to page 95; w-i-p is covered in pages 95—6; and finished goods are dealt with in pages 96—103. General considerations are described in pages 103—11.

FIFO

Introduction
FIFO stands for "first-in-first-out". It means that the first goods to be delivered into store are assumed to be the first to be issued to production.

Returns from production to store do *not* constitute new deliveries but merely the return of old deliveries. FIFO tends to follow the actual way goods in fact move in most factories, and therefore it conforms most closely to the Causative Rule. Issues are priced at the cost appropriate to the delivery being issued, and this ensures that units are charged only with the costs caused by such units. However, if the physical flow of goods does not follow a FIFO basis, the bookkeeping on the stock card and stock accounts should not do so either if the CR is to be obeyed.

The physical flow of goods

Throughout the pages following, up to page 95, we shall use a constant example of the physical flow of goods to illustrate the various bases of raw materials stock valuation. Below is the bin card for the first two weeks of September, showing the entry, exit and physical balance of stock item A 3456.

BIN CARD

Classification A   *Stock item no A 3456*
Maximum level 600   Reorder point level 100
Minimum level   20   Reorder quantity   200

Date	Receipts	Issues	Balance
1st			100
3rd	200		300
4th		100	200
10th		150	50
13th	200		250
14th	200		450
14th		200	250

The opening balance consists entirely of a delivery on 30th August costing £1,000, so the unit cost is £10.

The costs of the other deliveries are as follows:

Date	Cost (£)	Quantity	Unit price (£)
3rd	2,200	200	11
13th	2,400	200	12
14th	3,000	200	15

It can be seen that the purchase price is subject to galloping inflation. This assumption has been made to bring out as sharply as possible the effects of the different bases of valuation.

FIFO value of the closing stock

Under the FIFO assumption, the closing balance of 250 units consists of the last in, because the first in has already been issued as the first out.

Therefore 200 units came from the delivery on the 14th and the remaining fifty were delivered on the 13th.

The valuation schedule for the closing stock is as under.

Delivery date	Quantity	Unit price (£)	Total cost (£)
14th	200	15	3,000
13th	50	12	600
Closing balance	250	not applicable	3,600

The FIFO stock account
Stock accounts are debited with deliveries and credited with issues, but there is also a third column to show the quantity and cost of the running balance. Our presented example is accounted for thus:

STOCK A 3456 ACCOUNT

Date	Receipts			Issues to process 1			Balance	
September	Quantity	Price £	Cost £	Quantity	Price £	Cost £	Quantity	Cost £
1st							100	1,000
3rd	200	11	2,200				300	3,200
4th				100	10	1,000	200	2,200
10th				150	11	1,650	50	550
13th	200	12	2,400				250	2,950
14th	200	15	3,000				450	5,950
14th				50	11	550		
				150	12	1,800		
				200		2,350	250	3,600

FIFO cost of materials consumed
The FIFO cost of materials issued in the period is £(1,000 + 1,650 + 2,350) = £5,000. If these were sold in their raw state to realise proceeds of £8,000, our gross profit on sales under FIFO would be £3,000 or $37\frac{1}{2}$ per cent of sales. Our gross period profit sales less cost of sales is opening stock plus purchases minus closing stock. This is £(1,000 + 2,200 + 240 + 3,000) − 3,600 = £5,000, identical to the cost of issues. Gross profit as a percentage of sales is $37\frac{1}{2}$ per cent.

Disadvantages of FIFO

(*a*) The issue price does not reflect the impact of inflation, so that part of the FIFO profits are the passive result of selling old stock first.

(*b*) As different issue prices are used, it is hard fairly to compare the cost of jobs undertaken at different dates but in identical conditions.

(*c*) The material element in unit costs is heavily influenced by the time of issue, and this can be matter of place in a queue outside the store. This reinforces (*a*) above.

LIFO

Introduction

LIFO stands for "last-in-first-out". LIFO prices stores issues on the basis that the last items to be delivered are the first ones to be issued. Only rarely will LIFO follow the physical flow of goods, although materials with very short shelf lives might be moved on a LIFO basis. In such cases old stock left on hand would have to be written down to account for deterioration and the four stock control quantities would have to be reviewed with an eye to reducing them. The main justification for LIFO is that issues are priced at levels most closely fitting the cost to replace them, so any gross profits are largely clear of passive holding gains. However, the replacement cost argument justifies LIFO less than it justifies NIFO and current cost, which are outlined on page 94.

Tax authorities around the world tend to refuse to accept LIFO as a stock valuation base, partly because it rarely reflects the physical flow of goods and partly because, during inflation, it deflates profits (and therefore tax payable on profits) relative to FIFO and weighted average. The second and third FIFO disadvantages listed above apply also to LIFO. This leaves the main justification for LIFO as being a form of inflation accounting easier to use than NIFO or current cost.

LIFO value of closing stock

Under LIFO our closing stock of 250 units is attributed to the earliest possible deliveries. This involves working forwards through the issues in the period in order to determine such deliveries. The issue of 100 on the 4th is attributed to the most recent delivery, that of the 3rd. The issue of 150 on the 10th uses the remaining 100 from the delivery on the 3rd and takes the other fifty from the opening balance. This leaves fifty in stock from the opening balance. The issue of 200 on the 14th comes from the delivery of 200 earlier on the 14th. The closing balance of 250 therefore has 200 left from the delivery on the 13th and fifty still left from the opening balance. It is valued thus:

Delivery date	Quantity	Unit price (£)	Total cost (£)
1st	50	10	500
13th	200	12	2,400
Closing balance	250	not applicable	2,900

This value is £700 less than the FIFO valuation of £3,600.

The LIFO stock account

STOCK A 3456 ACCOUNT

Date	Receipts			Issues to process 1			Balance	
		Price	Cost		Price	Cost		Cost
September	Quantity	£	£	Quantity	£	£	Quantity	£
1st							100	1,000
3rd	200	11	2,200				300	3,200
4th				100	11	1,100	200	2,100
10th				100	11	1,100		
				50	10	500		
				150		1,600	50	500
13th	200	12	2,400				250	2,900
14th	200	15	3,000				450	5,900
				200	15	3,000	250	2,900

LIFO cost of materials consumed

Total materials issued cost under LIFO £(1,100 + 1,600 + 3,000) = £5,700. Again, assuming a sales value for these materials of £8,000, this gives a gross profit on sales of £2,300, or $28\frac{3}{4}$ per cent. This gross profit is considerably below the £3,000 or $37\frac{1}{2}$ per cent we calculated for FIFO.

During periods of inflation, both the value of closing stock and the gross profit are lower under LIFO than under FIFO. The exact oppostie would be true in a period of falling prices (when the tax authorities could be expected to approve LIFO and reject FIFO in order to maximise their tax collections).

Any accounting policy that depresses the reported cost of closing stock and reported gross profit is said to have a LIFO effect. Conversely, any policy inflating closing stock and gross profits is said to have a FIFO effect.

Weighted average cost (WAC)

Introduction

Under WAC, the balance after each delivery or issue is priced, and that price is used as the price of the next issue. This avoids the inflated profits of FIFO and the deflated profits of LIFO. Moreover, when the materials are held in liquid or gaseous form in large containers, each delivery mixes into the materials already held in the container. It is clearly not possible then to identify an issue with a specific delivery, and so WAC can be said to be a better reflection of the physical flow of liquid or gaseous stocks than either LIFO or FIFO. This, however, will not apply to deliveries of liquid or gas in small containers which are stored and issued in them. In this case the bottle, carton or cylinder is delivered and issued, and, since this is a solid object, it will probably move according to FIFO.

Disadvantages (*b*) and (*c*) of FIFO (*see* page 91) still apply to WAC, as each issue is priced at a different rate from its predecessors during inflation. Tax authorities accept WAC even though its profit effects are below FIFO during inflation. It is a reasonable compromise between FIFO's adherence to the Causative Rule when goods move in a FIFO manner and LIFO's reflection of cost inflation on reported profits. However, it *is* a compromise, and so it does not fully obey the CR on the one hand, or entirely reflect inflation on the other.

The WAC stock account

It is easier to understand the valuation of closing stock under WAC if we complete the Stock Account first. Note the inclusion of a price column in the balance block.

STOCK A 3456 ACCOUNT

Date	Receipts			Issues to process 1			Balance		
		Price	Cost		Price	Cost		Cost	Price
Sept	Quantity	£	£	Quantity	£	£	Quantity	£	£
1st							100	1,000	10
3rd	200	11	2,200				300	3,200	$10\frac{2}{3}$
4th				100	$10\frac{2}{3}$	1,067	200	2,133	$10\frac{2}{3}$
10th				150	$10\frac{2}{3}$	1,600	50	533	$10\frac{2}{3}$
13th	200	12	2,400				250	2,933	11.73
14th	200	15	3,000				450	5,933	13.184
				200	13.184	2,637	250	3,296	13.184

The balance price is found by dividing the balance quantity by the balance cost. The price changes only after a delivery, not after an issue. Thirds can be kept as fractions, but other recurring decimals are better recorded as such rather than being rounded, unless the number is irrational (such as 3.141234, etc. with no repeating pattern).

WAC closing stock and gross profit

We can see from the stock account that it would be rather awkward to compute the value of closing stock under WAC without first having priced the issues made in the month. The WAC closing stock of £3,296 is higher than LIFO's £2,900 but lower than FIFO's £3,600.

Gross profit we should also expect to be between LIFO's £2,300 and FIFO's £3,000. Cost of materials for WAC is £(1,067 + 1,600 + 2,637) = £5,304. On sales income of £8,000 this gives a gross profit of £2,696, or gross profit rate of 33.7 per cent. Our expectation is fulfilled. Because the price computed for issues is a weighted average taking into account the relative size of various deliveries, we should not be surprised that the WAC results are not exactly half-way between the LIFO and FIFO ones.

Although all three deliveries are of the same size at 200 units each, our early issues come partly from the opening balance of only 100 units. In this case the WAC results will be on the FIFO side of the mid-point between FIFO and LIFO.

Other valuation bases

Review

Although FIFO, LIFO and WAC are the most commonly used bases and the ones that are invariably set in exams, other bases are sometimes found. The more important of these are outlined below. Particular attention should be paid to those bases which do not suffer from FIFO's second and third disadvantages because, as we have seen, neither LIFO nor WAC is free of those disadvantages.

NIFO

NIFO stands for "next-in-first-out". It is the extreme version of LIFO in a way. NIFO makes no pretence of following the physical flow of goods, so breaches the Causative Rule. Issues are priced at the price of the next delivery after issue, so the Rule Against Anticipating is also broken. However,advocates of NIFO claim it is the price of the next delivery that best measures the replacement price of each issue. Thus the Realistic Value Rule is obeyed, they would claim, even if the other two rules are broken. NIFO in our example would value the issue on the 4th and the issue on the 10th at a unit price of £12 (the delivery price on the 13th), while the issue on the 14th would be priced at the rate of the next delivery after the 14th, say £20. This gives us total issue costs of £(12 × 250) + £(20 × 200) = £7,000. Gross profit is only £1,000 and the closing balance of 250 units is valued at the next delivery price of £20 to give a value of £5,000. This means gross profit on sales and gross period profit will diverge—an illogical and unsatisfactory outcome. The replacement cost will be captured by NIFO only if (and only if) stocks are replaced *as soon as* they are issued. Otherwise, NIFO overstates relacement cost as well as having a very extreme LIFO effect on profits. Disadvantages (*b*) and (*c*) of FIFO (*see* page 91) still apply.

Current cost

The current cost of stock is its true replacement cost. For our issues on the 4th, 10th and 14th, let us suppose that the true replacement price at the time of issue is £1 above the price of the most recent delivery. The issue prices will then be £12, £12 and £16 respectively. The 250 units of closing stock will be priced at £16 as well. Total cost of issues is £(12 × 250) + (16 × 200) = £6,200, which gives us a gross profit of £1,800. This current cost profit is the most accurate possible reflection of the impact on inflation. However, FIFO disadvantages (*b*) and (*c*) still apply.

HIFO

HIFO stands for "highest-in-first-out". This would give exactly the same results as LIFO in our example. It would give different results only when delivery prices go up, then down, then up, etc., in irregular runs. Issues would then be priced at the highest of the previous delivery prices, subject to the deliveries concerned not having been used up by previous issues. Closing stocks will be understated and gross profits low, as with LIFO. The HIFO justification is the financial accounting prudence convention which permits losses to be anticipated but not profits. In costing, however, such a breach of both the CR and the RAA is quite unjustifiable.

Average price

This method is similar to weighted average cost except that issues are priced at an unweighted average price. In our example, the issues on 3rd and 10th will both be priced at £$10\frac{1}{2}$, this being the simple average of £11 and £10. The balance after the delivery at £12 on the 13th is £$\frac{1}{2}$ $(10\frac{1}{2} + 12) = £11\frac{1}{4}$. After the delivery on the 14th at £15 it is priced at £$13 - 12\frac{1}{2}$. This method is simple but has a weaker justification than WAC, as it is a far weaker compromise between the FIFO and LIFO extremes. It too suffers from FIFO disadvantages (*b*) and (*c*).

Standard price

Under standard pricing, all stocks are assigned unit price for the period. All issues are priced at the standard price irrespective of the delivery prices' pattern. The standard price is set before the start of the period and will try to anticipate inflation. If the anticipation is accurate, closing stocks and gross profits will be similar to those reported WAC. This method enables inter-job comparisons to be made and is not susceptible to timing accidents. Here at last is a method not suffering from FIFO disadvantages (*b*) and (*c*). Standard price is widely used in decision accounting and performance evaluation. We shall have much to say about standard prices in Chapters 6 and 7. At this stage we should note that standards ensure comparability, but only at the cost of accuracy. No issue actually costs the standard price, and the difference between actual and standard costs creates variances that affect the size of the period profit. If standards are widely different from actuals, profit computations based on the former will be seriously misleading.

Work-in-progress

Process and uniform costing w-i-p

In manufacturing processes w-i-p is the value of semi-finished goods as shown in the production cost centre account. Process w-i-p has been amply explained in Chapter 3. Uniform costing w-i-p is simply the costs incurred to date by the semi-finished goods.

Service w-i-p

Service w-i-p is valued at the cost of any work done for customers before the period end but not yet billed to them at the year end. In job and batch costing the relevant amount will be the total of the balances carried forward on all the job and batch accounts.

Contract w-i-p

Contract w-i-p is work done but not yet certified. However, on the Balance Sheet of a contractor, the amount shown against the item "stocks and work-in-progress" will include all the balances carried forward except for accrued and prepaid expenses. In particular, profit in suspense forms part of this item. In the United Kingdom, Statement of Standard Accounting Practice No 9 (SSAP 9) explicitly allows this inclusion of profit in stock. Such a policy has a FIFO effect both on stocks and on reported gross period profits. However, SSAP 9 specifies that where the outcome of a contract cannot be assessed as certain to make a profit, then no credit to the Profit & Loss Account for profit realised is allowed. In this case provisions for possible losses, whether or not under penalty and retention clauses, should be made. The apportionment of such provisions between profits previously credited to the Profit & Loss Account (as prior year charges) and between w-i-p carried forward is a matter of financial accounting judgment and auditors' advice. Any use of profit in suspense to provide explicitly for losses will be offsettable against the value of w-i-p carried forward. Such provisions will reduce the reported value of w-i-p.

Finished goods

Inroduction

Many factories have finished goods warehouses. The physical flow of goods is from final production process to warehouse, thence to the customer. The accounting flow is from final process account to finished goods stock account to cost of sales account. If production costs have been rising through the production period, the manufacturing cost of later goods will be higher that that of earlier ones. Underlying this statement is the assumption that finished goods move on a FIFO basis from production through warehouse to customer. This must be true of the movement from production to warehouse, but it may not always be true of the movement from warehouse to customer. Following the Causative Rule, we should charge to cost of sales the actual cost incurred by the goods delivered to the customer. If in any particular case goods move from warehouse to customer in a LIFO manner, we must cost accordingly. In the case of such processed liquids as petroleum, weighted average cost will be most appropriate. For inflation accounting under the Current Cost Accounting Rules of Statement of Standard Accounting Practice No 16 (SSAP 16), finished goods are valued at replacement cost in both cost of sales at period end closing stock. In short, all the valuation bases considered for raw materials can apply also to finished goods. As before, FIFO is recommended for most occasions, as this usually represents the physical flow pattern.

Finished goods have a further complication not applicable to raw materials. This is the question of fixed cost absorption. So far in this book we have done our costing under the policy of recovering all costs from the cost unit. The point has now been reached where we need to evaluate the wisdom of this policy.

A review of absorption costing

In Chapter 2 we decribed how all overheads were allocated and apportioned to productive cost centres and then absorbed by the cost unit. We explained that the purpose of this procedure was to ensure that the unit price charged to the customer fully covered all costs. This procedure turns all period costs into product costs. We must emphasise, however, that this is a pricing procedure and not a bookkeeping one. In the books and in the financial accounts, office, administration and financial overheads are written off to the Profit & Loss Account as period costs. They are never debited to production cost centre accounts or work-in-progress or finished goods *in the books*. Full absorption costing may be recorded in the cost ledgers under an interlocking system, but it is more usual for non-factory overheads (even in interlocking systems) to remain as pure period costs.

Full absorption is done on costing schedules outside of the books and solely for the purpose of establishing a profitable price. If full absorption of all costs by the cost unit were carried out in the books, there could be no source of entries to the Profit & Loss Account. All overheads would be recovered in cost of sales, period end w-i-p and finished goods stocks. This would cause the Trading Account to show net profit rather than gross profit and there would be literally no nominal ledger accounts needing to be cleared to the Profit & Loss Account, for they would all have been cleared already to cost of sales, w-i-p or finished goods. There would, in short, be no period costs at all.

It is important to realise that this is *not* what happens under full absorption costing. Costs are fully absorbed on schedules not in the books. In the books themselves the ordinary conventions of period end financial accounting are observed. This means that office, administration and financial costs are cleared to the Profit & Loss Account as period costs. Selling and distribution costs are cleared to the Trading Account in so far as they can be considered to be costs of *goods sold*, and to the Profit & Loss Account otherwise. Factory overheads are cleared to the Manufacturing Account, and it is these overheads which become product costs rather than period costs *as far as the books and accounts are concerned*. The absorption of all costs by the cost unit we may term "absorption cost pricing". The absorption of *all production* and relevant *selling and distribution* costs by the cost unit in the books we may term "absorption cost accounting". Other textbooks do not make this distinction sufficiently clear for many students. Absorption cost pricing ensures that the cost unit is charged with a share of all the firm's costs and is performed outside the books of account. Absorption cost accounting charges the cost unit merely with all production and some selling costs and is performed inside the books of account.

In absorption cost accounting, cost units are dealt with *en masse*. The Manufacturing Account, as we saw in Chapter 1, discloses the cost of goods produced after absorption of production overheads and after accounting for the difference between opening and closing w-i-p. The cost of goods produced thus calculated is the full production cost but not the fully absorbed cost. In the Trading Account, cost of goods sold is calculated after accounting for the difference between opening and closing finished goods stocks and after adding on any selling and distributions incurred *up to* the point of sale and wholly attributable to the goods sold. This means direct selling costs such as warehousing, variable costs of transport outwards and consumable packaging are included as product costs, but such indirect costs as sales staff salaries, advertising and customer entertaining are excluded from product cost in the Trading Accounts (and written off as period costs in the Profit & Loss Account).

Production overheads include foremen's pay, factory rent and energy bills, factory plant maintenance and depreciation costs. These costs are direct to the factory cost centre but indirect to the goods produced—that is, to the cost unit. In absorption cost accounting overheads are defined relative to the production process, not relative to the production cost centre.

In most financial accounts, finished goods and costs of goods sold are valued inclusive of absorbed production and relevant selling overheads. In a minority of financial accounts, finished goods and costs of goods sold are valued instead on the marginal costing basis. After describing marginal costing, it will be necessary to compare it with absorption costing and evaluate the arguments for and against each method.

Marginal costing

Economists define the term "marginal cost" as the increase in total costs caused by the production and sale of one more unit of product than was produced and sold before. Every new unit incurs direct material and direct conversion costs. In any period short enough to exclude cost inflation, the direct cost of every finished unit should be uniform. The marginal cost will be the direct cost so long as no overheads can be uniquely attributed to the new product unit. However, variable overheads by definition vary in proportion to the volume of production and sales. Suppose ten extra product units in a particular situation cause variable overheads to rise by £1. It is reasonable to attribute to the cost unit 10p of variable overhead as a true component of its marginal cost. This is usual in marginal cost accounting. Marginal cost is usually interpreted to mean unit variable costs—that is, direct costs plus variable overheads. Fixed overheads are excluded. Rent, for example, is payable whether we produce 1,000 units, 100,000 units or none at all. Rent payable is not affected by production or sales volume. This, however, is not true in the long term. Suppose a factory has a maximum productive capacity of 100,000 units per week. So long as production is below or at this capacity, it is fair to measure marginal costs as consisting solely of variable costs. However, if consumer demand becomes great enough to justify production of 150,000 units a week, new machinery, extra labour-hours and very probably a new large factory will be needed. The extra costs of new machinery, labour and space are wholly attributable to the extra 50,000 units. Strictly speaking, we should be justified in apportioning all the extra costs between units 100,001 to 150,000 and inflating their marginal costs accordingly. Indeed, it could be argued that all the extra costs should be absorbed into the marginal cost of unit 100,001, because it is this unit that necessitates the big increase in capacity. In this event the marginal cost of unit 100,001 would far exceed its total cost under absorption costing!

Because of the inconvenience and impracticality of the previous conclusion, marginal cost accounting is performed on the assumption that extra product units can be made and sold within existing capacity constraints. In other words, marginal cost accounting carries the implicit assumption of capacity under utilisation. It cannot assume production at full utilisation of capacity because this would mean extra units would have to carry the fixed costs of the necessary extra capacity. We shall use the term "incremental costs" rather than "marginal costs" to mean all the extra costs inclusive of new capacity incurred by extra units of product. We shall restrict the term "marginal costs" to purely variable costs, with the associated assumption of capacity under utilisation.

Marginal cost accounting charges cost units only with their variable costs. Fixed overheads are accounted for as period costs, which means they are written off to Profit & Loss instead of being cleared to the Manufacturing or Trading Accounts. In the financial accounts, variable production costs are cleared to the Manufacturing Account, variable relevant selling costs to the Trading Account, but other variable overhead costs are still written off in the Profit & Loss Account. The cost of goods sold under marginal costing will be less than under absorption costing, and so too will be the value of finished goods. Gross profit shown in the Trading Account will therefore be more under marginal cost accounting than under absorption cost accounting. Marginal cost accounting has a FIFO effect. Absorption cost accounting has a LIFO effect on stock and *gross* profits.

Marginal cost pricing follows a different procedure from that described in the previous paragraph. Here the cost unit is charged with all variable costs, not just with variable production and relevant selling costs. The price is set to cover the marginal costs and it is the volume decision, rather than the price decision, which is responsible for ensuring that total costs are covered. This is a matter of ensuring that sufficient units are sold to cover fixed costs; or, in other words, ensuring that sales volume will pass the break-even point. This is discussed fully in Chapter 8.

Marginal cost pricing is performed on marginal costing schedules. These schedules are costing statements designed to show clearly:

(*a*) unit sales price;

(*b*) unit marginal cost (i.e. total variable unit cost as per the previous paragraph);

(*c*) unit contribution towards fixed costs and profits (unit contribution = unit sales price less unit marginal cost);

(*d*) anticipated total volume of units sold;

(*e*) anticipated total contributions from all products together;

(*f*) fixed costs in the period; and

(*g*) net profit (total contributions minus fixed costs).

An example, showing the usefulness of marginal costing in comparing product profitability, is given below.

MARGINAL COSTING STATEMENT

| | Products | | | |
| | A | B | C | Total |
	£	£	£	£
Sales price	5	10	15	—
Unit marginal cost	3	8	5	—
Unit contribution	2	2	10	—
Sales volume in units	1,000	3,000	500	—
Total contributions	2,000	6,000	5,000	13,000
Fixed overhead costs	—	—	—	10,000
Net profit	—	—	—	3,000

Using the above example we can compute marginal cost of sales for all three products as volume times marginal unit cost, thus A = £3,000, B = £24,000 and C = £2,500.

Although B has the highest marginal cost, it makes the largest contribution (£6,000) to fixed costs and net profits. However, it is not the most profitable product. That honour belongs to C, as it contributes £10 for every £15 of sales income. The ratio unit contribution to unit sales price is here 10:15 or $\frac{2}{3}$. This ratio is commonly, and rather confusingly, called the "Profit Volume Ratio" (PV ratio).

Finally, if we assume that one-tenth of anticipated sales volume actually ends up as closing stock at the period end, and if we further assume that £4,500 of the fixed costs are production overheads recovered on a unit basis, we can show the effects on stock valuation and gross profit of choosing marginal rather than absorption costing. This is done below.

Marginal versus absorption costing

We begin the comparison of the two methods by scheduling their effects on the previous example.

	Marginal costing		Absorption costing	
	£	£	£	£
Sales income		42,500		42,500
Less				
Variable costs	29,500		29,500	
Fixed production overheads	—		4,500	
Total	29,500		34,000	
Less				
Finished goods stock	2,950		3,400	
Cost of sales		26,550		30,600
Contribution				
Gross profit		15,950		11,900
Less				
Period costs		10,000		5,500
Net profit		5,950		6,400

The statements above bring out the major differences between marginal and absorption costing methods quite sharply. These are as follows:

(a) Stocks are valued higher under absorption costing.
(b) Costs of sales are higher under absorption costing.
(c) Gross profit (absorption) is lower than contribution (marginal).
(d) Period costs written off are lower under absorption costing.
(e) Net profit is *higher* under absorption costing than under marginal costing by the amount (£450) of fixed production overheads carried forward by the closing stock.

The last point is very important. Fixed production overheads are product costs, not period costs, in absorption cost accounting. This means that the closing stock absorbs those overheads rather than the Profit & Loss Account. In marginal costing all fixed overheads are charged in the period in which they were incurred. In absorption costing, fixed production overheads absorbed in closing stock units are charged in the period after the one in which they were incurred. Absorption costing can thus be argued to breach the Rule Against Deferrals.

Furthermore, fixed overheads cannot be directly allocated to cost units but have to be apportioned to centres, then absorbed by units. This results in units carrying costs they have not incurred in breach of the Causative Rule. Comparing product profitabilities is made more difficult when products are charged with fixed overheads, as the apportionment procedure is necessarily subjective. Comparing product contributions gives us a far more objectively precise view of product profitability than does comparing product gross or net profits.

With absorption costing, we have to forecast both total costs and total volume to obtain a recovery rate under the General Absorption Formula. This gives rise to the probability of under- or over-recovery of overheads, as volume forecasts rarely turn out to be exactly right. This cannot arise under marginal costing, as no attempt is made to recover fixed overheads from the cost unit, but instead unit contribution is established to derive a unit price attractive enough to customers to ensure that break-even volume is passed.

Under absorption cost accounting, overheads are absorbed by every unit produced. Any unsold units at the period end have their overheads carried forward until they are sold. Since closing stock is a deduction in the calculation of costs of sales, the larger the stock figure is, the greater gross profits will be. However, profits caused by large closing stock values are unrealised profits. They are not profits realised in sales income. If such stocks eventually prove unsaleable except for less than cost price, profits previously reported will have been overstated (i.e. fictitious). This danger is considerably reduced under marginal costing, as only variable costs can be carried forward through closing stocks.

Against this formidable case for marginal costing, some serious arguments can be adduced.

Marginal cost pricing can lead to low prices being acceptable during a recession in the hope of achieving sufficiently large sales volumes. However, when the recession lifts, customers may not necessarily be willing to pay higher prices.

Marginal costing assumes less than full utilisation of capacity. Because this is what it assumes, it is apt to become what it encourages, and this waste of resources carries both recordable costs and opportunity costs.

Fixed costs, especially fixed production costs, are a necessary part of running a business and hence of making and selling a product. Absorption costing recognises this necessity in charging the cost units, marginal costing does not. In this respect it can be argued to be marginal costing rather than absorption costing that breaches the Causative Rule. Moreover, it is often true that some fixed costs can be directly associated with a product. For example, a machine might be used wholly for product A and never for any other product. Under the Causative Rule, the maintenance and depreciation costs of the machine should be charged to units of product A, but this happens only under absorption costing.

Just as fictitious profits can arise through unsaleable stock under absorption costing, so fictitious losses can arise under marginal costing. This will happen when period costs are so high as to cause a net loss, but closing stock consists of entirely saleable products that bring in a huge profit in the next profit. If these stocks had been charged with fixed production overhead, the fictitious loss would not have arisen. In this situation it can be argued that marginal costing breaches the Rule Against Anticipating.

Marginal costing would exclude from product costs machine rental based on a fixed hire charge, but would include a rental based on the number of units produced. Since the product is identical under either financing basis, it seems inconsistent to cost the product differently. This type of anomaly does not occur under absorption costing.

The arguments do not allow us to say that one method is always preferable to the other. It depends on the circumstances. Generally marginal costing is better for product profitability comparison, but absorption costing is better for conservative and cautious pricing policy. In decision accounting, and control accounting and performance evaluation, the better choice is a matter of the precise objectives of the report concerned. We shall consider this further when we deal with the three areas mentioned.

STOCK MANAGEMENT EVALUATION

Introduction

Now that we have dealt with stock control and stock valuation methods, the next question we must tackle is how to assess the efficiency of stock management. As a first step we evolve criteria for judging stock management performance. Then we can compare actual performance against the predetermined criteria. In this section we discuss the choice of appropriate criteria.

Turnover periods

Stock turnover tells us how many times a year stock is used up and replaced. The greater the stock turnover, the more efficient the stock policy. An example will serve to clarify this point. Let us imagine two firms, A and B, both selling the same type of product at the same price and both realising £1 million a year in sales income. Neither firm has any cash but both satisfy their cash needs by borrowing from their banks on overdraft at 10 per cent interest. A has average stocks of £250,000 at sales value, B's average stock is £10,000. A's stock turnover is 4, B's is 100. To afford stock, A has to have an overdraft of £250,000, B needs only £10,000. A has to pay £25,000 interest a year, B only £1,000. It is clear that high stock turnover saves money.

$$\text{Finished goods stock turnover} = \frac{\text{Sales}}{\text{Average stock at sales value}}$$

$$\text{or} = \frac{\text{Cost of sales}}{\text{Average stock at cost}}$$

Either method of computation is acceptable but the latter is more often used in reviewing performance inside the firm.

$$\text{WIP turnover} = \frac{\text{Cost of goods produced}}{\text{Average w-i-p}}$$

$$\text{Raw materials stock turnover} = \frac{\text{Cost of materials purchased}}{\text{Average stocks at cost}}$$

All the above ratios can be inverted to give stock turnover periods. Turnover periods are more useful ways of expressing stock turnover, because periods can be added together to give a total turnover period for all stock. It is not possible to add turnovers together otherwise. In order to compute a turnover period from annual figures, we invert the fractions used for turnover itself and multiply the result by the number of working days in the year. In the case below, every day of the year is a working day.

Examples		*Firm X*	*Firm Y*
		£	£
(a)	Annual purchases	200,000	500,000
(b)	Annual cost of production	500,000	800,000
(c)	Annual cost of sales	600,000	1,000,000
(d)	Opening stocks —raw materials	15,000	75,000
(e)	—w-i-p	25,000	60,000
(f)	—finished goods	28,000	120,000
(g)	Closing stocks —raw materials	25,000	125,000
(h)	—w-i-p	35,000	100,000
(i)	—finished goods	32,000	180,000
(j)	Average stocks —raw materials $\left\{\frac{d+g}{2}\right\}$	20,000	100,000
(k)	—w-i-p $\left\{\frac{e+h}{2}\right\}$	30,000	80,000
(l)	—finished goods $\left\{\frac{f+i}{2}\right\}$	30,000	150,000
(m)	Stock turnover —raw materials $\left\{\frac{a}{j}\right\}$	10 times p.a.	5 times p.a.
(n)	—w-i-p $\left\{\frac{b}{k}\right\}$	$16\frac{2}{3}$ times p.a.	10 times p.a.

(o)	—finished goods $\left\{\dfrac{c}{l}\right\}$	20 times p.a.	$6\frac{2}{3}$ times p.a.

(p) Stock turnover periods

	—raw materials $\left(\dfrac{365j}{a}\right)$	$36\frac{1}{2}$ days	73 days
(q)	—w-i-p $\left(\dfrac{365k}{b}\right)$	$21\frac{9}{10}$ days	$36\frac{1}{2}$ days
(r)	—finished goods $\left(\dfrac{365l}{c}\right)$	$18\frac{1}{4}$ days	$54\frac{3}{4}$ days

(s) Total stock turnover period
$(p + q + r)$ to nearest whole day   77   164

We can see that X turns its stocks over in less than half the time it takes Y. We may conclude that X has the efficient stock management policies.

The turnover periods represent average time in store. Thus X holds raw materials in store for $36\frac{1}{2}$ days on average before issuing them to production; whereas Y holds them for twice this period, which seems rather excessive and expensive.

The w-i-p turnover period is alternatively termed the "production period" because it shows the average length of time taken by production to convert raw materials into finished goods. X takes nearly 22 days, Y takes $36\frac{1}{2}$ days. This period can be reduced by improving production methods.

The finished goods stock turnover period represents the average time finished goods are held in the warehouse before despatch to the customer. For X this is only $18\frac{1}{4}$ days, but for Y it is nearly 54 days. Y may be producing at a faster rate than can be readily absorbed by sales. Y may indeed have a problem in selling the product, and its directors should look into ways of improving sales volume.

The total stock turnover period represents the total time that materials arc on the firm's premises between the date of delivery of purchases and the date of despatch of sales. It is this total period that has to be financed—the longer it is, the more expensive.

Other criteria

Control quantities
Efficient stock management adheres to the four ruling control quantities for each stock item. Stock counts should never disclose actual stock to be below minimum or above maximum. In a two-bin system, opening the sealed bin should always cause a requisition to be placed with buying office for a replenishment order at the predetermined EOQ. All four control quantities should be reviewed for all stocks every year in the light of

changing usage patterns, and Class A stocks should have the control quantities reviewed at intervals no longer than quarterly. Perpetual inventorying should ensure that quantitative controls are adhered to and that bin cards, stock cards and stock ledgers all match each other and represent an up-to-date record of actual stocks counted.

Paperwork
New deliveries are ordered in writing on an authorised purchase order from the buying office to the supplier. Such an order should be issued only in response to a written requisition authorised by the stores or factory manager. Deliveries should be accompanied by a supplier's advice note, which should be an exact description of the material delivered. All deliveries should be inspected and checked with the advice note before the storekeeper issues a goods received note (one copy to the delivery driver, other copies to the relevant staff in the firm). The goods received note can serve also as an inspection note certifying the receipt of goods in satisfactory condition. The advice note and goods received note should be checked in the buying office against the order and any discrepancies immediately queried. The supplier's invoice should be passed in the buying office as correct before being cleared for payment. It should of course match the order and goods received note in every particular. If it does not, the buying office should raise a debit note for the discrepancy which the supplier should accept and respond by the issue of a credit note (acknowledging the amount to be deducted from the total owed to him as a result of the discrepancy). One copy of all the above documents should be sent to the accounts department bought ledger section in order to keep records up to date and enable the supplier's accounting and credit control queries to be dealt with efficiently and quickly.

All this is within the province of audit checks. Efficient paperwork is an inherent and important part of all management efficiency and is of particular importance in stock management, as so many parts of the firm are involved and so many stock items have to be properly accounted for.

Coding
Closely allied with paperwork efficiency in stock management is a materials coding system that helps rather than hinders the development of such efficiency. All documents mentioned above should be serially numbered. The order number should be quoted on all other documents relating to the order. Paperwork for orders not yet invoiced should be stored separately from completed order files. Once invoices have been cleared for payment, accounts should file the paperwork from order to invoice by invoice number, while other departments will file by order number—this reflecting the prime nature of the invoice to accounting but of the order to all the other functions.

For good storekeeping, stock accounting and materials management generally every type of item held in stock should have its own identity number. This material code number is to enable different materials to be precisely located. Verbal descriptions may need to be very long in order to be exact and, even then, confusion is still possible. Materials are coded by numbers to avoid confusion and minimise the difficulty of description.

A good coding system conforms to basic principles which demand that the code number should be:

(*a*) brief—long numbers are more liable to error;

(*b*) certain—no two types of item should share the same code;

(*c*) flexible—so that new types of item can easily be fitted into the existing coding system, for which reason it is that many code numbers in everyday use (such as bank account numbers) have so many noughts in them; and

(*d*) simple—alphanumeric codes (these have letters as well as numbers) are more easily remembered than purely numerical ones and have twenty-six possible digits (A to Z) per entry rather than only ten (0 to 9): easy enough to remember is Scotland Yard's former telephone number—Whitehall 1212—but it is rather difficult to handle 2221212.

The four qualities listed above are not always fully obtainable at the same time. Certainty must take priority, then flexibility, while simplicity and brevity are still important but perhaps not fundamental. To sum up, good stock management is facilitated by a good coding system and definitely hindered by a bad one.

Stock planning

Good management of any resources or of any situation is impossible without good planning. Stock planning involves planning in advance the following before each period begins.

(*a*) Production volume.

(*b*) Material usage and yield for the expected production volume.

(*c*) Expected levels of actual raw material stocks required to satisfy (*b*).

(*d*) Possible variations in (*a*) and (*b*) realistically likely.

(*e*) The four control quantities for the period in the light of (*c*) and (*d*) above.

(*f*) Cost of production.

(*g*) Expected w-i-p appropriate to (*f*) and the current production period.

(*h*) Unit cost of sales.

(*i*) Sales volume.

(*j*) Reconciliation of (*a*) and (*i*) to establish a satisfactory level of finished goods stock.

The most important issues raised by the above list are:

(*a*) the dependence of stock levels on planned volumes of production and sales;

(*b*) the dependence of the gap between maximum and minimum stock levels on the extent of expected variations of actual stock levels; and

(*c*) the need to plan stock levels via the control quantities rather than by attempting to specify what the actual stock level will be. We shall see in Chapter 6 that whenever future quantities of anything are beyond the firm's complete control or are subject to fluctuations, those quantities are best handled through control quantities rather than by direct specification of one figure. Control quantities specify the upper and lower limits between which actual quantities are permitted to fluctuate. Thus control quantities are essential to good planning. We plan the control quantities so that we may control the actual quantities.

Conclusions

Good stock management involves:

(*a*) good stock planning;

(*b*) good stock control through such measures as control quantities;

(*c*) good paperwork systems allied to good coding systems; and

(*d*) partly in consequence of the above, minimised stock turnover periods. Minimised turnover periods minimise stock costs. Management should periodically review stock costs to see where and how they may be reduced. One area that offers scope for such cost reduction is that of components. These are raw materials in the accounting sense (in that they are assembled or otherwise processed to make the firm's products), but are finished goods in the physical sense (in that they represent the fully finished end-product of the supplier's factory). Components are usually bought from suppliers. It may be cheaper in some instances for the firm to make them itself. The make-or-buy decision affects stock costs; it is the first example in this book of decision accounting and is dealt with below.

THE MAKE-OR-BUY DECISION

Fundamentals of decision accounting

Decision accounting is one of the most important parts of management accounting. In Chapter 1 we saw that a frequently read but rather narrow idea of the nature of management accounting was the provision of information to management in such a way as to enable managements to make optimum decisions. Optimum decisions are those whose results represent the most profitable outcomes of all the available alternatives. Thus, if we can make a component for a unit cost of £20 when we have to pay £25 to buy it, the optimum decision is to make it (because that cuts our costs so must raise our profits). In decision accounting we are confronted with two or more alternative courses of action and we have to compare them in order to ascertain which course will be our optimal decision.

In putting together figures to cost the alternative courses of action, two of the basic costing principles are of especial importance.

(*a*) The Realistic Value Rule, whereby all resources employed in each alternative course of action are valued not at their historic cost but at their economic value. Economic value will often be well represented by opportunity cost. Opportunity cost is the loss we make by choosing one alternative instead of another. If we buy a component at £25 when we could have made it for £20, buying has an opportunity cost of the loss of £5 profit. Loss here means lost opportunities, lost savings or lost income, *not normal accounting loss* as in the Profit & Loss Account. The alternative with the lowest opportunity cost is the alternative representing the optimum decision.

(*b*) The Causative Rule, whereby cost units are charged only with those items to which they have given rise. Closely related to the Causative Rule is a fundamental rule in decision accounting, namely: alternative courses of action are charged only with costs *relevant* to the choice between alternatives. This is the Relevance Rule (RR). The RR means that costs which are identical to all alternatives are excluded from costing each alternative, as they cannot affect the choice to be made. For example, if we are choosing whether to make Product A for £35 a unit or B for £30 a unit and they both need materials of £20 a unit, the materials cost is irrelevant. We should instead exclude the materials cost from both and compare A's *differential cost* of £15 with B's differential cost of £10. Thus we may express the Relevance Rule thus: the only relevant costs in decision accounting are differential costs.

Opportunity costs are always differential costs. Costs recorded in the books may or may not be differential. Sunk past costs are never differential and their exclusion in decision accounting obeys the basic Rule Against Deferrals.

The make-or-buy decision

The differential cost to buy is the purchase cost invoiced by the supplier plus any delivery and inspection costs, costs of buying office staff time, less any trade discount normally given by the supplier.

The differential cost to make has two parts.

(*a*) The incremental cost of making the component—that is, the full accounting cost of resources used to make the components. The incremental cost will equal the marginal cost if, and only if, factory capacity is *sufficiently under-utilised* before the make-or-buy decision is made *to render all fixed costs irrelevant* to the decision.

(*b*) The opportunity cost of making the component as measured by the total contribution that would have been earned by the most profitable product which could have been made by the resources used to make the component.

Make-or-buy decision example

Component XZ50B can be bought for £35 after trade discount. Total staff time attributable to each item purchased is costed at £1. The factory is currently working at 80 per cent of its machine capacity. The idle machines could make the component at the rate of 200 a week. The labour cost per week is £1,600 and the materials cost £400. Variable overheads of £200 per week would be incurred and fixed overheads of £1,000 per week would represent a fair apportionment to the idle machines. These figures exclude machine depreciation of £5,200 per year for all the idle machines.

Forty per cent of factory capacity (including the idle 20 per cent) could be used to make 500 components. To do this the firm would have to stop making by-product M or N. M has a sales price income of £20,000 per week and variable costs of £15,000. N has a sales income of £10,000 a week and variable costs of £2,000. The labour and variable overheads of M are £10,000 and could be used to make the component.

Should the firm use the idle machines to make the component? Should the firm turn over 40 per cent of its capacity to make the components instead of its existing policy of buying the component and making one of the by-products M or N?

Let us take the first decision to begin with. Fixed overheads are irrelevant because they have to be borne whether or not the firm decides to make the component. Machine depreciation is also irrelevant, as a sunk cost for it too has to be borne anyway. The differential cost to make the component with the idle machines is the direct costs plus the variable overheads. These total £2,200. As 200 components could be made a week, the unit differential making cost is £11. This is far cheaper than the cost to buy and clearly represents the optimal decision.

The second decision is more complex. Fixed overheads and machine depreciation are still irrelevant. However, for this decision we have to evaluate opportunity costs. This involves a further decision: whether to choose M or N as the by-product to drop. We subtract variable costs from sales income for each product to ascertain total weekly contribution. M contributes £5,000 a week, N £8,000. N is more profitable, so we would drop M. This means M is the relevant product to consider in our make-or-buy decision. N is more profitable than M, so we should not be sensible to drop N instead of M. Thus, although N represents the more profitable use of the capacity, we use M's figures in our make-or-buy decision because it will be M's not N's contribution that we prefer to lose.

The opportunity cost of making the component is M's weekly £5,000 contribution. The accounting cost is not just the £2,200 costs of using the

20 per cent idle capacity but a further £10,000 for labour and variable overheads transferred from M to the components. Moreover, 20 per cent of factory capacity could make 200 components, and 40 per cent can make 500. The capacity that is currently used to make M can be used to make 500 − 200 = 300 components. If 200 components had a materials cost of £400, it seems reasonable to suppose 300 will have a materials cost of £600. Total differential cost to make is thus:

	£
Opportunity cost	5,000
Idle capacity costs	2,200
M labour and variable overhead	10,000
Extra material	600
Total differential cost	17,800

This total is absorbed by 500 components to give a unit differential cost of £35.60. The differential cost to buy is the purchase price of £35 plus the attributable staff cost of £1, a total of £36.

We can see that making still represents a slightly cheaper alternative, but the difference is now very small. We might wish to view the attributable staff cost not as the allocation of a variable overhead. Since staff salaries of the buying office and inspection staff, etc., would have to be paid anyway, we could argue that the staff cost is actually irrelevant. If staff would *not* be made redundant by the decision to make rather than buy, the argument is right and the staff cost is indeed irrelevant. In that case, buying has a differential cost of £35 and now represents the optimal decision. This is even more strongly so, if by-product M could be sold at a higher price or made for lower variable production costs than as at present, since either would increase its contribution. If its contribution increases, the opportunity costs of making (rather than buying) the component also increase.

Thus the optimal decision with idle capacity is make, but the optimal decision when making involves switching resources from M to the component is buy.

SUMMARY

(*a*) Stock control involves establishing and adhering to four control quantities: maximum level, minimum level, reorder point level and reorder quantity for each stock item. A items which represent a minority of items but a majority of stock value should be supervised more intensively than other stock items. Economic order quantities should be calculated in determining reorder quantities and trade discounts should be taken into account. Minimum stock levels should be set after careful consideration of the costs and acceptability of stockouts. Often the best way of ensuring that reorder point levels are implemented is by the use of the two-bin system.

(b) Stock evaluation involves considering which of FIFO, LIFO, WAC, replacement price or standard price bases best represent the views of management about the value of stock, particularly raw materials. Only standard cost excludes timing accidents and facilitates inter-job comparison of labour and machine efficiency. Only replacement cost fully accounts for the impact of cost inflation on profit. FIFO, LIFO or WAC should be chosen under the Causative Rule, on the basis of which of these most accurately reflects the physical flow of goods. FIFO inflates profits, LIFO deflates them. Finished goods can be evaluated under either absorption or marginal cost accounting. Absorption costing has a FIFO effect, marginal costing a LIFO effect. Closing stocks under absorption costing defer the charging of fixed production overheads from the year of production to the year of sale. Absorption cost pricing is more conservative, since it charges cost units with a share of all the firm's costs. Marginal cost pricing ensures only that variable costs are covered and relies on adequacy of sales volume to cover fixed costs. Marginal cost accounting gives a sharper picture of comparative product profitability than absorption costing.

(c) Stock turnover periods are invaluable aids to appraising stock management efficiency. Long periods mean high carrying costs. Other criteria of managerial efficiency are: good stock planning; adherence to and review of stock control quantities; good paperwork and coding systems subject to regular audit. Good management reviews component costs regularly to see if it is optimising the make-or-buy decision.

(d) The make-or-buy decision involves comparing differential buy costs with differential make costs. Sunk costs and irrelevant fixed costs are excluded from the calculations. Opportunity costs of contributions lost by switching resources from making a saleable product to making the component are a relevant part of differential making costs.

QUESTIONS

1. What determines raw material stock usage?

2. Why should the level of w-i-p need to be minimised when other stock levels need only be above their minimum levels?

3. What is the case for using LIFO?

4. Contrast the case for replacement cost with the case for FIFO.

5. Why was distinction made in this chapter between absorption cost pricing and absorption cost accounting?

6. Appraise the choice between marginal costing and absorption cost in the light of the fundamental costing rules (the CR, RAA, RAD, RAE and RVR).

7. Explain the difference between marginal, variable, incremental and differential costs. What, if anything, do they have in common?

8. What is the Relevance Rule and why is it necessary?

9. If in a make-or-buy decision, the alternative "make" involves building a new factory with new machines in it, how does this affect the treatment in decision accounting of fixed costs in general and depreciation in particular?

10. Why does decision accounting use opportunity costs?

For numerical questions, see numbers 2, 4 and 9–13 in Appendix V.

CHAPTER FIVE

Working Capital

Pride does not wish to owe and vanity does not wish to pay.
La Rochefoucauld

OBJECTIVES

(*a*) To understand the nature of working capital.

(*b*) To be able to evaluate the factors most important in deciding the size and composition of working capital.

(*c*) To appreciate the relationship between solvency and liquidity.

(*d*) To perceive the nature and significance of credit control.

(*e*) To be able to calculate the savings attainable through improvements in credit control procedures.

(*f*) To evaluate the effectiveness of working capital management through interpretation of published accounts.

(*g*) To perceive the similarities and differences between stock management and cash management.

(*h*) To be able to calculate trading cycle lengths and to comment on their significance.

(*i*) To understand the uses and limitations of opportunity costing in working capital decisions.

(*j*) To appreciate the management accounting role of the funds flow statement.

THE NATURE AND VALUE OF WORKING CAPITAL

Nature of working capital

Working capital consists of current assets and current liabilities. Net working capital is the amount left after subtracting current liabilities from current assets. It is also known as "net current assets". We shall use the letters NWC to refer to net working capital.

Current assets consist of stocks, work-in-progress, debtors and prepaid expenses, quoted investments, trade bills receivable, cash at bank and cash in hand. This list is in order of increasing liquidity. Liquidity means the certainty and speed with which anything can be turned into cash. Cash in hand is perfectly liquid, as it is certain in amount and can be used immediately. Cash at bank on deposit account is certain in amount but we may have to give the bank seven days' advance notice before we can withdraw it, so it is not as liquid as cash in hand. Stocks are uncertain in amount, since we do not know how much cash they will bring in; and they are relatively slow to be realised in cash, as they first have to be processed, delivered and sold. They are thus not very liquid. Debtors may include bad debts, so they are not quite certain in amount, and they take varying times to pay, and thus their speed of transformation into cash is not as good as bank deposit accounts. Quoted investments consist of investments in securities traded on the stockmarket, and while they can be realised very quickly, we cannot be certain of the price at which we shall be able to sell them. Prepaid expenses like prepaid rates are a form of debtor. If we cease to occupy pemises for which we have prepaid the rates, the Rating Authority has to repay us the unused portion. The amount of cash we shall receive is uncertain, as we do not usually know well in advance when (if at all) we should cease to occupy the premises. Moreover, we cannot be sure how long the Rating Authority will take to refund us. So although debtors and prepayments are aggregated on the Balance Sheet, prepayments are usually less liquid than debtors. Finally, trade bills receivable are bills of exchange we have drawn on a customer who promises to pay us a specified sum either on a fixed date or on delivery. The amount of cash receivable is certain, but there is an interval from the date of drawing to the date of payment. Trade bills are more liquid than debtors and investments but not quite as liquid as bank deposit accounts. Debtors and prepayments, investments, trade bills and all forms of cash are regarded as *liquid assets*. Thus, liquid assets are current assets minus stock and w-i-p.

Current liabilities are any amounts a firm is obliged to pay within one year from the Balance Sheet date. Unlike the practice with current assets, current liabilities are not listed on the Balance Sheet in descending order of liquidity. The convention is to list them in the following order: trade creditors and accrued expenses; taxation; trade bills payable; proposed dividends (from current year profits); and bank overdrafts. There is no logical reason for this order and no compulsion in law or in accounting standards to follow it. What is interesting about it is that it starts with one of the most liquid liabilities—creditors (who expect to be paid in thirty days from invoice at exactly the invoiced amount). Bank overdrafts, listed last, are most liquid in legal form, since they are repayable on demand, but least liquid in economic substance, because most firms with overdrafts are able to treat them as a continuing loan with no maturity date. For management accounting purposes we shall need to divide the overdraft between its long-term component and its short-term one. The long-term component is the amount below which the overdraft never falls, so it represents long-term loan capital supplied by the bank even though it could legally be recalled tomorrow. The rest of the overdraft represents the firm's short-term borrowing needs and it fluctuates with those needs.

Net working capital, (NWC) is the excess of current assets over current liabilities. Since current liabilities are, by definition, short-term debts owed by the firm, NWC represents that part of the total current assets *not* financed by short-term debts. In other words, NWC is current assets financed by long-term liabilities—that is by loan and equity capital funds. Current assets are the result of the productive process and sales effort. Production produces stocks, sales convert stocks into debtors, trade bills and cash (some of which is used to buy quoted investments). Current assets thus arise from the work done in the firm. Since NWC is financed by capital, the term "working capital" can be seen as uniting the work embodied in current assets with the capital used to finance them. Capital is a rather confusing word whose meaning depends on its context. It is most usually used to describe the aggregate of shareholders' funds and deferred liabilities—that is, of "equity" capital and "loan" capital. The term *working* capital means that part of the equity and loan capital which finances assets embodying work done in the firm—namely, the current assets. The rest of the equity and loan capital is represented by fixed and intangible assets. This does not imply that the capital financing such assets is idle (in the sense of not working), but rather that such capital finances the *capacity* to do work—capacity being represented by buildings, machinery, furniture, etc.—rather than the *results of such work*.

These then are the conceptual roots of the term "working capital". Unfortunately, the term is widely used as if it meant current assets. It does not. It means that part of current assets which do not "represent" current liabilities but long-term capital. The reader is advised to reserve the term "working capital" to NWC only, in the interests of clear thinking. Working capital management involves deciding the optimum size of NWC, and this in turn involves deciding the composition and overall size of both current assets and current liabilities. It is this set of decisions that is the subject of the present chapter.

Costs of working capital

Since our review of working capital management is to enable the firm to *optimise decisions* about its size and composition, the rules of decision accounting will apply. This means we have to identify the opportunity costs incurred by holding assets in current rather than fixed form.

A firm buys fixed assets to generate the capacity to produce and sell its goods. This is most obviously the case with factory machinery. It will simplify matters (without unduly distorting them) if we assume that all fixed assets are productive. Suppose we can spend £1 million to buy a machine that will make a product whose contribution would average £200,000 a year. The machine would have a return every year of 20 per cent of its original capital cost. If instead we use the £1 million to finance NWC, that NWC has an opportunity cost of 20 per cent of £1 million per year, being the lost contribution from the forgone machine. The way in which £1 million can be made to finance NWC is by using the £1 million to *pay off current liabilities*. As current liabilities fall by £1 million, it automatically follows from the definition of NWC that net working capital has increased by £1 million. That increase has an opportunity cost of 20 per cent—£200,000 a year.

Let us suppose our long-term capital consists of £5 million loan capital on which we have to pay 10 per cent interest a year (£500,000), and also £5 million equity capital on which our shareholders require us to pay a dividend of 15 per cent a year (£750,000). Our total capital is £10 million and the total return we have to make every year is £1.25 million or $12\frac{1}{2}$ per cent. This $12\frac{1}{2}$ per cent is the firm's cost of capital. All assets incur this cost, since it is only through using or selling the assets that we can cover the cost of capital and so meet the requirements of our loan creditors and shareholders. The cost of capital thus represents the minimum return our assets must generate to satisfy our suppliers of capital. The fixed assets will have to generate this return by themselves, as only they represent the capacity to do work. The current assets merely represent the embodiment of past work, so are unproductive. However, a large part of current assets is financed by current liabilities. It is only the residue, the NWC, that is financed by long-term capital, so it is only the NWC that has to be attributed with the cost of capital.

The cost of capital is widely used as a substitute for the opportunity cost of forgone contribution of products that could have been made by machinery we could have bought instead. Thus cost of capital is itself an opportunity cost in the context of working capital, because it is used as a more accessible and more precisely measurable substitute for the true opportunity cost. In theory we should use true opportunity cost if we knew which machines we should have bought and also how much contribution its products would have generated. In practice, we can rarely know this, so we use cost of capital instead, representing as it does the *minimum* return the forgone machine would have had to generate.

Cash can earn interest when placed on deposit account, and quoted investments attract dividends and capital gains. All the other current assets lack this capacity to generate their own returns, so they have the opportunity cost of forgone income from the investments and deposit accounts that would otherwise have been held.

The two opportunity costs just described are combined as follows. Suppose investments earn 8 per cent (combined dividend and capital gain) while the firm's cost of capital is 15 per cent. This means stocks and debtors have an opportunity cost of 15 per cent but investments have one of 15 per cent *minus* 8 per cent = 7 per cent. It is quite wrong to add the 8 per cent to the 15 per cent and call the result the full opportunity cost of stock and debtors. This is because we could have spent the money used to finance stock and debtors *either* on machinery (15 per cent) *or* on investments (8 per cent), but not on both. Of course, we could have spent some on machines and the rest on investments, but if we had done so the combined return would be a weighted *average* of 8 per cent and 15 per cent, *not a summation* of them. Both stocks and investments could have earned 15 per cent if their money had been used for machines. Stocks earn nothing, so they are costed to the full 15 per cent. Investments earn 8 per cent so they have a lower opportunity cost than stocks—namely, the 7 per cent that represents the *extra* return machines would have made over the return achieved on investments.

Stocks, w-i-p and debtors all represent sales (potential or actual). They all therefore have costs of sales. However, these costs are already in the reported value of these assets and so do not have to be added in again when the costs of working capital are computed. To put it another way, in computing the costs of current assets for decision accounting purposes, we are primarily interested in financing costs, as these represent opportunity costs. Production costs and sales costs are not directly relevant to the decision as to how big NWC should be and what should be its optimum composition. Production and sales costs are, in this particular context, sunk costs.

We may consider that the ideal is no NWC at all, as this would avoid all the opportunity financing costs which NWC incurs. If we must have current assets at all, we may consider at this stage that they should consist of investments and cash on deposit account as far as possible, while stock, debtors, bills and cash on current account and in hand should be minimised. From the strictly cost minimising viewpoint, this is all quite correct. However, even the most dogmatic profit maximiser holds stocks, debtors and unproductive cash. This implies that there are important benefits associated with their costs. To these benefits we shall now turn our attention.

Benefits of working capital

A firm with no stocks is in a position of permanent stockout. Stockouts cause loss of goodwill, idle time costs while production stops for lack of essential materials, and cancellation of customer orders, since customers will not be prepared to wait for supplies they could get faster from a firm that holds stocks ready for sale. These stockout costs are avoided by holding stocks. A no-stock policy has the opportunity costs of stockouts. Conversely, the benefits of holding positive quantities of stock are represented by the opportunity costs avoided—that is, by the opportunity savings.

Debtors are the result of selling on credit. Firms choose to sell on credit because they generate more sales volume and sales income that way than they could expect from a strict cash sales only policy. Clearly, then, the opportunity cost of a no-debtors policy is the net income lost in forgone extra custom. The benefits of debtors are the savings in those opportunity costs. We shall look at this more closely later in this chapter.

Trade bills receivable are a generally accepted form of overseas trade financing. If we insisted on cheques instead we should lose some customers. The benefits are thus similar to those of holding debtors.

The benefits of quoted investments are their actual returns plus their relative liquidity. The benefit of cash solely resides in its liquidity. Liquidity is a major benefit in itself. A firm with insufficient liquid assets to pay its current liabilities in full, as and when they become due, will incur penalties. Unpaid suppliers stop deliveries, unpaid tax causes legal proceedings and fines, and if a firm fails to pay its proposed dividends the shareholders will be tempted to fire the directors or sell their shares. All these things bring costs with them. Unpaid creditors may go further than stopping supplies. They may sue the firm and follow a successful suit with a petition to wind up the company. If the latter is approved by the courts, the firm ceases trading. Thus bankruptcy is a risk attendant on failure to pay debts as they fall due. Such failure is a definition of technical insolvency. Its costs arise from the consequences listed above. Liquidity is the main defence against technical insolvency. Such a defence is a major benefit of working capital, and it is important enough to be discussed at some length below.

LIQUIDITY

Overtrading

Overtrading is explained most clearly by an example. A firm sells entirely on credit at a sales price of 10 per cent over absorption cost. In the first quarter it sells 1,000 units for £1,000, but receives orders for the next period of 2,000 units. It incurs £1,800 (90% of $2 \times £1,000$) in costs to make the units for the second order. In the second quarter it sells the 2,000 units for £2,000, but receives orders for the third quarter of 4,000 units, and these cost £3,600. In the final quarter sales and orders double again. This firm is experiencing explosive growth on sales and profits. Paradoxically it is also a leading candidate for bankruptcy. Let us suppose customers pay three months after invoice. This means the sales income of each quarter is not realised until the following quarter. This in turn means costs always run ahead of sales. Let us assume the firm has an overdraft facility. The table below shows how it will rise during the year.

Quarters:	1	2	3	4
	£	£	£	£
Sales income received	–	2,000	4,000	8,000
Cost of filling new orders	1,800	3,600	7,200	14,400
Net cash outflow	1,800	1,600	3,200	6,400
Overdraft at quarter end	1,800	3,400	6,600	13,000

We can see that the firm is getting deeper and deeper into debt even though it is making more and more profits. It is getting deeper into debt because it incurs costs ahead of receiving sales income and because both are rapidly rising. The increasing indebtedness is usually expressed as deteriorating liquidity. The phenomenon of rising profitable sales volume combined with deteriorating liquidity is what constitutes overtrading.

Overtrading puts pressure on NWC by causing current liabilities (particularly trade creditors and overdrafts) to rise. The associated fall in NWC is itself a symptom of illiquidity. The danger of illiquidity is that it can deteriorate into technical insolvency—inability to pay debts in full as they fall due—and that in turn can precipitate full bankruptcy. All this can happen despite the fact that the company is profitable and rapidly expanding. This highlights the important difference between making profits on the one hand and making money on the other. The former can be at the expense of liquidity as in overtrading; the latter requires both profitability and liquidity to be secured.

There are several alternative ways out of the liquidity trap of overtrading. One is to cut back on sales by raising prices enough to reduce the rate of new orders coming in. Another way out is to raise fresh long-term capital represented by cash. This is called funding of short-term debts, since it replaces current liabilities with long-term ones (or with new venture capital in the form of new shares). A third way out is to reduce the timing difference between cash outflow and related cash inflow. The interval between these two flows is variously known as the "cash cycle", the "working capital cycle", the "operating cycle" and the "trading cycle". The longer it is, the worse the firm's liquidity position. It is to this cycle that we shall turn our attention next.

The trading cycle

The term "trading cycle" is preferred to its rivals because it comes closer to describing the factors influencing the interval between cash outflow and associated cash inflow. "Cash cycle" is misleading because it implies that working capital items are solely responsible for cash flows generally, whereas long-term sources like loans provide some inflow and long-term applications like acquisition of fixed assets absorb some outflow. "Working capital cycle" suggests all current assets and current liabilities are brought into the picture, whereas in fact tax, dividends, investments and bank deposit accounts are excluded. "Operating cycle" suggests that the totality of the firm's operations are accounted for in calculating the interval, whereas in fact period costs, capital costs and long-term capital sources are excluded. "Trading cycle", however, focuses attention on the trading mechanism—buying materials, paying for their conversion and delivery and finally selling the finished product to the customer. Trading cycle thus best describes the interval between the date we pay for raw materials and the date we receive cash from the customer. It is this interval that affects our liquidity more than anything else *most of the time*, although major long-term inflows and outflows will affect it more every once in a while.

Computation of the length of the trading cycle involves very similar arithmetic to that used to calculate the stock turnover periods in Chapter

4. The full computation is as follows:

Stock turnover period + average collection period
Less average payment period = trading cycle period

The average collection period is the average time debtors take to pay their invoices. It is sometimes called "debtors' turnover period". It is equal to (average debtors divided by total annual sales) multiplied by 365. The result is also known as "the number of days' sales". The term "average collection period" describes it better.

The average payment period is the average time taken to pay suppliers and is sometimes called "creditors' turnover period" (but hardly ever "number of days' purchases"). It is equal to (average amount of creditors for *both* the raw materials *and* the expenses that are regarded as product costs rather than period costs divided by total annual purchases and the invoiced expenses which are regarded as product costs) multiplied by 365. In most examinations expenses are excluded from the calculation, as information is given only on purchases. That means the payment period is simplified to (average trade creditors divided by annual purchases of direct materials) multiplied by 365.

Here is a worked example of the calculation of a trading cycle period, followed by an analysis of what each element signifies.

Given date	*Opening position* £	*Closing position* £
Stocks—raw materials	2,500	3,500
—w-i-p	3,000	3,000
—finished goods	4,500	5,500
Creditors	12,000	18,000
Debtors	20,000	30,000

	Period flows £
Purchases and relevant invoiced expenses	90,000
Costs of production	150,000
Costs of sales	155,000
Sales	200,000

Workings	
Average stocks—raw materials	3,000
—w-i-p	3,000
—finished goods	5,000
Average creditors	15,000
Average debtors	25,000

TRADING CYCLE PERIOD *(to the neareast whole day)*

	Days	Workings
1. Raw materials Stock turnover period	12	$365 \times$ (Average stock ÷ purchases, etc.) $3 \div 90 = \frac{1}{30}$
Less		
2. Payment period	61	$365 \times$ (Average creditors ÷ Purchases etc.) $15 \div 90 = \frac{1}{6}$
Gives		
3. Period of free use of materials	(49)	
Add		
4. Production period	7	$365 \times$ (Average w-i-p ÷ cost of production) $3 \div 150 = \frac{1}{50}$
And		
5. Finished goods stock Turnover period	12	$365 \times$ (Average stock ÷ cost of sales) $5 \div 155 = \frac{1}{31}$
Gives		
6. Net stock turnover period	(30)	
Add		
7. Collection period *To obtain the overall*	46	$365 \times$ (Average debtors ÷ sales) $25 \div 200 = \frac{1}{8}$
8. Trading cycle period	16	

An explanation of raw materials stock turnover period and finished goods stock turnover period was made in Chapter 4. There we saw also that the average length of the production cycle from entry of raw materials to exit of finished goods to warehouse was represented by w-i-p divided by the cost of production.

The payment period has already been introduced above. In order to explain it in more depth, let us consider annual purchases and expenses of £300,000 and the average trade creditors of £50,000. Purchases are six times as large as creditors. This means that creditors are "turned over" by paying for purchases six times a year. It also means that creditors represent an average of one-sixth of a whole year's purchases. Since there are 365 days in a year, we can multiply $\frac{1}{6}$ by 365 to obtain the average time the firm takes to pay its creditors' invoices (sixty-one days).

What has just been said about the payment period applies equally well to the collection period. Our debtors are turned over in sales eight times a year. Average debtors equal one-eighth annual sales, and one-eighth of a year equals forty-six days.

Number three of the trading cycle period computation reads "Period of free use of materials". Some examples will help clarify what this means. Given a raw materials stock turnover of twelve days as in our trading cycle period computation, let us consider the effect of either reducing the payment to five days or extending it to eighty-one days. If we reduce the payment to five days, we pay for the materials before we use them in production. Raw materials take twelve days to be issued and payment is made in five days, so we pay seven days *before* we use the materials. Conversely, if we pay in eighty-one days, the payment period exceeds the raw materials stock turnover period by sixty-nine days. This means we have free use of the materials in the factory for sixty-nine days.

The net stock turnover period is the total period from *paying for* raw materials to producing finished goods. If it is negative, it means we do not pay for the raw materials until after we have produced the finished goods.

The total trading cycle period is the time elapsed from paying for raw materials to receiving money from the customers who purchased our finished goods on credit. The trading cycle period is the period during which the NWC has to be financed and during which it incurs opportunity costs. The longer the trading cycle, the more expensive is NWC to finance.

If a firm's cost of capital is 10 per cent, we can illustrate the remarks in the previous paragraph by comparing NWC financing costs for three different trading cycle lengths: two months, three months and four months. Let us suppose that NWC averages £100,000 in each case.

Trading cycle period	Financing cost
2 months	$100,000 \times 10\% \times \frac{2}{12} = £1,667$
3 months	$100,000 \times 10\% \times \frac{3}{12} = £2,500$
4 months	$100,000 \times 10\% \times \frac{4}{12} = £3,333$

Contrast these variations from those occurring if we have a constant trading cycle period of three months but vary the NWC itself by 25 per cent either way. Thus:

NWC	Financing cost
£75,000	$75,000 \times 10\% \times \frac{3}{12} = £1,875$
£100,000	$100,000 \times 10\% \times \frac{3}{12} = £2,500$
£125,000	$125,000 \times 10\% \times \frac{3}{12} = £3,150$

Note that a 25 per cent increase in NWC does not have as great an effect on financing costs in this example as raising the trading cycle period by 25 per cent.

Nevertheless, the cost of carrying NWC is affected by all three factors and all are important. These are: the trading cycle period; the size of NWC; and the cost of capital itself. In the short term the firm can do little to change its cost of capital, but it can reduce both its trading cycle period and the size of NWC. Generally, a reduction in the size of NWC will automatically reduce the trading cycle period. Reducing the level of stocks or debtors automatically reduces their turnover periods. Similarly, increasing the amount of trade creditors by taking longer to pay them reduces the trading cycle length. However, NWC also consists of quoted investments, cash and current liabilities other than trade creditors. These other ingredients of NWC do not enter into trading cycle computations. Any change in them will therefore have no direct effect on the trading cycle period. It follows that the areas for management to focus on in order to reduce NWC costs are stocks, debtors and creditors. We have already devoted the whole of Chapter 4 to stocks. We shall now turn our attention to the problem of creditors and debtors.

CREDIT FLOW

Credit flow concept

If we take sixty days to pay creditors while our customers take only thirty days to pay us, trade credit flows in our favour by thirty days. Conversely, if we have to pay creditors in thirty days but our debtors take forty-five days to pay us, credit flows against us by fifteen days. Negative credit flow increases trading cycle length and incurs NWC financing costs. Positive credit flow reduces trading cycle length and so reduces NWC financing costs.

It seems to be a good idea to take as long as possible to pay our trade creditors while ensuring that our own debtors pay up as quickly as possible. The larger a firm is, the more it is able to achieve this aim. Large firms can impose trading terms both on small suppliers and on small customers, since the small firm needs the large firm as a trading partner more than the large firm needs any *one* small firm. The effect of this is a tendency for credit to flow against smaller firms in favour of larger ones. It can be appreciated that this imbalance helps large firms grow still larger while making it hard for small firms to become medium ones.

Trade creditors

Introduction

To make the longest possible use of trade credit requires planning. Simply not paying invoices and ignoring reminders will lead to the supplier cutting off supplies, and/or refusing to trade on credit in future and/or issuing a writ. These three consequences merit some discussion.

Denial of supplies

In Chapter 4 we considered the ABC system of classifying stocks. C was the most numerous but least valuable, A the most valuable but least numerous. A firm can possibly afford indifference to a denial of C supplies, but a denial of A supplies can quickly cause a stockout, with its attendant costs. Once a supplier has cut off supplies, the firm has to find alternative sources and these may be more expensive than the source forgone. The difference between the forgone price and the new price represents the cost of a payment policy that results in supplies being denied. To this cost must be added stockout costs if the material in question cannot be obtained from an alternative source before stocks run out.

Cash terms

If a supplier stipulates that no further credit will be allowed, further trading is effected on a cash-on-delivery basis. The cost of this restriction is the cost of financing a longer trading cycle period. This will be clear from the following example. Suppose a firm has NWC of £250,000 and trade creditors of £50,000 on a payment period of sixty days. If the cost of capital is 10 per cent, NWC has an opportunity financing cost of £250,000 a year. If supplies have to be paid for entirely in cash, this adds £50,000 to the average burden of NWC and raises financing costs by £5,000 to £30,000 a year.

Writs and their consequences

If a supplier issues a writ for the amount owed, the customer is obliged to pay not only the basic amount owing but the court costs stated on the writ. If the writ is ignored, the court awards judgment for the creditor and the debt becomes a "judgment debt". The debtor is legally barred from disputing a debt once it becomes a judgment debt. He must pay in full plus the court costs (and possibly the creditors' solicitors' costs as well, if the court so orders). If payment is made, the creditor may still register the judgment debt on the central register in London. Future suppliers may be deterred from extending credit to any firm whose name appears on the publicly available register of judgment debts.

If the firm still does not pay after judgment has been awarded against it, the creditor has several further courses of action. The one most usually adopted is to apply to the court for an execution order. This instructs the court bailiff to seize sufficient goods of the debtor to enable the debt to be paid when the goods are sold. The bailiff can choose any assets for this purpose, irrespective of the debtor's convenience. If execution fails to satisfy the debt in full, or if the creditor prefers to avoid the delays often inherent in execution, the creditor can proceed directly from obtaining judgment to petitioning the court to issue a receiving order against the firm. This removes control of the firm from its directors and places them under the orders of a court-appointed receiver. The receiver may recommend to creditors that the firm be wound up, and, if they accept this the firm ceases trading and ceases eventually to exist at all.

In short, the issuing of a writ initiates a legal process whose ultimate sanction against a firm is a corporate death penalty. Even if the debt is paid on judgment, the debtor incurs legal costs and risks permanent loss of future credit as a result of public access to the register of judgment debts. Any debtor who does not pay a writ before it is heard in court is generally regarded as being unable to pay rather than being merely unwilling to pay.

Cash discounts

A supplier may try to encourage faster settlement of bills by offering a cash discount for payment within a stated number of days after invoice. The debtor has to weigh the cost of forgoing the discount against the cost of financing the extra burden of NWC that arises from taking the discount.

For example, a major supplier whose average credit balance with the firm is £60,000 (representing sixty days' purchases) offers a cash discount of 5 per cent for payment up to ten days after invoice. The firm would save 5 per cent of £60,000 = £3,000 on every two months' purchases. This means an annual saving of £3,000 × 6 = £18,000 per year. Against this saving has to be offset the cost of reducing creditors from an average of £60,000 to a maximum of £10,000 ($\frac{10}{60}$ of 60,000). The reduction in creditors of £50,000 increases average NWC by the same amount. If cost of capital is 10 per cent, the extra cost generated by the extra NWC is £5,000. This means that the savings from taking the discount exceed the costs of so doing and that therefore it is worthwhile accepting the discount. Later on we shall discuss the situation from the creditors' viewpoint.

Trade debtors

Principles of credit control

A good system of credit control minimises the firm's investment in trade debtors by reducing the collection period to as short a one as possible. This involves:

(*a*) vetting new credit customers;
(*b*) setting and enforcing credit limits and credit periods; and
(*c*) insuring as far as possible against bad debts.

Vetting new credit customers means obtaining from them satisfactory references from their bankers and other suppliers which have had credit relations with the applicant. These references are apt to be given "without responsibility", to preclude the possibility of a future negligence suit should the customer default. Even such references are better than none at all. Better still is an examination of the customers' financial accounts to date, explicitly to check for any pointers to liquidity dangers. (This topic is elaborated in pages 135–8. Finally, there are credit reference agencies that specialise in assessing creditworthiness, and investing in a report from them can be a wise precaution.

Setting credit limits is necessarily somewhat arbitrary. Applicants should be asked to estimate their average monthly purchases at the outset.

The credit limit should not be less than the estimated customer purchases, nor greater than twice this figure. Once set, the credit limit should be enforced.

Credit periods should be set not on a customer-by-customer basis, but on a global basis to bind all customers equally. Many firms stipulate in their published conditions of trading a given credit period, typically thirty days, without stipulating that the period runs from the invoice date. As a result, customers may prefer to regard the period as commencing from the beginning of the month following the invoice, especially if that is when the customer receives a statement. A planned credit period of thirty days thus becomes anything from thirty to sixty days.

There is seldom a good reason to exempt a customer from the credit period stipulation. Fear that the customer will buy elsewhere is often the reason why a credit period against a large customer is not enforced. Such a policy takes the firm out of its principal trading activity into the dangerous business of providing interest-free loans to its major customers.

Enforcement of credit periods and insuring against bad debts are achieved by similar mixes of policy. Bad debts arise when the customer is unwilling or unable to pay. The possibility of encountering a situation in which the customer is unable to pay is reduced by thorough credit vetting, not only at the start of the trading relationship, but on every occasion that the customer seeks to increase the credit limit. A situation in which the customer is unwilling to pay should be met by strict enforcement tactics and by the prompt and efficient recognition and resolution of disputed balances. These arise when the customer claims a refund against faulty or returned goods or when the customer's bought ledger is inadequately maintained. Such disputes are apt to become prolonged unless settled at a senior level between the two firms.

Strict enforcement involves not only sanctions against late payment but inducements to early payment. These aspects will now be discussed.

Payment inducements
Payment inducements are designed to reduce the firm's average investment in debtors by offering advantages to customers who pay invoices early. The main inducements are:

(a) cash discounts on early settlements;
(b) interest charges on overdue accounts;
(c) frequent oral reminders beyond the due date; and
(d) issuing writs when the account becomes three months' overdue.

Cash discounts
Cash discounts are most usually offered for settlement in ten days from invoice and entitle the customer to deduct a stated percentage of the total bill from the cash remitted. Examinations often include questions about

whether it is worthwhile offering customers a discount. The following is a worked example.

XY Ltd has £3 million credit sales a year and an average collection period of sixty days. The introduction of a 2 per cent cash discount for payment in ten days would be attractive to 50 per cent of existing customers (causing the average collection period to fall to thirty days). The firm's profit margin on goods sold is 20 per cent of sales, and its cost of capital is 10 per cent. The bad debt rate is 5 per cent and the introduction of cash discounts is expected to reduce the rate by one percentage point. Required: calculate the annual cost or saving from introducing the cash discounts.

In this type of problem we have to compute the cost of the customers' accepting the discount and balance it against the savings from a lower investment in debtors (including a reduction in bad debts). If the savings exceed the costs, it is worth introducing the discount.

First, the cost of the discount is 2 per cent of annual credit sales to those customers that take the discount. In this case the annual cost is:

$$2\% \text{ of } 50\% \text{ of £3 million} = £30,000$$

Next, the savings consist of the extra bad debts recovered every year plus the reduced cost of financing average debtors. Bad debts fall from 5 per cent of sales to 4 per cent—that is, a reduction of 1 per cent of sales = £30,000. This saving alone equals the annual cost of the discount. In addition, there is the reduced investment in debtors. At present the debtors are sixty days' sales. This is one-sixth of a whole year's sales—£500,000. The discount halves this balance to £250,000. The *opportunity* cost of these balances is 10 per cent so the opportunity saving is:

$$10\% \text{ of £}(500,000 - 250,000) = £25,000$$

However, the debtors' figures given above are in terms of sales income crystallised in the debtors; 20 per cent of those figures represent profits not yet realised in cash receipts. In calculating the carrying cost of the debtors, most authorities agree that the investment should reflect the cost of the sales represented by debtors, and not the full amount of the debtors inclusive of unrealised profit. The investment in debtors is thus seen as the cost of waiting for the recovery of expenses incurred in making and selling the sold products, and this cost excludes all unrealised profit.

In this case unrealised profits are 20 per cent of debtors. The cost of sales enshrined in debtors is 80 per cent of the debtors. Before discount this gives 80 per cent of £500,000 = £400,000, and after discount it gives 80 per cent of £250,000 = £200,000. The carrying cost of 10 per cent is applied to these figures, not to the total debtors' figures, in order to obtain the actual financing cost as opposed to the opportunity financing cost (which does include the profit forgone in waiting for debtors to pay). The calculation of savings from the reduction in debtors is thus:

Annual cost of capital × (cost of sales as a percentage of sales × the reduction in the debtors' balance)

$$= 10\% \text{ of } (80\% \text{ of } £500,000 - £250,000)$$
$$= 10\% \text{ of } 80\% \text{ of } £250,000$$
$$= 10\% \text{ of } £200,000$$
$$= £20,000 \text{ } actual.$$

In these questions it is the actual saving (£20,000) not the opportunity saving (£25,000) that is normally required, as the unrealised profit is caught by the Rule Against Anticipating.

The total solution as recommended for exam presentation is:

Cost of introducing discounts = 2% of 50% of £3m – £30,000 p.a.
Savings
  From reduction in bad debts = 1% of £3m   = £30,000
  From reduced debtor financing costs = 10%
      of 80% of (£500,000 – £250,000) = £20,000

                              Total savings   £50,000 p.a.

Net annual savings from introducing
    the discount   £20,000 p.a.

It should be noted that there is no need to reduce bad debts by the 20 per cent profit margin, because bad debts are written off *in full* against the Profit & Loss Account.

Overdue account interest charges
To deter debtors from late payments, the practice has arisen in recent years of making it a condition of trading that interest will be charged on overdue balances. If such a clause is clearly expressed in the conditions of trading made available to a customer before trading begins, interest is legally enforceable in the courts. The disadvantage of such a policy is that it might encourage some customers to seek other less stringent trading partners.

An example will illustrate the calculations necessary in deciding whether the interest policy is worthwhile. YZ Ltd has decided to increase its collection period from thirty days to sixty days to obtain more customers, but it will charge interest at 2 per cent per month (compound) on balances outstanding after sixty days. Annual sales are £2.4 million, profit on sales is 30 per cent and cost of capital is 20 per cent. The new credit policy will increase sales volume by 30 per cent, but the interest policy will deter 5 per cent of the increased volume from trading. The *average* collection period is expected to rise to sixty days, but one-tenth of the debtors are expected to suffer one month's interest charge and bad debts are expected to rise from 4 per cent of sales to $4\frac{1}{2}$ per cent.

Costs

　　Financing of increased debtors

　　20% of 70% of $\left\{\dfrac{£2.4m + 25\%}{6} - \dfrac{£2.4m}{12}\right\}$

　　　= 20% of 70% of £300,000　　　　　　= £42,000

　　Increase in bad debts written off

　　$4\frac{1}{2}$% of £3m *less* 4% of £2.4m

　　　= £135,000 − £96,000　　　　　　　= £39,000

　　　　　　Total increase in annual costs　　　　£81,000

Savings and extra income

　　Increased profit from increased sales

　　30% of (£3m − £2.4m)　　　　　　= £180,000

　　Income from interest on overdue balances

　　2% of 10% of £500,000　　　　　　= £1,000

　　　　　　Total additional income　　　　　£181,000

　　　　　　Net savings from new policy　　　　£100,000

Efficient enforcement routines

Statements are mere copies of the customers' accounts in the seller's sales ledger and have no legal force. They are useful, however, in assisting the debtor to reconcile the balance in his bought ledger with that shown on the seller's sales ledger. If statements are sent at all, they could best be sent one month after invoice, accompanied by a reminder that payment is now due.

The credit control officer should follow up the reminder and statement with a telephone call to the customer's bought ledger supervisor in order to establish that there is no disputed item and attempt to obtain a promise of immediate payment.

A written reminder should be sent when the account has become seven to fourteen days' overdue. If, when it has become twenty-one days' overdue, a telephone call does not bring forth immediate payment, the account should be marked as overdue. A letter should be sent, signed by the chief accountant, stating that credit will be suspended and legal proceedings taken if the account is not paid in seven days. If this fails to secure payment, a writ should be issued and credit stopped. Such practice should ensure that overdue accounts rarely fall more than one month behind.

Many firms take three months before threatening legal proceedings and even then merely transfer the process of enforcement to their solicitors. The solicitors may well take a further three months before issuing a writ. The costliness of such lax enforcement is self-evident.

CASH MANAGEMENT

The cash budget

Justification
Although there are several models to assist management to select an optimum balance of cash (in hand and at the bank in the current account), no model or decision rule will make it safe to dispense with a cash budget. The cash budget enables a firm to plan and control the timing and extent of its cash movements and thereby avoid liquidity crises on the one hand and excessive amounts of idle, unused cash balances on the other.

Preliminary steps
Since all cash flows arise from income and expenditure, in order to plan cash it is first necessary to plan income and expenditure. How to do this is the subject of the early part of Chapter 6. Having prepared an operating budget for income and expenditure budget on revenue account, the next step is to prepare a capital budget detailing the capital expenditure and asset disposals envisaged in the coming year. Finally, time lags must be attributed to each item on both the operating and capital budgets in order to identify the length of period between incurring a cost or a debt and the cash movement associated with it. Use is made of the periods calculated for trading cycles in order to derive the payment periods to trade creditors and collect periods from trade debtors.

Example of cash budget preparation

XY LTD'S OPERATING BUDGET SEPTEMBER–MARCH

	Sept £	Oct £	Nov £	Dec £	Jan £	Feb £	March £
Income (Sales)	8,000	8,000	9,000	10,000	10,000	12,500	12,000
Costs							
Materials	3,000	3,000	3,500	3,500	3,500	4,000	4,000
Labour	2,000	2,000	2,000	2,500	3,000	3,000	3,000
Expenses	1,000	1,000	1,000	1,500	1,500	2,000	2,000
Total	6,000	6,000	6,500	7,500	8,000	9,000	9,000
Trading profit	2,000	2,000	2,500	2,500	2,000	3,500	3,000

5 WORKING CAPITAL

XY LTD'S CAPITAL BUDGET FOR SEPTEMBER–MARCH (SUMMARY)

	£	£
Expenditure		
1 new ZFS 6000 computer	45,000	
Replacement of furniture	8,000	
Total		53,000
Financed by		
Proceeds of new share issue	25,000	
Bank loan (secured)	8,000	
Total		33,000
Difference financed from own resources		20,000

In addition to the above we have to provide for a payment of company tax in March of £30,000.

Sales are made 50 per cent for cash, 50 per cent on credit. The credit sales are divided thus: 10 per cent pay in the month of sale taking a 2 per cent cash discount, 60 per cent pay the month after sale and the rest pay in the second month after sale.

Labour and 50 per cent of expenses are paid when incurred. The balance of expenses is paid quarterly in arrears in early January, early April, etc. Twenty-five per cent of materials are purchased for cash, the balance being settled on average two months after purchase.

A 50 per cent down payment on the computer was made in December, the balance being payable in March. The furniture is purchased in December and paid for in February. The share proceeds are expected in February and the bank loan is receivable in March.

Required: a summary cash budget for the months from January to March, assuming a cash balance of £5,000 at the end of December.

Solution: the first step is to translate the operating budget into an operating cash budget, thus:

Sales	Sept	Oct	Nov	Dec	Jan	Feb	March
	£	£	£	£	£	£	£
Total per budget	8,000	8,000	9,000	10,000	10,000	12,500	12,000
Cash (50%)	4,000	4,000	4,500	5,000	5,000	6,250	6,000
Credit with discount*	392	392	441	490	490	$612\frac{1}{2}$	588
Credit—1 month							
(60% of 50%)	2,400	2,400	2,700	3,000	3,000	3,750	3,600
Credit—2 months							
(30% of 50%)	1,200	1,200	1,350	1,500	1,500	1,875	1,800

*Relevant sales 10% of 50% = 5% of total sales
Discount allowed 2%
So net receipts are 98% of 5% = 4.9% of total sales
and 9.8% of credit sales

Using the above analysis we can derive the cash inflows for the budget period thus:

	Jan	Feb	March
	£	£	£
Cash sales	5,000	6250	6,000
Sales attracting discount	490	$612\frac{1}{2}$	588
Sales on 1 month's credit	3,000	3,000	3,750
Sales on 2 months' credit	1,350	1,500	1,500
Total cash inflow expected	9,840	$11,362\frac{1}{2}$	11,838

We use the same process on the operating costs, thus:

	Sept	Oct	Nov	Dec	Jan	Feb	March
	£	£	£	£	£	£	£
Labour	2,000	2,000	2,000	2,500	3,000	3,000	3,000
Expenses paid in month	500	500	500	750	750	1,000	1,000
Expenses paid quarterly	500	500	500	750	750	1,000	1,000
Materials paid in month (25%)	750	750	875	875	875	1,000	1,000
Materials paid in 2 months	2,250	2,250	2,625	2,625	2,625	3,000	3,000

	Jan	Feb	March
	£	£	£
Cash outflows			
Labour	3,000	3,000	3,000
Expenses monthly	750	1,000	1,000
Expenses quarterly	1,750	–	–
Materials for cash	875	1,000	1,000
on credit	2,625	2,625	2,625
Total outflow	9,000	7,625	7,625 (excluding tax)

Finally, we incorporate the additional data from the capital budget summary and the tax payment to produce the summary cash budget, thus:

	Jan	Feb	March
	£	£	£
Opening cash	5,000	5,840	$26,577\frac{1}{2}$
Cash flows on revenue account			
Receipts	9,840	$11,362\frac{1}{2}$	11,830
Payments (includes March tax)	9,000	7,625	37,625
Net cash flow (= net outflow)	840	$3,737\frac{1}{2}$	(25,795)

	Jan £	Feb £	March £
Cash flows on capital account			
Receipts	–	25,000	8,000
Payments	–	8,000	22,500
Net cash flow	–	17,000	(14,500)
Total net cash flow	840	20,737½	(40,295)
Closing cash	5,840	26,577½	(13,717½)

We conclude that at the end of March XY Ltd will need an overdraft of £13,717.50.

A comparison of cash and stocks

Characteristics in common

(*a*) Part of the actual stock held at any one time represents safety stock, held as a protection against stockout. Part of the actual cash balances held are similarly attributable to the need to have a "safety stock" of cash to meet unforeseen payments. Such cash is held to satisfy what is known as the "precautionary" demand for cash.

(*b*) The principal reason for holding stock is to close the gap between production volume and sales volume. The principal reason for holding cash is to close the gap between sales receipts and expenditure outflows.

(*c*) Stock has carrying costs, a major element of which is the cost of financing. Cash has a carrying cost represented by bank charges. The opportunity cost of holding ready cash, however, is the return that could have been earned if the cash had been invested either in a bank deposit account or in the acquisition of high-yield securities.

(*d*) Just as there is an EOQ model for stock, so there is an EOQ model for cash devised by E.J. Baumol, the economist. His formula is designed to obtain the optimum amount of cash that should be transferred at any one time from deposit account (or from investment in securities) to current account. This optimum amount

$$Q^* = \sqrt{\frac{2bT}{i}}$$

where *b* is the cost of transferring money from deposit to current account (a transactions cost), *T* is the total demand for cash in the period concerned (the total anticipated net cash outflow less the initial cash balance) and *i* is the interest earned on deposit account (or alternatively the returns from holding securities) and represents the opportunity cost of holding cash. To illustrate the formula, let us imagine a firm makes 6 per cent per year on deposit account, has a monthly cash demand of £6 million and

[*]See "A model of the demand for money by firms", *Quarterly Journal of Economics* (Aug 1966), pp. 413–35.

each withdrawal from deposit account costs £100. We must first translate the annual interest of 6 per cent into a monthly one of $\frac{1}{2}$ per cent, as the period under review is a month not a year.

$$Q^* = £\sqrt{\frac{2bT}{i}} = £\sqrt{\frac{2 \times 100 \times 6 \text{ million}}{0.005}} = £489,898$$

The number of withdrawals in the month

$$= \frac{T}{Q^*} = \frac{6m}{489,898} = 12$$

The reason for the frequency of withdrawals is principally due to the small Q^* relative to the large T. The trouble with Baumol's adaptation of the stock EOQ is that it requires cash flows (T) to be smooth and predictable, and this rarely happens in real life.

(e) An alternative cash management model is the one devised by Miller-Orr* to take account of the unpredictability of cash flows. This model defines a cash level z which is used to specify an upper or maximum cash limit h. Optimally $h = 3z$ and $z = 3\sqrt{3b\sigma^2/4i}$ where b and i are defined as in the Baumol model, while σ^2 is the variance of daily cash flows about their mean level. When h is reached, $h - z$ amount of money is put into deposit account; while when a minimum cash level (≥ 0) is reached, z amount of money is taken from deposit account to current account. The Miller–Orr model assumes cash flow timings and amounts to be random, and the formula for z given above depends on the restrictive assumption that cash flows in such a random manner that at any time there is a 50 per cent chance of the next cash movement being positive (and 50 per cent of its being negative).

FUNDS FLOW

The funds flow statement

Introduction
The Funds Flow Statement, also known as the Statement of Sources and Applications of Funds, is part of the published final accounts. In the United Kingdom its format has to comply with the provisions of SSAP 10 and has to disclose fully all the sources of funds and the use made of them during the year.

The Funds Flow Statement is a key piece of evidence in evaluating managerial competence in liquidity management. It shows how operating earnings are transformed into working capital. It raises questions about the firm's perception of the conflict between short-term and long-term goals. These are large claims. Let us examine the arguments justifying them with two hypothetical examples.

*ibid.

FUNDS FLOW STATEMENTS FOR THE YEAR 1983

Sources		A Ltd		Z Ltd
Generated from operations		£		£
Net profit		70,000		130,000
Depreciation provided in year		130,000		70,000
Cash flow		200,000		200,000
Long-term sources				
Disposal of fixed assets	800,000		300,000	
Loans	–		500,000	
New shares issued	1,000,000		–	
Total		1,800,000		800,000
Total sources		2,000,000		1,000,000
Applications of funds				
Purchase of fixed assets	1,000,000		500,000	
Acquisition of subsidiary	1,500,000		–	
Total		2,500,000		500,000
Balance—Increase/(Decrease) in working capital		(500,000)		500,000
(Increase)/Decrease in creditors	(300,000)		(200,000)	
Increase/(Decrease) in Stocks	200,000		100,000	
Debtors	(200,000)		300,000	
Cash	(200,000)		300,000	
Total		(500,000)		500,000

Analysis of Funds Flow Statements

(*a*) Both A and Z generate £200,000 from operations, but A is losing liquidity while Z is gaining it. In other words, A is making profits but not making "money", while Z is making both.

(*b*) A generates £130,000 from depreciation, £800,000 from selling old assets—a total of £930,000. It has spent £1 million on acquiring new assets—just enough to replace the old assets with the balance of £70,000 being exactly accounted for by profit. In sum we have a picture of a firm just managing to stay the same size in terms of physical operating capacity (disregarding, at this stage, its acquisition of a subsidiary). Performing the same analysis on Z Ltd we compare its purchase of new assets at £$\frac{1}{2}$ million with its depreciation of £70,000 plus asset disposals of £300,000 (a total of £370,000) and conclude that its profit of £130,000 has financed (or, more accurately, been able to finance) a small expansion in operating capacity. Profits for Z *seem* to be associated with growth.

(*c*) A has acquired a subsidiary for £1$\frac{1}{2}$ million and issued shares for £1 million, the shortfall of £$\frac{1}{2}$ million being traceable to the fall in working capital, particularly the £200,000 cash decrease. This acquisition seems to have adversely affected A's liquidity, causing it to rely more on trade creditors, while its control of debtors shows a deterioration of £200,000 (although this could be due to larger sales rather than longer collection periods). Z, on the other hand, has raised a loan of £½ million which is associated (but has not necessarily caused) an equivalent rise in working capital. If such an association is in fact causative, Z has used the loan to fund its short-term liabilities, thereby trading possible liquidity problems for an increase in financial risk represented by the increased gearing.

(d) Both firms display confidence in their long-term future, A by acquiring a subsidiary, Z by committing itself to repayment of a loan. A's expansion by acquisition is associated with an increasing liquidity problem. Z's expansion is more modest but its liquidity is growing sounder.

(e) To put all the above in a proper perspective we should need the Balance Sheet. That would enable us to judge the materiality of the changes listed on the Funds Statement. We know that the changes are certainly material, relative to the reported profits.

(f) Generally the Funds Statements show us:

(i) the correlation between profits and movements in working capital;

(ii) the extent to which expansion is financed internally from operations and externally from long-term sources;

(iii) the extent to which working capital increases are accounted for by one-off sources such as loans and new shares—such sources are not available year after year and reliance on them in any one year points to potential financing problems in future years if profits should prove inadequate;

(iv) the extent to which long-term sources have financed long-term applications—ideally profit plus depreciation should equal or exceed the increase in working capital; and

(v) the changes in the composition of working capital between one period end and the next—in particular whether increasing trade creditors, stocks and debtors combine with decreasing cash to suggest possible overtrading.

Finally, a firm which maximises short-term gains at the expense of long-term prospects will show one or more of the following symptoms on its Funds Flow Statement.

(a) Long-term applications (asset and subsidiary acquisitions) will fall below long-term sources, as the firm is not concerned to expand its operating capacity.

(b) Trade creditors will tend to be used to the fullest extent as cheap finance.

(c) Depreciation plus asset disposals will tend to exceed asset purchases for the same reason as in (a) above.

Liquidity analysis

Conventional ratios
To evaluate the effectiveness of working capital management from accounts, the following ratios are commonly used.

(*a*) The "current ratio"—current assets over current liabilities. Acceptable current ratios exceed 1.75.

(*b*) The "quick ratio", also called the "acid test" or "liquid ratio"—current assets less all levels of stock over current liabilities. Acceptable quick ratios exceed 0.8. This ratio tells us whether all current liabilities could be paid off without having to realise stock on an emergency basis.

(*c*) Vulnerability—the percentage of the least liquid asset that must be sold to pay off current liabilities in full. It combines the previous two ratios in a single figure. An example will clarify this. A firm with current liabilities of £400,000 has £100,000 cash, £150,000 investments, £200,000 debtors and £500,000 stocks (total liquid assets £400,000; total current assets £900,000). Vulnerability is 100 per cent of debtors because, after using cash and investments, the whole of debtors would have to be realised to pay off current liabilities in full. Liquid ratio is 1 and current ratio is $9:4$ or $2\frac{1}{4}$. The vulnerability of 100 per cent of debtors conveys essentially the same information as the combination of the two ratios.

(*d*) Credit flow—collection period less payment period. This tells us whether the firm finances its own debtors or, on the contrary, uses its trade creditors as cheap finance.

(*e*) All the turnover periods considered earlier (*see* pages 120–4), especially the trading cycle itself.

Other useful figures in analysing liquidity

(*a*) The level of current liquidity is the number of days it would take to generate enough cash flow to pay off those current liabilities not covered by liquid assets. If a firm has a vulnerability higher than 80 per cent of debtors and has no unused overdraft facility, the level of current liquidity tells us how long it would take the firm to solve its liquidity problem from its own resources. The formula is:

$$\frac{\text{(Current liabilities less liquid assets)} \times 365}{\text{Cash flow generated from operations per year}}$$

(*b*) Similar to the level of current liquidity is the countdown period for a loss-making firm. The countdown period is the number of days a loss-making firm has from its period end to a liquidity crisis. A liquidity crisis is defined as the advent of inability to pay debts without recourse to external sources of funds. The formula is:

$$\frac{\text{(Liquid assets less current liabilities)} \times 365}{\text{Negative cash flow from operations per year}}$$

In both of the above formulae, cash flow is used in its Funds Statement rather than its cash budgeting sense. In short, cash flow equals net profits plus depreciation.

SUMMARY

(*a*) Working capital is held to protect the firm from insolvency—inability to pay debts as they fall due. It is a lubricator between the different pattern of outflows from that of inflows.

(*b*) The trading cycle period tells us how much time elapses on average from when we pay a creditor for material purchased to when a debtor pays us for selling him the converted material. The longer a trading cycle is, the more expensive it is to finance.

(*c*) The trading cycle period can be reduced by processing stock faster, by taking longer to pay trade creditors and/or by tightening up credit control procedures over debtors.

(*d*) Good credit control involves vetting all prospective debtors, enforcing credit limits and credit periods, and using tools such as cash discounts whose benefits in a particular firm exceed their full costs.

(*e*) Cash management is primarily a matter of cash budgeting, although models exist to help managers optimise cash levels, given predictability or randomness of cash flows.

(*f*) Funds Statements are important aids to assessing the effectiveness of liquidity management. Several ratios are commonly used to assist such assessment.

QUESTIONS

1. In what respects is cash unlike stocks and how far do such differences vitiate the usefulness of the Baumol and Miller–Orr models?

2. An analysis of the published accounts of M and P reveals the following, which you are asked to interpret for the benefit of a bank manager faced with a request for a large overdraft by both firms.

	M	*P*
Vulnerability	60% of debtors	20% of stock
Trading cycle period	120 days	140 days
Annual net profit	£80,000	£240,000
Credit flow	(10 days)	10 days
Fixed assets		
Less loans outstanding	£2 million	£3 million
Trend in finished goods stock levels	Steady	Up
Trend in sales volume	Up	Steady
Net working capital	£250,000	£750,000
Currently applicable cost of capital	$12\frac{1}{2}$%	$7\frac{1}{2}$%

State what other figures would be useful in your analysis and assume the requested overdraft is £1 million.

3. Why does credit tend to flow towards larger firms?

4. If a firm with a steady sales volume faces rising levels of bad debts, when would you recommend:

(a) the introduction of 5% cash discounts;

(b) the doubling of the credit period; and

(c) selling the debts to factor who charges 10 per cent of all debts foɪ the service of collecting the debts and paying the firm the money when (and only when) collected?

5. What remedies are available to a firm experiencing overtrading?

6. Explain how the requirements of profitability and those of liquidity may sometimes conflict.

For calculation questions, *see* numbers 14–17 in Appendix V.

CHAPTER SIX

Planning and Control Systems

*In relation to their systems most systemisers are like a man who
builds a castle and lives in a nearby shack.*

Kierkegaard

OBJECTIVES

(*a*) To understand the purposes of and differences between planning and control.

(*b*) To perceive the relationship between management philosophies and the principal planning and control systems.

(*c*) To apprehend the nature of budgeting and standard costing.

(*d*) To perceive the significance of the law of requisite variety.

(*e*) To understand the capacities and limitations of the following systems: internal control; corporate planning; budgeting; standard costing; and bonus incentive.

(*f*) To be able to present budgetary statements clearly and recognise their assumptions.

(*g*) To comprehend the nature of the planning cycle and its relationship to management by objectives (MBO).

(*h*) To comprehend the nature of all control systems and their relationship to management by exception (MBE).

(*i*) To be able to interpret simple operating statements.

FUNDAMENTAL TERMS AND CONCEPTS

Planning

The planning cycle is the series of operations that enable management to plan the growth and profits of the firm. The sequence of operations is as follows.

(*a*) Define the firm's mission—its reason for being in business and its ultimate aspirations.

(*b*) Specify the planning period, bearing in mind the nature of the firm's markets, capacity, history and environmental uncertainty. One year is the usual period for a budget; five years is common for corporate plans.

(*c*) Forecast the trends in sales, costs, capital inflows and outflows for the planning period on the assumptions of most probable environmental circumstances and of no change in management policies.

(*d*) Specify the firm's objectives by the end of the planning period for major accounting items including sales, operating costs, retained profits, capital expenditure, production volumes and working capital.

(*e*) Identify the gaps between (*c*) and (*d*) above and conduct "gap analysis" to obtain strategies for bringing the forecast and objectives closer together until they match.

(*f*) Produce a corporate plan (five years) or budget (one year) based on the results of the gap analysis.

(*g*) Instruct all staff of the content and implications of the plan.

(*h*) Execute the plan.

(*i*) Compare actual results with the plan and identify differences and their causes.

(*j*) Produce and execute strategies for reducing differences, either by operational changes or by plan revisions.

(*k*) Review the plan and its execution at the period end and go to stage (*c*) for the next planning period.

In sum, the above amounts to the following.

(*a*) Set objectives.

(*h*) Make strategic plans to achieve the objectives.

(*c*) Execute the plan.

(*d*) Compare plan with actual.

(*e*) Make new plans.

Planning enables management by objectives to take place. In MBO, top management agree objectives with each manager and supervisor, but leave the manager alone to achieve his objectives. At regular intervals actual performance is compared with objectives and top management intervenes only when objectives are regularly not met without adequate justification.

Forecasting

Introduction

Forecasts are not plans but merely predictions of future company results on stated assumptions. They form the necessary groundwork on which plans can be laid. Forecasts are prerequisites of plans if the latter are to be realistic. This means that the forecasts themselves must be realistic, and this in turn depends on the predictability of the principal independent variables, notably sales, materials, prices and labour earnings.

Techniques

Forcasting techniques are divisible into two broad classes.

(*a*) Time series analysis.

(*b*) Simulation.

Time series analysis reviews the past trend of a major variable such as sales and extends the trend line into the future. In its simplest form, this resembles completing an arithmetical progression. If, for example, sales for the previous six months to forecast are 3, 5, 7, 9, 11, 13, it takes no great insight to predict the next six months' sales as being 15, 17, 19, 21, 23, 25. The trouble is that this rate of increase may not be supported by the market or by the firm's productive capacity. A more general point arises from this. Time series analysis is as valid only as its underlying assumption that past trends will be continued to the end of a future planning period. This assumption is valid only in the most exceptionally stable business environments.

More meaningful forecasts can be generated from an analysis of the factors giving rise to changes in the sales and other major variables. Having isolated such factors, the forecaster makes explicit assumptions about their probable magnitude during the planning period. A pattern of sales figures, etc., can now be built on the assumed size of the causative factors. The identification of such causative factors and the quantification of their relationship to sales and other major variables are the essential work of simulation. Simulation tries to reduce the complexities of the business environment to a series of mathematically expressed statements that together constitute a *model* of the firm. The model is as good only as its key assumptions about the relationship between key variables like sales and their causative factors. For example, suppose a firm models its sales thus:

$$S = 0.2M_0 + 0.3(M_1 - M_0) + 8A$$

where S is sales volume in physical units

         M_0 is size of total production market now

         M_1 is size of total product one year ahead

and A is current costs of advertising

If in fact it turns out that the actual coefficient of A should have been 4 instead of 8, the planned sales volume will be over-ambitious and not achieved in reality. The fault will not lie with the marketing or advertising personnel so much as with the planning personnel who have misspecified the sales model. It is important for top management to apportion the blame correctly in these circumstances, so as to avoid demoralising and embittering the marketing and advertising personnel.

Predictability

There is no such thing as a perfect forecast. If the future were wholly predictable, there would be no need for plans at all after the first year of operations, since the first year's plan could be validly extended in the light of wholly foreseeable circumstances and its factor analyses need never be revised. Human beings are not wholly predictable as consumers, payers or anything else.

The unpredictability of human actions does not justify the complete omission to forecast as being a waste of effort. For business environments may not be wholly predictable, but they are never wholly unpredictable either. Forecasts based on careful factor analysis and simulation models will identify a significant proportion of the key items affecting the firm in the planning period. Some of the risks of misapplied effort and wasted expenditure arising from unpredictability can be reduced by applying probabilities to forecasts in the way described below.

Forecasting and probabilities
Suppose a planner knows that if the market is one state, sales will be 500, if in another 200, if in a third 1,000. The probability of state one is 40 per cent, of state two 35 per cent and of state three 25 per cent. If he puts sales into the plan at 500 because this level is more likely than the other two states individually, the forecast has a 60 per cent (100 per cent less 40 per cent) chance of being wrong, a 35 per cent chance of the error being 300 in one direction and 25 per cent chance of the error being 500 in the opposite direction. To handle this situation the planner should find the *expected value* of all three states, thus:

$$
\begin{array}{llll}
\text{State 1} & 40\% \text{ of } 500 & = & 200 \\
\text{State 2} & 35\% \text{ of } 200 & = & 70 \\
\text{State 3} & 25\% \text{ of } 1000 & = & \underline{250} \\
\multicolumn{3}{r}{\text{Weighted average outcome} =} & \underline{\underline{530}}
\end{array}
$$

The expected value of 530 is entered as the sales figure because it more accurately reflects the *three* possible outcomes than does the modal probability of 500. The value of 530 minimises the size of a possible error on the probabilities given. However, we know that sales will not in fact be 530, but will be 1,000, 500 or 200. We might prefer to have three different plans, one for each of the sales figures that could actually occur. If we adopt such a contingency planning approach we shall have to combine each of the sales figures with each of the possible cost of sales figures we expect. Suppose there are four cost of sales figures that could actually occur. This gives us twelve plans, as follows:

		Sales state	
Cost of sales	1	2	3
States 1	1,1	1,2	1,3
2	2,1	2,2	2,3
3	3,1	3,2	3,3
4	4,1	4,2	4,3

When we have as many as twelve alternative plans, we shall be in the dark as to which if any is the plan taken most seriously by the firm's directors. We may as well have no plan at all in these circumstances.

In general, plans based on forecasts of expected value are the most satisfactory. For although we know the expected value will not be the actual value of a variable, we know that actual will deviate less from expected than via any other forecasting technique, and we have the advantage of retaining one identified plan rather than several.

Control

Introduction

A forecast is an *objective* statement of what is expected to occur. A plan is a *subjective* statement of what the firm intends shall occur. The planning process has been briefly outlined above.

Some items can be planned directly. Rent can often be forecast and planned exactly, office staff costs similarly. Other items cannot be planned directly because they vary too greatly for one steady figure to be maintained. For example, stock levels depend on the level of production which can be quite tightly planned and also on the level of sales which cannot, as it is not possible to control or plan with precision what customers will do. To plan stocks, therefore, it is necessary to specify the maximum and minimum levels between which stocks will be allowed to vary. This means that actual stocks are planned to be between two permitted levels. The purpose of the two levels is to control the actual deviations of stock. The plan specifies an expected value for stock levels, given planned figures for production and expected values of sales volumes. However, the figure in the plan is a dependent variable which is a function of production and sales volumes, so it is not itself directly planned. The planned control levels, maximum and minimum, constitute the true means of executing stock plans. Thus control serves planning by ensuring that the deviations of actual stock from planned (expected) stock are kept within specified limits. Any item subject to fluctuations, whose extent and timing are not wholly predictable, is better planned by using a control system than by relying on the exact achievement of a figure specified in the planning statement.

Control systems defined

A control system is a system whose purpose is to achieve and maintain a desired state. A system can be defined as a set of activities linking inputs with a process of transformation, and linking that process with outputs. An essential condition to be fulfilled before a group of things and activities can constitute a system is that each ingredient should have a definite relationship with at least one other ingredient so that the complete set of ingredients has a unifying character of some kind. Thus the words "stepped dirt piece" do not constitute a system, but the words "he stepped on a piece of dirt" do constitute the system termed a "sentence".

For a system to constitute a control system, at least four different types of ingredient are necessary.

(*a*) A sensor—something which measures the input or output to be controlled, i.e. a tool for measuring "actuals".

(*b*) A standard—a specified desired value against which actuals will be set by means of (*c*).

(*c*) A comparator—compares the actuals derived from the sensor with the standard and, if the difference is unacceptable, this brings into operation (*d*).

(*d*) An effector—changes the inputs or output in question to bring it closer to the standard.

Control systems may be open or closed. Closed systems do not depend on outside intervention, as system output "feeds back" directly to system input. The usually cited example of a closed system is a thermostat. In a thermostat the sensor is a thermometer, the standard is the preset control temperature, the comparator is the device comparing the thermometer reading with the preset control, and the effector is the switch that turns on, if actual temperature is below control, or off if it is above. No outside intervention is needed to ensure that the effector switch does its job, so long as the thermostat is in sound working order. The input to the sensor is directly changed by the effector—this change being termed in systems language "feedback". When the actual equals the control, this is a state of equilibrium.

The effector in an open system does not feed back *directly* to systems input but utilises an outside agent, sometimes termed a "controller". Open systems are characterised also by equifinality, the ability to reach the same final state by a variety of alternative routes. A mechanical thermostat reaches its control temperature by one route only—the switch that turns the heater on or off. The bodily thermostat can bring excessively high skin temperature down to the equilibrium 98.4 °F level by sweating and panting on an automatic level, or by causing the person to go into a cool room or take a shower or go for a swim on a conscious level. The closed thermostat system has only one route to a control level; the open system has several, including many which involve outside effectors such as shower taps.

Most business systems are open systems. Closed systems have an inbuilt tendency towards equilibrium, a situation known as "homeostasis". Some open systems lack this tendency. For example, there is no homeostasis in the biological systems linking food with waste, as it is readily observed that the same person eating the same mix of food and drink will put on more weight on some occasions as a result than on others. The absence of homeostasis in certain open systems is linked to a tendency to absorb excess input as reserves—fat in the case of food, working capital in the case of firms realising more in income than they give out as expenditure. In certain cases the anti-homeostatic tendency becomes a drive to maximise the particular reserves arising from the unexpended inputs.

Positive and negative feedback

Under negative feedback the effector reduces the deviations between actual and control by taking action opposed to the direction of the input shown by the sensor. Thus, if the temperature is rising above the control, the thermostat takes action to reverse its rise.

Under positive feedback the effector takes action to reinforce the direction of the input quantities shown on the sensor. A business example of positive feedback is sometimes found in the area of bonus systems. Management offers labour 1 per cent of wage bonus for every ten hours saved in completing, say, a building project. This reduces total time by, say, fifty man-hours. Encouraged by this result, management offer 2 per cent for every fifteen hours saved, and total time on the next similar project falls by eighty hours. This positive feedback continues until no further savings are physically possible.

Positive feedback is a feature of systems designed to *maximise* some benefit. Negative feedback is a feature of systems designed to *stabilise* costs (and possibly benefits too).

Control accounting is largely concerned with negative feedback. A plan is laid down, actual results are compared with the plan and deviations are examined with a view to minimising them. However, if the deviations are largely favourable to the firm's profits, the system may then change its character from one of negative feedback to one of positive feedback. This is especially applicable to systems integrating incentive bonuses with normal control accounting.

MBO and MBE

Planning systems enable management by objectives (MBO) to be set in motion; control systems enable MBO to be maintained without further need for top management intervention. This enables top management to spend more time on strategic management and planning and to avoid becoming bogged down in detailed day-to-day operations. The setting of departmental and personal objectives that together best ensure the attainment of corporate goals is, under MBO, the central task of top management.

Management by exception (MBE) is really a description of the effector phase of an MBO control system. At regular intervals, typically monthly, actual performance is compared with the objectives set. Large variances are investigated and management intervenes as effector to ensure negative feedback:

(*a*) if the variances are regarded as unacceptable; and
(*b*) the explanations offered for them are unsatisfactory.

This intervention is thought to be exceptional—hence management by exception.

INTERNAL CONTROL

The purposes of internal control

Internal control is the organisation of accounting duties in such a way as to maximise the chances of accurate accounting and minimise the chances of undetected fraud occurring. These twin purposes dictate the types of bookkeeping and accounting systems that are available to any firm subject to audit. The purpose of audit is to ensure that the accounts show a true and fair view of the firm's income and assets. Auditors rely heavily on tests of the firm's internal control system in order to ensure the audit purpose is met.

Characteristics of internal control

To ensure accurate accounting, an accounting system must display the following characteristics.

(*a*) The books of account must be written up from vouchers that constitute the primary evidence of a transaction's having taken place.

(*b*) The vouchers themselves must accurately reflect transactions as regards:

    (*i*)   date;
    (*ii*) quantity;
    (*iii*) price;
    (*iv*) value (quantity times price); and
    (*v*) identity of the transacting parties.

(*c*) Aggregated accounts must equal the total balances of their component accounts. For example, the balance on the sales ledger control account must equal the total balances in the sales ledger.

(*d*) Final accounts must be drawn directly from the ledgers, according to generally accepted accounting principles, and must *fully* reflect ledger content. Thus secret reserves are precluded, as the resultant understatement of retained profit would not fully reflect the ledger content.

The characteristics of internal control systems designed to minimise the possibility of fraud are given below.

(*a*) No one person is responsible for more than one of the following aspects of any transaction.

    (*i*)   Authorisation.
    (*ii*) Recording.
    (*iii*) Realisation (through cash payment or receipt).

(*b*) The system is regularly tested (by internal and/or external audit) to ensure that the previous characteristic operates in practice, to ensure no dummy transactions can pass through the system undetected, and to detect any frauds that may occur through collusion between two or more people in the firm.

Internal control as a control system

The sensor
The actual accounting records and actual allocation of duties are read from the books, from the accounts manual (if one is kept), and from the

job specifications of each member of the staff. These records are verifiable by interview and inspection.

The standard
The characteristics of a properly functioning internal control system listed in above constitute the ideal or standard with which the actual system can be compared.

The comparator
The audit team compares the actual system with the ideal one and notes the differences, signifying their importance as potential subverters of accounting accuracy or as promoters of fraud.

The effector
Top management usually delegates to the chief accountant the task of correcting the weaknesses identified by the audit team.

Conclusion
Internal control is the oldest accounting control system. It arose in the Middle Ages when clerks acted as stewards to the lord of the manor and had to account to him for every penny with which they were entrusted. The tradition of stewardship is responsible for the present legal framework of financial accounting, wherein the directors as stewards are charged with presenting true and fair accounts to the shareholders as owners. The external auditors are appointed by, and report to, the shareholders rather than the directors (in theory). The internal control system is to ensure good stewardship of the shareholders' funds.

OPERATING STATEMENTS

Function of operating statements
Operating statements are comparators of actual results with standards. Their function is to provide feedback to management about the extent to which plans or standards have been achieved. They thus serve the purposes of MBO and MBE.

Preparation of operating statements
Every cost centre has records kept for it concerning its expenditure, physical inputs and outputs and income, if any, during the month. At the end of the month this information is transferred to monthly accounts, drawn up in the same way as final accounts but necessarily involving more estimates of accruals. The monthly income statements are presented on forms such as the one shown below.

AB LTD DIVISION M: OPERATING STATEMENT, MAY 1983

	Standard	Actual	Variance
Sales volume—physical units	50,000	40,000	(10,000)
Production volume—physical units	55,000	50,000	(5,000)
Finished goods stock movement	5,000	(10,000)	(5,000)
Finished goods stock on hand at month end	7,000	3,000	(4,000)
	£	£	£
Sales income	200,000	170,000	(30,000)
Stock at cost—finished	14,000	6,000	(8,000)
—in progress	7,000	5,000	(2,000)
—raw materials	2,000	4,000	2,000
Total stocks	23,000	15,000	(8,000)
	£	£	£
Material costs	15,000	7,500	7,500
Direct labour costs	8,000	4,000	4,000
Variable overhead costs	2,000	2,500	(500)
Total variable costs	25,000	14,000	11,000
Fixed costs	5,000	6,000	(1,000)
Total cost	30,000	20,000	10,000
Profit	20,000	20,000	–

In the above very simplified summary operating statement, each item has actual and standard compared and variance revealed. Often there is a fourth column, showing the variance as a percentage of standard, to help management identify the proportionately largest variances. In this case the variances with the highest percentage variances are:

(a) finished goods stock movement [(100%)];
(b) raw materials closing stock costs [100%];
(c) finished goods closing stock in units [$(\frac{4}{7}) = 57\%$];
(d) finished goods closing stock cost [$(\frac{8}{14}) = 57\%$];
(e) materials costs [50%]; and
(f) labour costs [50%].

All of the above would warrant management attention. As we shall see, however, the importance of variances in a situation such as the above is changed when we isolate certain common effects of the volume variances reported in the top row. At present, it is sufficient to note that an operating statement compares a plan or standard result with an actual one; but to achieve the most effective control system over costs, the figures entered for plan or standard variable costs may need to be adjusted in order to correct for the variance between the plan or standard production volume. The standard variable costs all arise from a standard production volume. If this volume fails to be achieved, the standard variable cost levels will correspondingly fail to be achieved.

Interpretation of operating statements

MBE governs the interpretation of operating statements. Only exceptionally do large variances need concern top management. Additionally, variances that mutually correlate need not concern management item by item. For example, if there is a large adverse variance of production volume, there will be consequent favourable variances of variable costs because the firm has produced *less* than plan, so variable costs are in necessary consequence *less* than plan. The concern of management here is not the saving in variable costs but the shortfall in production volume.

More specifically, we can tabulate the major variances and their possible type of explanation as an introductory guide to their interpretation.

Variance	*Possible explanations*
Unit sales volume	Product over/under priced, under produced, generally more/less successful than planned.
Unit production volume	Factory capacity use, labour efficiency, strikes, stockouts.
Stock movement	Difference between sales and production volumes above/below that planned.
Sales income	As per sales volume with slightly more emphasis on pricing policy.
Stock costs	Difference between planned and actual stock volumes or unit input costs.
Material costs	Difference in materials prices, usages, yields or ingredient mixes from those planned, or arising directly from production volume variance.
Direct labour costs	Difference in labour pay rates, hours at work, productivity or skills mix from those planned, or arising directly from production volume variance (itself possibly attributable to labour factors).
Variable overhead costs	Arising directly from same causes as labour variance when variable overheads are recovered against labour-hours or labour costs. Otherwise expenditure on variable overheads may be different from plan, recovery basis may be inappropriate (e.g. production volume used when sales volume is a more suitable base).
Fixed costs	Difference between planned and actual expenditure or between planned and actual production volume.
Total costs	Materials, labour, variable overheads and/or fixed costs and production volume variances.

Variance	*Possible explanations*
Profit	Total cost variance and sales income variance (which may, as in our example, cancel each other out. This does not necessarily mean actual profits are satisfactory, since with the *actual* level of sales volume achieved, management might well have required a different level of profit from that originally planned).

CORPORATE PLANS AND BUDGETS

Distinctions between plans and budgets

(*a*) Plans are general, budgets are detailed.

(*b*) Plans are strategic and long term, budgets are tactical and short term.

(*c*) Plans are to achieve corporate goals, objectives or visions of the future position of the firm; budgets are to achieve shorter term plans.

(*d*) Plans involve creative identification and exploitation of opportunities; budgets involve cautiously realistic targeting of attainable results.

(*e*) Plans are constrained by the underlying political, economic, social, market and resource environments but not by short-run scarcities; budgets are constrained by temporary limits imposed both by environments and the current endowment of internal resources.

(*f*) Plans usually generate policies and budgets; budgets operate *within* policies and generate feedback through operating statements.

(*g*) Plans depict corporate aspirations; budgets depict immediate corporate intentions.

(*h*) Cost and profit centre performance is not usually judged against the corporate plan but rather against the current budget.

Similarities between plans and budgets

(*a*) Both represent attempts to order the future course of events.

(*b*) Both are drawn up within resource or environmental constraints.

(*c*) Both are instruments for furthering corporate objectives.

(*d*) Both are widely held to be easier to achieve if prepared with the active participation of staff affected by them.

(*e*) Both are used to motivate staff to work for the attainment of corporate goals.

(*f*) Both are used to promote goal congruence—a convergence of corporate goals with the staff's personal aspirations—in the interests of team spirit and reduced interpersonal friction and reduced person–company alienation.

The planning process

Introduction

The first part of this chapter outlined the planning cycle and showed it to be a continual feedback mechanism. The planning process can be represented as an open system of modified feedback between the environment as mirrored in forecasts and the firm as mirrored in its objectives.

Ranking of objectives

A firm has a set of objectives, some deriving from its Memorandum of Association's objects clauses, some from the directors' view of the firm's image and identity, some from the universal necessities of business survival and some from the traditions laid down by past chief executives. At the outset of planning, these objectives are to be identified and ranked.

Suppose a firm's directors have identified the following objectives and now seek to rank them.

(*a*) Acquisition of land for building and subsequent sale (from the Memorandum).

(*b*) Maintain a reputation for high quality "executive" style housing in upper-middle-class areas (image).

(*c*) Improve dividends to shareholders (business environment).

(*d*) Raise market profile so that products are seen as quite distinctive from those of competitors (business environment and image).

(*e*) Maximise return on capital employed (business environment).

(*f*) Stay in top part of housing market (tradition).

(*g*) Recruit more managers from site supervisors (tradition).

(*h*) Minimise burden of external debt (tradition).

In ranking these objectives, the directors will have regard to the sources of the objectives. Image is as important only as the sales it generates, tradition as the profit it helps or hinders, and the Memorandum is merely the legal document stating what the company was originally formed to do. Since survival and growth is determined chiefly by business environment, it is this source that is most important. We have three objectives above springing from this source: improve dividends; raise market profile; and maximise return on capital employed (ROCE).

Maximising ROCE will enable dividends to be improved, while dividends can still be kept well covered by profits earned. This is the principal objective. Raising market profile represents a key *strategy* for maximising ROCE rather than an objective in itself. This strategy is consistent with the second listed objective—that of maintaining quality—and in fact that objective operates as a *constraint* on the strategy, for it precludes the firm from raising its market profile by going down-market. The same applies to objective (*f*). It is also a constraint operating the same way as objective (*b*)—keeping the firm up-market. Objective (*a*) is irrelevant, as it would be impossible to achieve high quality housing without the acquisition of land for development. Objective (*g*) is a *major factor* to be taken into account in achieving the *strategy* but not so important as to interfere with the primary ROCE objective. If the firm has a choice between recruiting an outside manager or promoting one from its own supervisors, it will prefer the latter, but only if the candidate is seen as being no less likely than the outsider to improve operating profitability.

Objective (*h*), the minimising of the burden of debt, looks at first sight like a facilitator of the principal objective. Greater borrowing might enable the firm to take on bigger and more profitable jobs, although profits will be reduced by the payment of interest on loans. The debt minimising objective seems quite consistent with the ROCE objective. Minimising debt involves not only minimising interest costs but reducing the proportion of total assets financed by shareholders. Return on shareholders' capital can be increased by the taking on of loans, *so long as* the profitability of loan-funded projects is high enough *both* to cover interest and to generate profits at least as good as the firm's previous projects. To illustrate this, let us suppose the firm has £2 million of shareholders' funds and an annual average profit of £200,000. This is a 10 per cent ROCE. It is worthwhile for the firm to take on loans if they can earn 10 per cent *plus* their interest cost. Suppose a £500,000 loan at 10 per cent interest can be used to finance an operation yielding profits of £200,000 a year. The yield after deduction of £(10% of 500,000 =) 50,000 interest is £150,000 or 30 per cent. This represents a better ROCE than the firm's current 10 per cent. It shows that debt burdens do not necessarily have to be a constraint on maximising ROCE but can, on the contrary, help achieve better returns. This in turn means that the objective of minimising debt may constrain maximising ROCE, and the directors should not lightly entertain such a constraint. Objective (*h*) could be reformulated thus: keep the debt burden down to the level that the profitable exploitation of opportunities justifies.

In sum, the primary objective is to maximise the return on capital employed, the primary strategy to achieve which is the raising of the market profile. This strategy is to be conducted without an *undue* increase in the debt burden and without the use of outside managerial recruits when suitable managers can be found from among currently employed site supervisors.

Gap analysis

Suppose the directors wish to raise ROCE from the 10 per cent currently experienced to 15 per cent by the end of a five-year planning horizon, but environmental analysis has led the forecasters in the planning office to show that a return of only 12 per cent is to be expected. The gap of 3 per cent must now be analysed. It could be due to one or more of the following.

(*a*) The forecast expects the total market for quality housing in the region to grow very little.

(*b*) The forecast expects the firm's market share to remain at its present level.

(*c*) The forecast identifies a scarcity of a particular resource—for example, bricks or site supervisory labour that constrains the maximum possible growth rate of the firm's returns. Such a resource that constrains fulfilment of corporate objectives is known as a "limiting factor".

(*d*) The forecast assumes previous managerial aversion to debt will continue.

(*e*) The forecast assumes economic conditions will constrain the firm in some other way not covered above.

The planners and directors will consider each of the above in turn and determine which of the assumptions or expectations of the forecast can realistically be amended. For example, increased advertising (of the right sort) could increase the firm's market share, as could commencing operations in parts of the country not yet covered by the firm. Raising loans to enable the firm to take on larger projects might also be a way of closing the gap.

Of special importance is the limiting factor. The shortage of a critical material might be eased by paying a higher price to suppliers, by seeking alternative materials or by taking over a supplier to ensure more direct access to the scarce material. The shortage of supervisory labour might be eased by training promising foremen or by recruiting widely from outside. However, once the directors have examined and begun to adopt all the most promising steps to ease resource shortages, there will still remain one or more resource that chiefly constrains the firm's possibilities of growth. This is where the plan actually starts. Given the existence of a limiting factor, the need is *to maximise the productivity of that factor*. It may be that after an outline plan has been drawn up by the planning office to comply with this need, the maximum ROCE is 14 per cent. In this case the directors will have to accept 14 per cent as a realistic maximum instead of the 15 per cent they originally sought. At that stage the planning office can expand the outline plan into a full five-year corporate plan, showing how each cost and profit centre is expected to contribute to the directors' objectives.

Rolling plans

After a corporate plan has been drawn up, it is necessary to spell out its detailed requirements for the upcoming year. This is the task of the budget. Plans are generally drawn up for at least three years ahead; five years is usual and ten years not unheard of. After the first year, the directors may wish to alter the plan to make it more realistic (or more ambitious) in the light of changed conditions since the plan was conceived.

The same sequence of objectives, forecast, gap analysis and outline plan drawn round the principal limiting factor will apply. The result might be an entirely new plan.

Even if the existing plan is not seriously modified, it will be "rolled over" for a further year. Thus, for a five-year planning system, at the end of year 1 there are four more years to go and the planners will outline figures for a fifth year, so that the planning horizon remains consistent at five years instead of five in the first year, four in the second year, etc. By adding an extra year to the plan at the end of each year of experience a rolling plan is achieved. Rolling plans enable major changes to take place smoothly and keep planning horizons consistent. There would be considerable upheaval in the firm if, instead of rolling its plans, it waited until near the end of one five-year block before laying quite different plans for the next five-year block.

Budgets

The planning context

Budgets are detailed plans for one year of operations. In firms with long-range plans, they are the instruments that enable such plans to be achieved. In firms with no explicit long-range plans (those too small to have planning offices or in a commercial environment so unpredictable that long-range planning would make no sense), budgets have to fulfil the functions of plans as described above. Thus budgets begin by identifying limiting factors and are drawn up to ensure that those factors display maximum productivity. Production and sales volumes are budgeted and variable operating costs built up on the assumption that the budgeted volumes are achieved. Fixed costs are budgeted on the assumption of capacity usage consistent with budgeted production volumes and on what, it is hoped, are realistic judgments of price increases to be faced in the coming year.

Operating budgets

The production and other operating costs are related to budgeted sales incomes for each month for the purpose of compiling monthly budgeted income statements known as "operating budgets". These budgets should be *phased*—that is, they should fully reflect expected seasonal variations in sales and costs and not merely be annual figures partitioned into twelve equal monthly amounts. This is in the interests of realism.

Capital budgets

Each department of the firm has a requirement to replace or extend its stock of fixed assets every year. Every request for such expenditure should be justified in writing by the department head, using at least one of the capital expenditure appraisal methods we shall examine in Chapter 9. The directors will accept some, defer others to a future year and reject the rest. In a well-planned firm, major capital expenditures are explicitly specified in the corporate plan and all capital expenditures are authorised by inclusion in the approved annual capital budget. This means a department cannot request capital expenditure during a budget year unless it has provided for it in the budget, save in very exceptional circumstances (e.g. destruction of an asset by fire). After the directors have reviewed the departmental submissions, they will determine how much money each individual department will be allowed as its capital allocation for the budget year. The total of all departmental budgets will constitute the corporate budget.

Cash budgets

After operating and capital budgets have been approved, the finance director's staff can draw up a cash budget. To do this, the finance director must ensure that funds are available to meet major approved capital expenditures and identify their sources and costs. Funds flow statements can be derived for the year and detailed monthly cash budgets drawn up using the techniques outlined in the previous chapter.

Master budgets

The master budget is the budget for the whole firm, or for each division of the firm, that summarises the data from the departmental budgets. Thus there is a master operating budget (sometimes called the master "profit" budget), a master capital budget and the cash budget (itself a summary of cash flows from all profit centres in the firm or division). From the master budgets, a budgeted Income Statement and Balance Sheet for the year can be drawn up showing what the firm plans to report to its shareholders next year if the budget is achieved.

Planned Programme Budgeting

Traditionally budgets are drawn up for each cost and profit centre, then summarised to make the master budgets. In American firms the general practice is to budget not only by way of traditional departments but more importantly by way of "programmes". A programme is some form of corporate output, products, services or activities. The advantage of the programme approach is that it concentrates the focus of budget planning on what the firm sells, and adjusts inputs to fit output requirements. The disadvantage of the approach is that many departments may contribute to a programme (e.g. several sequential factory processes to produce one type of product) and programme budgeting weakens the identification of responsibility for particular costs in the interests of getting the overall programme profile correct. More seriously, a focus on outputs in the planning system *may* put pressure on planners to understate the importance of a limiting factor and so render the budget unrealistic from the outset. In the United Kingdom, budgets serve MBO and each centre that incurs costs is given the responsibility for staying within its budgets. The budget and its matching monthly operating statement are seen as an instrument of *responsibility accounting*. The focus on outputs in the United Kingdom accounting context comes partly from the technique of standard costing. In budgeting we focus on cost centres but do not ignore cost units; in standard costing we focus on cost units but do not ignore cost centres.

STANDARD COSTING

Types of standards

(*a*) Ideal standards—the costs and profits achievable under wholly ideal conditions (no idle time, no holidays, no breakdowns, no adverse markets, etc.). These are inherently unrealistic and few firms would contemplate their use.

(*b*) Capacity standards—the costs and profits achievable under conditions of no wastage of any resource machine or paid labour-hour. These are not realistic for most firms, in which holidays, breakdowns, strikes and idle time are an integral part of business experience.

(*c*) Past standards—the costs and profits achieved in previous years used as a standard to judge those achieved now. These tend to be insufficiently ambitious for most firms, as most firms expect nominal (if not real) profits to rise with every passing year.

(*d*) Normal standards—the average level of costs and profits expected over a future period. These are realistic, if their underlying forecasts are, but not sufficiently ambitious.

(*e*) Basic standards—costs and profits, expressed in real terms, that represent the desired levels for the foreseeable future. These are like ideal standards if the levels "desired" are inadequately grounded in studies of what can realistically be achieved.

(*f*) Expected standards—costs and profits expected to be achieved, given current capacity and working methods. These are more realistic than other standards (except normal and past standards), but can be drawn up to represent an improvement over the current situation.

Thus we may define a standard as the required value of an item given current capacity and working methods. Standards are set and revised at regular intervals, ideally each year when the budget is prepared and corporate plan is rolled over. Then the firm can ensure consistency of approach and convergence of effect between plan, budget and standards. In the final section of this chapter we shall look further at the reconciliation problems involved.

Standards are required values. Standard costs represent expected costs, not necessarily those desired. A zero variance of product costs against standard means actual costs are *running at a satisfactory level,* neither better nor worse than that; just as zero variance of departmental running costs against budget means actual running costs are *running according to plan.* The foundation of the standard costing system is the standard hour. Its value as a control system depends critically on the realism of the original composition of the standard hour. It is as crucial to standard costing as correct identification of the limiting factor is to budgeting.

The standard hour

Work study

Every routine task in a factory can be analysed into a sequence of necessary individual actions the worker needs to take. Time-and-motion studies break down the factory jobs into their component actions. Then they time by stop-watch the duration of each action by each of a sample of factory operatives. The results are analysed by means of work study techniques, and improvements to working routines may be proposed. If these improvements are adopted by the workers, there will be a period of settling in to the new routines. During this period the workers become increasingly familiar with the new routines and their speed of task completion correspondingly increases. This situation is known as the "learning curve". After the settling-in period the time taken to complete a task stabilises at a level reflecting the workers' mastery of the routines involved. In work study jargon, the learning curve is said to "level out". The time-and-motion men observe a further sample of workers at this stage and note the duration of each activity in the production process. (In service industries and offices generally, the equivalent of work study is organisation and methods, and both approaches are well-established branches of management science. The purpose of work study is not only to improve work methods but *to establish what the standard work output is for an average worker working at an average pace. The average work output per man-hour so established is what constitutes the standard hour.*)

Use of the standard hour

Let us suppose a firm makes six products and each product has its own single process cost centre. The output of each centre in May is as under.

Centre	Output	Centre	Output
1	30,000 cans	4	250 square metres
2	50,000 tonnes	5	6,000 boxes
3	150,000 litres	6	30,000 kilograms

These outputs are all measured differently, so we cannot directly compare them. The outputs are said to be incommensurable. After work study, however, we know how much output should come from each man-hour.

We can therefore convert the outputs into standard hours of production (SHP) and immediately see which centre has been the most prolific (not necessarily the most productive, as will be explained shortly). The conversion is shown below.

Centre	Output as given	Output per standard hour	Output in SHP
1	30,000 cans	600 cans	50
2	50,000 tonnes	50 tonnes	1,000
3	150,000 litres	750 litres	200
4	250 m^2	$2\frac{1}{2}$ m^2	100
5	6,000 boxes	120 boxes	50
6	30,000 kilograms	1,500 kilograms	20
		Total corporate output	1,420

It is apparent from the above that centre 2 has been most prolific in terms of standard hours. We should expect this to be the case because it employs the largest number of people.

Productivity

Output measured in SHP tells us how many man-hours should have been used to make the actual output physically generated by the centre. Given the actual man-hours worked, we can quickly see whether the centre's workers have shown greater or less productivity than standard. Standard hours divided by actual hours will give us the productivity ratio, an indicator of the efficiency with which the workers have laboured in the month in question. The table below shows this.

Centre	SHP	Actual man-hours	Productivity ratio
1	50	50	100%
2	1,000	1,250	80%
3	200	175	114%
4	100	140	71%
5	50	30	167%
6	20	25	80%
Total	1,420	1,670	85%

The firm's labour force has been only 85 per cent as productive as standard. Centre 2, as the largest producer, is largely to blame for this, with a productivity ratio of 80 per cent. The least efficient centre is centre 4, with a ratio of 71 per cent, while the most efficient one is centre 5, with a ratio of 167 per cent. The director will require convincing explanations of these large variations in labour efficiency.

Standard unit costs

Constructing the standard cost profile

Work study gives us the SHP—how much physical output to expect from a man-hour. This enables us to determine the labour content of a cost unit. Similar studies are made by production engineering experts to determine the optimum material content of a cost unit. Management accountancy expertise is needed to review the expenses and overheads, so as to identify their most suitable recovery bases. This has been considered in Chapter 2.

After all the above preliminary work has been done, we can build up the standard variable unit cost. The full standard unit cost involves fixed cost apportionment, and this in turn involves integrating standards with budgets. First, let us focus on the variable costs.

The standard unit cost of direct materials for a unit of X can be put together as shown in the table below.

Ingredient	Price per unit	Standard usage of ingredient per unit of X	Standard cost in £ (price times usage)
A	25p per oz	8 oz	2.00
B	10p per g	4 g	0.40
C	15p per ml	3 ml	0.45
Can	15p	1	0.15
	Total standard unit material cost		3.00 (per can)

The standard unit labour cost is derived in a comparable way as shown next.

SHP per grade of labour in cans of X	Standard time per can	Standard basic hourly pay rate	Standard cost in £ (time times rate)
Unskilled—10	6 min ($\frac{1}{10}$ hr)	£6.00	0.60
Skilled—20	3 min ($\frac{1}{20}$ hr)	£8.00	0.40
	Total standard unit labour cost		1.00 (per can)

Finally the variable expenses and variable overheads may be recovered at, say, £2 unskilled labour-hour. This means the variable expense per can is 20p ($\frac{1}{10}$ of £2). Thus the variable cost per can is £3 materials, £1 labour, plus 20p expenses, which totals £4.20.

If budgeted standard unskilled hours are 200 a month and if fixed costs are recovered against standard hours at £1 per hour, standard fixed costs per can are 10p. The total standard cost of a can of X would be £4.20 plus 10p, equalling £4.30.

If the price charged to customers is £5 per can, our summary standard cost profile for a can of X is as follows.

	£
Materials	3.00
Labour	1.00
Expenses	.20
Variable costs	4.20
Fixed costs	.10
Total costs	4.30
Profit	.70
Sales price	5.00

Reporting against standards

Just as we exercise MBO for cost centres through operating statements comparing actual with budget, so we exercise MBO for cost units through operating statements, comparing actual with standard for each product or service sold to customers.

Actuals can vary from standards either because of prices or quantities. Price variances arise when sales price, material prices per unit of ingredient, basic hourly rate of pay or total monthly overhead expenditure deviates from the original plan. Quantity variances arise when sales volumes or production volumes differ from *budget* or when materials usage, labour productivity or usage of labour or machine capacity differ from *standard*. Chapter 7 examines variances in detail, but at this stage we should note that reporting against budget need take no account of standard costs, but that reporting against standards—especially under absorption costing—must take account of the budget. This is because standards relate to individual cost units, while budgets relate to the *total* number of cost units planned to be produced by each cost centre. This means standards can ignore output volumes but budgets cannot. It also means control of unit costs by standards and departmental costs by budget must be seen as twin subsystems within the overall management control system. The reconciliation of subsystems is covered in pages 165–7. Before we address that question, however, we need to consider a further system—the motivation system.

MOTIVATION AND INCENTIVES

Introduction

Behavioural accounting is the name for a new branch of accountancy that examines how accounting affects behaviour. One of its central concerns, is the impact of budgets on performance (and vice versa, to a lesser extent). Implicit in early behavioural accounting literature was the assumption that people perform better if they are involved in participating in any plans that affect their working life. This assumption is related to the theory Y view of management that believes people are motivated more through personal involvement than monetary reward. Theory X holds the reverse view. Wise management will assume both theories are true in different contexts for different workers. Their motivation system will reflect both theories. Bonus payment systems reflect theory X rather than Y but are quite compatible with the latter.

Bonus systems

Bonus systems reward workers for working more efficiently and productively than the basic requirements. In the crudest systems this amounts simply to working faster. Time saved is rewarded by extra earnings. For example, if 600 cans equal sixty SHP but the actual hours taken to make the cans is only fifty, there is a time saving of ten hours. If bonuses are paid at the full basic rate for half the time saved and if the basic rate is £9 per hour, workers will receive a bonus of $\frac{10}{2} \times £9 = £45$.

Some bonus systems reward at half the time saved, some for a third and others reward for the full time saved but at a bonus rate usually below the basic rate of pay. For the system to motivate workers to work faster, they have to be able to gain more in bonuses than they lose in overtime. Suppose each extra hour over thirty-five per week is paid at time and a half (150 per cent of the basic rate). If a worker on a basic of £9 an hour can earn overtime at £13.50 an hour, he will prefer to make extra cans by working extra hours to working only the basic hours but working harder. For saving ten hours the worker in our above example earned £45. For working ten extra hours he would earn £135. Only a fool would prefer the bonus to the overtime in these circumstances. Clearly, for the bonus system to motivate effectively, each hour saved must be rewarded at a greater amount than a normal overtime hour. However, if time saved is paid at, say, £14 an hour, this time is now *more* expensive to the firm than an overtime hour at £13.50.

The way out of this dilemma is for management to take into account the associated costs of overtime hours such as machine electricity, supervisory time and all the other costs arising from keeping open the factory beyond clocking-off time. If these associated costs total over 50p an hour, it is still worthwhile to value time saved at £14. Should they not do so, it is still sensible to value time saved at *no less than* £13.50 if workers are to be motivated to save any time at all. Few of the traditional bonus systems took this rather basic point into account.

Managerial incentive systems

Just as the directors pay workers for productivity beyond the basic, so many firms pay profit centre managers a bonus for their performance.

Some firms give managers shares so as to motivate them to make greater profits and thus boost the value of the shares in the firm. Other firms charge each centre a capital sum, the basic required profit to earn a target ROCE, and reward the manager for any "residual income" after deducting that capital sum from profits. Still others pay a bonus on profits, on returns on investment, on increases in sales or on increases in cash flow. These systems are compatible with theory X (more money for better results) and theory Y (creating incentives for managers to become more involved in, and committed to, improved performance).

For such systems to motivate rather than demoralise, it is necessary for profits to be largely the result of managerial effort. If the manager of centre A experiences large profit growth while manager B makes a loss, it seems reasonable to pay manager A a bonus but not manager B. However, let us suppose manager A is an inexperienced newly promoted trainee benefiting from a market explosion to which he has contributed nothing, while B is highly experienced but operates in a shrinking market from which the directors have refused permission for him to diversify and, moreover, B's loss is far lower than it would have been under a manager like A. In this situation a bonus will demoralise and embitter B, while A will take credit for skills he has yet to prove he really possesses.

All of this shows the importance of recognising the impact of environmental constraints in rewarding managers. Rewarding the manager for the centre without regard for his market conditions and other constraints is unwise. Moreover, if a manager is rewarded for residual income, ROCE or sales increases, he will concentrate his efforts on the area of reward. This is fine when the motivation system is tied to the budgeting system; but if it is not, the manager will disregard the budget as irrelevant to his personal earning of a bonus. The theory X manager will treat the rewarded target (residual income, etc.) as the budget *for him*, while the actual budget is merely paid lip-service. The theory Y manager will feel demotivated by the tension between his responsibility to the actual budget's fulfilment and his desire to earn his managerial bonus—this tension between conflicting objectives being termed "goal dissonance".

Once again we can see how important it is to prevent systems conflict, especially between the motivation system and the planning and control systems. Systems integration is essential to the effective operation of any set of systems *in any context,* but fundamental to long-term profitable survival in the business context.

SYSTEMS INTEGRATION

Contingency theory

Contingency theory's central postulate is that the optimum organisation of any systems group is contingent on the various environments in which the systems operate. It is clearly therefore a theory of open systems only.

The nature of the systems' contingency or dependence on their environments is twofold.

(*a*) The greater the differences between the environments in which a system, such as a budgeting one, must operate, the greater needs to be the *differentiation* between the way the system operates in various contexts. For example, a budget needs to be prepared and operated in one way in a London factory with highly trained and unionised labour, in a different way in a South Korean factory with less unionised labour but less inventive supervisors perhaps, and in yet another way in a Yugoslav factory where the social and political attitudes to work and money are quite unlike those in the United Kingdom. Failure to differentiate the budgeting system is exemplified by the American multinational that used to send out an identical set of printed budget forms to all centres throughout the world and place equal credence on all the completed returns (many of which did not even add up correctly).

(*b*) The greater the variety of programmes (products, services and activities) and of environments, the greater the need for *integration* of the systems to ensure goal congruence both between the profit centres themselves and between the profit centres and central headquarters. Integration between the corporate plan, the budget, the standard costs and the incentive and bonus targets is particulary important both within each centre and for the corporation as a whole. Integration does not mean uniformity; it is not in conflict with differentiation. It means each system must dovetail with neighbouring, overlapping and complementary systems. Such dovetailing is to systems design as sound foundations are to house building. Dovetailing systems means modifying each system so that its interface with other systems is as smooth as possible. The interface between systems is smoothed by applying appropriately the Law of Requisite Variety.

The Law of Requisite Variety
W.R. Ashby in his book *Introduction to Cybernetics* (1956) propounded the Law of Requisite Variety. In its simplest form, this systems law states that "only variety can destroy variety" (Ashby, Chap. 11, sect. 1.7). In a closed mechanical system such as a thermostat, the variety of actual outside temperatures can be reduced within control limits only if the regulator can adapt to all the outside temperatures experienced—it is no use if it melts when the outside temperature exceeds 90 °F. Conversely, if the regulator responds to *every* variation in temperature with just one reaction— namely, cooling the air—it is not a regulator at all but a cooler. The regulator must display sufficient (requisite) variety of reactions to meet the variety of stimuli. The variety of data input to a system through its sensor must be matched by equivalent variety in the comparator and effector. Thus, if input data are in tonnes, litres, etc., but standards are in SHP,

the comparator must transform tonnes, litres, etc., into SHP before comparison can be made.

The application of the Law of Requisite Variety to the interface between motivation, planning and control systems is slightly different. Our aim is goal congruence between these differentiated systems, and our strategy is sufficient integration of those systems to ensure that they all facilitate fulfilment of the directors' primary objective. To integrate motivation with planning, it is necessary to make rewards contingent on fulfilment of plans (in particular, profit centre budgets), but also to make directorial approval of plans contingent on participation (ideally on agreement) of managers in setting their own budget targets. To integrate planning with control, it is necessary to ensure that standards and budgets match by reviewing both at the same time, by using standards in the budget and by using data in the budgets to derive capacity data for the standards. The law of requisite variety means that if the motivation is simple—say it is a straightforward 10 per cent of all residual income—while the budgeting system is very thorough and complex, dealing with all the revenue and capital account items passing through every cost centre, then integrating motivation with budgets necessitates either reducing the budgets to residual profit centre income or, conversely, examining the detailed income and cost implications for each centre of its residual income target. In short, integration requires that the variety of the two systems should be matched before conflicts between them can be reconciled.

Goal congruence and motivation

Integration of the five-year plan, the budget, the standard costing profiles and the motivation systems requires not simply the arithmetical matching posited to be necessary by the law of requisite variety. In addition, it requires clear communication by the directors of the corporate goals that constitute the point and the spirit of the systems. The motivation system must be integrated into the planning and control systems and also display the requisite variety of responses to the manifold variations in the psychology of the people to be motivated. This particular aspect of requisite variety is, in principle at least, illuminated by the concepts of expectancy theory. This theory analyses motivation into two components: valence and probability. Valence is the value or importance of any outcome (time saved, residual income realised, etc.) to the individual. The higher the valence of an outcome, the more motivated a person is to achieve it. However, if the outcome is seen as very improbable, motivation is lost, but so is it if the outcome is seen as certain. For if an outcome is guaranteed, there is no need for effort to be wasted in achieving it. A budget target which motivates is one whose outcome is high valent (because of bonuses, promotion or praise associated with it) and probable enough to be realistic, but not so likely as to require no effort.

Finally, the five-year plan is best employed as the instrument for communicating the directors' goals and wider range perspectives on the business. The budgets are instruments for achieving the plan, centre by centre. Standard costs are instruments for achieving the plan, programme by programme. Operating statements are instruments for controlling actual performance—that is, for making actuals conform to plans. Bonus payments are among the instruments for motivating staff to achieve the plans.

SUMMARY

(*a*) The planning cycle is a closed loop feedback system which consists of setting objectives, making forecasts, reconciling the two through gap analysis, drawing up the plan, executing the plan, comparing the actual performance with the plan, changing the performance and/or the plan and beginning the cycle once again.

(*b*) All control systems seek to reduce deviations between actuals (read by a sensor) and standards (such as a budget) by means of an effector taking appropriate action in order to reduce those deviations shown by a comparator (such as an operating statement).

(*c*) Management by objectives involves managers in achieving directors' objectives their own way and in management by exception, the directors only intervening when large variances persist.

(*d*) The corporate plan is the quantitative expression of directors' strategy for achieving their chief goals. The budget is the detailed elaboration for one year of the plan by responsibility centre. Standard costs are the elaboration of the plan by programme.

(*e*) Motivation systems reflect theory X or theory Y to a greater or lesser extent. They need to be integrated with the planning and control systems, so they all convey the same message. Expectancy theory can help design motivation systems integrated appropriately. Contingency theory postulates the need to integrate systems enough to promote goal congruence, yet to differentiate them in such a way as to reflect the environments (especially the human ones) in which they have to operate.

QUESTIONS

1. In what respects do internal control and budgeting meet the basic requirements of a control system?

2. If you were a manager of a profit centre on a fixed salary, what package of rewards from the directors would most motivate you to achieve your budget?

3. How far does the unpredictability of consumer demand make long-range planning pointless?

4. How far should standard costing take account of limiting factors?

5. How does the concept of standard hours help us distinguish between a prolific centre and a productive one?

6. A budget detailing inflows and outflows exists for all twenty-six centres of a firm. The firm produces three products and has a standard marginal costing system for each one (note marginal not absorption). Centre managers are paid an annual bonus of 5 per cent of any increase in net profits over the previous year. What relevance has the law of requisite variety to this situation and what other factors are important to integrating the systems involved?

7. A firm has two centres, each making the same three products. Centre A is managed and motivated according to theory X, centre B according to theory Y. What differences in performance might arise from this, if any, and what effect might it have on the design of motivation systems?

8. The directors of company M identify as an important goal the increase of the market share from 20 per cent to 25 per cent over the next five years. The company planners identify in their forecast a fall in the market share from 20 per cent to 15 per cent, arising from previous policies of selling only for cash, a shrinkage of the total market by 5 per cent, and the increasing outdatedness of the company's products. Outline the gap analysis process that should now follow.

9. An operating statement for May shows an adverse profit variance against budget of 50 per cent. Sales income shows an adverse variance of 60 per cent. What does this *imply* about cost control during May?

10. Accounting, costing, planning and motivation can be seen as *systems*. What is the importance of the law of requisite variety in integrating these systems?

Calculation questions are to be found in Appendix V questions 18–22.

CHAPTER SEVEN

Performance Evaluation

Nothing is enough to the man for whom enough is too little.
Epicurus

OBJECTIVES

(*a*) To develop skills in interpreting operating statements and variance analyses so as to be able to judge fairly when performance is to be applauded or deplored and when poor planning is responsible for revealed variances.

(*b*) To appreciate the impact of volume effects on budgetary control systems, on standard absorption costing and on standard marginal costing.

(*c*) To be able to prepare a detailed variance analysis in various environments.

(*d*) To be able to prepare computations in order to determine whether particular variances are worth investigating and correcting.

(*e*) To be able to analyse published accounts by selecting the ratios most significant to evaluating corporate performance.

(*f*) To understand the special difficulties attendant on evaluating divisional performance.

(*g*) To evolve control accounting skills generally, and a sense of analytical judgment in particular, as a crucial step in progressing from management accounting to management accountancy.

THE VARIANCE ANALYSIS FRAMEWORK

Budgetary allowances

A budget is a detailed plan for the firm's cost centres. The monthly operating statement against budget shows how far the plan has been realised in practice. However, an important secondary purpose of a budget is to control actual costs. The requirements of budgetary planning and of budgetary control can sometimes conflict, especially when actual outputs seriously deviate from budget.

Suppose for May we budget sales and production volume at 1,000 units, selling units for £5 each to realise a total sales income of £5,000. Each unit is to make a budgeted profit of 70p; 30p per unit is budgeted for fixed costs, £1 for variable expenses, £1.50 for labour and £1.50 for materials. Actual results for May are: sales income, £6,000; fixed costs, £400; variable expenses, £800; labour costs, £2,000; and material costs, £1,500. The resultant operating statement follows.

OPERATING STATEMENT FOR MAY

(Adverse variances in brackets)	Budget	Actual	Variance	
	£	£	£	£
Sales	5,000	6,000	1,000	20
Materials	1,500	1,500	–	
Labour	1,500	2,000	(500)	(33)
Expenses	1,000	800	200	20
Total variable costs	4,000	4,300	(300)	(1½)
Fixed costs	300	400	(100)	(33)
Total costs	4,300	4,700	(400)	(9)
Profit	700	1,300	600	86

The above operating statement shows actual profit to be 86 per cent above budget, sales income 20 per cent above, and total costs (adversely) 33 per cent above. This seems to contain more good news than bad, as the increase in costs is more than offset by the increase in sales volume to give the large favourable variance in profits.

However, on the assumption that all variable costs vary linearly in direct proportion with volume, we should expect these costs to show the same percentage deviation against budget as actual volume shows against budgeted volume. Therefore, in order to give an effective control standard for variable costs, we should calculate what the variable costs ought to have been if we had been able to predict correctly our actual output volume. The resultant *flexible budgetary allowances* (or allowances, for short) replace the originally budgeted targets for all variable costs, in the interests of finely tuned (therefore maximally effective) control accounting. If actual volume is half-budgeted volume, allowances for variable costs will be half the originally budgeted figures. In the above example volume was 20 per cent over budget, so variable cost allowances will be 20 per cent greater than originally budgeted. We do not recompute budgeted fixed costs, as by definition they do not vary with output volume. Our operating statement shows the allowances and reports variances against them and not against the original budget. The result for our May example is as below.

This operating statement is still good news, with a favourable profit variance of 44 per cent. The total cost and variable cost variances are now also favourable, because the allowances take into account the greater resource requirement occasioned by the larger volume. The only adverse variances are on labour costs and fixed costs, and these require explanation. Note that in reporting against allowances, the sales variance disappears—hence the need to show the original sales budget on the left. If there had been a sales price variance, this would be reflected in the allowance. Suppose the sales price had been £6 instead of £5, the allow-

OPERATING STATEMENT FOR MAY

Original budget		Budgetary allowance		Actual		Variances	
£		£		£		£	£
5,000	Sales	6,000		5,000		–	–
1,500	Materials	1,800	1,500		300		17
1,500	Labour	1,800	2,000		(200)		(11)
1,000	Expenses	1,200	800		400		33
4,000	Total variable costs	4,800		4,300		500	10
300	Fixed costs	300		400		(100)	33
4,300	Total costs	5,100		4,700		400	8
700	Profit	900		1,300		400	44

ance would still be £6,000 (to reflect actual volume in units), but actual sales income set against the allowance in the actual column would be £6 × 1,200 = £7,200.

The general framework for variance analysis

Operating statements show sales, then costs, then profits; variance analysis statements begin with profits, usually continue with sales and end with costs. This is because the variance analysis statement addresses data in order of importance, with profit being regarded as the key figure. Profit variances arise from a combination of sales variances and total cost variances.

Sales variances and cost variances both subdivide between price variances and quantity variances. Thus:

(a) sales price variance plus sales quantity variance = sales variance; and

(b) cost price variances plus cost quantity variances = cost variances.

There are general formulae for calculating these variances either against allowance or against standard cost: $PV = AQ(SP - AP)$ and $QV = SP(SQ - AQ)$ where P is price, Q is quantity, V is variance, A is actual and S is standard (but could also be budgetary allowance). These formulae should be learnt. It should be noted that the two formulae are asymmetrical. The price variance formula multiplies the price variance *per unit* by the *actual* quantity of units. The quantity variance, however, multiplies the quantity variance in *units* by the *standard* unit price. To illustrate these formulae and their effects, let us consider the sales variance.

A product has a sales price at £5 standard. The budgeted sales volume is 1,000 units. Actually sold in June were 1,400 units at £4 each. The sales variance is the difference between budgeted sales income at standard price and actual sales income. Budgeted income was £5,000, while actual income is £5,600. There is a sales variance of £600—favourable, as profits should be up £600 in consequence of the improved sales. Analysing this variance using the formulae, we have:

PV = AQ(SP − AP) = 1,400(5 − 4) = £1,400—adverse
because the *unit* price variance of £1 is a price cut
which suggests an equivalent cut in profits
QV = SP(SQ − AQ) = 5(1,000 − 1,400) = 5 × 400 = £2,000—favourable
because actual sales volume exceeds budget

Combining the two, we have sales variance = price plus quantity variance = (1,400) + 2,000 = £600. This confirms that the adverse price variance is more than offset by a favourable quantity variance. This means that the price cut has resulted in sales volume growing to such an extent that sales income itself rises. In economists' terms this reflects a high price elasticity of demand.

Notice that, for sales variances, SP − AP and SQ − AQ can give positive or negative answers. If the answer is *positive*, as in the price variance above, the variance is *adverse*. If the answer is *negative*, as in the quantity variance, the variance is *favourable*. The test of whether a computed variance is adverse or favourable is the profits test: does the variance mean profits are above or below budget/standard as a result of the variance? If above, the variance is favourable; if below, it is adverse and is usually shown in brackets.

The genealogy of variances
Figure 8 shows how the profit variance on the operating statement is subdivided. The diagram should be learnt. It applies to any budgeting or standard costing system *using absorption costing*. Later, we shall see how it has to be modified to handle marginal costing.

Explanation of variances

(*a*) The *profit* variance—total variance of actual profit from budgeted or standard profit.

(*b*) The *sales* variance—the variance of actual sales income from standard or budget.

(*c*) The *cost* variances—the variances of actual costs from the standard or budget.

(*d*) Sales price variance—the gain or loss over standard/budget owing to the *unit* sales price variance being applied to the full amount of the actual quantity sold.

(*e*) Sales volume variance—the sales quantity variance; the effect on profits of the actual quantity of units sold varying from budget.

(*f*) Sales mix variance—that part of the sales volume variance arising from selling more of one product, less of another, etc., relative to the budgeted *proportions* of those products in the original budget's sales mix.

(*g*) Sales yield variance—that part of the sales volume variance arising from the *absolute* quantities sold being different from budget.

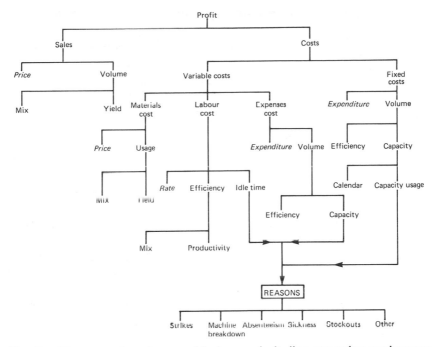

Fig. 8. *Diagram of variances. Variances in italics are price variances; all other variances, except for those with the word cost in them (and the two leading variances of profit and sales) are quantity variances. The quantity variance formulae, modified as shown in the text, apply.*

(*h*) Materials price variance—the difference in unit prices between standard/budget and actual applied to the actual quantity of materials consumed. It is usually adverse, as inflation causes prices to rise above the levels applying when the budgets/standards were formulated.

(*i*) Materials usage variance—the materials quantity variance: the variance arising from using more or fewer units of material input than budgeted/standard to produce the *actual* quantity of units output.

(*j*) Materials mix variance—that part of the materials usage variance arising from the *proportions* in which material inputs are used being different from the proportions at budget/standard. The idea is identical to the sales mix variance.

(*k*) Materials yield variance—that part of the materials usage variance arising from the materials process losses being different from budget/standard. In other words, it is the *ab*normal gain or loss.

(*l*) Labour rate variance—the difference between the actual and budget/standard hourly rate of pay applied to the actual hours paid. This is the price variance for labour costs.

(*m*) Labour efficiency variance—the difference between actual working and standard hours (*never* budgeted hours) to produce the actual output. Labour has no single quantity variance akin to the sales volume and materials usage variances. Its quantity variances consist of efficiency and idle time, both of which can be further subdivided.

(*n*) Labour idle time variance—the difference between budgeted hours *paid* and actual hours *worked*. Idle time is often budgeted at zero, so that any idle time causes an adverse variance.

(*o*) Labour mix variance—defined identically to sales mix and materials mix variances, except the ingredients here are different grades and types of labour input.

(*p*) Labour productivity variance—akin to the materials yield variance, it shows the variance caused by the standard mix of labour producing more, or less, than expected.

(*q*) Variable expenses expenditure variance—the expenses price variance—the difference between standard/budget expenses in the month and actuals applied to the *actual* recovery volume (*not* to the standard/budgeted volume).

(*r*) Expenses volume variance—the expenses quantity variances arising from the volume against which expenses are recovered being different from standard/budget.

(*s*) Fixed cost expenditure and volume variances are defined as for expenses.

(*t*) Efficiency variance, for expenses and overheads—that part of the volume variance arising from labour productivity variances when expenses and overheads are recovered against labour-hours.

(*u*) Capacity variance—that part of the volume variance arising from idle time.

(*v*) Calender variance—that part of the capacity variance arising from the incidence of holidays or from the number of days worked in the month being different from budget (e.g. February having twenty-eight days when the budget assumes all months have thirty).

(*w*) Capacity usage variance—that part of the capacity variance arising from idle time not explained by calender differences.

(*x*) Capacity usage variances can be analysed further into their individual components, each one reflecting particular causes of idle time such as strikes, machine breakdown or stockouts which the budget did not envisage.

DIRECT COST VARIANCES

Materials variances

The problem

A firm budgets an output of 20 tonnes of X for June. The standard input per tonne of X is 10 tonnes of A, 6 tonnes of B, 9 tonnes of C and 10 litres of a catalyst, D. Standard prices per tonne are £1 for A and for B, £5 for C and 50p per litre of D. In June 40 tonnes of X were produced using 25 tonnes of A, 10 of B, 15 of C and 30 litres of D. Prices were 90p per tonne of A, £1.25 per tonne of B, £6 per tonne of C and £1 per litre of D. The budgeted cost of X for June is as under, for an output of 20 tonnes.

Input	Price	Usage	Budgeted cost
A	£1	10	£10
B	£1	6	6
C	£5	9	45
D	50p	10	5
		Total cost	£66

The actual cost of X for June, reflecting an output of 40 tonnes, is as under.

Input	Price	Usage	Cost
A	90p	25	22.50
B	£1.25	10	12.50
C	£6	15	90.00
D	£1	30	30.00
		Total cost	£155.00

At first sight we have a materials cost variance of £155 − £66 = £(89), a very serious matter. However, we are not comparing like with like but the budgeted cost of 20 tonnes with the actual cost of 40. We need to compute the budgetary allowance for 40 tonnes. In an integrated control system the result will be the standard cost of 40 tonnes of X, thus:

Input	Standard price	Standard usage	Allowance/standard cost
A	£1	20	£20
B	£1	12	12
C	£5	18	90
D	50p	20	10
		Total cost	£132

The allowances/standards form our true standard for computing our variances. The difference between the originally budgeted £66 and the allowance of £132 is £66, and is sometimes termed a "revision variance", because it represents the variance arising from revision of the budget to take account of actual output volume.

The materials cost variance is allowance less actual = £132 − £155 = £(23) which is adverse.

Price variance

The price variance is the total of the price variances for each ingredient, thus:

Input	Standard price	Actual price	Unit price variance	Actual usage	Total price variance
A	£1	90p	10p fav	25	£2.50
B	£1	£1.25	(25p) adv	10	(2.50)
C	£5	£6	(£1) adv	15	(15)
D	50p	£1	(50p) adv	30	(15)
			Total materials price variance		£(30) adverse

This shows that even after correcting the budget for volume being double the budget figure, we have a large price variance. It is in fact larger than the total materials cost variance. The two inputs chiefly responsible are C and D, and this is not only because of their unit price variances but because their actual usages are high. Price variances apply to the whole actual quantity used, so the *larger the usage variance, the larger the associated price variance*. Some people have said that this causes variance analysis to be biased in favour of price effects, while quantity effects are apt to be undervalued. In fact, of course the bias is towards a quantity *effect*, as the price difference is applied to the whole of the actual quantity. While this undoubtedly spreads the price variance across all the quantities, it remains a quantity effect. The quantity variances, on the other hand, are valued at the standard unit price. The *fixity* of standard price as a multiplier constrains the size of quantity variances in a way not applicable to price variances, which are multiplied by the infinitely *variable* actual quantity.

Usage variances

To return to our example, the materials usage variance follows the QV formula: $QV = SP(SQ - AQ)$. Q, in the case of the usuage variance, means the *standard quantity of inputs* associated with the *actual level of output*. In other words, Q is the allowance for inputs. The usage variance is computed as shown below.

Input	Standard usage	Actual usage	Difference	Standard price	Cost
A	20	25	(5) adverse	£1	£(5)
B	12	10	2 favourable	£1	2
C	18	15	3 favourable	£5	15
D	20	30	(10) adverse	50p	(5)
			Total usage variance		£7 favourable

We should now check that the usage variance and the price variance add up to the total materials cost variance, thus: Usage + price = 7 + (30) = (23) = materials cost variance as originally computed.

Mix and yield variances

The mix and yield variances are subdivisions of the usage variance. This means that they are both valued at the standard unit price and follow the QV formula: $QV = SP(SQ - AQ)$.

The mix variance's SQ is the input quantities that represent actual usage in the standard proportions, while AQ is actual input quantities. The simplest way to derive the SQ of the standard mix is to treat all the inputs as commensurable even though D is measured in litres while the others are in tonnes. Standard usage proportions for A:B:C:D are 20:12:18:20 respectively, and these proportions simplify to 10:6:9:10 when they add up to 35. Thus A should represent $\frac{10}{35} = \frac{2}{7}$ of total units input, B $\frac{6}{35}$, C $\frac{9}{35}$ and D $\frac{2}{7}$. Actual inputs of A:B:C:D were 25:10:15:30 respectively, making a total of 80 units. If those 80 input units had been constituted in the standard proportions we should have used $\frac{2}{7} \times 80$ units of A and of D, $\frac{6}{35} \times 80$ of B and $\frac{9}{35} \times 80$ of C. We can now calculate the mix variance as shown below.

Input	Standard mix	Actual mix	Difference	Standard price	Difference × price
A	$\frac{2}{7} \times 80 = 22.86$	25	(2.14) adv	£1	£ (2.14)
B	$\frac{6}{35} \times 80 = 13.71$	10	3.71 fav	£1	3.71
C	$\frac{9}{35} \times 80 = 20.57$	15	5.57 fav	£5	27.85
D	$\frac{2}{7} \times 80 = 22.86$	30	(7.14) adv	50p	(3.57)
	Total 80.00	80	nil		
				Total mix variance	£25.35 favourable

The above shows a favourable mix variance largely owing to savings on the most expensive input, C.

Finally, we come to the yield variance which is the same as abnormal loss or gain discussed in Chapter 3 in the context of single inputs. For multiple inputs as we have here, the QV formula again applies, with Q meaning output yield. So the yield variance is the difference between standard and actual yield valued at the standard price of the output. Standard price of output means standard unit cost and *not* standard sales price. Actual yield is simply the actual output of 40 tonnes. The standard yield is the output we should have obtained from our *standard mix of inputs*. Thirty-five units are expected to produce 20 tonnes, as we know from original budget data where the input units added up to 35. Therefore 70 units would be expected to yield 40. The actual input of 80 units should yield $1\frac{1}{7}$ of 40 tonnes, which is 45.71 tonnes (correct to two decimal places). We can now find the yield variance applying the QV formula thus: $QV = SP(SQ - AQ) = £\frac{66}{20}$ (per tonne) $\times (45.71 - 40) = £3.3 \times 5.71 = £18 - 84$. This is adverse, as actual yield is below standard.

Now we must check that the mix and yield variances add up to the usage variance.

Mix + yield = 25 − 85 + (18 − 84) = 25.85   minus   18.84 = £7.01
Usage variance = £7

We can permissibly round up the yield variance to £(18.85) to get rid of the rounding error and thereby ensure a perfect match of the mix and yield total with the usage variance.

Labour cost variances

The problem
A firm makes product Y using skilled and unskilled labour. For June it budgets 500 man-hours, with no idle time, to produce 100 tonnes of Y at a standard pay rate of £5 per hour for unskilled men and £8 per hour for skilled men. The skilled men account for 20 per cent of the budgeted man-hours. No overtime is budgeted.

In June the skilled man-hours paid totalled eighty and the unskilled 450. Overtime at time and a half was payable for fifty unskilled hours. However, ten skilled and forty unskilled man-hours were idle owing 50 per cent to machine breakdown and 50 per cent to stockouts caused by strikes in the suppliers' factory. Nevertheless, 105 tonnes of Y were produced. Hourly earnings excluding overtime were £6 for unskilled men and £10 for skilled men.

To produce the labour cost variance we proceed similarly to the way we did with materials. First we tabulate the original budget thus:

Labour grade	Budgeted hours	Standard rate	Total cost
Skilled	20% of 500 = 100	£8	£800
Unskilled	Balance = 400	£5	2,000
	Standard labour cost of *100 tonnes* is thus		£2,800 for June

Actual labour cost of *105 tonnes* is as follows:

Labour grade	Actual hours paid	Actual rate	Total cost
Skilled	80	£10	£800
Unskilled—basic	400	6	2,400
—overtime	50	$1\frac{1}{2} \times 6 = £9$	450
	Actual labour cost for June is thus		£3,650

The labour cost variance against the original June budget is thus seen to be £3,650 − £2,800 = £850 adverse. However, because actual output is 5 per cent over budgeted output for June, we need to compute the budgetary allowances for 105 tonnes thus:

Labour grade	Allowance in hours	Standard rate	Allowed cost
Skilled	105% of 100 = 105	£8	£840
Unskilled	105% of 400 = 420	5	2,100
		Allowed labour cost is	£2,940

The labour variance is now £3,650 − £2,940 = £(710) adverse. This is both the variance against budgetary allowance for June and the variance against the standard cost of 105 tonnes. The difference between this variance of £(710) and the original £(850) variance against the "fixed" June budget of £140 favourable is the labour cost revision variance. It is, of course, the £(710) variance that counts and that is to be further analysed into rate, productivity, idle time and mix variances.

Rate variance

The labour rate variance follows the price variance formula, $PV = AQ(SP - AP)$. In this case it is easier to apply the formula by multiplying it out thus: $PV = AQ.SP - AQ.AP$ where P is the labour rate and Q is the total hours paid. AQ.AP is actual hours paid times actual rates; in other words, the actual labour cost which we computed above at £3,650. SP is the standard hourly pay rates of £8 for skilled men and £5 for unskilled. AQ is actual hours paid, eighty for skilled and 450 for unskilled. We now compute $AQ \times SP$ for each grade thus:

$$\text{Skilled: AQ.SP} = 80 \times £8 = £640$$
$$\text{Unskilled:AQ.SP} = 450 \times £5 = £2,250$$
$$\therefore \quad \text{Total AQ.SP} \quad\quad - £2,890$$

We can now apply the formula thus: $PV = AQ.(SP - AP) = AQ.SP - AQ.AP = £2,890 - £3,650 = £(760)$ adverse, owing partly to the overtime hours. Fifty hours of overtime earned a premium of £3 over basic minus a total extra cost of $50 \times £3 = £150$.

The increase in basic rates for unskilled men was £1 and this applies to their 450 hours paid to give £450. The increase in rates for skilled men was £2 and their eighty hours paid to give £150. Check: $150 + 450 + 160 = 760$ total rate variance.

We can see that the principal component of the adverse rate variance is the £1 increase on basic unskilled rates because, although it is the smallest in unit hourly terms, it applies to the greatest number of actual hours paid. This is an example of the large quantity effect of a small unit price variance.

Labour efficiency variance

The labour efficiency variance results from labour's taking more time to produce actual output than standard, or taking less. To compute this variance we have to convert tonnes of actual output into SHP and compare the SHP with the actual man-hours worked. Note that the comparison is between standard and actual hours *worked*; hours *paid* are wholly irrelevant to this variance. The difference between SHP and actual hours worked is valued at the standard rate of pay. The quantity variance formula applies—QV = SP(SQ − AQ)—only it might help to rewrite it thus: Ef . V = SR(SHP − AHW), where SHP is standard hours produced, AHW actual hours worked and SR is standard hourly pay rate.

For skilled men, SHP is the allowance of 105 hours and for unskilled the allowance is 420 hours. Actual hours worked are found by subtracting actual idle time from actual hours paid, thus:

Skilled: paid − idle = 80 − 10 = 70 hours
Unskilled: paid − idle = 450 − 40 = 410 hours

We can now apply the formula thus:

Skilled: SR(SHP − AHW) = £8 × (105 − 70) = £8 × 35 = £280 fav
Unskilled:SR(SHP − AHW) = £5 × (420 − 410) = £5 × 10 = £50 fav

Labour efficiency variance   £330 fav

Thus although more hours were *paid* than were budgeted, fewer hours were *worked* to produce 105 tonnes than standard, which means that both grades of labour worked harder in their working hours than expected—a creditable performance that might well merit a bonus payment, except for the fact that the savings of £330 on efficiency are more than offset by the £(760) adverse rate variance and by the existence of unbudgeted idle time. The efficiency variance can be further analysed into a mix variance and a productivity variance.

Idle time variance

Since no idle time was budgeted, any actual idle time represents an adverse variance, computed thus:

Labour grade	*Idle hours*	*Standard rate*	*Rate × hours*
Skilled	10	£8	£(80) adverse
Unskilled	40	5	(200) adverse
		Total idle time variance	£(280) adverse

Because we know that 50 per cent of idle time was caused by machine breakdown and 50 per cent by stockouts, we can further analyse the idle time variance thus:

> Idle time variance £(280) adverse
> > of which £(140) arose from machine breakdown
> > and £(140) arose from stockouts

Labour mix variance

The procedure for finding the labour variance closely resembles that for finding the materials mix variance. The actual mix is the actual hours worked: seventy for skilled and 410 for unskilled, a total of 480. The standard mix divides the 480 actual hours worked into the proportions applicable under the allowed hours to produce 105 tonnes—namely, 105 skilled and 420 unskilled, a ratio of one skilled to every four unskilled hours. In the standard mix, the total hours should be split $\frac{1}{5}$ skilled and $\frac{4}{5}$ unskilled. Applying this to 480 actual hours worked gives us standard skilled hours of

$$\frac{480}{5} = 96 \text{ hours and } \frac{480 \times 4}{5} = 384 \text{ unskilled hours.}$$

We can now compute the mix variance, using the QV formula: $QV = SP(SQ - AQ)$ where P is standard hourly rate and Q is mix. The tabulation is as below.

Labour grade	*Standard mix hours*	*Actual hours*	*Difference*	*Rate*	*Difference × rate*
Skilled	96	70	26 fav	£8	£208 fav
Unskilled	384	410	(26) adv	5	(130) adv
	480	480	nil		
			Labour mix variance		£78 fav

The favourable mix variance is caused by the higher value of the 26 skilled hours saved relative to twenty-six unskilled hours extra.

Labour productivity variance

Actual output is 105 tonnes. The standard output to be expected from actual hours *worked* of 480 subdivided into the standard mix of ninety-six skilled and 384 unskilled is different. The budget tells us that 500 hours are expected to produce 100 tonnes of output. It follows that 480 hours should produce $100 \times \frac{480}{500} = 96$ tonnes. We now have standard output minus actual output = $SQ - AQ = 96 - 105 = 9$ tonnes favourable (favourable because more is produced than standard).

Before we can apply the QV formula in full we need a standard price per tonne of output. The budget tells us that the standard labour cost of

100 tonnes is £2,800, so the standard labour cost per tonne is £28. This figure is our standard "price" for the QV formula: $QV = SP(SQ - AQ) = £28 \times 9 = £252$ favourable.

Finally, we must check that the productivity variance and the mix variance sum to the efficiency variance: $EV = MV + PdV = 78 + 252 = 330$ as required.

Labour cost control statement
We can check that all the labour variances add up correctly and also give management a synopsis of the individual variances by presenting them in control statement form as shown below.

LABOUR COST CONTROL STATEMENT FOR JUNE

	£	£
Budgeted labour cost for 100 tonnes		2,800
Revision variance		(140)
Allowance/standard cost of 105 tonnes		2,940
Rates		
Skilled basic	(160)	
Unskilled basic	(400)	
Unskilled overtime	(200)	
Total rate variance		(760) adv
Idle time		
Machine breakdown	(140)	
Stockouts	(140)	
Total idle time variance		(280) adv
Efficiency		
Labour mix	78	
Labour productivity	252	
Total efficiency variance		330 fav
Total labour cost variance		(710) adv
Actual labour cost of 105 tonnes		3,650

This statement tells the reader at a glance that the labour worked harder than standard (favourable efficiency variance) but that the benefits were offset by idle time (adverse) and were reversed by large adverse rate variances, especially the increase in basic rates of unskilled pay. The question raised next is who is responsible for these variances. Labour has done well, but idle time has to be investigated, and the rates increases have masked a basically good performance by the workers. In the pages following we shall discuss when variances reflect on the planners rather than on operations.

Variable expenses and variable overheads

Variable expense variances follow a pattern similar to that of materials and labour. The original budget must be transformed into an allowance; the materials usage and labour efficiency variances have their counterpart in the variable expenses efficiency variance; and the labour idle time variance is matched by the variable expenses capacity variance. Two features we have not met before. First, instead of a price variance or rate variance, we have an expenditure variance. Second, the efficiency and capacity variances add up to a volume variance—a master quantity variance. The problems are similar to those involving fixed overheads, and are discussed below.

VARIANCES AND VOLUMES

Absorption and marginal costing

Recapitulation

Under absorption costing, the cost unit is charged with its variable costs and also with an apportionment of fixed costs. Under marginal costing, the cost unit is charged only with its variable costs. Absorption costing has sales minus costs equals profit; marginal costing has sales minus variable costs equals contribution. The standard absorbed cost is the standard "full" cost; and the standard marginal cost is only the standard variable cost.

Fixed costs

Under standard absorption costing, fixed costs can display both expenditure and volume variances. Under standard marginal costing they can display only expenditure variances. This is because marginal costing treats fixed costs as period not product costs, so does not recover them from each cost unit produced. Because absorption costing does recover fixed costs from units produced, volume variances will arise whenever the budgeted cost centre overhead is over- or under-recovered. Fixed overhead variances are explored in pages 188–91.

Sales

Under standard absorption costing, the sales variance divides between a sales price and a sales volume variance. Under standard marginal costing the sales variances are calculated by means of the unit contribution instead of the unit sales price. To complicate matters further, standard absorption costing has increasingly tended, over the past decade, to measure sales variances not by reference to the standard sales price but rather by reference to the standard unit profit. These practices are explored in pages 184–8.

Variable overheads

Variable overheads are assumed to be incurred only during working hours. Idle time is therefore irrelevant to their computation and they can thus *never* show a capacity variance. The volume variance on variable overheads will be entirely consequent upon efficiency variances.

It is common to recover overheads, both fixed and variable, against direct labour-hours. This means hours worked, not hours paid. If there is a labour efficiency variance in these circumstances, there will always be an equivalent variable overhead efficiency variance. For example, five standard labour-hours produce 1 tonne of output, but in July 200 tonnes were produced in 950 hours. Variable overheads (and expenses) are recovered at £2 an hour. Applying the QV formula, the variable overhead efficiency variance is: £2 × (SHP − AHW) = £2 × (1,000 − 950) = £100 favourable.

The variable overhead expenditure variance is the difference between the expenditure allowance for the actual hours worked and the expenditure actually incurred. Continuing the example in the previous paragraph, given an actual expenditure on variable overheads of £2,250, we have an allowance of SR × AHW = £2 × 950 = £1,900. The expenditure variance of £2,250 − £1,900 = £(350) adverse.

The variable overhead cost variance is the sum of the efficiency and expenditure variances, thus: £350 − £100 = £(250) adverse. We check this result by comparing *actual* overhead *expenditure* with *standard* overhead *recovery*. We shall do this through a modified presentation of the cost control statement that should clarify exactly what the variances mean.

	£
Variable overheads actually expended	2,250
Expenditure variance and adverse	(350)
Variable overhead allowance for 950 hours	1,900
Efficiency variance—favourable	100
Budgeted variable overhead for 1,000 hours	2,000

Note how the allowance is applied to the recovery basis—hours, not to the output units—tonnes.

Sales variances

The problem

In July, a firm's sales budget is as follows.

UNIT SALES *(£)*

Product	Sales volume (units)	Price	Variable costs	Contribution	Fixed cost	Profit
J	1,200	10	6	4	1	3
K	800	20	15	5	3	2

TOTAL SALES *(£)*

	Income	Contribution	Profits
	12,000	4,800	3,600
	16,000	4,000	1,600
Totals	28,000	8,800	5,200

Actual results in July were as follows.

Product	Sales income	Contributions	Profits	Sales volume
	£	£	£	
J	15,000	5,500	3,000	1,000 units
K	17,000	4,500	3,500	1,000 units
Totals	32,000	10,000	6,500	

Sales price variances

The sales price variances are computed the same way under marginal and absorption costing, simply following the PV formula: $PV = AQ(SP - AP)$. For J and for K, $AQ = 1,000$ units. J's standard price is £10, K's £20. $AQ \cdot AP$ = actual sales income = £15,000 for J and £17,000 for K. We can compute the sales price variances using the multiplied out formula $PV = SP \cdot AQ - AP \cdot AQ =$

for J: $(10 \times 1,000) - 15,000 = £5,000$ favourable

and

for K: $(20 \times 1,000) - 17,000 = £(3,000)$ adverse

to give a total price variance of £2,000 favourable. This means company profits will be £2,000 above those expected as a result of J's price being higher than standard to such an extent that it outweighs the effect of K's price being lower.

Sales volume variance

The sales volume variance in units is the difference between actual and budgeted units sold. For J this difference is (200) adverse and for K it is 200 favourable. Under absorption costing these variances are valued at the *standard unit profit* and under marginal costing they are valued at the *standard unit contribution*. Because they are valued that way instead of at standard unit price, they are often called the "sales *margin* quantity variances". Applying the modified QV formula, we have $QV = SP(SQ - AQ) = S$ Profit $(SQ - AQ)$ for absorption costing and S contribution $(SQ - AQ)$ for marginal costing. The results can be tabulated thus:

ABSORPTION COSTING

Product	Volume variance in units	Standard profit	Volume variance £
J	(200) adv	3	(600) adv
K	200 fav	2	400
		Total volume variance	(200) adv

MARGINAL COSTING

Product	Volume variance in units	Standard contribution	Volume variance £
J	(200)	4	(800)
K	200	5	1,000
		Total volume variance	200 fav

The two costing systems give opposite results for the sales volume variance. This is because absorption costing profits follow accounting for fixed costs, whereas marginal costing contributions precede it, and the burden of unit fixed costs is greater on K (60 per cent of unit contribution) than on J (25 per cent of unit contribution).

Sales mix and yield variances—units method
The sales mix and yield variances are subdivisions of the volume variance and are calculated similarly to the materials mix and yield variances. The results for products J and K are as below.

ABSORPTION COSTING

Product	Actual/mix	Standard mix	Difference	Standard profit	Variance
J	1,000	1,200	(200)	3	(600)
K	1,000	800	200	2	400
				Total mix variance	(200)

This is identical to the volume variance and we need go no further. The marginal costing mix variance will be the same as the marginal costing volume variance. The total of budgeted units to be sold = 1,200 + 800 = 2,000; actually sold were 1,000 + 1,000 = 2,000. Since the same *total* units appear in actuals and budgets, there is no yield variance at all, so the entire volume variance is attributable to the sales mix.

Revenue method
Mix and yield variances calculated by the units method employed above closely resemble the method used for materials mix and yield. In practice,

however, many firms calculate these variances by means of the revenue method, as this controls the proportions of revenue obtained from each product in the sales mix rather than the (less important) proportions of units sold. The revenue method mix variance formula is:

$$\text{MixV} = \text{SP}(\text{SQ} - \text{AQ}) \times \text{Unit profit (or contribution): Sales ratio}$$

AQ here is the actual mix *valued at the full* **standard** *price*. To obtain SQ we divide the £30,000 AQ into the *budgeted* proportions for *total* revenue, namely £12 of J for every £16 of K—a ratio of 3J : 4K. £30,000 ÷ 7 = £4,286 (to the nearest £), so J is three times this, £12,858, and K is four times = £17,144, but these must be rounded to £12,857 and £17,143 to make them total the required £30,000.

This time we shall exemplify the method using standard marginal costing, so shall focus on unit contribution rather than unit profit.

MIX VARIANCE—REVENUE METHOD

Product	Actual mix	Standard mix	Difference	Contribution: Sales ratio	Mix variance
	£	£	£		£
	AQ	SQ	(SQ − AQ)		
J	10,000	12,857	2,857	$\frac{4}{10} = 40\%$	(1,143) adv
K	20,000	17,143	2,857	$\frac{5}{20} = 25\%$	714 fav
	30,000	30,000	nil	Total variance	(429) adv

This mix variance of £(429) adverse directly reflects the lower sales revenue but greater unit profitability (under marginal costing) of J compared with K. It is a quite different result from the units method. This time we shall have a yield variance. The marginal costing sales volume variance was £200 favourable. The difference between volume and mix variances of £629 favourable is the required level of the yield variance by the revenue method.

The budgeted contribution is £8,800 and the budgeted sales income totals £28,000, an overall contribution: sales ratio of 88:280 − 31.43 per cent. We use this ratio to reduce the yield variance in revenue terms to contribution terms, thus:

Budgeted sales income	£28,000	
Actual sales at standard price	£30,000	(AQ in the mix above)
Yield variance—revenue	£2,000	favourable
C:S ratio	31.43%	
Yield variance—contribution	£629	favourable

Check: Volume V = Mix + Yield = (429) + 629 = 629 − 429 = 200 favourable.

Summary of sales variances

The overall sales variance is the difference between budgeted and actual sales incomes. In our example this is the difference between a budgeted £28,000 and an actual of £32,000 = £4,000 favourable. However, the *allowance* for sales is the actual sales volume of 2,000 units total valued at the standard sales prices, to give a total allowance of £30,000. The sales variance against allowance is thus only £2,000 favourable and it consists entirely of sales price variance. In operating statements against budget that deals with the sales variance.

The revision variance of £2,000 between budget and allowance is a quantity variance. We sold 200 less J at an SP of £10 and 200 *more* K at an SP of £20. This means J realised £2,000 less and K £4,000 more than budgeted—a volume effect of £2,000 favourable. In preparing operating statement against standards, we deal with *both* the price and the volume variances. Under standard absorption costing we reduce the £2,000 overall volume effect to an *adverse* £(200) profit effect, and under marginal costing to a favourable £200 contribution effect. The latter we further analysed into mix and yield variances. Under absorption costing the volume variance arose entirely from mix. Under marginal costing using the revenue method we had a £(629) adverse mix variance and a £429 favourable yield variance.

The information orginally given on *actual* contributions and *actual* profits is wholly irrelevant to computing sales variances. We are interested only in the profit or contribution effects of variances in sales income. Any variance in profits or contribution not explained by sales variances must arise from cost variances, and so actual contributions and profits never enter into any of the sales variance computations.

FIXED COST VARIANCES

Marginal costing and absorption costing

Under marginal costing, there can be no such thing as a fixed overhead volume variance. This greatly simplifies overhead variance analysis. Consider the following situation. Product A has a standard sales price of £5, variable costs of £3 and unit contribution of £2. In August 20,000 units of A are budgeted to be sold and £5,000 fixed costs are to be incurred. Actually 25,000 units were sold at £6 each with variable costs of £4, and £6,000 fixed costs expenditure took place. The operating statement for August under marginal costing is as under.

AUGUST OPERATING STATEMENT

Fixed budget £		Allowance/ standard £	Actual £	Variance £	Remarks
100,000	Sales	125,000	150,000	25,000	Price variance— £1 per unit
60,000	Variable costs	75,000	100,000	(25,000)	Labour
40,000	Contribution	50,000	50,000	–	efficiency
5,000	Fixed costs	5,000	6,000	(1,000)	Expenditure variance
35,000	Profit	45,000	44,000	(1,000)	Fixed costs adverse

The statement shows that although contribution was on target—with sales price effects exactly offset by variable cost variances—profit was £1,000 below allowance/standard because of the fixed cost variance. Note that fixed budget and flexible budgetary allowance for fixed costs are identical.

Contrast the above with the following operating statement prepared on the absorption basis. Because absorption costing apportions fixed costs to cost units, over- or under-recovery will arise when actual sales differ from budget. Fixed budgeted costs are flexed, just like sales, to give a fixed cost allowance, but this does not get rid of the volume variance (as a revision variance) in the way we saw happen for sales variances against the budget (but not against standard).

AUGUST OPERATING STATEMENT

Budget £		Allowance £	Actual £	Variance £	Remarks
100,000	Sales	125,000	150,000	25,000	Price £1 per unit favourable
60,000	Variable costs	75,000	100,000	(25,000)	Labour efficiency adverse
40,000		50,000	50,000	–	
5,000	Fixed Costs	6,250	6,000	250	Expenditure (1,000) adverse Volume 1,250 favourable
35,000	Profit	43,750	44,000	250	

Here we have a £250 *favourable* profit variance, again wholly because of fixed overheads. Actual overheads of £6,000 are as per the marginal costing statement, but the allowance is £1,250 over the fixed budget, so the variance is 250 favourable compared to the marginal costing adverse variance of £(1,000). The difference of £1,250 favourable is the volume variance which is computed by multiplying the volume variance in units of 5,000 by the standard recovery rate of 25p. The resultant £1,250 is the "revision" variance between fixed budget and allowance. The allowed cost under marginal costing is exactly as per the fixed budget—hence no volume variance; but the allowed cost under absorption costing is the standard recovery rate multiplied by the actual quantity sold $= 25\text{p} \times 25,000 = £6,250$. This identity of the volume variance with the revision variance is comparable with what we saw happen with sales volume variances.

We can now examine the subdivisions of the fixed overhead volume variance, remembering that volume variances on fixed costs occur only under absorption costing.

Analysis of fixed overhead volume variances

Efficiency and capacity variances
The £1,250 favourable overhead volume variance above is the result of production being well above budget. Efficiency and capacity variances determine the reasons for the extra production. Let us suppose fixed overheads are recovered, not against output units but against direct labour-hours, and let us further suppose that output per standard hour is five units. The 5,000 unit variance becomes a 1,000 variance in hours. Since the recovery rate is 25p per unit, it must be $5 \times 25\text{p} = £1.25$ per hour.

The SHP equivalent of the 25,000 units of output is 5,000 hours. The SHP equivalent of 20,000 units originally budgeted is 4,000 hours. The difference is our volume variance of 1,000 hours. Actual hours worked were 6,000 hours. Hours paid are irrelevant, just as for variable overheads. The difference between budgeted hours, 4,000, and actual hours, 6,000, gives the capacity variance, which arises from the time worked being above budget (and has nothing to do with idle time directly). The difference between the standard hours or allowed hours, 5,000, and the 6,000 actual, gives an adverse efficiency variance, as 1,000 hours more were taken to produce the output than standard.

Efficiency V = SR (SHP − AHW) = £1.25 (5,000 − 6,000) = £(1,250)
                                                                         adverse
Capacity V = SR (budgeted hours less actual) = £1.25 × 2000
                                              = £2,500 favourable
                    Fixed overhead volume variance   £1,250 favourable

Clearly the favourable capacity variance of 2,000 hours over budget requires an explanation. Let us suppose that the original budget divided the annual fixed overhead budget into twelve equal monthly divisions and that the budgeted working month contains twenty working days and that each day contained 200 hours. In August, however, a great deal of work was done at the week-ends so that twenty-four working days occurred. There is a calendar variance of $24 - 20 = 4$ working days $= 4 \times 200 = 800$ hours and these recover fixed overhead at £1.25 an hour. The calendar variance is thus $£1.25 \times 800 = £1,000$.

The calendar variance of £1,000 subtracted from the capacity variance of £2,500 still leaves £1,500 unexplained. The calendar has supplied 800 of the 2,000 extra hours worked. The remaining 1,200 hours, we may assume, came from the number of employees being higher than budget. The budgeted working day of 200 labour-hours at eight hours per man gives us a budget of twenty-five labourers. We know twenty-four days were worked in August and we still have to explain 1,200 hours. Twelve hundred hours over twenty-four days is the equivalent of fifty hours a day. If six men were hired at the start of August and one more near the end of the month, this explains the conversion of the extra fifty hours a day into $\frac{50}{8} = 6\frac{1}{4}$ men per day average. Thus the favourable capacity usage variance is explained by recruitment of new labour. (This same recruitment may also explain the adverse efficiency variance as the new men take time to learn the job.)

VARIANCE ACCOUNTING

Bookkeeping

All costs are entered into the ledgers at standard. Sales are recorded at actual income. Budgeted figures are kept out of the ledgers altogether. Production cost variances are cleared from the different variance accounts in the cost ledgers to the Manufacturing Account, selling cost variances are cleared to the Trading Account and other cost variances are cleared to the Profit & Loss Account. Adverse variances are debited, favourable variances credited, in the three Income Statements. An example will clarify.

AUGUST OPERATING STATEMENT: SUMMARY

Fixed budget £		Allowance/ standard £	Actual £	Variance £		Remarks £
50,000	Sales	55,000	50,000	5,000	5,000	fav price variance
20,000	Cost of sales	22,000	25,000	(3,000)	(2,000)	materials
					(1,000)	labour
30,000	Gross profits	33,000	35,000	2,000		
15,000	Admin expenses	16,500	18,000	(1,500)	(500)	variance expen.
					(800)	fixed efficiency
					(400)	fixed capacity
					200	fixed expen.
15,000	Net profits	16,500	17,000	500		

INCOME STATEMENTS IN THE LEDGERS

Manufacturing and Trading Account

Cost of sales (standard)	£22,000	Sales	£60,000
Materials cost variance	2,000		
Labour cost variance	1,000		
Gross profit c/d	35,000		
	£60,000		£60,000

Profit & Loss Account

Administrative expenses	£16,500	Gross profit b/d	£35,000
Variable expenditure variance	500	Fixed expenditure	
		variance	200
Fixed efficiency variance	800		
Fixed capacity variance	400		
Net profit	17,000		
	£35,200		£35,200

Stock variances

Finished goods

Stock variances arise when actual stock values vary from budget. Budgets frequently assume that production and sales volume will keep in step. If they fail to do so, stock volume variances will arise. If there is any variance at all in production costs, finished good stock price variances will arise. An example follows.

	Production	Sales	Stock
	£	£	£
Budget	100	90	10
Actual	120	80	40
Variances	20 fav	(10) adv	30

Unit cost of sales are budgeted at £5 but are actually £7. The stock is budgeted at $10 \times £5 = £50$ but is actually $40 \times £7 = £280$—giving a stock variance of £230, which is favourable because the higher the value of closing stock, the higher are reported *period* profits. The stock volume variance is $30 \times £5 = £150$ and the stock price variance is $40 \times £(7 - 5) = £80$.

Raw materials

If actual labour hours paid exceed hours worked, we shall expect an idle time variance to arise. If the quantity of materials purchased exceeds the quantity used in production, there is idle material—in other words, raw material stocks. If the purchase price is above standard, there will be a stock price variance; if there are unused stocks at all there will be a stock quantity variance (unless there is an explicit budgetary allowance for raw material stocks). Finally, when the materials variance is being calculated, the raw materials stock variance must be included, and the materials price variance will apply to materials *purchased* not just to materials consumed, so will include any stock price variance.

To illustrate the above, the March budget envisages materials expenditure of £5,000 on 500 tonnes of material to yield 400 tonnes of output.

Actual output was 300 tonnes from 450 tonnes of material inclusive of 50 tonnes closing stock and the materials cost £5,000.

The budgetary allowance for 300 tonnes of output is $\frac{3}{4}$ of $500 = 375$ tonnes of material input costing $\frac{3}{4}$ of £5,000 = £3,750.

Variances:

Materials cost: Allowance less actual = £3,750 − £5,000   = *£1,250*
Materials price: AQ(SP − AP) = AQSP − AQAP = £4,500 − £5,000
                                                       = £(500)

Materials usage: SP/SQ − AQ) = £10(375 − 400) = £10 × (25)   = £(250)
Stock quantity: SP(SQ − AQ) = £10(nil − 50) = £10 × (50)   = £(500)
(The stock price variance is included *within* the materials price variance).

Variance analysis statements

Operating statements compare allowance/standard with actuals to give the main sales and cost variances. Variance analysis statements reconcile budgeted profit with actual profit as shown in the example below.

MARCH VARIANCE ANALYSIS STATEMENT

	£	£	£	£
Budgeted profit				5,000
Sales price variance			(1,000)	
Sales volume variance			2,000	
Sales variance				1,000
Actual sales *less* Standard cost of sales				6,000
Materials price variance	(3,000)			
Materials usage variance	1,500			
Stock quantity variance	(500)			
Materials cost variance		(2,000)		
Labour rate variance	(2,000)			
Labour efficiency variance	4,000			
Labour idle time variance	(1,000)			
Labour cost variance		1,000		
Variable expense expenditure variance	100			
Variable expense efficiency variance	400			
Variable expense variance			500	
Total variable cost variances			(500)	
Fixed cost expenditure variance		500		
Fixed cost volume variance		1,500		
Fixed cost variance			2,000	
Total cost variances				1,500

Finished goods stock price		1,100
Finished goods stock volume		(600)
Finished goods stock variance		500
Actual profit		8,000

The principal variances in the above statement are these:

Variance	Remarks
4,000 Labour efficiency	This suggests the standard hour needs recalibrating
(3,000) Materials price	This is usually regarded as an "uncontrollable variance.
2,000 Sales volume	Sales volume is over budget, but the existence of a finished goods stock variance suggests production is still further over budget which suggests misplanning.
(2,000) Labour rate	This variance is also often regarded as uncontrollable, but even if the basic rate is beyond a manager's control, the approval of overtime hours is not.

Clearly we need now to consider which of the variances really were the responsibility of the profit centre manager and his section heads and which were truly uncontrollable. Only controllable variances should be taken into account in appraising managerial performance. As a general rule, materials price, labour rate and some types of labour idle time are widely regarded as uncontrollable. Furthermore, given a variance between allowed input quantities and actual inputs all the quantity variances will display a degree of mutual correlation. This means that fully controllable variances boil down to just these.

(*a*) Sales price—a matter for the sales manager.

(*b*) Sales volume—also a matter for the sales manager.

(*c*) Finished goods stock—a matter of co-ordinating sales and production.

(*d*) Controllable idle time—a matter of effective factory management.

(*e*) Efficiency (labour and overheads)—a matter of motivation, methods and supervision.

(*f*) Capacity—a matter of manpower planning.

(*g*) Raw materials—a matter of planning EOQs and co-ordinating buying opportunities with consumption needs.

Materials price, labour rate and overhead expenditure variances can arise largely from market forces beyond the control of line management. The question is whether these variances are also beyond the foresight of the planners. This will be discussed below.

VARIANCE EVALUATION

The foundations of planning variances

The traditional variances we have looked at in this chapter have been criticised by a number of university professors of accounting. They say that the control effectiveness of allowances and standards is vitiated by planning errors and by unavoidable mistakes in forecasting. Demski argued that opportunity costing provides the foundation for effective control.* The proper standard to be used in computing variances, he maintained, is one based on actual conditions—that is, the conditions that would have been incorporated into the original budgets and standards if they had been known in advance. For example, if material A has a standard unit input price of £5 but world-wide shortages cause its average price in the budget year to rise to £8, then £8 not £5 is the realistic standard. This realistic standard is known as the "attainable standard" or the "ex-post standard". Allowances are an ex-post standard corrected for volume. The opportunity costing approach proposes to go further and correct also for price.

The differences between actual results and ex-post standard are called "operating variances" and they can be divided into the conventional classifications we have already explored above. The differences between the ex-post standard and the original standards/budgets are called "planning variances". Planning variances are thus *restrospective* revision variances revising not only volumes but prices. The planning variances are classified into three broad categories: avoidable, possibly avoidable and unavoidable. Avoidable planning variances represent poor planning.

The hoped-for result of adopting the opportunity cost approach to control accounting is the more accurate allocation of responsibility for reported variances than is possible with traditional variance analysis. The disadvantage of the approach is that it allows managers an opportunity to excuse themselves for poor operating variances on the grounds that they are really planning variances.

Examples of the opportunity costing approach

Materials

A budget specifies the use of 5 kg of XA at £2 a kilogram to produce 4 kg of output. Actual usage was 11,000 kg of XA at a cost of £33,000 to produce 10,000 kg of output. Now, 5 kg of XB perfectly substitutes XA and its average price has been £2.50 a kilogram.

*J. S. Demski, "Variance analysis using a constrained linear model" in D. Solomons (Ed), *Studies in Cost Analysis*, 2nd edition, Sweet & Maxwell, London, 1968, pp. 526–40. See also M. Bromwich, "Standard costing for planning and control", *Accountant* (19/26 Apr and 3 May 1969).

Since the actual price of XA was

$$\frac{£33,000}{11,000} = £3 \text{ a kilogram,}$$

the planners would have specified the use of XB if they had foreseen the 50 per cent inflation afflicting the XA price. However, the ex-post standard is the *actual XA* price of £3.

Operational variances
  Usage: $SP(SQ - AQ) = £3 \ (12,500 - 11,000) = £3 \times 1,500 = £4,500$
                                                                 favourable
  Price: $AQ(SP - AP) = 11,000 \ (3 - £3) = 11,000 \times £(0) = \text{NIL}$
Planning variances: Price
  Avoidable by using XB instead of XA:
          $SQ(P_{XA} - P_{XB}) = 12,500 \times (3 - 2.5)$
                         $= £(6,250) \text{ adverse}$
  Unavoidable arising from difference between actual XB and planned
          XA price: $SQ(P_{XA} - P_{XB}) = 12,500(2.5 - 2) = £(6,250)$

Control Statement	£	£
Standard cost allowance of 10,000 kg output		
(12,500 × £2)		25,000
Operational variance—usage	4,500	
Avoidable planning price variance	(6,250)	
Unavoidable planning price variance	(6,250)	
Total variances		(9,000)
Actual cost of 10,000 kg of output		33,000

Labour
During February a factory has an output budget of 2,000 tonnes. Standard sales price is £20, unit materials cost £9 and unit labour £6 (one man-hour), to give a standard unit contribution of £5. The actual output was 1,500 tonnes produced in 1,800 hours out of 2,100 hours paid. Unit materials costs, hourly labour rates and sales price all realised their standard costs. Had the union not resisted management work-improvement recommendations, hours worked would have been 1,600, the ex-post standard.

Traditional variance analysis would be:	£	£
Labour cost allowance: £6 × 1,500 =		9,000
Actual labour cost: £6 × 2,100 =		12,600
Labour cost variance comprising:		(3,600)
Idle time (£6 × 2,100 − 1,800) =	(1,800)	
Efficiency (£6 × 1,800 − 1,500) =	(1,800)	
		(3,600)

The 300 idle hours and the 300 hours excess over standard represent a loss of 600 tonnes of output—a foregone contribution of £5 × 600 = £3,000. This lost contribution represents a further cost of the adverse labour variances: their opportunity cost.

The difference between 2,000 hours budgeted and 1,500 hours allowed is the familiar revision variance—valued at £5 per hour to become a planning variance of 2,500.

The difference between the 1,500 hours allowance and the 1,600 hours that the new method would have involved is a methods variance and was, in the circumstances, unavoidable—it too is a planning variance.

The difference between the 1,600 hours it should have taken using the new method and the 1,800 hours actually taken is an operating variance, as the planners could not have foreseen this.

The idle time is an operating variance, on the assumption that it was not foreseeable.

Putting the above together we have the following.

(a) *Labour cost allowance*
Operating variances:

Idle time	(1,800)	
Efficiency (1,600 − 1,800) × 6	£(1,200)	
Planning variance:		
Methods (1,600 − 1,500) × 6	(600)	
Total labour cost variances		(3,600)
Actual labour cost		£12,600
(b) *Budgeted contribution* (£5 × 2,000)		10,000
Planning variance revision:		
production volume (£5 × 500 tonnes)		(2,500)
Contribution allowance (£5 × 1,500 tonnes)		7,500
Labour cost variances as above		(3,600)
Actual contribution in the month		£3,900
(c) *Actual contribution*		£3,900
Opportunity cost of excess hours	£3,000	
Labour cost variances	3,600	
Full cost of excess hours		6,600
Ex-post attainable standard contribution		£10,500

Variance investigation

It is worthwhile investigating variances only if the benefits of doing so outweigh the costs. The costs consist of staff time spent on the investigation and management plus labour time spent on correcting the variances. The benefits consist of the savings made from correction at their expected value. The expected value is found by applying a decimal probability to the net benefits (benefits less costs). An example will illustrate.

A labour efficiency variance of £(2,000) would cost £300 to investigate and £300 to correct but could result in savings with 0.5 probability of being above £1,800 and 0.5 probability of being above £2,400. There is a two-thirds chance that the variance is controllable.

The expected value of *gross* savings is $(0.5 \times 1,800) + (0.5 \times 2,400) =$ £2,100. The net benefits, if and—only if—the variance is controllable, are £2,100 − £300 = £1,800. As there is only a two-thirds chance that the variance is controllable, the expected value of the net benefit is two-thirds of £1,800 = £1,200. However, there is a one-third chance that the variance is uncontrollable, in which case the £300 spent on investigation would be wasted.

Thus the expected value of the net benefits from investigation are:

$$\tfrac{1}{3} \times £(300) = £(100)$$
$$\tfrac{2}{3} \times £1,800 = \underline{£1,200}$$
$$\text{Value of benefits} = \underline{\underline{£1,100}}$$

Since the benefits have a positive value of £1,100, it is worthwhile undertaking the investigation and risking the one-third chance that the £300 investigation cost will be wasted. The fact that the £1,100 benefit is below the £2,000 adverse variance being investigated is wholly irrelevant—the variance itself is a sunk cost.

Variance evaluation

Variance evaluation consists of seeing beyond the bare figures in an operating and variance analysis statement to the possible underlying causes and the extent to which they are controllable or avoidable. It involves distinguishing the true exception in which MBE is interested from the cumulatively large deviation caused by, say, persistent inflation in materials factor markets. The latter requires the isolation and classification of planning variances. The former requires calculating the net benefits of variance investigation, whose value depends very much on the accuracy of estimated costs, estimated savings and ascribed probabilities. As a broad rule of thumb, variances over 10 per cent of allowance or standard are candidates for investigation, especially if the variances concerned are sales volume, materials usage, labour idle time or any of the efficiency variances.

In comparing the performance of one cost centre with another, it can be helpful to compare the centres' main standard costing ratios. These are:

$$(a) \text{ the activity ratio} = \frac{\text{Standard hours produced in the period}}{\text{Working hours budgeted}} = \frac{\text{SH}}{\text{BH}};$$

(b) the capacity ratio $= \dfrac{\text{Actual hours worked}}{\text{Working hours budgeted}} = \dfrac{\text{AH}}{\text{BH}}$; and

(c) the efficiency ratio $= \dfrac{\text{Standard hours produced}}{\text{Average hours worked}} = \dfrac{\text{SH}}{\text{AH}}$.

The ratios are expressed as percentages, the activity ratio always equalling the capacity ratio times the efficiency ratio. An example is given below.

		HOURS			RATIO	
Centre	Budget	Actual	SHP	Activity	Capacity	Efficiency
A	1,000	1,000	2,000	200%	100%	200%
B	1,000	2,000	1,000	100%	200%	50%
C	1,000	500	500	50%	50%	100%

We can see from the above that A is the best performer in both efficiency and activity terms. B is very inefficient so has recruited extra men or worked overtime hours to fulfil its budget. C is as efficient as standard but has a large burden of idle time, causing it to fail to fulfil its budget altogether.

In conclusion, variance analysis and costing ratios help us to evaluate managerial fulfilment of corporate objectives and managerial performance compared both with allowances and other cost centre managers. Operating statements and variance analysis focus on income statements. To evaluate a firm or division fully we need to consider not just the income statements but the Balance Sheet and Funds Flow Statements. The considerations this entails are outlined in the pages following.

CORPORATE PERFORMANCE EVALUATION

The criteria of good performance

Investors
A potential investor in a company is widely believed to require that the value of his investment will grow in real terms. This in turn means the company must earn a high enough return on capital employed to ensure:

(a) stable or growing dividend payouts; and
(b) sufficient profits are retained in order to conserve or increase the asset value of the firm.

The investor is thus keenly interested in ensuring that the return on capital employed is at or above his requirements. Return on capital employed

(ROCE) is the primary ratio in corporate evaluation. It is usually defined as:

$$\frac{\text{Net profit } before \text{ interest and tax}}{\text{Net tangible assets}}$$

Closely associated with ROCE is return on investment (ROI), defined as:

$$\frac{Earnings \text{ (net profits after interest, tax and preference dividends)}}{\text{Shareholders' capital (either book value of shareholders' funds or market value of issued ordinary shares)}}$$

The ROI tells the investor if his investment is performing competitively. If ROI from a firm is 7 per cent while bank deposit accounts offer 9 per cent, the investor would do better to sell his shares and put the proceeds in a bank deposit.

The primary ratio, ROCE, and the ROI are closely correlated. Both depend on the activity of the firm and the profitability of its sales. The former is measured by dividing sales income by net tangible assets, and the resultant capital-turnover ratio should exceed 100 per cent. The latter is measured by the average profit margin ratio found by dividing gross period profit by sales income, the result offering a crude picture of manufacturing and selling cost control success.

Creditors

A potential lender likes the firm to be profitable, showing good ROCE and ROI. He also prefers to lend to firms showing stability in their profit and asset growth record to date. Creditors prefer making secured rather than unsecured loans. This requires that the borrowing firm should not be too highly geared already and to have significant equity in tangible assets. Equity in tangible assets is defined as: tangible assets less wholly or partly secured loans outstanding. Tangible assets are fixed assets, *net* current assets plus any trade investments.

Gearing, called "financial leverage" in the United States, describes the relationship of long-term debt to total capital employed. It can be variously measured, but the definition recommended here will be widely found in practice among financial analysts.

$$\text{Gearing} = \frac{\text{Long-term external debts outstanding}}{\text{Shareholders' funds plus long-term debts}}$$

Gearing levels of over 40 per cent are apt to be regarded by potential lenders as risky, unless the firm is a property company holding under-valued land.

Lenders are interested in the firm's continuing solvency—its ability to pay debts, especially loan interest as they fall due. A picture of the firm's solvency is found from a combination of the messages conveyed by:

(*a*) gearing level;
(*b*) equity in tangible assets;
(*c*) the pattern to date of the ratio—*retained* earnings:net assets;
(*d*) the liquidity ratios (*see* Chapter 5);
(*e*) funds flow statement (*see* Chapter 5); and

(*f*) interest cover $- \dfrac{\text{profit before interest and tax}}{\text{annual interest payments}}$

—which should exceed 4 in most circumstances.

Labour and its trade unions

Labour seeks from the firm job security and the prospect of ever-rising earnings (among other things). Job security is partly a function of corporate solvency and profitability, which was briefly considered above. The other things it depends on—such as automation, which replaces men by machines, the impact of take-overs or diversification and unforeseen collapse of consumer demand—cannot be illuminated by accounts analysis. The prospect of rising earnings depends on:

(*a*) increased productivity;
(*b*) promotion prospects;
(*c*) availability of overtime;
(*d*) corporate profitability; and
(*e*) trade-union bargaining power.

Accounts analysis can help in forming a picture of (*a*) and (*d*) but not of the rest.

Productivity can be derived from final accounts in a number of ways, including:

(*a*) output per man—total volume ÷ average number of employees;
(*b*) income per man—sales income ÷ average number of employees; and
(*c*) value added per man—

$$\frac{\text{Sales income less materials and invoiced expenses}}{\text{Average number of employees}}$$

—or more crudely from

$$\frac{\text{VAT paid in the year} \times \dfrac{100}{\text{current VAT rate}}}{\text{Average number of employees}}.$$

Some left-wing commentators suggest an "exploitation ratio" defined as: value added per man divided by average earnings per man. The implicit assumption here that value added is available to pay higher wages rather than higher dividends, more directors' perks, etc., ignores the need for value added to finance replacement and augmentation of factory capacity and machines.

All in all, accounts as currently published are of strictly limited use to trade unions. Trade unions can argue about profit growth exceeding wages growth, but will find it hard to use accounts to *prove* the presence of *unnecessary* costs and profits that could be diverted to wages. Management, on the other hand, have access to the ledgers and management accounting statements, so can readily draw on evidence to refute any contention of excess profits or unnecessary costs. There is no sign of this situation changing in the near future.

Society

Society wants its business firms to provide employment for the maximum but to sell its products for prices at a minimum. Through the Government, its interest in accounts is as a taxation base and to ensure compliance with relevant government legislation. Some writers have argued that firms should present social accounts showing what the firm has cost, and how it has benefited society as a whole. Pollution would exemplify a social cost; sponsorship of football matches would exemplify (to many people anyway) a social benefit. This approach is drawn from welfare economics—that part of economics which tries to devise measurements of social costs and benefits.

The welfare economics based technique of cost benefit analysis is a crucial part of public sector accounting. It has not yet entered the mainstream of financial or management accounting because of the difficulties of measuring either expected costs or expected benefits with acceptable degrees of verifiable precision. Moreover, private sector accounting is still suffused with its "stewardship" inheritance from the Middle Ages and there is a consequential tendency among people to believe that the only benefits that count are those definable in ROCE and share price growth terms. This belief is not conducive to the growth of social accounting in the private sector.

Human capital

Some writers, following Flamholtz (1974), argue that really meaningful accounts would capitalise on human resources so that a return on human capital employed could be derived. They argue that labour has long ceased to be a variable cost because of increasing job security and that the labour force constitutes a capital asset just as much as a factory machine does. Factory capacity can be constrained just as readily by labour shortage as by numbers of machines or factory space. Football teams sell footballers for a fee reflecting the players' capital value in the market. So much for the case in favour of HRA (human resource accounting).

The case against HRA begins with the comment that labour costs do not become fixed with job security—they are still variable to production centres and direct to the cost unit. Second, traditional assets are acquired at explicit cost; human assets are acquired only at the cost of recruitment and training. Training and recruitment costs do not necessarily represent the present value of future benefits to be gained from employing someone, whereas machine acquisition cost is supposed precisely to represent the current value of benefits, as we shall see in Chapter 9. (Note that the word here is "represent" not "equal".) Finally, while football has established a market for its human resources with transfer fees representing market value, private sector businesses have not. Unless the slave-trade is reintroduced, it is unlikely that businesses will emulate football in introducing market values for human beings. HRA is likely to remain a matter of purely academic concern, therefore, for the foreseeable future.

A worked example of ratio analysis

We shall compare the accounts of two companies from the viewpoints of investors, creditors, labour and government.

INCOME STATEMENTS   (£000s)

	AB Ltd Last year	AB Ltd This year	XY Ltd Last year	XY Ltd This year
Materials consumed	300	400	600	900
Factor labour costs	400	600	600	800
Factory expenses	100	100	200	200
Direct cost	800	1,100	1,400	1,900
Factory overhead	500	800	600	1,100
Cost of goods produced	1,300	1,900	2,000	3,000
(Increase) Decrease in stocks of finished goods	700	(300)	500	(500)
Cost of sales	2,000	1,600	2,500	2,500
Sales income	3,500	4,200	5,000	4,500
Cost of sales	2,000	1,600	2,500	2,500
Gross profit	1,500	2,600	2,500	2,500
Overhead variances	–	100	(625)	(300)
Office costs, etc.	500	700	2,000	1,500
Interest	500	800	125	500
Total P.&L. charges	1,000	1,600	1,500	1,700
Net profits	500	1,000	1,000	800
Taxation	250	500	500	400
Dividends	100	100	200	220
	350	600	700	620
Retained profits	150	400	300	180

BALANCE SHEETS   *(£000s)*

	AB Ltd		XY Ltd	
	Last year	*This year*	*Last year*	*This year*
Share capital	3,000	3,000	3,000	3,000
Reserves	2,000	2,500	1,000	1,500
Shareholders' funds	5,000	5,500	4,000	4,500
Loans	4,000	5,000	1,000	2,000
Lease obligations	1,000	1,500	–	1,500
Long-term liabilities	5,000	6,500	1,000	3,500
Capital employed	100,000	12,000	5,000	8,000
Represented by:				
Fixed assets at net book value	6,000	7,500	3,000	4,000
Stock and WIP	2,400	3,000	2,000	4,000
Debtors	2,000	2,000	1,000	4,000
Cash	400	–	1,000	500
	4,800	5,000	5,000	8,500
Less Current liabilities	1,200	1,500	3,000	5,000
Net current assets	3,600	3,500	2,000	3,500
Tangible assets	9,600	11,000	5,000	7,500
Goodwill	400	1,000	–	500
Net assets	10,000	12,000	5,000	8,000

RATIOS DERIVED FROM THE ACCOUNTS   *(£000s)*

	AB		XY	
	Last yr	*This yr*	*Last yr*	*This yr*
1. ROCE $\dfrac{\text{Profit before interest and tax}}{\text{Net tangible assets at year end}}$	10.4%	18%	22.5%	17.3%
2. Profit margin (Gross profit ÷ Sales)	42.9%	61.9%	50%	55.6%
3. Capital turnover (Sales ÷ Tangible assets)	36.5%	42%	100%	60%
4. ROI (Net profit after tax ÷ Shareholders' funds)	5%	9.1%	12.5%	8.9%
5. Gearing (Long-term debt ÷ debt plus shareholders' funds)	50%	54.2%	20%	43.8%
6. Interest cover (Profits before interest and tax ÷ Interest)	2	2.25	9	2.6
7. Dividend cover (Profit after tax ÷ Dividends)	2.5	5	2.5	1.8
8. Equity in assets (Tangible assets *less* Long-term debts)	£4,600	£4,500	£4,000	£4,000
9. Retained profits ÷ Net tangible assets	1.6%	3.6%	6%	2.4%

10. Current ratio (Current assets ÷ Current liabilities)	4	$3\frac{1}{3}$	$1\frac{2}{3}$	1.7
11. Liquid ratio (Liquid assets ÷ Current liabilities)	2	$1\frac{1}{3}$	$\frac{2}{3}$	0.9
12. Debtors turnover period (Debtors ÷ Sales, times 50)—weeks	28.6	23.8	10	44.4
13. Stock turnover period (Stock ÷ Cost of sales, times 50)—weeks	34.3	35.7	20	44.4
14. Labour costs ÷ Total costs	17.4%	17.1%	17.1%	17.0%
15. Labour costs ÷ Profit before interest and tax	40%	$33\frac{1}{3}$%	53.3%	61.5%
16. Labour costs ÷ Dividends	4	6	6	3.64

Interpretation of the ratios

Interpretation for investors

(a) ROCE for AB has substantially improved over the year, while for XY it has declined. The comparison of ROI tells a similar story, but with AB showing 9.1 per cent and XY 8.9 per cent, neither firm shows a brilliant return compared with bank deposits.

(b) Dividend cover is satisfactory for AB but not for XY.

(c) Activity, shown by capital turnover and by the turnover periods, is grossly unsatisfactory for both firms. This means sales are very slow, perhaps because of declining markets. Activity is so poor, however, that it poses serious questions about both firms' possible survival.

(d) Sales volumes could be increased if sales prices were cut. The high profit margins of both firms suggest that this might be possible.

(e) All in all, neither firm seems a very good investment, but AB is not quite as bad as XY.

Interpretation for loan creditors

(a) Equity in assets for AB is slightly over that for XY, but neither shows any increase over last year despite significant increases in tangible assets. AB's gearing is very high at over 50 per cent, and XY's has jumped dramatically in one year from 20 per cent to nearly 44 per cent. Considerable financial risk, therefore, is associated with both firms.

(b) Interest cover is rather weak for both firms. In neither case is it high enough to justify any further loans with any confidence.

(c) Retained profits as a proportion of AB's assets are improving, while XY's are deteriorating. Current and liquid ratios are better for AB than XY; both seem overstocked. XY seems to be drifting into illiquidity.

(d) Both firms' asset growth over the year has been largely debt financed and is not reflected in significantly greater sales or profits. Neither firm is attractive to new lenders.

Interpretation for labour and trade unions

(*a*) As has been indicated above, both firms are poor prospects for investors and creditors, with a weak solvency picture and dangerously low levels of activity. This indicates dangers to the labour force of future redundancies caused by the sales declines, which will quite soon cause either firm to cut back massively or to be taken over.

(*b*) Labour costs are a stable 17 per cent of total costs, indicating little improvement in relative earnings. They are a falling proportion of AB's profits but a rising proportion of XY's. This, however, reflects more on XY's profits than on its labour force's earnings. However, XY's labour cost ratio to dividends has shrunk, while AB's has risen. This suggests XY's shareholders have been protected from the effects of its deteriorating position, a possibility which is reinforced by the decline in XY's dividend cover. XY's trade unions may want to use this to argue for equivalent protection of their members' jobs.

Interpretation for the Government

(*a*) The poor prospects of both firms threaten the Government with a loss of corporation, income and value added tax revenue, and possible social security payments to redundant labour. It might save public funds in the long term to give both firms development grants now conditional on implementing consultants' recommendations concerning marketing strategies and possible mergers with healthier firms. Neither firm seems big enough to warrant being "saved" by nationalisation.

(*b*) Government agencies may be able to buy up the enormous stockpiles at a discount if they have a use for them. This will improve activity levels.

(*c*) The appalling credit control record of both firms could be changed with the help of consultants from government agencies such as the Industrial and Commercial Finance Corporation or the small firms' advisory services.

DIVISIONAL PERFORMANCE EVALUATION

The problem

A corporate division may be a subsidiary of the group holding company, a large group of operations in a particular geographical area or a significant profit and investment centre. It will have its own board of managers, or possibly even directors, who are accountable to the central board of directors for divisional performance. Ideally, a division's performance is evaluated in the same way as is an independent company's—that is, as described above.

The more integrated the division is with the group, the less valid it is to evaluate it as if it were independent. The degree of integration is shown by the answers to the following questions.

(*a*) Does the division need central board permission to undertake capital expenditure? If so, what proportion of its annual capital expenditure requires such permission?

(*b*) What proportion does the division have of total sales and purchases in relation to other members of the group?

(*c*) What proportion of intragroup trading is at prices not equal to open-market prices?

(*d*) To what extent does group headquarters control working capital and cash management operations?

(*e*) To what extent are divisional managers' budget submissions amended by group directors?

The greater the extent of group control over the above and other divisional matters, the more integrated and less differentiated is the division. At one extreme, the division is just a profit centre whose managerial performance is most fairly monitored by operating statements and the correction of adverse *controllable* variances. At the other extreme, the division is an investment by the central board to be monitored by ROCE and the other criteria appropriate to an independent enterprise. The problem is gauging how far the division's situation is closer to one extreme rather than the other.

Possible solutions

(*a*) The use of ROCE as an appraisal measure should be divided into two parts: full ROCE to gauge divisional performance as an investment comparable with any other investment; and controllable ROCE to form a picture of managerial performance within the constraints imposed by central board policies. Controllable ROCE would include in the capital base only those assets over which the division has full control, and the earnings denominator would be profits *plus* those charges imposed or dictated by central board orders.

(*b*) Residual income is often used in the United States to measure divisional performance. Central office imposes a capital charge on each division reflecting the central board directors' required return on group capital employed at the division. Any profits over the capital charge represent residual income on which divisional managers may earn bonus payments or some other reward. The fairness of this appraisal method depends critically on the perceived justice of the capital charge and on the impact of group policies on all divisions being of roughly equal effect. For such policies to be of equal effect, each division should have similar degrees of control over its trading environment and a similar proportion of intragroup trading.

(*c*) Rewarding managers for favourable *controllable* variances can be just as effective for virtually independent divisions as for fully integrated ones. This is subject to the qualification that budgets are prepared on a fully participative basis, with due inspiration from expectancy theory, and that standards are seen to be attainable. In the present writer's view, only this method of appraising divisional performance conforms with the systems requirement of contingency theory for a balance between integration and differentiation of subsystems. The previous two solutions run the risk of creating goal dissonance between divisions and within them, as the budgets may be disregarded in the interests of maximising ROCE or residual income *at the expense of other divisions*. This danger is less when divisions operate to fulfil integrated budgets and focus *as much* on controlling efficiency and usage-based costs as on increasing sales volume.

SUMMARY

(*a*) Performance evaluation is a matter of establishing criteria (standards), measuring actual performance (input of actuals through a sensor) and of compring them fairly (operating statements against allowances and ex-post standards as comparators). It is thus a matter dependent on the existence of effective control systems.

(*b*) Variances arise either from price or quantity. Price variances are magnified when actual quantities exceed allowed quantities, because they are applied to the whole of actual quantities. This has led some writers to think that variance analysis has a price bias.

(*c*) Quantity variances on cost reflect on the efficiency of input use and the extent to which capacity constraints have been worse or better than expected. Quantity variances on sales reflect contribution (under marginal costing) or profit (under absorption costing) gained from positive variances or lost from adverse ones.

(*d*) Overhead variances reflect both expenditure variation from allowance and volume, under absorption costing. Variable overheads show only efficiency as a volume variance; fixed overheads also show capacity. Fixed overheads in marginal costing show only expenditure variances. Overhead allowances are found by flexing the original budget, not for output volume, but for the recovery base—usually direct labour-hours. The allowed direct labour-hours determine the allowed overhead costs.

(*e*) Planning variances *purport* to divide traditional variances between those for which operational managers are responsible (operating variances) and those for which they are not (planning variances). Planning variances nobody is to blame for are unavoidable, while avoidable ones are the fault of the planners.

(*f*) It is worth investigating variances only if the expected value of net benefits is positive. The greater the probability of a variance being controllable, the greater the probability of net benefits being positive.

(*g*) Company performance evaluation is facilitated by computing *at least* the following ratios in every case: ROCE, profit margin, gearing, a liquidity ratio and two activity ratios. Profitability, stability, growth, solvency and activity are the key criteria for all interested parties, but different accounts users will rank these criteria differently.

(*h*) Divisional performance evaluation, while partly reflecting the criteria for company evaluation, is often more fairly achieved using the profit centre evaluation techniques of operating statements and variance analysis. This area is subject to a great deal of controversy and argument among academics and has no uniquely "right answers".

QUESTIONS

1. How would you judge whether a variance was controllable enough for the profit centre manager to be held responsible for it? In your answer consider whether any variance is every wholly controllable.

2. Why are sales mix and yield variances different, using the revenue method rather than the units method? Which method is likely to be useful for practical control accounting?

3. Variances against budget are shorn of much of their volume effects as a result of using the allowance as the standard of comparison. To what extent do materials price planning variances reduce the importance of price effects in gauging profit centre performance?

4. Is the ex-post standard for labour efficiency actual efficiency or the efficiency that should have been displayed? Contrast your answer with the ex-post standard for materials price.

5. Outline the causes of stock variances and say how you would evaluate their seriousness.

6. How is it possible to have materials mix variances unless the materials concerned are perfect substitutes for each other in the production process?

7. Outline possible reasons for favourable capacity and idle time variances.

8. Are all calendar variances avoidable planning variances in essence?

9. In company evaluation, how would you determine the firm's long-term survival prospects solely from its published accounts?

10. As a trade-union negotiator with access to divisional records, how would you determine which divisions could best afford to pay higher basic hourly rates?

For calculation questions, see numbers 23–7 in Appendix V.

CHAPTER EIGHT

Price and Volume Decisions

Few have the virtue to withstand the highest bidder.
George Washington

OBJECTIVES

(*a*) To be able to prepare, interpret and understand break-even and profit/ volume (PV) charts.

(*b*) To understand the limitations of break-even charts.

(*c*) To be able to prepare contribution profit/volume (CVP) analysis statements useful to management decisions.

(*d*) To understand the decision accounting treatment of scarce resources.

(*e*) To understand the uses, limitations and assumptions of graphical linear programming.

(*f*) To appreciate the effects of economic environment on price and volume decisions.

(*g*) To comprehend the nature, advantages and disadvantages of pricing techniques commonly found in industry.

(*h*) To understand the difficulties involved in interdivisional transfer pricing and to be able to assess the validity of frequently encountered attempts to solve such difficulties.

BREAK-EVEN CHARTING

The basic calculations

The key terms

Throughout this section we shall consider a firm whose standard unit variable costs are £3, standard sales price is £5 and annual fixed costs are £10,000.

Just to cover fixed costs requires a total contribution of £10,000. Unit contribution = sales price less variable costs = SP − VC = £2. The required contribution will be achieved by selling £10,000 ÷ £2 = 5,000 units. This is the break-even volume.

Generally, to find break-even volume we can apply the break-even volume formula: BE Vol = FC/UCb where FC is period fixed costs and UCb is unit contribution.

To find the sales income generated by the break-even volume—that is, the break-even sales value—we can of course multiply the BE Vol of 5,000 by unit sales price of £5 to obtain the answer, £25,000. We do, however, require an alternative method of deriving break-even sales value to cover the situation when unit prices and unit costs are not available. Suppose, for example, fixed costs as above are £10,000 and the only other datum we are given is that variable costs are 60 per cent of sales revenue. From this it follows that the contribution:sales ratio (sometimes, rather misleadingly, called the "profit/volume ratio" or "PV ratio") is 100% − 60% = 40%. The contribution required to cover £10,000 of fixed costs is, of course, £10,000. Contribution is 40 per cent sales revenue, so the required contribution of £10,000 is 40 per cent of the required sales value. Thus the break-even sales value is £10,000 × $\frac{100}{40}$ or $\frac{5}{2}$ × 10,000 = £25,000. Generally the break-even sales value is FC/C:S ratio, and we must remember either to decimalise the C:S ratio or to keep it as a percentage but *multiply* the fixed costs by 100.

If actual sales were 8,000 units, we have a margin of safety over break-even volume of 3,000 units. This is often expressed in percentage terms to give the percentage margin of safety or safety factor. In this case it is

$$\frac{3,000}{8,000} = \frac{3}{8} = 37\tfrac{1}{2}\%.$$

The general formula for the safety factor is

$$\frac{\text{Actual volume less breakeven volume}}{\text{Actual volume}} \times 100.$$

A simple application
We can use the data above to assess the impact of changes in sales price or cost changes. Suppose that a change in production methods would reduce unit variable costs by 50p but raise annual fixed costs by 20 per cent. Assuming no change in sales price or demand, we can calculate the effect of the changes in cost on profit, on break-even volume and on the safety factor. We can also assess at what sales volume the new methods become profitable. The results are shown below.

		Current methods		New methods	
Unit sales price		£5		£5	
Unit variable cost		3		2.50	
Unit contribution		2		2.50	
Units sold	8,000		8,000		
		£			£
Total contribution		16,000			20,000
Fixed costs		10,000			12,000
Profit		6,000			8,000
BE Volume		5,000	$\left\{\dfrac{12,000}{2.5}\right\} = 4,800$		
Safety factor		$37\tfrac{1}{2}\%$	$\left\{\dfrac{8 - 4.8}{8} \times 100\right\} = 47\tfrac{1}{2}\%$		

It is clear that the new methods are more profitable than the current ones for sales of 8,000 units. Also break-even volume is achieved 200 units earlier with the new methods. Profit increases £2,000 as a result of the new methods, and contribution increases by 50p per unit. The new methods become more profitable than the old at £2,000 ÷ 50p = 4,000 units below actual sales volume of 8,000 units—that is at 4,000 units. At that level contribution under the old methods = £8,000 (2 × 4,000), which is £2,000

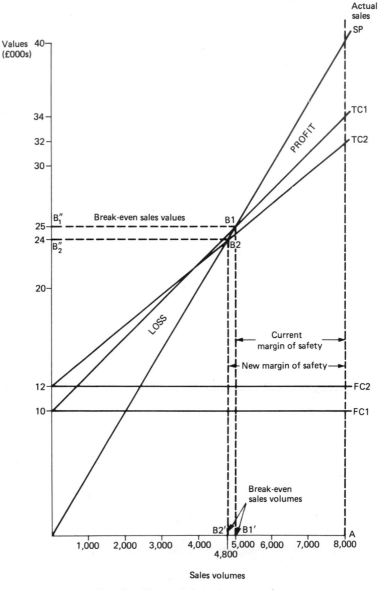

Fig. 9. *Type 1 break-even chart.*

short of fixed costs; while contribution under the new methods = £10,000 ($2\frac{1}{2} \times 5,000$), which is also £2,000 short of (new) fixed costs. For sales below 4,000 units, the old methods are more profitable; for sales above 4,000, the new methods are more profitable.

Simple charting

Type 1 charts

Figure 9 shows the previous calculations in graph form on a break-even chart. There is one SP line, as there is only one sales price. There are two FC (fixed costs lines), FC1 representing current methods and FC2 new methods. There are two TC (total cost lines), TC1 representing current methods and TC2 new methods. There is no line on a type 1 chart for variable costs. They are represented by the vertical distance at any point between the TC and FC lines. If variable costs increase, the slope of the TC lines will become steeper; if they decrease, the slope flattens—as is the case moving from TC1 to TC2. B1 is the current methods break-even *point* which is associated with a sales volume of $0 - B_1'$, 5,000 units and a break-even sales value of $0 \quad B_1''$—£25,000. Similarly B2 is the new methods break-even point with volume $0 - B_2'$, 4,800 units and value $0 - B_2''$, £24,000. Actual sales volumes are shown by distance $O - A$, with the current margin of safety being $B_1' - A$, 3,000 units and new margin being $B_2' - A$, 3,200 units. The type 1 break-even chart is the type usually encountered.

Type 2 charts

Precisely the same data are reflected in Fig. 10 as in Fig. 9. The difference lies in the presentation of variable costs at VC1 and VC2, and fixed costs as the vertical distance between the TC lines and their associated VC lines. Although type 2 charts are less often seen than type 1, they are more useful because they give an immediate view of contribution which is not available with type 1 charts. The vertical distance between the SP line and the VC line is the contribution for any given volume of sales. This is useful information.

PV charts

Simpler to read than either break-even chart is a profit volume chart. It has sales volume on the x-axis, and £ of net profit or loss on the y-axis. At zero sales, the loss equals the fixed cost because there are no variable costs if there is no volume. The contribution line, Cb, shows the profit or loss at each level of sales: Cb1 for the current methods, Cb2 for the new methods.

The greater clarity and simplicity of PV charts is achieved at the expense

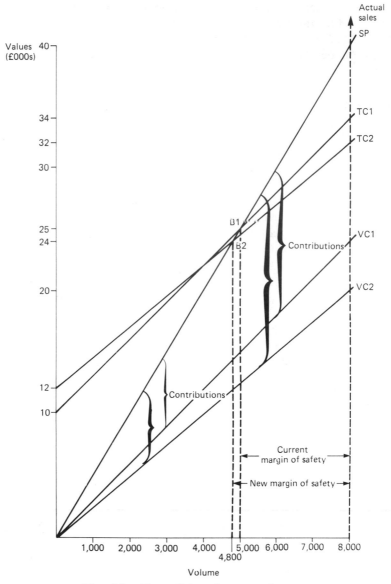

Fig. 10. *Type 2 break-even chart.*

of losing information about the sales revenue and variable cost data behind the contribution.

Where Cb1 crosses Cb2 is the indifference point of 4,000 units which partitions sales volume into 4,000+ where Cb2 is higher, and 4,000− where Cb1 is higher. The higher contribution line at any one point reflects the greater profitability of the underlying method of production, current methods for Cb1 and new methods for Cb2.

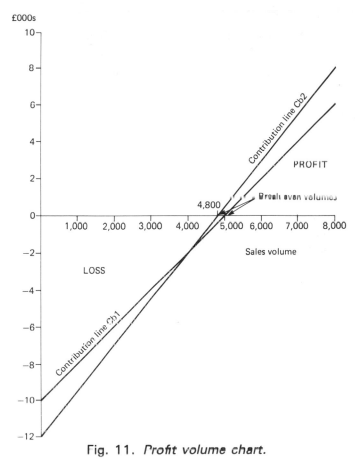

Fig. 11. Profit volume chart.

Product profitability comparisons

The problem
Suppose a firm has a choice of manufacturing three products—A, B and C. Product A is the one we already know with a sales price of £5, unit variable costs of £3 and with fixed costs attributed to it of £10,000 per year. Product B has a sales price of £10, unit variable costs of £5 and annual fixed costs of £20,000. Product C has a sales price of £50, unit variable costs of £20 and annual fixed costs of £150,000. Existing production capacity can be used in one of the following ways.

(*a*) Devote all production to C and produce 50,000 units.

(*b*) Devote one-third of the facilities to A to produce 8,000 units and two-thirds to B to produce 15,000 units.

(*c*) Devote one-third to A (8,000 units), one-third to B (7,500 units) and one-third to C (25,000 units), but incur extra fixed costs on B of £5,000.

General fixed costs of £30,000 must be covered by each proposal.

The solution

The alternative showing the highest profits and highest safety factor will be chosen. The alternatives are evaluated as under.

Unit profile	A	B	C
Sales Price	5	10	50
− Variable cost	3	5	20
= Contribution	2	5	30

Fixed period costs attributable to the product

	A	B	C
Break even volume (FC/VCbn)	$\left(\dfrac{1,000}{2}\right)$ 5,000	$\left(\dfrac{20,000}{5}\right)$ 4,000	$\left(\dfrac{150,000}{30}\right)$ 5,000
Actual volumes under proposal 1	−	−	50,000
Margin of safety resulting units	−	−	45,000
Actual volumes under proposal 2	8,000	15,000	−
Margin of safety resulting—units	3,000	11,000	−
Actual volumes under proposal 3	8,000	75,000	25,000
Margin of safety resulting	3,000	35,000	20,000

		Proposals	
	1	2	3
	£	£	£
Contribution from			
margin of safety units A	−	6,000	6,000
margin of safety units B	−	55,000	17,500
margin of safety units C	1,350,000	−	600,000
Total contribution	1,350,000	61,000	623,500
General fixed costs and B's extra costs	30,000	30,000	35,000
Profits	1,320,000	31,000	588,500

It is dramatically clear that proposal 1 is far the most profitable. Product C should be the sole product. Not only is its C:S ratio higher than the other two, its absolute value of units contribution is far higher, and it is this fact that causes it to dominate the other products.

A further example

The data for four products are as follows.

	E	F	G	H
Sales price	5	50	8	100
Unit variable cost	3	30	5	75
Maximum possible sales in units per year	5,000	2,000	30,000	1,000

Given general fixed costs of £20,000 per year; break-even volumes are as shown below. Margins of safety of maximum sales in units are also given.

	E	F	G	H
Break-even volumes	10,000	1,000	$6,666\frac{2}{3}$	800
Unit margins of safety	(5,000)	1,000	$23,333\frac{1}{3}$	200
Profits (Units safety margins × Unit contribution)	Loss	£20,000	£70,000	£5,000

If we can make only one product, that product would be G.

A charted example
S1, VC1 and TC1 show the position for product G above, with line A1 showing the maximum sales volume, in Fig. 12. S2 shows the effects of a £2 price rise. Break-even point falls from B1 to B2. TC3 shows the effect of a £1 increase in unit variable costs (but with the new price S2 still ruling). Break-even point rises from B2 to B3.

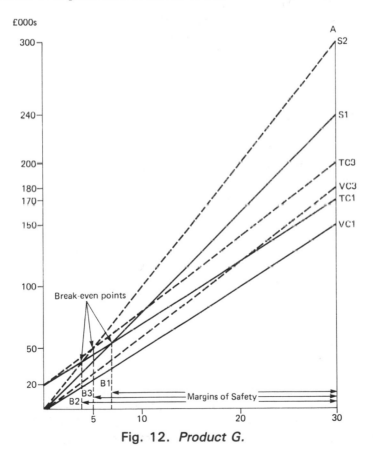

Fig. 12. *Product G.*

Plotting a break-even chart—type 1

To plot break-even charts given unit sales price, unit variable cost, period fixed costs and actual sales volume, the easiest method is as follows. Plot the x-axis so that its extreme right is the nearest round figure over the actual sales volume. If the actual sales volume were 36,557, the figure on the extreme right should be 40,000. The more thickly lined squares between the origin and 40,000 should be a round figure like 5,000, so each small square represents 500 units. Eight large squares would be used on the x-axis.

For the y-axis, first determine the overall range by multiplying the upper sales volume on the x-axis, 40,000, by the sales price—say £5—to give an upper y-axis value of £200,000. If there are twenty large squares available lengthways, each one can represent £10,000; if only ten are available, each represents £20,000. However, if fifteen are available, each large square could represent £15,000, but it is preferable for each large square to be 10,000 or 20,000, as both are easier to follow. Therefore, it looks better to use ten squares only out of the possible fifteen and use the remainder to provide space for labelling the whole diagram.

Having scaled both axes, the next task is to draw in the sales line. This always starts at the origin. We already know the upper sales volume (40,000) and sales value (£200,000). On the graph we mark the point representing the £200,000 value and 40,000 volume. We join this point to the origin with a straight line. Next we mark two points for the FC line, one on the y-axis and one vertically below the top end of the sales line, and we draw in the FC line between them.

Finally, to draw in the TC line we calculate the total variable costs associated with our maximum sales of 40,000 units. We add the result to fixed costs to obtain total costs. We mark the point representing total costs of maximum sales vertically below the top end of the sales line and join this point to the point where the FC line cuts the y-axis—that is, to the FC line intercept.

APPLICATIONS OF CVP ANALYSIS

Capacity usage

No scarce resources

Contribution analysis is useful in order to determine whether to use spare capacity to make new products. Thus if a firm has general fixed costs of £100,000 and contributions from current sales are £80,000, it is worthwhile making and selling a new product if its total contribution can cover the remaining £20,000 of fixed costs. Moreover, suppose existing sales come entirely from product A with a unit sales price of £16 and unit contribution of £8, so 10,000 units of A are currently sold. An additional product B could be sold for £20 with a unit contribution of £10. Not only would we need to sell just 2,000 units of B to cover the fixed costs left unrecovered by A, but it could well pay us to replace A by B altogether. This is because to cover £100,000 of fixed costs requires

$$\frac{100,000}{8} = 12,500 \text{ units of A but only } \frac{100,000}{10} = 10,000 \text{ units}$$

of B. This conclusion is valid, however, only if B consumes no more *scarce* resources per unit of output than A does. If this holds true, we should prefer to produce the product with the lower break-even point. The treatment, when one resource is scarce, is described below.

One limiting factor

X Ltd makes two products, J and K, and their unit variable costs are as follows.

	J	K
	£	£
Materials	1	3
Labour (£5 per hour)	10	5
Expenses	1	1
Total	12	9

J sells for £18 a unit, K for £13, and sales demand for J is expected to be 3,000 units, for K 5,000 units. During the budget period only 8,000 labour-hours will be available and fixed costs are to be £20,000. We now wish to determine the profit maximising product mix.

At first sight it may seem that X should make as many units of J as it can sell, because J's unit contribution of £6 is higher than K's of £4 by 50 per cent. Thus 3,000 Js would bring in a contribution of £18,000, while the other £2,000 of fixed costs would be covered by selling 500 units of

K $\left\{\dfrac{2,000}{4}\right\}$, which is only 10 per cent of K's anticipated demand.

However, labour is scarce. To meet the demand for 3,000 units of J would require $3,000 \times 2 = 6,000$ labour-hours, and to meet the demand for 5,000 of K requires 5,000 hours—a total requirement of 11,000 hours when only 8,000 are available. After applying 6,000 hours to J, 2,000 are available to K to make 2,000 units. This is above K's break-even point, but is it the most profitable use of resources? The 1,500 K units over break-even bring in profits of $£4 \times 1,500 = £6,000$.

J's unit contribution is £6, but J uses 2 labour-hours per unit, while K's unit contribution is £4 but K uses only one labour-hour. J has a contribution per labour-hour of $£\frac{6}{2} = £3$, and that is *below* K's £4 per hour contribution. Because K makes the bigger contribution *per unit of limiting factor,* it is more profitable to make K than J. As a general rule, when one limiting factor exists, products should be ranked in descending order of contribution per unit of limiting factor. We produce and sell as much as we can of the most profitable until we reach its sales limit, when we produce and sell as much as we can of the second most profitable, and so on.

Applying the ranking rule to J and K we use 5,000 hours of labour to make 5,000 units of K, which earn a total contribution of $5,000 \times £4 = £20,000$—precisely the sum of fixed costs to be covered. The remaining 3,000 hours will yield 1,500 units of J with a total contribution of £9,000—which is pure profit, as fixed costs were covered by K. This is £3,000 more profit than arose from satisfying all J's demand and using the balance of labour-hours on K. It can be seen how important it is to allocate resources not in descending order of unit contribution but rather in descending order of contribution per unit of limiting factor.

Order acceptance

Principles
As a general rule, new orders should be accepted if they increase profits. When no spare capacity is available, the order can be accepted only if resources are switched from current production, and any such switch involves a relevant opportunity cost which is to be charged to the proposed order. The measure of opportunity cost here is the contribution lost from no longer making and selling the relevant quantity of the old product.

Example
A firm makes a single product for which demand is unlimited. The product takes two labour-hours at £3 per hour to make, uses £4 of materials per unit and absorbs £2 of variable overhead. The sales price is £20. Production is at full capacity with no labour-hours to spare. A customer is willing to pay £5,500 for a special order which would use £2,000 of materials and 500 labour-hours. Variable overhead is recovered at £1 per labour-hour.

To decide if the order is to be accepted, we need to deduct from its £5,500 value all relevant costs, including its opportunity costs. Labour is scarce and would have to be diverted from normal production to fulfil the order. The product contribution is $£20 - £12 = £8$ per unit. Contribution per unit of labour-hour is $£8 \div 2$ (hours) $= £4$.

Costs of the order	£
Materials	2,000
Labour (500 × £3)	1,500
Variable overheads (500 × £1)	500
Total cash costs	4,000
Opportunity costs (500 × £4)	2,000
Total relevant costs	6,000
Value of order	5,500
Loss incurred if order accepted	(500)

We can see that the opportunity costs have made all the difference to the decision. They are not mere abstractions. The £2,000 contribution *is* earned from current labour use in making the current product and would fail to be earned if the 500 hours were switched to the order. In other words, the firm really would be £2,000 worse off but for the value of the order; and even given the value of the order, the firm would still be £500 worse off. The order should clearly be rejected unless the customer is prepared to raise the price to *over* £6,000.

Closure decisions

Product profitability comparisons

To compare the profitability of different products sold by a firm we can compare their respective total contributions. However, if any product has fixed costs uniquely attributable to it, such costs are relevant charges against its contribution. In closure decisions, the products whose production is to be stopped are those whose contribution to general fixed costs is the least.

Example

Results for a year for sales of four products show the following.

	L	M	N	O	Total
	£	£	£	£	£
Total contributions	10,000	(1,000)	2,500	7,000	18,500
Attributable fixed costs	–	1,000	3,000	–	4,000
Net contributions	10,000	(2,000)	(500)	7,000	14,500
			General fixed costs		12,000
			Profit		2,500

Product M should be abandoned forthwith, as it cannot even cover its variable costs, so is a pure loss-maker.

Product N does cover its variable costs but not its attributable fixed costs. If savings of £500 (N's negative net contribution) can really be made by closing N's production facilities, it is worthwhile ceasing production of N. However, if the fixed costs will still have to be met (e.g. factory rent, machine lease payments), abandoning N would not alleviate the burden of the £3,000 fixed costs but would deprive the firm of N's contribution of £2,500. The cost of the abandonment would be that lost contribution of £2,500, so although the firm now loses £500 on N, after abandonment it would lose £3,000 (the fixed costs which continue after abandonment). However, if N's facilities could be employed to make a product whose contribution *exceeds* £3,000, so as to generate a *positive* net contribution to general fixed costs, it is worth while stopping to make N and to substitute the new product.

Pricing

CVP principles
All products have a price elasticity of demand—that is, a specific relationship between price changes and volume effects. A demand elasticity of 1 means every price change is exactly offset by a volume change in the opposite direction and sales revenue is always constant. Elasticity of above 1 means volume effects outweigh the price changes, so a price increase causes such a large volume decrease that sales revenue falls. Elasticity below 1 means volume effects do not fully match price changes, so any price increase will increase sales income as volume falls by too little to offset the price increase. CVP analysis can help management select a profit maximising price.

If fixed costs are constant (unstepped) over the full range of possible sales volumes, optimum sales price is the price which maximises total contribution. Price rises raise *unit* contribution but may decrease *total* contribution as a result of volume effects. It is total contribution's maximum that fixes optimum sales price.

Example
A new product has a marginal cost of £2 per unit and market research indicates that 8,000 units would be sold at a sales price of £2.75 but demand would fall by 450 units for every 5p increase in the sales price. We are required to find the optimum sales price. This we do by preparing a table as shown below.

Sales price £	Unit contribution	Sales volume	Total contribution £
2.75	75p	8,000	6,000
2.80	80p	7,550	6,040
2.85	85p	7,100	6,035
2.90	90p	6,650	5,985
2.95	95p	6,200	5,890
3.00	£1	5,750	5,750

The table makes it clear that contribution is maximised at £6,040, which arises from a sales price of £2.80, the optimum price. Any higher price reduces total contribution as volume effects outweigh price ones.

ADVANCED CHARTING

Semi-fixed and semi-variable costs

In the real world only direct costs are wholly variable and very few overheads are wholly fixed. Break-even charts can handle this situation. Suppose a firm has £10,000 a year of fixed costs, unit variable costs are £3 and unit sales price is £5, but in addition there are semi-variable costs whose variable component is 50p per unit and whose fixed component is £5,000 per year. The type 1 break-even chart depicting this situation is shown in Fig. 13 below.

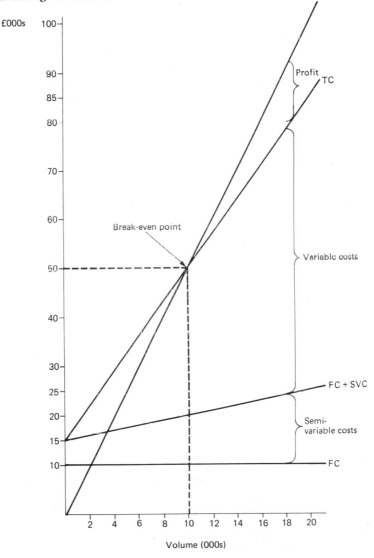

Fig. 13. *Semi-variable costs.*

Semi-fixed costs can also be charted as is done in Fig. 14 below. Note the stepping in fixed costs causes consequential stepping in total costs and creates three break-even points, of which only the highest one is safe to rely on. Profits are maximised just before a step increase and minimised just after one.

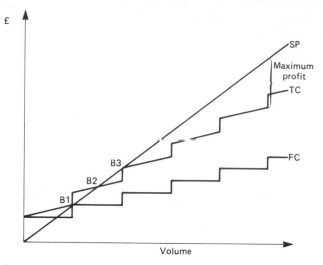

Fig. 14. *Semi-fixed costs. B1, B2 and B3 are all break-even points, but only beyond B3 is the firm sure to make profits.*

Cash costs and notional costs

Certain costs such as machine depreciation are notional in that they do not give rise to a related cash outflow equal to the cost. Once cash costs (that do require cash outflows) have been covered by sales income, the firm

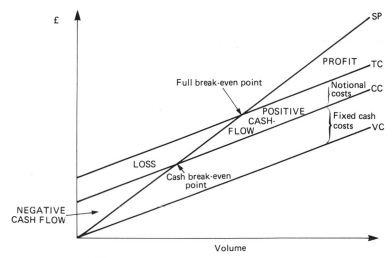

Fig. 15. *Cash break-even chart.*

begins to experience positive net cash flow. The point where sales revenue covers cash costs is the cash break-even point. This occurs at an earlier and smaller sales volume than the full break-even point. Between the two break-even points, the firm is "making money" without yet making profits. This situation is depicted in the type 2 chart (*see* Fig. 15).

Accounts charting

It is quite possible to present final accounts in graphical form using type 1 or, better, type 2 break-even charts. The main components of variable

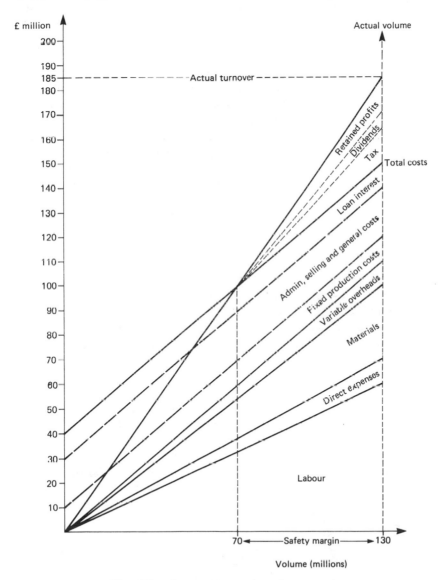

Fig. 16. *Accounts on break-even charts.*

and fixed costs can be shown (with stepped and semi-variable costs if desired). Cash and full break-even points can be made clear with the margin of safety achieved by actual sales. Appropriations of profit between tax, dividends and retentions appear as slices inside the profit angle. This is illustrated by Fig 16.

UNCERTAIN SALES

Expected value

Forecasts are usually of expected values—that is, of the weighted average of all reasonably probable alternative levels that sales might achieve. The source of the weighting is the planners' estimate of how probable is a given level of sales.

Suppose a product has a unit contribution of £4 and annual fixed costs of £10,000, its break-even volume is 2,500 units. The schedule of probable levels of sales in the forecast year is such that there is a 40 per cent chance of selling 3,000 units, a 20 per cent chance of selling 2,000 and a 20 per cent chance of selling 4,000, and a 10 per cent chance of selling only 1,000 and also a 10 per cent chance of selling as much as 5,000 units. The expected value is (40% of 3,000) + (20% of 2,000 + 20% of 4,000) + (10% of 1,000 + 10% of 5,000) = 3,000 units, and this expected value of sales volume is put into the forecast. However, there is a 10 per cent chance of selling only 1,000 units and a 20 per cent chance of selling only 2,000, and at either level the firm fails to break even. There is, in short, a 30 per cent chance of the firm's making a loss and management must be made aware of this, as they may find such a high probability of loss unacceptable. They may prefer to make a product whose expected value of sales volume only just passes break-even point but which has only a 5 per cent chance of making any losses. Such a preference would signify managerial "risk aversion". The risk attached to a product is largely a reflection of its loss-making chances. Another way of appraising this risk is to calculate the coefficient of variation.

The coefficient of variation

The coefficient of variation is found by dividing standard deviation by expected value. The standard deviation from the 3,000 expected value is found for the situation described above, thus.

Probability	Sales units	Mean deviation (d) units	d^2 million units	Probability $\times d^2$ million units
0.1	1,000	(2,000)	4	0.4
0.2	2,000	(1,000)	1	0.2
0.4	3,000	nil	nil	nil
0.2	4,000	1,000	1	0.2
0.1	5,000	2,000	4	0.4
		Total = The variance (σ^2)		1.2

Standard deviation $(\sigma) = \sqrt{\text{variance}} = \sqrt{1.2 \text{ million}} = 1,095$ units. The coefficient of variation

$$\frac{\sigma}{\text{ExpVal}} = \frac{1,095}{3,000} = 0.365 = 36\tfrac{1}{2}\%.$$

The coefficient of variation tells by what percentage expected value is likely to vary. The higher the coefficient, the greater the risk attached to the value concerned. However, a $36\tfrac{1}{2}$ per cent coefficient simply *represents* the possible variation. It does not define the absolute limit of the variation. In the above example actual sales could be as little as $66\tfrac{2}{3}$ per cent below expected value or $66\tfrac{2}{3}$ per cent above it. The range of variation is thus almost double the coefficient of variation in either direction. However, standard deviation and its resultant coefficient of variation are the normally used measures of dispersion and variation, as they reflect the low probabilities of extremely large deviations, whereas the crude range does not. It would, nevertheless, be very useful if we could use standard deviation and coefficient of variation themselves to tell us the probability of making a loss. There is one very important circumstance when we can do just that, and we shall describe it below.

The normal distribution

Nature of a normal distribution
In the text above, the expected value of 3,000 units was only one out of five possible values that sales could take. It is very unlikely that the sales would vary in discrete 1,000 unit lumps—that is, that would be either 1,000 or 2,000 or 3,000 or 4,000 or 5,000 but would not be anything in between, such as 1,500 or 3,003. Unless sales volumes depend on fulfilling individual 1,000 unit orders, sales could actually take *any* value from 0 to, say, 5,500. The 40 per cent probability of sales being 3,000 is then really a 40 per cent probability of sales being between 2,500 and 3,500. Since the probability of 2,000 and 4,000 units was 20 per cent, the probability of 2,500 and 3,500 themselves is half-way between 20 per cent and 40 per cent—namely, 30 per cent. The values represent continuous data; meaning they could take any value between 0 and 5,500, and so must their associated probabilities. Thus the probabilities rise by 1 per cent for every 50 units increase in sales from 2,500 to 3,000 units, thus:

Probability (%)	Sales units
30	2,500
31	2,550
32	2,600
33	2,650
34	2,700
35	2,750

Probability (%)	Sales units
36	2,800
37	2,850
38	2,900
39	2,950
40	3,000

Similarly they fall by 1 per cent for every 50-unit increase in sales from 3,000 to 3,500. The distribution of probabilities across all the possible values of sales shows the following properties.

(*a*) Continuity—there are no step increases or gaps.

(*b*) Symmetry—the rises in probability up to 3,000 units match the decreases after 3,000 units.

(*c*) Unimodality—there exists only one value (3,000) with the maximum probability (40 per cent), and this one value divides both probabilities and values into two matching halves.

The qualities just listed describe the "normal" distribution which is represented graphically by a symmetrical bell-shaped curve, as shown in

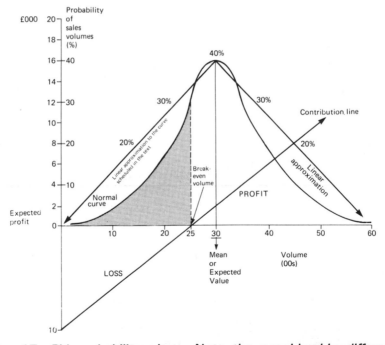

Fig. 17. *PV probability chart. Note the considerable differences between the linear probabilities scheduled in the text above and those derived from the normal curve. The shaded area represents the probability of making a loss.*

Fig. 17. The normal distribution curve is so called because it describes many phenomena, not because it represents some standard distribution from which all others are deviations. Its original name of "Gaussian distribution" is less misleading but now rarely used.

Figure 17 shows a PV chart with a normal distribution of possible actual sales *volumes*. The contribution line crosses the horizontal axis at the break-even point; the normal curve is at its highest where expected probability is highest. The point where the contribution line crosses the normal curve is a mere accident of scaling and has no significance whatsoever.

Properties of a normal distribution

The important property of a normal curve is that there is a distinct and constant relationship between the standard deviation of any value from its mean and the area underneath the curve. Thus 68.26 per cent of the area lies above the *x*-axis between one standard deviation below and one above the mean. Normal distribution tables enable us to look up the area between any given standard deviation and the mean. Such tables are not given in terms of the standard deviation itself, because this will vary with the data concerned, but rather in terms of *z*, which is the mean deviation (actual value less mean or expected value) divided by the standard deviation. Thus our expected value is 3,000, the *z* value of 4,095 units given a standard deviation of 1,095 units is

$$\frac{4,095 - 3,000}{1,095} = 1.$$

To use the normal distribution table in Appendix I , we look up 1.0 in the *z* column and find the area given against it is 0.3413. As per Fig. 18, 34.13 per cent of the area of the curve lies between a vertical line drawn from the mean of 3,000 and the next vertical line drawn from 4,095 units.

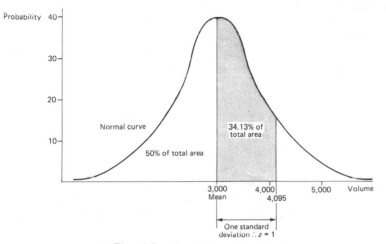

Fig. 18. *Z value and area.*

The importance of area is this: it exactly reflects probability. Thus half the area under the curve is to the left, half to the right of the mean 3,000 value. This means that there is a 50 per cent chance of sales having a value below 3,000 (to the left of 3,000) and 50 per cent chance of sales being above.

Applying the area:probability identity to 4,095 units, we have discovered from the table in Appendix I that the area between 4,095 units and 3,000 units is 34.13 per cent of the total area. We know also that 50 per cent of the area under a normal curve lies to the left of the mean. Therefore, the area to the left of 4,095 units is $50 + 34.13\% = 84.13\%$. This means there is an 84.13 per cent chance of sales being less than (left of) 4,095 units. The chances of sales being above 4,095 units are $100\% - 84.13\% = 15.87\%$.

Applying the same technique to Fig. 17, we can answer this question: what are the chances of the firm making a loss? The chances are given by the area of the curve to the left of the break-even point on the PV chart. The break-even volume is 2,500 units. Its z value is its mean deviation over the standard deviation:

$$z\ (2,500) = \frac{(2,500 - 3,000)}{1,095} = \frac{500}{1,095} = 0.4566$$

The table Appendix I tells that the area between the mean and $z = 0.4$ is 0.1554 and between the mean and $z = 0.5$ is 0.1915. The distance between the mean and $z = 0.4566$ is going to be slightly over half-way between the two above results. By linear interpolation we find its area to be

$$0.1554 + \left[\frac{0.4566}{1.0000} \times (0.1915 - 0.1554)\right] = 0.1554 + 0.0165$$

$= 0.1719 = 17.19\%$ of the area. The chances of making a loss are 17.19 per cent less than the chances of obtaining the expected mean value, $50\% - 17.19\% = 32.81\%$—nearly a one-in-three chance.

Uncertainty analysis is increasingly important in management accountancy and is seen more and more often in examinations. The use of normal curve properties is perhaps the most often tested uncertainty analysis technique. The reader is advised to read the above exposition of this topic as often as necessary until it is thoroughly understood. The next chapter uses the technique and the final chapter develops it further.

GRAPHICAL LINEAR PROGRAMMING

Principles and assumptions

Like break-even charting and contribution analysis, linear programming assumes linear relationships to hold between costs and volumes. Thus straight lines rather than curves are used on the relevant graphs to show costs rising with volumes. We shall hold this assumption while discussing the topic below.

The basic principle of linear programming is that whenever two or more resources are limited there is an optimum mix of products that can be calculated so as to maximise total contribution and hence total profits. The simplex technique of linear programming enables an optimum mix of two or more products to be calculated. All basic management science textbooks cover the technique, but it is extremely rare for it to be required in management accountancy exams. However, the graphical technique is quite often required, as it can be used within the strict time budget of an exam question, unlike most simplex problems. The weakness of the graphical technique compared to simplex is that it can handle a product mix of only two products, although it can handle any number of resource constraints.

The graphical LP technique
Where a firm has only one limiting factor, we have already seen that profits are maximised and the product mix optimised when contribution per unit of limiting factor is itself maximised. Where a firm has more than one limiting factor, the product mix is optimised when maximum use is made of the two most severely constraining factors. Which two factors are most severely constraining depends partly on their maximum capacity and partly on the contribution per unit of limiting factor available from each of the two products.

The linear programme (LP) graph has lines showing how much of the two products can be made, using every available unit of limiting factor. Every limiting factor has its own line, called a "constraint line". In addition, there is a contribution line showing, for each total contribution in £s, the possible combinations of the two products that can yield the contribution. The further away from the origin is the contribution line, the greater the contribution and therefore the greater the profit. However, once the contribution line passes beyond any constraint line, it enters an "infeasible region"—so called because insufficient resources of limiting factor are available to generate the product mix indicated by the points along the contribution line. That part of the graph between the origin and the innermost constraint lines defines the feasible combinations of the two products and is therefore termed the "feasible region". The optimum product mix always lies on the boundary of the feasible region, usually where two constraint lines cross. Its precise location on the feasible region boundary depends on the slope of the contribution line.

Plotting an LP graph

The problem
A firm makes two products, A and B, with unit contributions of £2 and £3 respectively. Monthly capacity is limited to 2,400 hours, sales of A cannot exceed 1,400 units at current prices and sales of B are similarly limited to 3,000 units. Both products use ingredient J, of which only 2,000

kg are available every month. Uses of limiting factors by each product are as below:

	A	B	Available maximum
Unskilled labour-hours	0.6	0.8	2,400
Skilled labour-hours	0.4	1.2	2,400
Finishing machine-hours	0.8	0.6	2,400
Kg of ingredient J	0.5	1.0	2,000

We restate the above data in LP formulae terms. First, we state the objective function, the formula for what it is our objective to maximise—namely, the contribution. Objective function: Max $2a + 3b$. Second, we list the constraint inequalities. Unskilled labour-hours, for example, must be equal to or below ($\leq$) 2,400 hours. Note that a is the number of units of A to be made, b the number of units of B, and the number of A and B we can get from 2,400 labour-hours is $0.6a + 0.8b$. The constraint inequality is $0.6a + 0.8b \leq 2,400$. Sales are not a resource but are constrained, so we need to specify the sales constraint inequalities as well. The full set of formulae are as follows.

> Objective function: Maximise $2a + 3b$
> Subject to:U (unskilled hours constraint) $0.6a + 0.8b \leq 2,400$
> S (skilled hours constraint) $0.4a + 1.2b \leq 2,400$
> F (finishing hours constraint) $0.8a + 0.6b \leq 2,400$
> J (ingredient J constraint) $0.5a + 1.0b \leq 2,000$
> A (sales of A constraint) $a \leq 1,400$
> B (sales of B constraint) $b \leq 3,000$

To draw the constraint lines, we must translate the inequalities into maximum a and maximum b values capable of solving the inequality. Thus, constraint J has $0.5a + 1.0b \leq 2,000$. If $b = 0$, the inequality could be satisfied by

$$a \leq \frac{2,000}{0.5} = 4,000.$$

If $a = 0$, b would be $\leq 2,000$. We use this result to plot the constraint line J between the intercept 4,000 units on the y-axis which represents values of a and the mantissa 2,000 units on the x-axis which represents values of b. Similar translation of the inequalities for all six constraints gives the following table.

Constraint	a	b
U	4,000	3,000
S	6,000	2,000
F	3,000	4,000
J	4,000	2,000
A	1,400	–
B	–	3,000

Finally, to plot the contribution lines $2a + 3b$, we assign a series of random but round £000 values to total contribution. For example, to earn £2,000 we make the objective function into the equation $2a + 3b = 2,000$. We then translate the equation into maximum values for each variable if the other were zero, just as we did with the constraint inequalities. In the case of $2a + 3b = 2,000$, a can be as large as 1,000 and b as large as $666\frac{2}{3}$. The following table develops this further.

Contribution (£)	Maximum a	Maximum b	Line
3,000	1,500	1,000	C1
6,000	3,000	2,000	C2
9,000	4,500	3,000	C3
12,000	6,000	4,000	C4

We use the tables to plot the lines. Line C4 has amount of A = 6,000 and amount of B = 6,000, and over the line is written the objective equation $2a + 3b = 12,000$. Figure 19 is the LP graph that results from the above data.

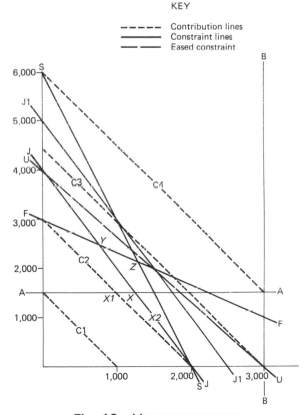

Fig. 19. *Linear programme.*

LP graph interpretation

The innermost constraint lines on the graph are A and J, so they are the frontiers of the feasible region. Only 1,400 units of A can be made, as no more than that can be sold. No more than 2,000 units of B can be made, as that is the maximum yield of B from ingredient J. Constraints A and J dominate all other constraints. The other four constraints may as well not exist, since A and J limit production possibilities more than any other constraints. Point X where A and J cross has $a = 1,400$ and $b = 1,300$. Checking this with the formula for line J we have:

$$J: \quad 0.5a + 1.0b \leq 2,000$$
$$0.5\,(1,400) + 1,300 = 2,000$$
$$700 + 1,300 = 2,000$$

So our graphical solution is correct. The question is, whether 1,400 A and 1,300 B give the maximum contribution that is feasible, given resource constraints. The contribution formula is $2a + 3b$. The contribution to be derived from 1,400 A and 1,300 B is thus £$(2 \times 1,400) + $£$(3 \times 1,300) = $ £6,700. Areas outside the feasible region are not available, so we must choose alternative mixes from along the feasible boundary and see if they contribute more than the mix at point X. At X1, $a = 1,400$ and $b = 1,000$. This must yield a lower contribution than point X because point X has 1,300 B while X1 has only 1,000. At X2, $a = 1,000$ and $b = 1,500$. Contribution is £$(2 \times 1,000) + $£$(3 \times 1,500) = $ £6,500—not as much as the contribution from the mix at point X. Point X thus represents the optimum mix of A and B, and £6,700 the maximum contribution under existing constraints.

However, if constraint A were to disappear because demand for A becomes unlimited for some reason, the feasible region would enlarge. The innermost constraint lines would now be lines F and J. The A and B values at point Y where F and J cross are hard to read exactly from the graph because they seem to involve non-round numbers. We can find out if contribution at Y is greater than that at X by using a ruler. Taking a ruler with its right-hand edge along contribution line C2 we carefully move it outwards, keeping it parallel to C2 until it just touches point X. If the contribution from Y is greater than it is from X, Y will appear to the right of where our ruler is now—signifying that Y lies on a higher contribution line than X. This is indeed the case and it means Y now represents the optimum product mix. This means we need to know the exact values of a and b at point Y.

Simultaneous equations

When we cannot read off exact values for a and b from the graph, we can use simultaneous equations to calculate their values instead. To use this technique involves knowing which constraint lines are involved and, as we need the graph for this, simultaneous equations do not do away with the need for the graph. The two constraint lines involved at point Y are lines F and J. We turn the inequalities for lines F and J into equations, then solve them for a and b, as follows.

$$
\begin{aligned}
\text{F}:0.8a + 0.6b &= 2{,}400 \\
\text{J}:0.5a + b &= 2{,}000 \\
\text{F} \times 10: \qquad 8a + 6b &= 24{,}000 \\
\text{J} \times 6: \qquad 3a + 6b &= 12{,}000 \\
(\text{F} \times 10) - (\text{J} \times 6): \qquad 5a &= 12{,}000 \\
a &= 2{,}400 \\
\text{J}:1{,}200 + b &= 2{,}000 \\
\therefore \ b &= 800
\end{aligned}
$$

Check with F: $0.8 \times 1{,}200 + 0.6 \times 800 = 1{,}920 + 480 = 2{,}400$: correct.

Optimum product mix is now $a = 2{,}400$ and $b = 800$. Contribution from this mix is £$(2 \times 2{,}400) +$ £$(3 \times 800) = $£7,200, some £500 more than the contribution at point X.

Shadow prices

Removal of constraint A resulted in an extra contribution of £500. The shadow price, also termed the "dual price", of any resource is the change in the total contribution received by the firm as a result of an increase or decrease of one unit of the limiting factor. This applies only while the resource is a dominant limiting factor that bounds the feasible region and does not apply outside it.

Constraint J operates at both points X and Y, so it would be useful to know its shadow price—that is, the contribution per unit (kg) of ingredient J; in other words, its unit opportunity cost. The total availability of J is 2,000 kg. At point Y we found $a = 2{,}400$ and $b = 800$ and in equation J we had: $0.5 (2{,}400) + 800 = 2{,}000$.

We now rework the simultaneous equations for point Y but with 1 kg added to make 2,001, thus:

$$
\begin{aligned}
\text{J}: \qquad 0.5a + b &= 2{,}001 \\
\text{F}: \qquad 0.8a + 0.6b &= 2{,}400 \\
\text{F} \times 10: \qquad 8a + 6b &= 24{,}000 \\
\text{J} \times 6: \qquad 3a + 6b &= 12{,}006 \\
5a &= 11{,}994 \\
a &= 2{,}398.8 \\
\text{J}: \ (2{,}398.8 \div 2) + b &= 2{,}001 \\
b &= 801.6
\end{aligned}
$$

Contribution from above values for a and b is £$(2 \times 2{,}398.8) +$ £$(3 \times 801.6) = $£4,797.6 + £2,404.8 = £7,202.4. Contribution from J = 2,000 was £7,200, therefore the shadow price of 1 kg of J = £2.40.

The shadow price of J is its unit opportunity cost. Every kilogram of J above 2,000 kg would be worth £2.40 in contribution made possible to the firm. It follows that it is worth paying up to £2.40 more than the current price per kilogram to obtain extra supplies of J. For example if the current price is £5 it is worth paying £7 to obtain an extra, say, 500 kg of J. The extra contribution will be £2.40 less £2 × 500 = £200. The increased price does not offset the gross increased contribution, so there is a net benefit.

Moreover, 500 extra units of J will move Y's constraint line outwards to J1 on Fig. 19 above. This removes J from the feasible region altogether. The feasible region is now bounded by lines F and S and the new optimum mix is given by point Z. This in turn means we needed only enough J to move its line to point Z—the extra J was a waste of money because we could not use it, since we do not have enough finishing-hours (F) or skilled labour-hours (S) to make use of the extra J. The reader should now apply the previous techniques:

(*a*) to define the mix at point Z;
(*b*) to translate that mix into required kilograms of J; and
(*c*) to compute the shadow price per finishing-hour.

PRICE VOLUME ECONOMICS

Optimal volume

The optimal output volume of the firm is the output which has minimum unit average absorbed costs. At this output unit costs are as low as possible with existing capacity, so profit is maximised. Figure 20 below is the cost curve diagram reflecting this situation. As volume rises the recovery base for fixed costs rises, so *unit* fixed costs fall. Variable unit costs initially fall, since volume rises reflecting such matters as quantity discounts, but then begin to rise as limiting factors such as labour's basic working week come into play and it is necessary to pay overtime, bonuses and premium prices for scarce raw materials. Marginal cost is not now merely variable cost but the difference between *total* costs of producing x units and the total costs of producing $x + 1$ units at each level of output. Where the marginal cost curve, MC, cuts the average cost curve, AC, unit costs are minimised. At that point MC = AC. Before that point MC < AC, so the marginal cost of one extra unit is below the average cost of previous units, and thus the average falls still further. After that point MC > AC, so increases in MC cause *increases* in AC. The point M in Fig. 20 defines minimum AC, and the line MN indicates the volume, ON, which generates this minimum.

Line P1 is a price line and is drawn to make P = MC = AC. At price P1, the firm will just cover its costs, so M then defines the break-even point.

Line P2 is a lower price line drawn to make P = MC = AVC, and here

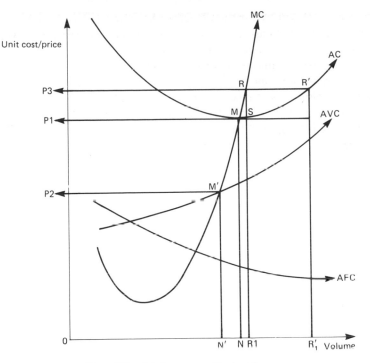

Fig. 20. *Volume optimisation.*

sales price equals only average variable cost, so there is no unit contribution to fixed costs. At this point, M', it is not worth making the product, so point M' is the shut-down point and its corresponding output volume is ON'.

Line P3 is a higher price line, cutting the MC curve at R and the AC curve at R'. If volume OR'₁ is produced, the P3 price will equate to unit average cost and R' will merely provide a new break-even point where no profit can be made. However, if volume OR₁ is produced, P3 price equals only marginal cost but exceeds the relevant average cost indicated by point S on the AC curve. The vertical distance between R and S signifies the profit per unit that derives from producing volume OR₁ at price P3. This volume is the profit maximising volume and is uniquely defined by the point where price equals marginal costs.

Profit maximising under perfect competition

On Fig. 20 above we had three price lines, all flat and parallel to the x-axis. This meant price did not need to change when volume changed. Consumers were prepared to pay the same price irrespective of the quantity offered to them. This situation reflects perfect competition, a situation where there are so many firms supplying a product and so many customers demanding that none of them can affect its market price. This means that each individual firm is very small relative to the total size of the industry and each individual customer represents only a tiny fraction of the total market.

Since the firm cannot decide sales price, as it must comply with the prevailing price to stay in business, it can maximise profits only by its volume decision. Given price P1 it produces volume ON and break-even. Given price P2 it shuts down altogether, as it cannot cover fixed costs at that price. Given price P3 it produces volume OR_1 and makes profits of $RS \times OR_1$. In all situations it can increase profits only by reducing costs, and for any given cost structure it maximises profits by producing the volume dictated by the point where the prevailing price equates exactly with the marginal cost.

Monopoly pricing

Homogeneous market

If marginal and average costs always fall, say because of technological improvements, it is worthwhile for the firm to produce more and more until it dominates the market. Government ownership of an industry creates another situation where one seller uniquely supplies the entire market. The volume at which costs are minimised is still the lowest AC point. If the monopoly eventually faces rising marginal costs (owing to the pressure of limiting factors of production), the MC = AC rule for dictating cost minimising volume will apply. However, the monopoly will not necessarily produce at the MC = AC volume, because it is now in a position to control not only volume but price. It can control price because it is the only supplier of the product to the market. To sell more, though, it will have to reduce its price. The price line is no longer horizontal but shows negative slope, so that volume varies *inversely* with price. The gradient of the line is determined by consumer perceptions of the necessity to have the product and of the ease and cheapness by which the product could be replaced by another. The more necessary and irreplaceable the product, the steeper and more nearly vertical will be the price line. A very steep line enables the supplier to make very small cutbacks in volume and charge very large consequential increases in price. The price line is actually a demand line and shows average unit revenue associated with each level of volume. Because average revenue per unit falls as volume rises, the revenue from selling one extra unit—the marginal revenue—will fall in turn. Marginal revenue is the addition to total revenue resulting from the sale of one more unit. It continually falls because price has to keep being reduced to make an extra sale. Where price reductions reach the point where total revenue itself falls, marginal revenue becomes negative.

The monopoly firm maximises profit at the point where marginal cost just equals marginal revenue. This is point E in Fig. 21 below. The volume

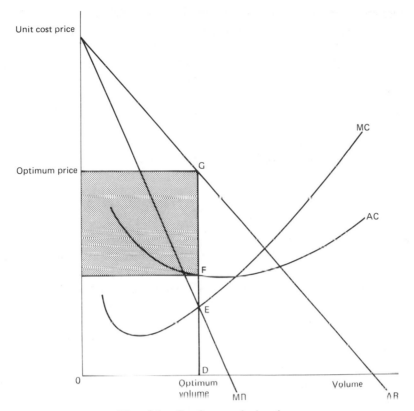

Fig. 21. *Profit maximisation.*

dictated by point E is OD and the price dictated is G—the point on the
demand or AR line lying vertically above point E. Point F shows the
average unit cost to produce OD units. Since price G is well above cost F,
unit profit of FG will be made and total profits are represented by the area
of the shaded rectangle. *MR = MC uniquely determines profit maximising
volume and price for all firms, not just monopolies.* Study of Fig. 21 will
show that at E the size of the profit rectangle is larger than it could have
been elsewhere.

A firm may not choose to maximise profit but instead decide to sell a
given volume or charge a given price. The firm can use a diagram like Fig.
21 to find out what volume it should produce in order to enforce its chosen
price, or what price it should choose in order to sell its available volume.
What no firm, even a monopoly, can do is try to dictate both volume and
price as if they were mutually independent. One must be the independent
variable and the other dependent, or else stockpiling will occur with too
high a price to clear a given volume or unfilled orders with too low a price.
A monopoly can dictate either price or volume in the market but not both
simultaneously.

Oligopoly

Figure 21 applies to all firms, because it is dependent for its validity not on the existence of absolute monopoly but on the existence of "U-shaped" cost curves and negatively sloping revenue lines. All firms experience these and perfect competition is hardly ever even approximated in the real world. Thus all firms maximise profits by finding the point where $MR = MC$ and making both price and volume decisions accordingly.

The steeper the demand line, the greater the power of the firm over price and volume (and therefore over revenue). It is thus in a firm's interest to be as dominant in its product markets as possible and enjoy the profits deriving from monopoly power. Firms attempt to achieve this by marketing and advertising strategies designed to achieve "product differentiation"—consumer perception of the uniqueness and irreplaceability of a product. This "monopolistic competition" may eventually result in the market's being shared by only a few firms, a situation termed "oligopoly" (meaning few sellers). Oligopoly firms have less monopoly power than pure monopolies but enough to ensure a reasonable margin of price (AR) over average unit cost (AC). Unlike monopolies, they need to be sensitive to the possible responses of rivals to any change in production or marketing policies. It is no use cutting prices by 5 per cent to gain 10 per cent more sales volume if rivals immediately follow suit and every firm ends up worse off by 5 per cent. The situation is rather like a game of poker and a whole branch of management science, game theory, has evolved to assist oligopoly firms make optimum decisions. It is, at the present time, beyond the scope of management accountancy textbooks.

Management accountancy inside an oligopoly firm puts considerable weight on increased market penetration. This must be achieved (to increase monopoly power) in a way that is proof against rivals' retaliation and at a cost that is not so high as to offset the benefits in extra revenue from increased market power.

Discriminatory pricing

An oligopoly or monopoly may not face a homogeneous set of consumers. For example, a telephone company has business customers that use telephones largely between 9 a.m. and 5 p.m., and private customers who use telephones at any time of day. Effectively there are two markets, a peak-hours' market and an off-peak market. The peak-hours' market regards telephones as more necessary and difficult to replace than does the off-peak market. The demand line for the peak-hours' market will therefore be steeper than the off-peak demand line. The firm can charge peak-hour users a higher price than it charges off-peak users and justify such discrimination by claiming it is trying to ration peak demand and encourage off-peak demand. This discriminating pricing applies to telephones, public transport, postage and holiday packages, among other things, so it is clear that an absolute monopoly is not required for a firm to take advantage of differentiated demand.

The mechanics of discriminatory pricing are shown in Fig. 22 below. Peak demand is depicted by line D1 and its associated marginal revenue line MR1. Off-peak demand is shown by D2 and the associated MR2. Combined marginal revenues from both demands is the marginal revenue for the whole firm, shown by line MRT. Where MRT cuts the firm's marginal cost, curve MC defines optimal prices and volumes for the whole firm. Line EE is extended left from this point, point E, to the *y*-axis. Where EE cuts MR1 defines the optimal price and volume for peak demand at P1 and Q1 respectively. Where EE cuts MR2 the optimal price P2 and volume Q2 for off-peak demand are defined. Volumes OQ1 + OQ2 = OQ3, the firm's overall optimum volume. However, the revenue rectangles delineated by P1Q1 and P2Q2 are greater than the profit rectangle EEQ3O that the firm would attain wihout price discrimination. Thus price discrimination leaves optimum volume unchanged but partitions it in such a way as to raise maximum profits through having two optimal prices instead of only one.

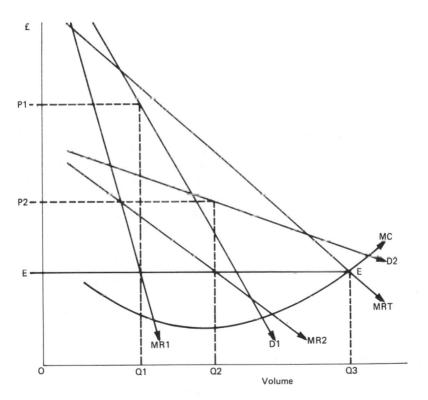

Fig. 22. *Discriminatory pricing.*

REAL WORLD PRICING

Cost-plus pricing

Principles

Economic theory as outlined above is normative, giving us rules for profit-maximising firms that know what their demand and cost curves look like. Real world firms have only an imperfect idea of their demand curves and cost curves, and may not always seek to maximise profits. Their price and volume decisions are based on easily available data rather than on the ideal data needed to make decisions strictly adherent to normative economics. The data most readily available are current actuals for unit product cost. The practice of using unit cost as a pricing base is therefore widespread.

With full-cost pricing, a profit mark-up is added to the fully absorbed unit cost in order to give the sales price. The size of the mark-up reflects a required return on capital tied up during the production process. Thus the longer the operating cycle, the higher the required return. Suppose £1 million of net assets are tied up during production and management require a return of 20 per cent on those assets, £200,000. If costs are £4 million, £200,000 required return will be generated from a mark-up of 5 per cent.

Disadvantages of full-cost pricing

(*a*) Full costs include absorbed fixed overheads, so unit cost is subject to forecasting error, both of expenditure and volume.

(*b*) The basis for apportioning overheads between different products may not be valid, especially if they have a common base such as labour-hours but are incurred on quite different bases.

(*c*) Opportunity costs, especially shadow prices, are wholly ignored, so the full cost of making one product rather than another, or using one resource rather than another, is overlooked.

(*d*) Short-term opportunities may be missed because contracts that cover marginal costs but not full costs as computed will be rejected.

(*e*) Demand conditions are wholly ignored, so the price may be quite unrealistic or suboptimal in economic terms. This objection and objection (*c*) also apply to marginal-cost pricing.

(*f*) Recovering overheads as a percentage of direct costs may greatly exaggerate errors in estimates of direct costs. For example, direct labour incurred by Ferranti to make missiles for the British Government was overestimated by £732,000. An overhead recovery of 564 per cent of labour cost was applied, and this resulted in overpricing of just under £5 million.

Competitive pricing

Competitive pricing takes demand and competitors into account. It requires price to cover marginal cost and generate a reasonable contribution, but is concerned to increase market penetration or obtain a contract in order to make use of currently spare capacity. The calculations necessary form part of decision accounting, some simple examples of which we looked at earlier in the chapter. More complex examples will be discussed in Chapter 10.

Minimum pricing

Principles

Minimum pricing is a limiting case of competitve pricing. The minimum price just covers the marginal costs of making the item plus the opportunity costs of resources consumed. If no resources are limited, opportunity costs are zero.

Example

Product A has a sales price of £25, contribution of £10 and labour costs of £5 per unit. Product B has labour costs of £4 per unit and total variable costs of £16. The minimum price to charge for B if labour is scarce is £16 plus the labour opportunity cost. A has £10 contribution per £5 of labour, so B must show an £8 contribution for its £4 of labour to match the return per unit of the limiting factor experienced with A. Thus minimum B price is £16 + £8 = £24.

Purpose

The minimum price is the price below which a firm should not make a product. It is the minimum acceptable price only, not an optimal price, and certainly not a profit-maximising price in most circumstances. It is useful when a firm has surplus stocks to sell, excess capacity to use or a new product to market. A new product may need to be sold initially at a minimum price in order to attract buyers. Once they are habituated to the product and want to repeat their orders, prices can be raised—because the demand line has become steeper.

Contract pricing

Tenders

In the building and engineering industries, cost units consist of large unique and high value contracts. The firm obtains contracts from clients by having its tender accepted. Most clients will prepare a bill of quantities listing the materials to be used on the contract, and the rival contractors then price each material listed. They calculate labour and overhead costs and submit the completed tender to the client. Thus the client is not merely quoted a total contract price but has the price analysed into its cost elements and constituent activities. Usually the client accepts the lowest tender but will not do so if it seems unattainable or so low as to jeopardise the contract through too many cost-cutting tactics or through the contractors' liquidation when progress payments continually fail to cover costs.

Time costs

Contract costs depend to a considerable extent on the time taken from start to finish of the contract work. Not only are many overheads time related, but direct labour costs vary directly with hours of site attendance. The contractor's optimum "volume" is thus the shortest possible time to complete the contract at normal costs per unit of resources. Network diagrams of each job to be done in order to complete the contract will be prepared and total contract time forecast. Reviewing the diagram, one particular chain of sequential activities will be seen to dictate the minimum possible contract time. This chain of activities is called the "critical path", because its duration is critical to the duration of the entire contract. Management effort is now directed to shortening the time taken by activities on the critical path, by rescheduling some that are currently done sequentially to be carried out simultaneously instead, and by investigating the possibility of reducing the time taken for specific activities. Eventually no further opportunities to save time can be identified and the firm has a time budget which will form the basis of its cost budget and its tendered prices.

Crash costs

Some activities can be made to take less time only if management is prepared to pay premium prices for resources. For example, fifteen hours may be required to clear a small building site to a standard adequate to lay foundations. This time could be reduced to thirteen hours if management were prepared to pay a bonus of £2 for each hour saved—that is, to pay a crash cost. If overheads accrue at *less* than £2 an hour, it is worthwhile to pay the bonus.

Contract duration is minimised if crash costs are incurred for all resources possible, but contract costs are minimised at the point where marginal crash costs equal marginal costs saved from one hour's reduction in work time. This is a special form of the general MC = MR rule for profit maximising. The contractor, once the contract is signed, is like the perfectly competitive firm, in that the price is given and unalterable; so profits can be maximised only by minimising costs at the optimum contract duration.

Setting contract prices

If all rival tendering firms add the same percentage mark-up on the same direct costs in their tenders, the lowest contract price will come from the firm expecting to complete the contract in the shortest time. Thus time competition is an integral part of price competition for contractors.

Cost-plus pricing is general and it is usually on a full-cost basis, as marginal-cost pricing is considered to leave overhead recovery too unplanned. However, fixed price contracts are now rare and most long contracts include clauses that allow the contractor to raise prices in order to pass on the effects of cost inflation.

The level of mark-up depends on:

(*a*) management's required return on assets;

(*b*) game theory type models of competitors' probable mark-ups and their chances of obtaining the contract at various levels of mark-up;

(*c*) the extent to which the contract will be inflation proof; and

(*d*) the firm's reputation, monopoly over certain types of service to date, its experience of similar work and its forecast of cost movements.

Once the contract is signed, the expected revenue from any one phase of the contract is proportional to the duration of that phase. Thus, if the first phase of a contract takes 20 per cent of contract total time, then, so long as resources are constant in cost terms throughout the contract, the revenue expected from the first phase is 20 per cent of the contract price.

TRANSFER PRICES

Nature of the problem

Transfer prices are those at which one profit centre sells its product or service to another profit centre inside the firm. Transfer price levels affect the distribution of total group profits among divisions, subsidiaries and profit centres at every level. Because transfer prices affect both allocation of resources and distribution of profits within the group, they are a very important decision variable. Each profit centre has an interest in selling at the highest possible price and buying at the lowest. Central board management has an interest in ensuring that transfer prices are set at a level likely to maximise group-wide profits. This last requirement involves minimising costs to all parts of the group because intragroup profits are eliminated on consolidation so do not benefit group shareholders at all.

At first sight, therefore, it seems that central management could require interdivisional trading to be at cost. However, divisional managers will be reluctant to sell to other divisions at zero profit and will prefer to stockpile output until it can be sold at normal profit to a customer outside the group. If the group is an international concern, its head office will not find it easy to prevent overseas divisional managers from subverting group transfer pricing policies. It is clearly better to attain goal congruence on transfer prices, so the aspirations of central management and divisional management are both met as far as possible. A number of ideas have been put forward to promote such goal congruence.

Market pricing

If transfer prices are set at the same level as prices for units sold to customers outside the group, neither profit centre can argue about the unfairness of the price. The buying division might expect better service, greater flexibility and reliability of supply and lower administration and procurement costs than would occur with an outside supplier. The selling division benefits from lower administration and selling costs while making no sacrifice in price. In practice, firms transfer at market prices where possible. However, market value pricing has certain disadvantages. It might involve the seller in selling below current actual unit cost. It might mean prices change with every change in market price, making budgetary control for both buyer and seller very difficult. In practice, however, the main situation where market value is not used is when it cannot be, because no open market exists, since the product is of a very specialised nature.

Standard cost-plus pricing

Actual costs cannot be used wisely for transfer prices. If they were, all the disadvantages mentioned above apply and, in addition, selling divisions have no incentive to control product costs, as any cost increases can be passed on to the buying division. If high unit costs reflect gross inefficiency and idle time, actual cost pricing is perceived as unfair by the buying division. Moreover, it encourages group-wide costs to run over budget and jeopardises corporate profit objectives.

Transfers at standard cost impose cost control discipline on selling divisions and enable buying divisions to plan with the security of certain prices for transferred inputs. A mark-up is added to standard cost to provide the selling division with an interest in making the sale. Such a mark-up has to be virtually uniform throughout the group to be perceived as fair, but a uniform mark-up could well mean wide variations in divisional ROCE. Low asset holding divisions benefit from uniform mark-up policies; highly capitalised divisions suffer and will resist their performance being evaluated in ROCE terms in the face of uniform mark-ups.

Shadow pricing

Transfers could follow LP rules and be based on shadow prices plus actual costs of resources used per unit of output—that is, on minimum prices as per pages 235–6 above. If cost volume profit relationships are all linear, such "minimum" prices should maximise overall group profit. LP can be used to identify the optimum volumes for given transfer prices. LP with applied economics can be used to delineate the price zone where the MC of the buying division equals the MR of the selling division. In theory, LP pricing techniques offer the most efficient solutions to the divisional transfer pricing problem in terms of overall group profits. That LP very rarely provides the basis of transfer prices in the real world reflects the instability and non-linearity of cost volume relationships and the high initial costs of identifying all the relevant cost data. As computers become more and more involved in management decisions rather than merely in record keeping, it is possible that LP pricing techniques will become more accepted.

Negotiated prices

If divisions are free to negotiate transfer prices with one another, the resultant agreements may not be in the group's interest even though they satisfy the two divisions involved. They may be different from LP minimum price and from market price. Negotiated prices depend also on the divisions involved being able to reach agreements. Valuable managerial time can be wasted in fruitless negotiations. This time would have been saved if any of the other bases for transfer pricing had been used. Disagreement is especially likely if either side expects a change in the market price of the product soon, or if the two divisions are unequal in bargaining power, so the weaker is sensitive to the possibility of being exploited by the stronger.

Profit-sharing approach to transfer pricing

Introduction

The transfer pricing bases outlined above have been largely orientated to optimising production sales and resultant group profits. A quite different approach is to prepare divisional budgets based on final product prices and input costs to the group as a whole (and, *at this stage*, to treat transfers as occurring at budgeted cost only). LP can be used to optimise output volumes for each division, bearing in mind each division's resource constraints. Cost of goods produced for sale by each division can be derived. Let us suppose that for a particular firm the resultant contribution from a given product is £150,000 and group profit after fixed costs is £100,000. We can now allocate the profit between the divisions and derive transfer prices from the results. A common method of apportionment is the Massachusetts Formula, outlined below.

The Massachusetts Formula

Let us suppose the product generating the £100,000 profit is made by three divisions in the firm—A, B and C. The profit is apportioned to each division in proportion to its:

(*a*) capital intensity;
(*b*) payroll size; and
(*c*) responsibility for sales.

Capital intensity is represented by net tangible assets, payroll by total labour cost and sales by budgeted sales to customers *outside* the group at market prices. The figures for these three categories are calculated after accounting for and eliminating the resources and sales of any by-product or service offered by one division only. The resultant figures are given in the table below.

DIVISIONS

	A	B	C	Total
	£	£	£	£
Assets	1 million	2 million	0.5 million	3.5 million
Labour costs	200,000	500,000	300,000	1 million
Sales	zero	zero	3 million	3 million

Only division C sells the product to the public, but A and B process the ingredients necessary to make it. Profit is allocated between the divisions, using the Massachusetts Formula (MF) thus:

$$\text{MF profit} = \frac{1}{\text{no of divisions}} \times \left\{ \frac{\text{divisional}}{\text{total}} \text{ assets} + \frac{\text{divisional}}{\text{total}} \text{ labour cost} \right.$$

$$\left. + \frac{\text{divisional}}{\text{total}} \text{ sales} \right\} \times \text{total profit}$$

Applying the MF to our example gives the results tabulated below.

$$A \ \pounds\tfrac{1}{3} \left(\frac{10}{35} + \frac{2}{10} + \frac{0}{3} \right) \times 100,000 = \quad 16,190$$

$$B \ \pounds\tfrac{1}{3} \left(\frac{20}{35} + \frac{5}{10} + \frac{0}{3} \right) \times 100,000 = \quad 35,714$$

$$C \ \pounds\tfrac{1}{3} \left(\frac{5}{35} + \frac{3}{10} + \frac{3}{3} \right) \times 100,000 = \quad \underline{48,096}$$

$$\text{Total} \quad \underline{\underline{\pounds100,000}}$$

Transfer pricing from the MF
The transfer prices derived from the profit allocations above are quite easily calculated. They are simply unit divisional costs plus unit share of allocated profit. Let us assume that C sells 8,095 units to the public and that unit conversion costs are £4 for each division except for A, which has conversion costs of £2 and material costs of £2. The transfer price of output from A to B is £4 plus allocated profit of £2 per unit = £6. Complete results are tabulated below.

	A	B	C
	(£)	(£)	(£)
Unit cost from last process	nil	6.00	14.41
Unit materials + conversion costs	4.00	4.00	4.00
Profit allocation per unit*	2.00	4.41	5.94
Transfer price of goods conveyed to next process	6.00	14.41	24.35

*Computed thus: A $\frac{16,190}{8,095}$ = £2, B $\frac{35,714}{8,095}$ = £4.41, C $\frac{48,096}{8,095}$ = £5.94

C's transfer price of £24.35 is the budgeted sales price of finished product units. The MF technique is predicated on the assumption that strong central management dictates budgets (on LP principles) and from its master budget arises a group profit from each product, of which central management can dictate the allocation to each division. The more differentiated and decentralised the group is, the more difficult will it be to enforce any central rule—such as MF-based transfer prices. The technique is used in some large American corporations and does offer a way of sharing profits among divisions on a rational basis. There is no requirement to use assets, payroll and sales in order to weight the apportionment. Other measures could be used instead or in addition if central management desire, in the interests of fairly reflecting the factors most influencing divisional profit-earning capacities.

SUMMARY

(a) Break-even volume is found by dividing total fixed costs by unit contribution. Break-even sales value can be found by dividing total fixed costs by the contribution:sales value. The safety factor of actual sales is the difference between break-even and actual sales volumes divided by actual sales volumes.

(b) Break-even charts depict fixed (type 1) or variable (type 2) costs, total costs and sales price. From all break-even charts, break-even volumes and margins of safety can be easily read, but only from type 2 charts can we read contribution directly.

(c) Contribution analysis can be applied to decisions about accepting new orders, using spare capacity or extending existing capacity, stopping production of specific products and finding an optimum sales price. These decisions involve balancing the costs, including opportunity costs, of taking a particular course of action against the increased contribution to profits in order to derive the net benefit or net loss.

(d) Management can see the entire final accounts in a break-even chart. They may prefer the simpler message of the PV chart, which has only one line—the contribution line. The PV chart can be combined with a curve showing the relative probabilities of achieving various levels of sales volume. If such a curve is a normal one, we can use normal distribution tables to determine the probability of achieving a given level of sales (at most or at least).

(e) When one limiting factor exists, profits are maximised if the product mix maximises returns per unit of the limiting factor. Products are ranked in descending order of return to the limiting factor. Production is allocated first to the product with the highest such return, then to the product with the next highest, and so on.

(f) When more than one limiting factor exists, graphical linear programming shows us the optimum product mix in a two-product case. The exact quantities to be produced of each product can be found by solving the simultaneous equations of the two innermost constraint lines of the feasible region.

(g) Classical economics tells us that costs are minimised when we produce the volume which has marginal cost equal to average cost. Profits are maximised at the price and volume dictated by the point where marginal cost equals marginal revenue. Profits can be further increased by discriminatory pricing which charges a higher price for peak demand than for off-peak demand.

(h) Many firms price on a cost-plus basis because the data needed for cost-plus pricing are easily available. Other techniques, notably those derived from economics, are more theoretically valid.

(i) Transfer pricing is a difficult matter. Market value is the predominant basis, but where no market price is available, cost plus, or negotiated prices, tend to be used. LP-based prices are theoretically more valid for allocating resources optimally but harder to implement in practice. Profit apportionment via the MF formula enables transfer prices to be calculated that share group profits on a centrally planned basis.

QUESTIONS

1. Which of the techniques discussed in Chapter 8 do not depend on the assumption of linear cost volume relationship?

2. Constrast the coefficient of variation with the variable z needed to use normal distribution tables. Which measure is more useful?

3. What is the relationship between operating leverage and safety factors?

4. (a) What is a shadow price?

   (b) Has everything got a shadow price?

   (c) What is the use of knowing a shadow price?

5. Why are profits maximised when marginal cost equals marginal revenue?

6. Advise the directors of a new firm of building contractors how its tenders should be priced.

7. When should a group's central board of directors favour negotiated prices as the method of transfer pricing?

8. In what circumstances do you advise a firm to base its transfer pricing on the Massachusetts Formula approach?

9. (a) Is opportunity cost a notional cost or a cash cost?

   (b) Why are opportunity costs not recorded in ordinary ledgers?

   (c) In what sense could all costs be considered to be opportunity costs?

10. Discuss the significance of corporate policy on finished goods stock levels to price and volume decisions.

For numerical questions, see numbers 28–33 in Appendix V.

CHAPTER NINE

Capital Expenditure Appraisal

It is better to have hen tomorrow than an egg today.
Thomas Fuller

OBJECTIVES

(*a*) To be able to take all the necessary steps in order to appraise proposals for capital expenditure in a business context.
(*b*) To understand the uses and limitations of the main project appraisal techniques.
(*c*) To understand the effects of inflation on project appraisal and be able to quantify them.
(*d*) To comprehend the nature and effects of risk and uncertainty on project appraisal.
(*e*) To understand the uses and limitations of the main risk-handling techniques, especially sensitivity analysis, decision trees and mean variance analysis.
(*f*) To be able to handle the effects of capital rationing.
(*g*) To understand the role of portfolio theory in appraising a set of risky projects.
(*h*) Generally to comprehend the special problems and techniques involved in capital expenditure.

INTRODUCTION

Recognition of capital

Capital expenditure appraisal concerns decisions as to whether or not to undertake specified capital projects. A project is a capital project if it displays one or more of the following characteristics.

(*a*) *Fixed asset purchases.* For the project to be undertaken, it will be necessary for the firm to buy a new factory or new equipment or new offices or new machine attachments, or acquire a business that already owns the relevant assets.
(*b*) *Financial outlay.* For the project to be undertaken, the firm will have to spend money it would otherwise not have spent. If in a will Mr Smith leaves his factory to Growth Ltd, it constitutes a "free gift" to the firm and the newly acquired property is thus not a capital project.
(*c*) *Significant outlay on the Capital Account.* The financial outlay on the project must be for either new fixed assets as in (*a*) above or new holdings of shares in another business, and it must cost enough for the appraisal exercise to be worthwhile. This means that outlay on stocks, components, raw materials and overheads, however large it may be, does not bring the expenditure into the category of capital projects because the above are all

ordinary Profit & Loss Account items—that is, they are on Revenue Account not Capital Account. It also means that spending, say, £500 on new office furniture is excluded because the sum is too small to justify the staff man-hours involved in the appraisal exercise. Not all capital projects are susceptible to the appraisal methods to be described in this chapter. For capital expenditure appraisal to be applied to a project a fourth condition is necessary, namely (d) below.

(d) *Identifiable income and expenditure on Revenue Account*. This means that the project must be one whose material, labour and expense costs can be estimated, and also one where income flows are expected from new production or new services offered to customers. This condition excludes a large number of capital projects in the public sector of the economy such as bridges, roads, state hospitals and state schools, because these projects do not charge the users the "full economic rate". In other words, they have little or no income on Revenue Account to set against their revenue costs or capital costs. Such projects are evaluated using cost-benefit analysis, and that is not generally thought to be a management accounting technique but rather one of applied welfare economics, so it is regrettably beyond the scope of the present book.

The role of the management accountant in project appraisal

The most important function of the management accountant in industry is to provide information that managers can use for making effective and efficient decisions about the firm's resources. The preparation of the annual budget and monthly operating statements is the prime example dealt with so far of the management accountant's output to his employers. It will be recalled that the master budget includes summary data about capital expenditure planned to occur during the budget period. It is usual in industry for each cost centre to be allowed to spend on the Capital Account up to a specified sum in any one month (say £1,000) without its needing to go through full project appraisal procedures. Such small items of capital expenditure are controlled similarly to overheads, in that there is a set limit to accumulated capital expenditure on small items that the cost centre manager is forbidden to exceed. Capital items above the set limit will be subject to the full project appraisal procedure. Here the management accountant will be responsible both for the design of the appraisal system in the firm and for the detailed financial appraisal of each large project proposed by cost centre managers. He will design the appraisal forms, ensure that line managers understand the system and be responsible for slotting in the figures.

The management accountant gathers the data concerning all the income and expenditure expected to arise from the project, applies appraisal techniques to those figures, and forwards completed appraisal forms to the finance director for the approval or rejection of the board. If the board approves the project, it becomes part of the capital budget for the year.

In many firms the project will have to be approved twice by the board: first, as part of the capital budget; and second, during the year when the board may refuse permission for the project to begin because of circumstances unforeseen when the budget was prepared.For example, a sudden cash crisis could arise, causing a stop on all new capital expenditure. Thus it is not uncommon for a project to be approved for starting in year 1 as part of year 1's capital budget but for it never to start at all or to start in year 2 or later.

The figures relevant to a capital project will be:

(*a*) the capital outlays in each year;

(*b*) the revenue outlays in each year and the resultant net profit; and

(*c*) the costs of financing the capital outlay (such as bank interest), which are always segregated from the other revenue outlays.

Basic appraisal techniques

In the simplest appraisal technique total outlays are merely deducted from total inflows. If the result is that inflows exceed outflows, the project is worthwhile. Table I shows six different projects, all worthwhile except number 4 which breaks even only while the rest have net inflows. The question of which project is the most attractive is not quite so easy. Below are the possible choices with reasons.

(*a*) Project 1, as it costs less than the others at only £350,000.

(*b*) Project 2, as its inflows are nearest to being the same every year, so it is perhaps the safest investment.

(*c*) Project 3, because its net return of £2 million is $2\frac{1}{2}$ times its capital cost of £800,000—a better return than any other project.

(*d*) Project 6, because its net return of £3 million is bigger than the return from any other project.

TABLE I.   SIX CAPITAL PROJECTS

Projects	(£000s—all figures net)					
	1	2	3	4	5	6
(Outflows)/Inflows						
—first day	(350)	(500)	(800)	(1,000)	(1,000)	(5,000)
Year 1	100	50	400	(500)	(250)	(1,000)
Year 2	150	200	600	–	250	–
Year 3	250	250	800	500	500	3,000
Year 4	250	250	1,000	1,000	750	–
Year 5	250	–	–	–	1,000	6,000
Total inflows	1,000	750	2,800	1,500	2,500	9,000
Total net inflows	650	250	2,000	–	1,250	3,000

Using the simplest basic appraisal technique gives us four different best projects from a total of six projects under consideration. This is not very helpful as a guide to the board as to the best decision it should take. It seems that more sophisticated techniques are required, and we shall now turn to these.

Average rate of return (ARR)

The average rate of return technique is almost as simple as the basic technique and is still quite widely used because of its simplicity. The technique consists of the following steps.

(a) Tabulate the capital outlays for each year of the project.

(b) Divide the total capital outlay by the number of years over which it takes place in order to obtain the average annual capital outlay. (N.B. Year 1 is treated as one full year *after* day one.)

(c) Tabulate net inflows on revenue account for each year.

(d) Total the net inflows and divide that total by the number of years of project life in order to obtain the average annual return.

(e) Divide the average annual return by the annual average capital outlay, and then multiply the resultant decimal by a hundred in order to obtain the percentage average annual rate of return.

Table II applies these steps to the projects in Table I.

The project with the highest average rate of return is project 3 at 87.5 per cent, so it is "best" by this technique. Another interesting result is that

TABLE II.   AVERAGE RATES OF RETURNS

Projects	*1*	*2*	*3*	*4*	*5*	*6*
			(£000s)			
Step 1—Capital outlay, day 1	350	500	800	1,000	1,000	5,000
Capital outlay, year 1	–	–	–	500	250	1,000
Step 2—Total capital outlay	350	500	800	1,500	1,250	6,000
Number of years outlay	1	1	1	2	2	2
Average annual outlay	350	500	800	750	625	3,000
Step 3—Inflows year	100	50	400	–	–	–
year 2	150	200	600	–	250	–
year 3	250	250	800	500	500	3,000
year 4	250	250	1,000	1,000	750	–
year 5	250	–	–	–	1,000	6,000
Step 4—Total inflows	1,000	750	2,800	1,500	2,500	9,000
Project life in years	5	4	4	4	5	5
Average annual return	200	187.5	700	375	500	1,800
Step 5—Average annual return	200	187.5	700	375	500	1,800
Average capital outlay	350	500	800	750	625	3,000
Return as % of outlay	57	37.5	87.5	50	80	60
i.e. the annual average rate of return						

the break-even project, project 4, is now showing a very respectable 50 per cent rate of return. This is because its capital outlay occurs on day 1 and in year 1, so that its total outlay has been halved in order to obtain an average outlay. The reason for this is that day 1 is treated as being the present day while year 1 is treated as being one year ahead, so that outlay in year 1 is *assumed* to occur one full year after the present day. The percentage rates of return shown by all six projects seem very attractive compared with a return of less than 15 per cent from a bank deposit account or 10 per cent from the dividend yield on an ordinary public company share. Clearly the projects all seem good investments using this technique, but the technique ignores the break-even nature of project 4 and says nothing at all about the risks associated with each project.

Payback period

The purpose of the payback period technique is to discover how long it takes each project to generate enough inflow in order to recoup the initial outlays. The time taken to recoup is termed the "payback period", and it is desirable for it to be as short as possible. The longer the payback period, the longer is money tied up in the project and the greater the chances of adverse circumstances jeopardising project profitability.

Calculating payback is very easy.

(*a*) Step 1. Total the capital outlays.

(*b*) Step 2. Deduct from total capital outlay, first the year 1 inflow (if any), then year 2, then year 3 and so on until the result of any further deductions will be negative. The number of years' inflow deducted so far will be the payback period in years.

(*c*) Step 3. Take the next year's inflow and divide it into the balance of capital outstanding from step 2. The result of this division is the fraction of a year to be added to the payback period in step 2 to give the *exact* payback period. This process is called "interpolation".

Once again the six projects from Table I are used to calculate payback periods as shown below. It is recommended that particular attention be paid to step 3—the interpolation step—as it is easier to understand this process by example rather than from the verbal description just given. Notice that interpolation for projects 2 and 4 was not strictly necessary, as their payback periods came at the end of years 3 and 4 respectively, so there was no real need to use step 3 at all on those projects.

Project 3 has the shortest payback period, so it is the "best" project by this technique, just as it was by the average rate of return technique.

All six projects had uneven flows—that is, the flow in any one year was not the same as the flow in every other year. In Table IV are three projects with even flows. Such projects are termed "annuities".

The importance of annuity projects is that a constant relationship exists between their average annual rate of return and their payback period,

TABLE III. PAYBACK PERIOD

				(£000s)		
Projects	1	2	3	4	5	6
Step 1—Total capital outlays	350	500	800	1,500	1,250	6,000
Step 2—Deduct inflows—Year 1	100	50	400	–	–	–
—Balance	250	450	400	1,500	1,250	6,000
Deduct year 2 inflow	150	200	600	–	250	–
—Balance	100	250	Neg.	1,500	1,000	6,000
Deduct year 3 inflow	250	250	800	500	500	3,000
—Balance	Neg.	Zero	Neg.	1,000	500	3,000
Deduct year 4 inflow	250	250	1,000	1,000	750	–
—Balance	Neg.	Neg.	Neg.	Zero	Neg.	3,000
Deduct year 5 inflow	250	–	–	–	1,000	6,000
—Balance	Neg.	Neg.	Neg.	Zero	Neg.	Neg.
(x) Year of first negative balance	3	3	2	4	4	5
(y) Year before that	2	2	1	3	3	4
Step 3—Interpolation Inflow in year x	250	250	600	1,000	750	6,000
Balance end of year y	100	250	400	1,000	500	3,000
Balance ÷ by inflow	$\frac{2}{5}$	1	$\frac{2}{3}$	1	$\frac{2}{3}$	$\frac{1}{2}$
Payback in years from y above	2	2	1	3	3	4
Balance ÷ by inflow	$\frac{2}{5}$	1	$\frac{2}{3}$	1	$\frac{2}{3}$	$\frac{1}{2}$
			1 yr 8 m		3 yrs 8 m	4 yrs 6 m
Exact payback period	2.4 yrs	3 yrs	8 m	4 yrs	8 m	6 m

(N.B. Two-thirds of a year equals 8 months; $\frac{1}{2}$ a year equals 6 months.)

namely: the average rate of return of an annuity is the reciprocal of its payback period. Thus:

for A:2 = 1 ÷ $\frac{1}{2}$(50% as a fraction)

for B:1.6 = 1 ÷ $\frac{1}{0.625}$ (62$\frac{1}{2}$% as a fraction)

TABLE IV. ANNUITIES

		(£000s)	
Projects	A	B	C
Initial capital outlay	1,000	2,000	3,000
Annual inflow	500	1,250	750
Project life in years	4	4	8
Total inflow by project end	2,000	5,000	6,000
Net inflow (basic technique)	1,000	3,000	3,000
Average annual rate of return	50%	62$\frac{1}{2}$%	25%
Payback period	2 years	1.6 years	4 years

and:

$$\text{for C:} 4 = 1 \div \tfrac{1}{4}(25\% \text{ as a fraction})$$

Conversely:

$$\text{for A } \tfrac{1}{2} = 1 \div 2$$
$$\text{for B } \tfrac{5}{8} = 1 \div 1.6$$
$$\text{for C } \tfrac{1}{4} = 1 \div 4$$

This means that it does not matter for annuities whether one uses average rate of return or payback period, as both methods will produce the same order of preference of projects—in this case B then A then C.

DISCOUNTED CASH FLOW

The accruals conventions and the cash-flow approach

Basic technique, rate of return and payback period constitute the simple techniques of capital expenditure appraisal. The techniques are built on financial projections of capital costs, revenue costs and revenue incomes. These costs and incomes include notional costs, such as provisions for bad debts, notional incomes, such as discounts receivable, plus all accruals and prepayments as at each year end. In addition, they will also include the very important notional revenue cost of depreciation if the fixed assets purchased for the project are intended to be replaced at the end of the project. Notional costs are any costs not represented by cash outlay, and depreciation is usually the largest of them. While it is usual for the simple techniques to be based on the accruals conventions of accounting (including all notional costs), it is not necessary for this to happen. It is quite possible, and many would argue it to be preferable, for the simple techniques to use cash flows only and therefore to exclude all accruals, all prepayments, all depreciation and all other notional items. The justification for adopting the cash-flow approach rather than the accruals approach is as stated below.

Depreciation is merely capital cost (less terminal scrap value if any) divided by the number of years of project life, so that to include it with the other revenue costs is to double count the original capital outlay. Furthermore, accruals and prepayments arise only as an accident of year end cut-off so do not really affect the continuing flows of outlays and incomes. Henceforth, therefore, we shall deal with project appraisals on a strictly cash-flow basis and shall no longer need to make a distinction between outlays on Capital Account and outlays on Revenue Account. All we shall need to know from the basic project data is the net cash flows for each year.

Discounted cash-flow techniques (DCF)

In the techniques so far considered, £100,000 receivable in year 5 has been treated identically to £100,000 receivable in year 1, as if the value of

TABLE V. COMPOUNDING

To the end of year	Initial capital (£)	10% annual interest (£)	Year end balance (£)
1	100,000	10,000	110,000
2	110,000	11,000	121,000
3	121,000	12,100	133,100
4	133,100	13,310	146,410
5	146,410	14,641	161,051

money were immune to time passing. In the real world, the purchasing power of money diminishes all the time as prices rise under the inflation endemic to our time. Even if inflation did not exist, money receivable now would be more valuable than money receivable in five years' time because there is an opportunity cost attached to waiting for it. This opportunity cost is represented by the interest that a bank would have paid by the end of five years on the money if it had been received now, or by the interest a building society or any other institution might have paid in the interval. Let us suppose that this opportunity cost of money was exactly 10 per cent per year and we wish to calculate the cost of receiving £100,000 in five years' time. We can proceed as follows.

We begin one day with £100,000. Interest at 10 per cent a year means that at the end of year 1 we should receive £10,000 interest. Our total wealth is now £110,000, the whole of which is entitled to 10 per cent interest by the end of year 2, and 10 per cent of £110,000 is £11,000. We can set this out more formally, as shown below.

In five years, our initial £100,000 has grown to £161,051—a growth of £61,051, which represents the opportunity cost of receiving £100,000 in five years' time instead of now. The sum of £100,000 *compounded* up at 10 per cent a year becomes £161,051 after five years. The converse of the previous sentence is also true—namely, £161,051 *discounted* at 10 per cent over five years gives a *present value* of £100,000.

The essence of discounted cash-flow techniques is the ascertainment of the *present value* of future cash flows by using discounting.

The present value is found either from tables (as explained on page 260) or by applying the basic discounting equation below.

$$PV = \frac{CF}{(1 + r)^n}$$

PV stands for present value
CF stands for cash flow in the year concerned
r stands for annual interest rate expressed as a decimal not a percentage
and *n* stands for the year number concerned

For example, the present value of £121,000 discounted at 10 per cent received in year 2 can be found from the equation thus:

$$PV = \frac{CF}{(1+r)_n} = \frac{121,000}{(1+0.1)^2} = \frac{121,000}{(1.1)^2} = \frac{121,000}{1.21} = 100,000$$

The net present value technique (NPV)

The most commonly encountered DCF technique is the NPV technique. This consists of simply adding the present values of all the cash inflows and deducting from them the present values of all the cash outflows. Expressing the previous sentence in an equation:

$$NPV = \sum_{n=0}^{n=x} \frac{CF}{(1+r)^n}$$

The equation is identical to the one in the previous section except that instead of dealing with only one year's cash flow, it deals with all the cash flows throughout the project's lifetime. The notation

$$\sum_{n=0}^{n=x}$$

means add up the present values

$$\frac{CF}{(1 \div r)^n}$$

from the project start, $n = 0$, to the final year (year x), $n = x$, in order to obtain the NPV of the whole project.

An alternative to the discounting formula are the discount tables which can be found in most books of statistical tables. An extract from a discount table is reproduced as Table VI. Full tables will be found in Appendixes II and III. These tables are used in the following manner. The columns refer to percentage discount rates, and the rows to years of project life. The figures in the middle of the table are the resultant *discount factors* and these give the PV of £1 discounted at the relevant per cent over the relevant number of years. So, to find the PV of £1 discounted by $7\frac{1}{4}$ per cent from year 6, we look up the column headed $7\frac{1}{4}$ and row 6 to find the result *0.6886*. This is the discount factor. To find the PV of £749 in year 6 discounted at $7\frac{1}{4}$ we multiply £749 by the discount factor of *0.886* and obtain the answer *£515.76*.

TABLE VI.   DISCOUNT TABLES EXTRACT

Discount rates	5%	6%	7%	8%	9%	10%
Years—1	0.9524	0.9434	0.9346	0.9259	0.9174	0.9091
2	0.9070	0.8900	0.8734	0.8573	0.8417	0.8264
3	0.8638	0.8396	0.8163	0.7938	0.7722	0.7513
4	0.8227	0.7921	0.7629	0.7350	0.7084	0.6830
5	0.7835	0.7473	0.7130	0.6806	0.6499	0.6209

We are now ready to use the NPV technique on a complete project. We shall assume a discount rate of $8\frac{1}{2}$ per cent. Project cash flows are as follows.

	Outflow £	Inflow £	Net cash flow (outflows in brackets)
Day 1	5 million		(5m)
Year 1	3 million	1 million	(2m)
Year 2	5 million	6 million	1m
Year 3	6 million	8 million	2m
Year 4	7 million	10 million	3m
Year 5	8 million	10 million	2m

The NPV calculation is set out in tabular form thus:

	Net cash flow (£) (a)	Discount factor (8%) (b)	Present values (£000s) (a) × (b)
Year 0	(5m)	1	(5,000)
1	(2m)	0.9259	(1,852)
2	1m	0.8573	857
3	2m	0.7938	1,588
4	3m	0.7350	2,205
5	2m	0.6806	1,361
	Total PVs – Project's NPV –		(841)

The project NPV is negative, so the project fails the appraisal test. Applying the NPV technique to the six projects in Table I (*see* page 254), discounted at 8 per cent gives the present values shown in Table VII.

Project 4, the break-even project, has negative NPV, so would be rejected. Project 3, which had the highest average rate of return ($87\frac{1}{2}$ per cent) and the shortest payback period of twenty months, also has the highest NPV. Clearly project 3 is the most attractive project.

TABLE VII.   NPV OF PROJECTS AT 8% DISCOUNT

Projects	Present values (£000s)					
	1	2	3	4	5	6
Year 0	(350)	(500)	(800)	(1,000)	(1,000)	(5,000)
1	93	46	370	(463)	(231)	(926)
2	129	171	514	–	214	–
3	198	198	635	397	397	2,381
4	184	184	735	735	551	–
5	170	–	–	–	681	4,084
NPVs	424	99	1,454	(331)	612	539

The internal rate of return (IRR)

Identification of the IRR

If the present values of a project's inflows total £2,000 and the present value of outflows is also £2,000, the project's NPV is zero. The discount rate that gave rise to the equivalence of inflow PVs to outflow PVs is the internal rate of return. The internal rate of return is also known as the "marginal efficiency of capital" and the "DCF yield". It is defined as the discount rate which causes project NPV to be exactly zero. It tells us the maximum cost of capital a project may incur without making a loss (i.e. without its NPV becoming negative). The higher the IRR the more attractive the project.

Calculation of the IRR

(*a*) Step 1. Sum the inflows, sum the outflows and express the outflows as a fraction of the inflows, e.g. if total inflows are £7,500 and outflows £5,000, the fraction required is $\frac{2}{3}$.

(*b*) Step 2. Use the fraction to determine the initial discount rate that will be used in seeking the IRR. With outflows two-thirds inflows, inflows need to be reduced by one-third to equal outflows. However, a test discount rate of $33\frac{1}{3}\%$ will be too high, as the inflows do not yet show the time related costs of money. Therefore 25 per cent is more likely to prove satisfactory.

(*c*) Step 3. Work out the project NPV using the rate from step 2.

(*d*) Step 4. If the result of step 3 is a large positive NPV, repeat step 3 using a discount rate some 3 to 5 percentage points higher than the one used first. If the result is a large negative NPV, repeat step 3 with a discount rate some 3 to 5 percentage points lower than the one used first.

(*e*) Step 5. Repeat step 4 using different discount rates until the two rates are found which give the smallest negative project NPV and the smallest positive NPV. Let us suppose we find 7 per cent gives a positive NPV of £4,000 and 8 per cent gives a negative NPV of £2,000.

(*f*) Step 6. Find the IRR by linear interpolation between the two discount rates in step 5. Thus if 7 per cent gives an NPV of £4,000 and 8 per cent gives (£2,000), the rate that gives an NPV of zero is

$$\frac{2,000}{4,000 + 2,000} = \frac{1}{3}$$

of the distance from 8 per cent to 7 per cent. The RR is $8\% - \frac{1}{3}\% = 7\frac{2}{3}\%$

IRR of the projects previously listed

The six projects considered in the preceding text will all have different IRRs. We should expect project 3, the most attractive under previously examined techniques, to show the highest IRR, and project 4 to show the lowest.

Let us suppose the company's cost of capital can rise to 20 per cent. At a discount rate of 20 per cent, projects 1 and 3 still show large positive NPVs, so their IRRs must be considerably over 20 per cent. Project 5 shows an NPV of £18 at 20 per cent so its IRR is only just over 20 per cent. Project 2 turns negative at 16 per cent and its IRR by interpolation is 15.09 per cent. Project 6 has an IRR of 10.73 per cent and Project 4 breaks even with no discounting at all, so its IRR is zero per cent. Thus only projects 1, 3 and 5 could justify a 20 per cent cost of capital.

Comparison of rankings and techniques
We can now compare the attractiveness of the six projects under the four techniques we have learnt: average rate of return (which is also known as accountants' rate of return), payback period, NPV and IRR. This is done in Table VIII.

If we wished to adopt only one project, project 3 emerges as the most attractive under all four appraisal techniques. However, if we could afford two projects, we have a problem in identifying the second most attractive one. We have two different answers to the question—which project is the second most attractive after project 3. Project 5 has an average rate of return of 80 per cent which is very good, but that is because of its very high inflows in its later years. The more uncertain we are of the future value of money, the less confidence we can repose in that 80 per cent being achieved. If our main concern is to get our money back as quickly as possible, we shall prefer to select project 1 with its payback period of 2.4 years (a full year better than project 5). However, although project 1 returns its original capital in just under $2\frac{1}{2}$ years, it does not perform very brilliantly in years 3 to 5 compared with project 5. NPV endorses the ARR ranking and makes project 5 the better bet, but IRR endorses the payback ranking and makes project 1 seem better. Payback period and IRR have an important quality in common: they are both proportional measures which do not comment on the absolute size of project reward. ARR also shares this quality. Only NPV gives us some idea of the value of a project after accounting for the opportunity cost of money. The more important absolute cash values are to us, the more inclined we shall be to prefer project 5 to project 1. However, project 5 could not show much profit if we had to finance it by a 20 per cent loan. Its NPV would then be only £18 compared with £203 for project 1. At a cost of capital of 8 per cent, project 5 is more attractive than project 1; at 20 per cent, project 1 is more

Projects	1	2	3	4	5	6
Rankings:						
ARR	4	6	1	5	2	3
Payback	2	3	1	5	4	6
NPV	4	5	1	6	2	3
IRR	2	4	1	6	3	5

TABLE VIII.   PROJECT RANKINGS

attractive than project 5. Our decision as to which one we should prefer will be greatly influenced by the actual financing costs of the two projects. If we are not sure in advance what this will be, we can use a technique called the "incremental rate of return" to help us decide between the two projects. This technique is described below.

Incremental rate of return

When NPV and IRR appraisals rank a set of projects differently, we use the incremental rate of return technique to decide which ranking is the more valid. The aim of the technique is to identify the discount rate that causes the two competing projects to show identical NPVs. This rate, the incremental rate of return, is the rate at which we are indifferent between the two projects. We find the rate by deducting the cash flows of one project from those of the other year by year. The incremental cash flows so found are then put through the internal rate of return procedure. The IRR of the incremental flows is itself the incremental rate of return for both projects. We shall illustrate the technique on projects 1 and 5 and then interpret the result.

By linear interpolation the required IRR is

$$\left(13 + \frac{6}{6 + 26}\right) \% = 13.19\%.$$

An incremental rate of return of 13.19 per cent between projects 1 and 5 means that both projects are of equal attractiveness if the cost of capital is 13.19 per cent. At costs below 13.19 per cent, project 5 is more attractive and the NPV ranking applies (which used 8 per cent discount rate, considerably below the incremental rate of 13.19 per cent). At costs of capital above 13.19 per cent, project 1 is the more attractive and the IRR ranking applies. To choose between projects 1 and 5 we need only know if our cost of capital is likely to be above or below the incremental rate of 13.19 per cent. If the cost of capital were exactly 13.19 per cent, we should prefer the IRR ranking, because any uncertainty in the cash-flow forecasts or any slight increase in financing costs should cause us to view current cost of capital as a minimum likely to be exceeded.

TABLE IX.   INCREMENTAL RATE OF RETURN

	Project cash flows		Difference—incremental CFs	Present values of ICFs	
	5	1		(at 13%)	(at 14%)
Years 0	(1,000)	(350)	(650)	(650)	(650)
1	(250)	100	(350)	(309)	(307)
2	250	150	100	78	77
3	500	250	250	173	168
4	750	250	500	307	296
5	1,000	250	750	407	390
			NPVs	6	(26)

The incremental rate technique applies to pairs of projects only, not to groups of three or more. To use it, it is therefore necessary to group projects into competing pairs. Generally, however, projects compete owing to budgetary constraints, and in pages 267–70 we shall describe the techniques appropriate for selecting projects under regimes of limited funds.

Annuities under DCF

Properties of annuities
We have already considered annuities in the context of ARR and payback period. Annuity payback period is simply the reciprocal of annuity ARR. The NPV of an annuity is given by the following equation:

$$P_0 = \frac{R[1 - (1 + i)^{-n}]}{i}$$

where:

P_0 is annuity present value
R is the annual cash flow (which is constant for an annuity)
i is the interest or discount rate
n is the number of years the annuity lasts

For example, the present value of £2,000 net annual inflows for eight years at 10 per cent is:

$$£2,000 \frac{[1 - (1.1)^{-8}]}{0.1} = £10,670$$

We could have obtained the same result by using the table in Appendix III. This table gives "cumulative present value factors", often called "annuity factors". It is used just like the present value factor table in Appendix II, in that columns are for discount rates and rows are for years.

IRR calculations are easier for annuities than projects with irregular cash flows. As we have seen, normal project IRR calculations involve tedious searches for discount factors for each year of project life. With annuities we need only look up the row for the final year of the project to find the factor by which to multiply the annual cash flow so as to obtain project present value. Thus examination questions on IRR calculations tend to use annuities rather than normal projects, just to ensure candidates have enough time to finish the question!

IRR annuity example
Given an initial outlay of £100,000 and a five-year annuity inflow of £25,000 per year, we are required to find project IRR. The annuity factor we require will multiply 25,000 by just enough to equal exactly 100,000. The required factor is obviously 4. To find the discount rate that yields an annuity factor of 4 in year 5, we look up row 5 in Appendix III and note the two factors nearest to 4. Linear interpolation then yields the IRR,

thus:

	Annuity factor year 5	Discount rate
	4.100	7%
	3.993	8%
Difference	0.107	1%

$$\text{IRR} = 7\% + \tfrac{7}{107}\% = 7.07\%$$

Delayed annuities

Sometimes examinations specify that either cash flows or discount rates will be constant for a limited time, then change. In these circumstances we divide the project into its component annuities and discount the cash flows by the appropriate annuity factors for each part. For example, to find the annuity factor at 8 per cent for constant cash flows from years 4 to 8 inclusive, we simply subtract the annuity factor for year 3 from that for year 8 and treat the result as the annuity factor required.

For instance, in years 1 to 3 £2,000 a year will be received. Thereafter £3,000 a year will be received to the end of the project in year 10. Cost of capital is expected to be 8 per cent to year 5, but 10 per cent from year 6. NPV is calculated in Table X.

Perpetuities

An annuity that continues indefinitely is called a "perpetuity". In evaluating quoted companies, the dividend or the earnings are often regarded as perpetuities. Loans usually have to be repaid so are rarely perpetuities (except for undated loans to government such as $3\tfrac{1}{2}\%$ War Loan bonds). Projects like new factories have definite life expectancies. Companies, however, could theoretically go on for ever. The present value of a perpetuity is simply the annual inflow divided by the discount rate (as a decimal). So if a company has maintainable annual earnings of £2 million and the applicable cost of financing an investment in, or take-over of, the company is 20 per cent, the present value of the company is £2

TABLE X.   DELAYED ANNUITIES

Years	Final CPV* factor	Initial CPV* factor	Difference	Annual inflow (£)	Present value (£)
1–3	2.577	nil	2.577	2,000	5,154
4–5	3.993	2.577	1.416	3,000	4,248
6–10	6.145	3.791	2.354	3,000	7,062
			PV of inflow		16,464
			Initial outflow		10,000
			Project NPV		6,464

*CPV = Cumulative present value

million ÷ 0.2 = £2 million × 5 = £10 million, and that is the price a bidder would be prepared to pay to acquire the company—many other things being equal.

CAPITAL RATIONING

Single period capital rationing

Divisible projects
Capital rationing always applies in the real world but applies only sometimes in accounting examinations. It is a situation where project selection is limited by the amount of cash available. Assuming projects may be started at any point in the year, capital rationing can be handled by delaying start dates so that outflows do not exceed cash limits. For example, if the most attractive project has an outlay of £2 million but we have only £1.5 million to spend this year, we can defer £$\frac{1}{2}$ million of the outlay until next year. This is something we can do only if the project is financially divisible—that is, if there is no requirement that the outlay all occurs on day 1 (year 0).

Given capital rationing and six proposals for projects along the lines of the six projects we compared earlier, we have to rank the projects in descending order of attractiveness. We have already seen that the four evaluation techniques gave four different rankings. We noted that only NPV took absolute size of the projects explicity into account. However, even NPV does not take account of the limiting factor—money. We need a technique that will tell us the returns per unit of limiting factor. This we can obtain by computing the inflows per £ of outflow—at present values. The result is termed in some quarters the "profitability index", and in other quarters—including the present volume—the "benefit cost ratio" (BCR). The BCR is simply the PV of inflows divided by the PV of outflows, all discounted at a common rate. Table XI computes the BCRs at 8 per cent for the six projects with which we have already become acquainted.

TABLE XI.   PROJECT BCRs

Projects	1	2	3	4	5	6
PV of inflows (£000s)	774	599	2,254	1,132	1,843	6,465
PV of outflows (£000s)	350	500	800	1,463	1,231	5,926
BCR	2.21	1.20	2.82	0.77	1.50	1.09
Ranking	2	4	1	6	3	5

Coincidentally the BCR ranking is identical to the IRR ranking in Table VIII. This is only a coincidental result.

We use the BCR rankings to maximise the returns per £ of outflow under capital rationing as shown in Table XII. The BCR minus one gives the return per £ of outflow, £1.82 for project 3, but only 9p for project 6.

TABLE XII.   ALLOCATION OF FUNDS TO PROJECTS

Cash limit year 0	Projects selected
£1,000,000	3—outlay £800,000 plus $\frac{4}{7}$ of 1—outlay £200,000 (other $\frac{3}{7}$ deferred)
£3,000,000	3, 1, 5 and 2—outlay £2,650,000 plus 7% of 6—outlay £350,000
£5,000,000	3, 1, 5 and 2—outlay £2,650,000 plus 47% of 6—outlay £2,350,000
£10,000,000	3, 1, 5, 2 and 6—outlay £7,650,000. Invest the balance in quoted securities rather than project 4, which has a BCR of less than one.

Indivisible and complementary projects

The reader may be relieved to learn that we shall now leave the six projects behind for the rest of the chapter. Not all projects are divisible; some must be fully financed on day 1. Such indivisible projects cannot be part undertaken, but must be wholly adopted or wholly deferred. Other projects, called "complementary projects", may be undertaken only if another project is as well. For example, one cannot extend a factory without first building the factory. Nor can one invest in specialised tools and dies without also investing in the right machine for them to fit.

Table XIII lists seven projects in descending order of BCR, but we cannot select them in strict BCR order because so many of them are indivisible or complementary.

TABLE XIII.   INDIVISIBLE AND COMPLEMENTARY PROJECTS

Project	BCR	PV outflows (£)	PV inflows (£)	Initial outlay (£)	Remarks
A	5	3 million	15 million	3 million	Complementary to F
B	4	6 million	24 million	5 million	Complementary to G
C	3	10 million	30 million	8 million	Indivisible
D	2.5	1 million	$2\frac{1}{2}$ million	1 million	Indivisible
E	2	4 million	8 million	4 million	Indivisible
F	1.5	10 million	15 million	8 million	
G	0.8	10 million	8 million	8 million	

Because A cannot be undertaken without F nor B without G, Table XIII cannot be used for project selection. We should consider A and F as a single project and B and G similarly. Project AF has inflow PV of 30, outflow PV of 13, which gives a BCR of 2.31. Project BG has inflow PV of 32, outflow PV of 16 and a BCR of 2.

The revised ranking is as follows.

Project	BCR	Initial outlay (£)
C	3	8m
D	2.5	1m
AF	2.3	11m
E	2	4m
BG	2	13m

If we have between £9 million and £20 million available, we select C, D and AF. AF is divisible subject to our not undertaking A without also undertaking F. However, if we have less than £8 million we cannot undertake project C, as it is indivisible. We have to go to the next one on the list, D, and spend the rest of our allowance on AF.

In the following list all projects are indivisible.

Project	BCR	PV inflows	PV outflows	Initial outlay
		£	£	£
I	3.2	32m	10m	10m
II	3	30m	10m	5m
III	2.5	50m	20m	15m
IV	2	40m	20m	5m
V	1.5	$7\frac{1}{2}$m	5m	5m

If we have less than £10 million but more than £5 million to spend, we take project II. If £10 million to £15 million, project I. At £15 million we take I and II. At £20 million we take either I, II and IV or II and III. To decide which group is better, we have to see if the aggregate BCR of I, II and IV is better or worse than that of II and III. Since project II is common to both selections, we can ignore it and need only compare the BCR of III, 2.5, with the combined BCR of I and IV. Combined inflow PV is £72m and combined outflow PV is £30 million, so the BCR is 2.4. As this is worse than III's BCR of 2.5, the better use of our £20m is on projects II and III rather than on I, II and IV.

The above grouping procedure is almost always required in examination questions on capital rationing.

Multiple period capital rationing
When money for capital expenditure is limited in successive periods, the restraint imposed on each year's outlay is amenable to linear programming treatment. If only two projects are involved and both are fully divisible, we can use graphical LP to indicate to optimum mix in each year. For example, a firm can invest in trucks and/or cars to fulfil its transport needs for a particular purpose. Data for the problem follow.

	PER VEHICLE (£)	
	Cars	Trucks
NPV	200	500
Year 1 outlay	200	100
Year 2 outlay	100	300
Undiscounted total costs	300	400

Funds available: year 1—£40,000; year 2—£30,000

The objective function is $2c + 5t$ (c for cars, t for trucks) and this has

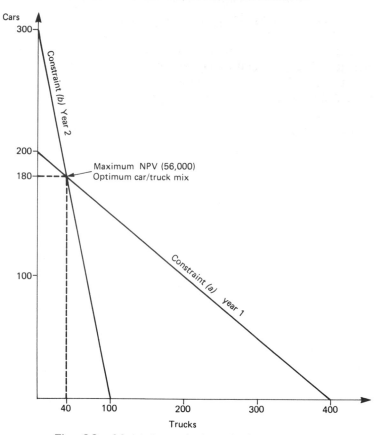

Fig. 23. *Multiple period capital rationing.*

to be maximised to obtain maximum overall NPV. The constraints are:

(*a*) year 1: $2c + t \leq 40{,}000$; and
(*b*) year 2: $c + 3t \leq 30{,}000$.

The graph of this problem is shown in Fig. 23 above. From Fig. 23 we can see that NPV is maximised (at £56,000) with 180 cars and 40 trucks being purchased. We could add further constraint lines for future years and derive a new optimum mix.

For more than two projects, simplex LP would need to be used.

RISK MEASUREMENT

Risk, uncertainty and inflation

Certainty and causes of uncertainty
Cash flows in project appraisal are all estimates and, like all estimates, they are subject to error. The techniques described so far take no account

of the possibility of forecasting error. Such errors will occur in real life because:

(*a*) inflation reduces the value of money, increases interest rates and costs;

(*b*) demand is never wholly predictable and inflow forecasts must therefore be regarded as less than certain; and

(*c*) many costs are time based, but the time taken to complete a project can be affected by unforeseen bad weather, inefficiency or idle time of any sort.

Risk and uncertainty

Uncertainty means we do not know what will happen. In this sense everything is uncertain, as we can never be 100 per cent confident than any forecast will turn out exactly as specified. In a narrower sense uncertainty means we cannot even specify the probabilities attached to various possible outcomes. A third meaning of uncertainty is that we do not know which of several outcomes will happen, but we are quite certain that one of them will. In this, and only in this, sense we can quantify uncertainty through the attribution of probabilities.

Risk, in common parlance, is almost synonymous with danger—or more precisely, with the possibility of danger. In the actuarial world of insurance companies risk is measured by previous frequency of a given danger. If six out of every 100 cigarette smokers die before the age of fifty, there is a 6 per cent chance that any smoker will not reach fifty and his life assurance premiums will be appropriately higher than those of non-smokers. The risk that a given forecast will not be achieved, however, cannot be based on past frequencies, as each new forecast is unique. Instead we have to use *subjective* probabilities and attribute to each possible outcome a guess as to its probability of occurrence. The actual measurement of risk is a topic we shall analyse in pages 274–7.

Inflation in project appraisal

Constant rate inflation

Let us consider a project whose initial outlay is £100,000 and which yields £35,000 every year for five years. Cost of capital is 10 per cent. The NPV of the project will be (£35,000 × CPV factor for 10%, year 5) less £100,000 = £32,685. However, let us now suppose 5 per cent inflation is expected to persist throughout the next five years. The purchasing power of the £35,000 annual inflow will be 5 per cent less every year and the project's *real* NPV has been overstated in our previous calculation. The discount rate has to be raised to incorporate inflation. The raised discount rate is termed the "*monetary* cost of capital" as opposed to the *real* cost of capital we have used so far. The formula for finding monetary cost of capital is as follows:

$$(1 + m) = (1 + r)(1 + i)$$

where m is the monetary cost of capital
r is the real cost of capital
and i is the inflation rate.
In our example, r is 10%, i is 5%, so
$$(1 + m) = (1 + 10\%)(1 + 5\%)$$
$$= 1.1 \times 1.05$$
$$= 1.155$$
$$\therefore \quad m = 15\tfrac{1}{2}\%$$

Applying the monetary cost of capital to the annuity above we multiply £35,000 by 3.313 to obtain £115,955. Project NPV falls from £32,685 to £15,955—that is, by over 50 per cent.

Increasing rates of inflation

Retaining the same annuity project as above, we shall add the complication that inflation is expected to increase by 1 per cent every year from 5 per cent in year 1. We can tackle this either by calculating five different monetary costs of capital for each of the five years and discounting each year separately. The trouble with this approach is that it will yield discount rates not easily handled by conventional present value tables. For example, in year 3, monetary cost of capital will be 17.7 per cent—a rate not conveniently handled by interpolation.

An alternative approach is to recalculate the purchasing power of the £35,000 to reflect the inroads of increasing inflation and then discount the results by the 10 per cent *real* cost of capital. This is done in Table XIV.

TABLE XIV.   INFLATION ADJUSTED PROJECT APPRAISAL

	Inflation rates		*Value of money as % of year 0 value*	*Cash flow* (£)	*Year 0 purchasing power* (£)	*PV factor* (£)	*PV* (£)
Year	*Annual*	*Cumulatively compounded**					
0			100%	(100,000)	(100,000)	1	(100,000)
1	5%	5%	95%	35,000	33,250	9,091	30,228
2	6%	11.3%	88.7%	35,000	31,045	8,264	25,656
3	7%	19.1%	80.9%	35,000	28,315	7,513	21,273
4	8%	28.6%	71.4%	35,000	24,990	6,830	17,068
5	9%	40.2%	59.8%	35,000	20.930	6,209	12,995
					Project NPV =		7,220

*To obtain these figures, multiply the annual rate by the previous year's cumulative rate, e.g. year 2's 11.3% × year 3's 7%—1.113 × 1.07 = 1.191, so year 3's cumulative rate is 19.1%.

Differential inflation rates

A project has an initial outlay of £1 million and lasts five years. Real cost of capital is 5 per cent. Sales are forecast at £1 million a year but prices will be raised 10 per cent every year to pass on the effects of cost inflation. Labour costs are forecast at £300,000 a year but are expected to rise by 12 per cent a year. Material costs are £100,000 a year but inflate at 5 per cent. Expenses and overheads are £200,000 but inflate at 8 per cent. We are required to calculate project NPV.

In this case we need four monetary costs of capital reflecting four inflation rates. We apply the formula $(1 + m) - (1 + r)(1 + i)$ thus:

$$\text{Sales:} \quad (1 + m)_S = 1.05 \times 1.1 = 1.155 \quad \therefore \quad M_S - 15\tfrac{1}{2}\%$$
$$\text{Labour:} \quad (1 + m)_L = 1.05 \times 1.12 = 1.176 \quad \therefore \quad M_L = 17.6\%$$
$$\text{Materials:} (1 + m)_M = 1.05 \times 1.05 = 1.1025 \quad \therefore \quad M_M = 10\tfrac{1}{4}\%$$
$$\text{Expenses:} \quad (1 + m)_E = 1.05 \times 1.08 = 1.134 \quad \therefore \quad M_E = 13.4\%$$

Cumulative PV factors from Appendix III for year 5 give us the basis for linear interpolation as follows.

Rate	CPV factor nearest below	CPV factor nearest above	Difference	Interpolation	Required CPV factor CPV below less interpolation
M_S 15$\tfrac{1}{2}$%	(15) 3.52	(16) 3.274	0.078	0.039	3.313
M_L 17.6%	(17) 3.199	(18) 3.127	0.072	0.043	3.156
M_M 10$\tfrac{1}{4}$%	(10) 3.791	(11) 3.696	0.095	0.024	3.767
M_E 13.4%	(13) 3.517	(14) 3.433	0.084	0.034	3.483

Applying the above to the project to obtain the NPV:

		£	£
PV of sales inflow	3.313 × £1 million		3,313,000
Less			
PV of labour costs	3.156 × £300,000	946.800	
PV of material costs	3.767 × £100,000	376.700	
PV of expenses	3.483 × £200,000	696.600	
PV of revenue costs			2,020,100
equals			
PV of net inflows			1,292,900
Less initial outlay			1,000,000
gives Project NPV			292,900

Alternatively we could have deflated the cash flows year by year and applied the real cost of capital, as we did in page 272. This would have involved more work and so opened up greater possibilities of arithmetical error than adopting the method used above.

Interpolation of discount factors as above is not absolutely accurate and factors do not decrease *linearly* with discount rate increases, but in most real life (and all examination) situations the amount of error arising from linear interpolation of discount factors can safely be regarded as immaterial. In real life situations a computer program would eliminate even those errors.

Risk

Certainty equivalents
We learnt in Chapter 8 how to calculate expected values, standard deviations and coefficients of variation in the context of sales volumes. Precisely the same calculations can be made in the context either of cash flows or the present values of cash flows. When a project has a variety of possible cash-flow streams to which we can attach subjective probabilities, the *expected* NPV of the project is the sum of the discounted cash flows' "certainty equivalents" for all outcomes. Certainty equivalent is a phrase with two meanings. One derives from utility theory and is dealt with below. The other simply means the result of multiplying a cost or income by the decimal probability attached to it. Thus the certainty equivalent of an 0.05 chance of winning £1 million is £1 million × 0.05 = £50,000. Utility theory posits that £50,000 is the certainty equivalent of a 5 per cent chance of obtaining £1 million only for the person to whom the certainty of £50,000 and a 5 per cent chance of £1 million really are equivalent. In such a case the person would be just prepared to stake £50,000 on the 5 per cent chance of winning £1 million.

Utility theory
Let us consider two projects, I and II. Project I has an 80 per cent chance of success which would yield an NPV of £1 million, but also has a 20 per cent chance of failure with an NPV of £minus 2 million. Its expected NPV is (£1 million × 0.8) − (£2 million × 0.2) = £400,000 (positive). Project II has an 80 per cent chance of success as well, but the associated NPV is only £$\frac{1}{4}$ million, while the 20 per cent chance of failure means a negative NPV of £$\frac{1}{2}$ million. The expected NPV is £100,000.

Although the expected NPV of project I is four times greater than that of project II, a prudent business man will nevertheless prefer project II. This is because it is far easier to recover from a loss of £$\frac{1}{4}$ million than from one of £2 million. This example shows how capital expenditure decisions are so affected by attitudes to risk that a minority chance of a large loss can be more important than a majority chance of a large profit. In this case a £1 of negative NPV is more important to the decision-maker than a £1 of positive NPV and has therefore a larger utility. This situation is portrayed in Fig. 24 below.

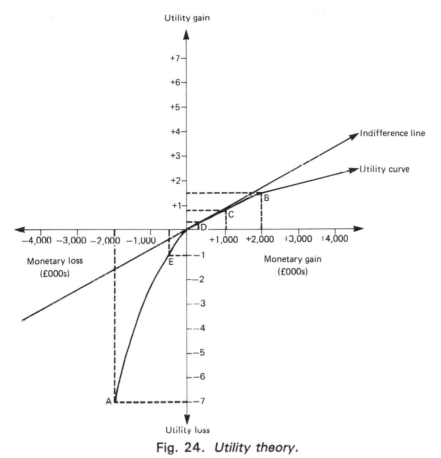

Fig. 24. *Utility theory.*

The indifference line shows what the utility curve would have looked like if the decision-maker regarded every £1 of NPV as equal to every £1, whether negative or positive. The actual utility curve is much steeper than the indifference line for negative NPVs and much less steep for positive NPVs. £1 saved from loss-making projects has a far higher utility than £1 made from profitable ones. This "risk averse" utility curve is widely held to represent how firms actually view risk in real life.

TABLE XV.   PROJECT APPRAISAL AND UTILITY THEORY

Project	Outcome £	Outcome utility	Probability	Weighted utility
I	+ £1m	+ 0.75 (point C)	0.8	+ 0.6
I	− £2m	—7 (point A)	0.2	− 1.4

Sum of utilities is negative at − 0.8, so reject the project.

Project	Outcome £	Utility	Probability	Weighted utility
II	+ £¼m	+ 0.25 (point D)	0.8	+ 0.2
II	− £½m	− 1 (point E)	0.2	− 0.2

Sum of utilities is non-negative at zero, so II is preferable to I,

Applying Fig. 24 to project evaluation, we look up the utilities of the two outcomes, weight them by their probabilities, then total the results to obtain project utility. This is done in Table XV.

Mean variance analysis

If business men do not act on expected values alone, they need from the management accountant some idea as to the risk inherent in, or the uncertainty associated with, the expected or mean NPV. Utilities are subjective and not amenable to external measurement. The variability of the NPV under different conditions is used instead. The principal measure of such variability is the standard deviation of all the possible outcomes around the mean (i.e. the expected) NPV. Dividing the standard deviation by the expected NPV gives us the project coefficient of variation. A risk-averse management will select projects with the lowest coefficients of variation. Note that the calculations are all probability weighted, so the resultant expected NPV represents not the most probable outcome but the best estimate of the actual outcome. The standard deviation represents the uncertainty (in the third sense) of that outcome, and the coefficient of variation represents the "riskiness" of the project.

If the probability distribution conforms to the bell-shaped curve of the normal distribution, we may translate the standard deviation into its z value and look up the probability of the NPV being less than a specific figure, often zero. Readers who have forgotten what any of these terms mean are recommended to turn back to pages 227–30 before proceeding further.

Mean variance analysis of capital projects involves the computations described above. The results can be graphed as shown in Fig. 25.

Projects A and B both have the same expected NPV of £5,000. B's NPV could be as low as £2,000 or as high as £8,000. A's NPV could be as low as minus £2,000 or as high as £12,000. A is clearly the riskier of the two and risk-averse management will prefer project B, *even though maximum possible profits are lower than A's*. This is a very important assertion. It means profit maximisation has been constrained by risk aversion, indeed dominated by it. It is a basic assumption of management accountancy and of financial management that such dominance occurs. It reflects the utility theory postulate that loss avoidance has higher utility than profit-seeking. To put it another way, it is held more important to survive (avoid loss) than (unstably) to grow.

Project C has an expected NPV of £10,000, twice that of project B, but it has a huge probability spread and may even make a loss. The comparison of B and C is rather like our comparison of projects I and II above. Risk averse management will select B over C because:

(*a*) B will certainly not make a loss, C might;
(*b*) B's coefficient of variation is far below C's; and

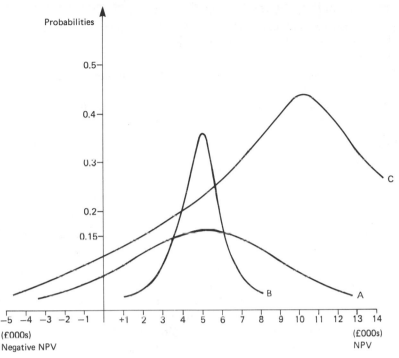

Fig. 26. *Mean variance analysis.*

(*c*) C's greater possibility of high profit does not compensate risk averse management adequately for the previous two points mentioned.

Given that risk exists and mean variance analysis can help identify its extent, the next question is how management can handle risks, which is the subject discussed below.

RISK HANDLING

Sensitivity analysis

Sensitivity to risk

Sometimes uncertainty is so bad that it is impossible to ascribe even faintly valid probabilities to possible alternative streams of cash flow. We have to make a best guess, then see how sensitive the project is to forecast error at any point. Such sensitivity is measured by the percentage change necessary in any cost or income to reduce project NPV to zero. The cost or income with the smallest percentage change is the one requiring the tightest control, as it is the one most likely to subvert the project forecast. It is the one to which the project is most sensitive and it is thus the item with the greatest risk.

Sensitivity analysis calculations

A project with £100,000 initial outlay has the following revenue costs and sales on an annuity basis over five years.

	Annual flows £	CPV factor (10%)	Present values £		Project NPV ÷ item PV
Sales	150,000	3.791		568,650	2.4%
Materials	60,000	3.791	227,460		6%
Labour	40,000	3.791	151,640		9%
Expenses	10,000	3.791	37,910		35.9%
Total costs	110,000	–		417,010	
Profit	40,000	–			
				151,640	
Initial outlay				100,000	51.6%
Project NPV				51,640 ÷ 3.791 = £13,622	

This is the sum by which annual sales would need to fall, or any cost item to rise, to reduce project NPV to zero. The final column tells us the project's sensitivity to each of the listed items. Since the project is an annuity, the percentage changes in present value given apply also to the undiscounted cash flows. Sales is the most sensitive item because these need fall by only 2.4 per cent to wipe out the project's profitability. A 5 per cent forecasting error on sales volume could therefore be fatal to the project. Since an error of such small magnitude is by no means unlikely, the project looks rather too risky at present.

Sales or initial outlay are usually the most sensitive items. Sales almost always are with annuities. This is not surprising, since they are the largest value item cumulatively, so NPV will represent a smaller proportion of sales than of anything else. Nevertheless, sensitivity analysis is not justified by telling us the obvious—that the largest item is the most sensitive one—but rather by telling us *exactly how sensitive various items are to normal forecast error*. A sensitivity of less than 10 per cent on any item might well cause risk-averse management to reject the project.

Risk, inflation and discount rates

If project A is thought to be twice as risky as project B but subjective probabilities cannot readily be applied for some reason, project appraisal literature is not silent on techniques for handling the situation. Project A's greater risk can be reflected either by halving its cash flows before discounting or by doubling the discount rate. This punitive treatment of project A's figures is supposed to reflect the *opinion* that A is twice as risky as B. Unfortunately the adoption of either technique will cause a more than twofold effect on the differential NPVs. Let us suppose A and B have identical cash flows and lifetimes, with initial outlays of £100,000, constant annual net cash inflows of £40,000 and five-year lifetimes—

exactly like the projects considered earlier. Project NPV at 10 per cent discount is £13,730. Risky project A is now deemed to have cash inflows of only £20,000 a year and these have a present value of £56,865, which is far below the £100,000 initial outlay and yields a negative NPV of £43,135. The new NPV is slightly below the size of the old one but in the opposite direction—a strange reflection of its being only two times as risky. The situation is little better if we discount A's cash flows by 20 per cent instead of 10 per cent. The annuity factor at year 5 for 20 per cent is 2.991, which gives a present value of the £40,000 annual profit as £119,640 and NPV of £19,640. This NPV is considerably less than half the size of the original one. Once again, although A is only twice as risky as B, B has an NPV (the original figure computed of £51,640) well over twice that of A. This is because discounting magnifies differences between projects more and more as cash flows recede further and further into the future. Project A is thus being more than doubly penalised for being doubly risky. Neither the inflated discount rate technique nor the reduced cash-flow technique can be defended as being fair or reasonable. Far better in this situation is it to present a brief verbal report with the DCF calculations explaining why A is thought to be riskier than B and why subjective probabilities cannot usefully be ascribed. Since sales are the most sensitive item, the report should pay particular attention to the possible causes of failure in order to achieve sales forecasts in the case of each project.

Abandonment value analysis
If at, say, year 3 of a project its remaining net cash inflows are discounted to give a present value of, say, £20,000, but the tangible assets involved in the project have an immediate resale or scrap value of £30,000, it pays the firm to abandon the project and sell the assets. By so doing, it will be £10,000 better off. This is a technique for determining the opportunity cost of continuation. It is seldom useful before a project is selected, as it is rare that future resale values of assets can be forecast. The risk that the abandonment value of a project may exceed its "going concern" value is one that should be considered by the management accountant as early as possible, even if it cannot initially be quantified. Projects involving expensive materials or plant of rapidly rising replacement value are especially vulnerable to the possibility of gains from abandonment. Abandonment value calculations are necessary in repair or replace decisions, as we shall see in pages 285–6.

Decision trees
To use decision trees we must be able to ascribe both £ values and subjective probabilities to all the possible final outcomes. Examination questions always give both; real life seldom clearly reveals either.

Let us consider a decision whether or not to invest in factory capacity in order to rectify spoilage. That is our primary decision and is represented by decision point 1 in Fig. 26 below. If we decide to rectify the spoilage, the rectification has to pass quality control. Even after installing the specialised machinery, we gauge there to be only a 50 per cent chance of the material passing quality-control tests. This is represented by outcome point A. If the material fails quality control, we can abandon it and lose £100,000, which we would have to write off, or alternatively we can sell the materials as scrap. This decision is made at decision point 2B. The sales of scrap can face high, medium or low demand, as shown at outcome point C.

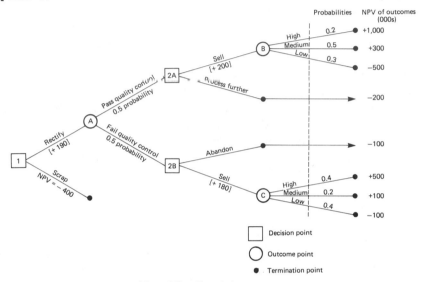

Fig. 26. *Decision tree.*

If the material passes quality control we have to decide whether to process it further or sell it "as is", and this decision is represented by decision point 2A. If we sell it, the possible outcomes are as shown right of outcome point B.

We are given the NPVs of all the possible outcomes and their probabilities. These are shown to the right of the dotted line in Fig. 26. We draw the decision tree first, put in the probabilities and outcome NPVs next and then, finally, evaluate the decisions. Such evaluation is always done by starting at the right-hand side of the tree and systematically working leftwards until we arrive at decision point 1.

The calculations involve simply finding the expected value of each decision. The expected value is of course the sum of the certainty equivalents (in the *non*-utility theory sense) of each outcome. Thus the expected value of selling material at point 2A = (1,000,000 × 0.2) + (300,000 × 0.5) + (0.3 × minus 500,000) = £200,000 positive. The expected values are placed on the appropriate branches of the decision tree and the results of this are shown within square brackets in Fig. 26.

At 2A the better decision is sell, as its expected value is +200, whereas processing further has a cost (negative value) of 200. At 2B the better decision is also sell, as +180 is better than −100. At outcome point A we evaluate the effect of having chosen to sell at 2A or 2B. The value of rectifying at decision point is (0.5 × +200) + (0.5 × +180) = +190, and as this greatly exceeds the NPV of scrap at −400, we recommend investment in the rectification plant. As we move left along the decision tree we ignore the values of the decisions we did *not* make—namely, processing further at 2A or abandonment at 2B.

The decision tree technique helps management make decisions in complex situations, is frequently required in examination questions, but suffers from the important limitations in practice imposed by the need to know (or guess accurately) the probabilities and values of all ultimate outcomes. It can be too readily manipulated at the right-hand side both on values and on probabilities in order to justify a decision that management want to make on "intuitive" grounds. Its validity depends quite critically on the accuracy of its ascribed probabilities and ultimate outcome values. It is therefore a technique whose sophistication is apt to disguise its tendentiousness.

Game theory

The minimax rule for costs
Although game theory is beyond the scope of this book, it is sufficiently important to the question of handling risk for a brief outline of two of its procedures to be given here. Suppose a firm is choosing one project from three possible ones and has prepared figures showing three possible total costs for each project under pessimistic, neutral and optimistic assumptions. The highest costs will, of course, be the most pessimistic. The maximum cost is minimised by selecting the project whose maximum cost is lower than that of the other two projects. The maximum cost is thus minimised.

The maximin profit rule
Similar to the minimax cost rule is the maximin profit rule. A matrix is drawn up of profits (or NPVs) for each project with different outcomes, based on different assumptions about the market, shown in columns. We

TABLE XVI. MAXIMUM PAY-OFF MATRIX

| | *Net present values under outcomes* | | | |
	I	II	III	*Minimum*
Projects A	90	10	50	10
B	300	200	− 10	− 10
C	15,000	5,000	− 2,000	− 2,000

then select the project showing the highest (maximum) of the minimum profits shown. Table XVI shows an example of this.

Project A is selected under the maximin rule because the worst it can threaten is a positive NPV of 10, whereas B and C could incur losses. It can readily be seen that the rule favours extreme risk aversion and is open to the criticism that the probabilities of the outcomes are not given. If outcome II is only 10 per cent likely, outcome III 5 per cent but outcome I 85 per cent, even quite conservative management might well opt for project C with its NPV of 15,000.

The minimax regret rule
If we select project A under the maximin profit rule but outcome I takes place, we have suffered an opportunity loss of 14,910 by not selecting project C. We may construct a regret matrix to highlight possible opportunity loss. We do this using the profit pay-off matrix above and subtracting each figure from the highest figure in the same column. Thus the entry row project A outcome I is 14,910. The regret matrix in full is as follows.

TABLE XVII.   REGRET MATRIX

	Net present values under outcomes			
	I	*II*	*III*	*Minimum*
Projects A	14,910	4,990	0	14,910
B	14,700	300	60	14,700
C	0	0	2,010	2,010

The project offering the smallest possible maximum regret—the minimax regret—is C, and we select this project rather than A. This does, of course, expose us to the possibility of an opportunity loss of 2,010 if outcome III occurs, but that is a much lower exposure than choosing A or B if outcome I occurs (and significantly lower than A or B under outcome II).

PORTFOLIO THEORY

Risk and diversification
All the techniques described in the preceding pages had certain limitations and none of them actually reduced risk itself; they merely enabled us to recognise risk and take defensive measures. The most important defensive measure we can take is to diversify. If we are in the business of selling hot dogs, our sales will show great seasonal variation with high sales on cold days but low sales on hot days. Sales will show a high coefficient of variation and investors may be deterred from buying our shares because of our business risk. If we diversify into sales of ice-cream, our sales pattern should stabilise, because on hot days we shall sell more ice-cream and on cold days more sausages. Our sales variability will decrease and with it our business risk and relative unattractiveness to shareholders.

In project appraisal we can apply the same approach. If we have three projects and wish to select only two, we choose the two whose cash-flow patterns are least alike. Consider Table XVIII.

TABLE XVIII.   CASH FLOWS FOR THREE PROJECTS

Projects	I	II	III
Years 0	(100)	(100)	(50)
1	–	(50)	150
2	–	–	500
3	300	400	200
4	500	600	50

We can see that the timing of cash flows for projects I and II is quite similar. Projects I and II together would show larger variation and therefore larger risk than either of them combined with project III. To decide which one should be combined with project III, we add their cash flows individually to those of project III and see which looks more attractive. This is done below.

TABLE XIX.   COMBINED CASH FLOWS

Years	0	1	2	3	4
Projects I and III	(150)	150	500	500	550
Projects II and III	(150)	100	500	600	650

Projects II and III together offer greater rewards, but only in years 3 and 4. Projects I and III are better in year 1. The higher the cost of capital, the more attractive is year 1 compared with years 3 and 4. The choice will therefore depend on the cost of capital: the higher it is, the more inclined we shall be to prefer I and III over II and III.

Share acquisitions and portfolio theory

An important reason for capital expenditure can be to acquire shares in other companies, with a view to reducing business risk or simply to make working capital more profitable. If we intend to hold over 5 per cent of the shares in any one company, the investment is of a capital nature. The optimum set of investments will be the set that offers the highest aggregate return for the lowest aggregate risk. In other words, we should choose investments with the best coefficients of variation. These will be the most "mean variance efficient" investments we could choose.

At any one time there is a unique set of investments that offers the greatest return for a given risk. In Fig. 27 the crosses indicate the returns (capital gain plus dividends) and the risk (standard deviation of the returns) for any one investment or portfolio (group) of investments. An investment has a greater return for a given risk than any investment vertically below it. It has a lower risk for the same return than any investment horizontally to the right of it. The most mean variance efficient investments at different levels of risk are those on the upper boundary. This

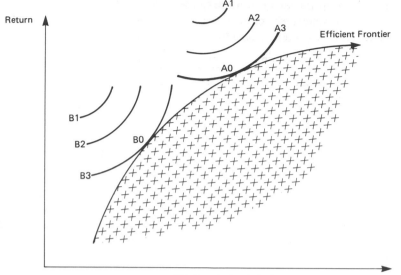

Fig. 27. *Portfolio theory. The crosses indicate any investment or portfolio. The A and B curves are investor indifference curves.*

boundary is called the "efficient frontier". The portfolios and investments on it are the "best" (most return per unit of risk) currently available.

The investor should select his investment portfolio from one on the efficient frontier. The particular one to choose depends on the investor's degree of risk aversion. Indifference curves can be drawn for an investor showing the combinations of risk and return he regards as being equal. Investor A regards any combination along curve A1 as of equal utility but prefers A1 to A2 and A2 to A3 because A1 offers higher return per unit of risk than A2 or A3. However, A1 and A2 lie in an area where no *actual* investments exist, as they all lie on or below the efficient frontier. A3 is the best investor A can do, and where A3 just touches the efficient frontier is where A's best investment lies. This is at point A0 and it uniquely defines A's optimum portfolio of investments. Investor B is far more risk averse than A, so his indifference curves are steeper and further left than A's. B's optimum portfolio lies at point B0. B0 offers lower returns than A0, but B does not mind that as he is unwilling to take the risks associated with being at A0.

Portfolio theory thus defines the optimum portfolio—the group of investments offering the highest return per unit of risk consistent with the individual investor's risk tolerance. Portfolio theory is sometimes called the "Markowitz model" after its creator.

Capital asset pricing model
An extension of portfolio theory was developed in the mid-1960s, termed the "capital asset pricing model". It is generally considered a central topic

of financial management rather than a peripheral topic of management accountancy. However, it does have some important postulates on project risk. The key measure of risk in the model is beta, a coefficient of the covariance of an investment's return with that of the stock market as a whole. If a security has a beta of 2, it means when the market as a whole shows a 2 per cent better return than before, the investment will show a $2 \times 2\% = 4\%$ better return. Such beta risk is important because the model specifies that beta risk is endemic to the stock-market system and such "systematic" risk cannot be diversified away. The risks that can be diversified away by prudent selection of investments whose returns show mutual negative correlation are called "alpha risks" or "unsystematic risks". It is alpha risks that we have dealt with here. Alpha plus beta should equal portfolio standard deviation or total risk. Thus, in the context of capital expenditure on buying shares, alpha and beta are both important measures of risk itself and also important indicators of how risk can be handled (by diversifying alpha and requiring a fair reward for accepting beta).

DECISION ACCOUNTING APPLICATIONS

Repair or replace decisions

Principles
A decision closely associated with project appraisal is the decision whether to repair or replace ageing assets. This decision really involves finding the optimum replacement interval for assets—that is, their true economic life. We want to *minimise* the present value of future costs. The replacement interval that does this is the optimum one.

Example
Table XX shows the maintenance costs and scrap (or abandonment) value of a machine over each of its maximum of four years' lifetime. The initial outlay is £20,000. First, we compute the present values of the differential costs associated with keeping the machine for different periods from one year to the full four years. In year 1 we can scrap the machine for £12,000 or maintain it for £6,000, so we have a differential cost of retention of $6,000 - 12,000 = -6,000$. In year 2 we have $8,000 - 9,000 = -1,000$; in year 3 +4,000; and in year 4 +10,000. These are tabulated in Table XXI.

TABLE XX. REPLACEMENT DATA

Years	0	1	2	3	4
Maintenance costs (£)	—	6,000	8,000	10,000	12,000
Scrap value (£)	—	12,000	9,000	6,000	2,000

TABLE XXI.   DIFFERENTIAL COSTS OF DIFFERENT RETENTION PERIODS

		Life		
Year	1 year	2 years	3 years	4 years
0	20,000	20,000	20,000	20,000
1	(6,000)	6,000	6,000	6,000
2		(1,000)	8,000	8,000
3			1,000	10,000
4				10,000

The present values of the differential costs at 10 per cent cost of capital are as follows. For:

(a) one year PV   = 14,545;
(b) two years PV = 24,629;
(c) three years PV = 32,817; and
(d) four years PV = 46,166.

To compare these present values in order to assist us in our repair or replace decision, our next step is to find the equivalent annuity (constant annual sum) which gives a present value equal to continuing cycles of one-year replacement, two-year replacement, etc. The *annual equivalent annuity factor* is found in statistical tables (or given, in examination questions) and is entered in the middle column of Table XXII below. We finally multiply the present values found above by the annual equivalent annuity factors in order to obtain the actual value of the annual equivalent annuity. The replacement cycle with the smallest equivalent annuity is the least expensive to us and represents our optimum replacement interval. In this case it is three years.

TABLE XXII.   EQUIVALENT ANNUITIES

Replacement interval	Present value of one cycle	Annual equivalent annuity factor	Value of equivalent annuity
Years	(£)	(from tables)	(£)
1	14,545	1.1000	16,000
2	24,629	0.5762	14,191
3	32,817	0.4021	13,196—lowest
4	46,166	0.3155	14,565

Lease, hire-purchase or buy decisions

Principles

As with repair or replace decisions when we have to choose between leasing, hire-purchase or buying (usually financed by a loan), our objective is to select the option that maximises NPV. We perform NPV appraisals of each option as if each option were a different project. That would be easy enough, but in this area the complication usually introduced is taxation.

Taxation and DCF

Tax charges, reliefs and allowances, together with any government grants, are relevant cash flows in DCF computations of different methods of financing an asset.

Capital allowances should be entered as inflows at the end of the year of purchase (i.e. year 1). Corporation tax on year x profits should be entered as an outflow in year $x + 1$. Tax saved on lease payments and the interest portion of hire-purchase payments is entered in the year subsequent to the payment and at the amount saved. Thus interest of £2,000 in year 2 will save in year 3 £1,000 at a 50 per cent tax rate, £800 at a 40 per cent rate or £1,200 at a 60 per cent rate. Grants are inflows in the year received, and terminal scrap value is an inflow in the final year subject to corporation tax the year *after* the end of the project.

Example

A machine costs £20,000 and has a five-year life with a £5,000 residual value. It will generate net cash flows of £5,000 a year for five years before accounting for tax or financing costs. The decision to acquire has already been made. It can be purchased with an 18 per cent bank loan, leased at £5,000 a year for each of the five years and payable in advance or acquired on hire-purchase for an initial deposit of £7,000 and subsequent year end payments of £4,000. The interest element in the instalments in years 1 to 5 are respectively, £2,000, £1,500, £1,300, £1,000 and £700, according to the finance company. Corporation tax is 50 per cent, corporate cost of capital 10 per cent, and a grant of 20 per cent of cost is available with the purchasing option.

The present value of the buying option is found by tabulating its associated *relevant* cash flows and discounting them at the after-tax cost of borrowing (50% of 18% = 9%). *Corporate cost of capital is irrelevant because the decision to acquire has already been made.*

		BUYING		
Year	*Item*	*Cash flow (£)*	*PV factor (9%)*	*PV (£)*
0	Outflow	(20,000)	1	(20,000)
0	Grant	4,000	1	4,000
5	Residual value	5,000	0.6499	3,250
6	Tax on residual value	(2,500)	0.5963	(1,491)
			PV =	(14,241)

Note that interest and project cash flows are ignored. The former is taken care of by discounting the project at the after-tax interest cost *and* by applying the same discount rate to the other two financing alternatives. The latter is ignored, as project cash flows are common to all three forms of financing and we are concerned only with the cash flows that are unique to each financing method—that is, with the *differential* cash flows.

LEASING

Year	Item	Amount (£)	(C)PV factor (9%)	PV(£)
0–4	Subsequent payments	(5,000)	3.240	(16,200)
1–5	Annual tax savings	2,500	2.973	7,433
			PV =	(8,767)

HIRE PURCHASE

Year	Payments (£)	Tax savings (50% of interest) (£)	Residual value and tax (£)	(C)PV factor (9%)	PV (£)
0	(7,000)	–		1	(7,000)
1–5	(4,000) a year			2.973	(11,892)
1		–	–	–	
2		1,000		0.8417	842
3		750		0.7722	579
4		650		0.7084	460
5		500	5,000	0.6499	3,574
6		350	(2,500)	0.5963	(1,282)
				PV =	(14,719)

Note that the grant is not available under the hire-purchase option but the advantage of trade in value is.

Leasing has the lowest negative NPV—that is, the highest present value of its net differential costs, so we advise the firm to lease rather than buy or hire-purchase.

THE PHILOSOPHY OF PROJECT EVALUATION

In this chapter we have considered a variety of techniques for assisting management to decide which projects to select for capital expenditure. In practice many firms believe the future to be so uncertain and forecasts so subject to error that they adopt the payback period method on the grounds that the sooner their capital outlay is returned, the safer they are. A slightly more sophisticated approach works out the payback period using present values rather than cash flows and the project with the lowest "DCF payback period", as it is called, is selected.

The accountants' rate of return method (ARR) enables the project to be easily compared with other applications of capital money, such as investment in shares. However, it is not as popular as the payback period because it does not tell management how long their money is tied up.

DCF techniques are used by large firms and other firms with computer facilities, but it is not clear that decisions are made according to the results of these techniques rather than to the reassuring payback method. Forecasts are made of cash flows, but the use of probabilities to assess and handle risk seems less widespread. The subjective element in ascribing probabilities is the culprit here. Risk-handling techniques help clarify thinking, however, by enabling firms to work out the consequences of alternative *assumptions* about the chances of various outcomes. We have seen the importance of risk aversion in managerial evaluation of the results of risk-handling techniques.

Portfolio theory is not widely used in management accounting in industry, although mutual negative correlation of project cash flows is regarded as important. In stock-market analysis of share investments, however, the capital asset pricing model is widely used and some stockbroking firms regularly calculate the beta risk of heavily traded shares.

The extent to which a firm prefers one technique to another and the investment it makes in the acquisition of forecasting data are a specialised topic in themselves, dealt with briefly in Chapter 10. Project appraisal is an area where academics and examinations are rather ahead of real life practitioners, it seems. This is partly explained, no doubt, by the fact that practitioners have to live with the results of misspecified probabilities and values, whereas examination candidates and their lecturers do not.

Nevertheless, lip-service is almost universally paid to DCF techniques and risk-handling methods. Even communist countries use them to appraise the present value of capital projects. They should perhaps best be regarded as aids to clarifying and quantifying thoughts about the future rather than as authoritative prophecies of what the future will bring.

SUMMARY

(*a*) Four basic techniques are used to appraise capital expenditure: the average or "accountants'" rate of return, payback period, net present value and internal rate of return.

(*b*) The DCF techniques, NPV and IRR, take explicit account of the time value—the opportunity cost—of money. Cash flows are discounted at the applicable cost of capital to obtain NPV, while the IRR gives us the maximum cost of capital we can afford to incur.

(*c*) When money for capital expenditure is scarce, projects must be ranked in descending order of return per £1 of outlay. The BCR, benefit cost ratio, does this and is found by dividing the PV of inflows by the PV of outflows. For multiperiod rationing, LP techniques are useful.

(*d*) Risk is measured by the standard deviation of possible NPVs about the mean or expected NPV. The coefficient of variation (standard deviation over mean) shows project riskiness in a single figure.

(e) Sensitivity analysis highlights the extent to which cash-flow streams are exposed to risk. Decision trees assist us to make decisions between projects if we have confidence in the ultimate outcome values and their attributed probabilities. Risk adjusted discount rates are a poor way of handling general risk, but inflation adjusted discount rates are a good way of handling the effects of inflation risk.

(f) Portfolio theory tells the optimum investment in shares to make *given* knowledge of investor indifference curves and the identity of the shares and portfolios of shares along the efficient frontier.

(g) The optimum replacement interval for an asset can be found by computing the annual equivalent annuities of the present values of the differential costs of the alternative replacement period. Annuity equivalent factor tables are required to do this.

(h) Taxation is relevant in deciding between leasing, buying and hire-purchase. Often on such decisions rest the relative tax advantages of different forms of financing. *All* financing forms are discounted at the most expensive form of financing given—implicit lease interest, hire-purchase interest or bank interest. Project cash flows are irrelevant in so far as they are common to all financing forms.

(i) Although DCF and the risk techniques associated with it are more precise and sophisticated than the payback period technique, the latter retains its popularity, since firms regard forecasts as too subject to uncertainty for sophisticated techniques to be relied on confidently. In particular, the ascription of subjective probabilities is an area regarded by many firms with considerable reserve.

QUESTIONS

1. Justify the practical use of the NPV technique to a firm that is still wedded to payback period appraisals.

2. Apart from inflation, what else contributes to the time value of money?

3. In what respects is there any meaningful difference between the concepts of risk and uncertainty?

4. When can there be such a thing as an *objective* probability in forecasting cash flows, if ever?

5. If the probability distribution of a project's outcomes is normal, specify how you would compute the chances of its having a BCR of at least 2.

6. Why is the utility of £1 of negative NPV likely to be higher than the utility of £1 of positive NPV?

7. Which techniques described in Chapter 9 are valid and useful even when the future is almost wholly unpredictable?

8. How would you guard against the dangers of telling management

what it wishes to hear when ascribing outcome values and probabilities at the right-hand end of decision trees?

9. How far do the arguments advanced in Chapter 6 in favour of planning justify the use of subjective probabilities?

10. Some academic accountants believe that "true" value is net present value. Discuss the case for and against this belief.

For quantitative questions, see numbers 34–8 of Appendix V.

Evaluation and Evolution in Management Accountancy

Seek simplicity and distrust it.
Whitehead

OBJECTIVES

(*a*) To perceive the overall range of management accountancy.

(*b*) To become acquainted with the problems currently being studied on the frontiers of the subject.

(*c*) To ponder what are the essential elements in management accountancy.

(*d*) To develop further skills in control and decision accounting.

(*e*) To revise the principles of costing.

(*f*) To revise the key concepts in management accountancy.

(*g*) Generally to round off previous studies as a possible foundation for tackling the more rigorous material listed in Appendix VI.

SEMANTICS AND COSTS

Introduction

The purpose of this final chapter is to integrate the material dealt with in previous chapters. In so doing, loose ends will be tied up and underlying patterns in management accountancy will be suggested. We begin by reviewing costing and its rules, then we review and extend our study of decision accounting, and next consider recent developments in control accounting. We move on to look at new areas being explored in the literature of management accountancy and then try to identify the core concerns of the subject. Finally, we discuss briefly the goals and future direction of management accountancy.

Semantic analysis of costs

Synonyms and antonyms generally

Costs have so many different descriptions that some firm guidance is needed, else one can find oneself not being able to see the wood for the trees. To assist revision, this section reviews all the main types of cost, and orders them in a logical sequence. First, there are the classifications that apply to all costs. Table XXIII lists these costs and briefly describes the criteria for deciding whether a given cost is in the first category or the second. All the costs in the table are mutually exclusive. A cost is either in the first category or the second but cannot be in both at once *in any given context.*

TABLE XXIII. MUTUALLY EXCLUSIVE COSTS

Categories 1 2	Criteria
Direct or indirect	*Direct,* if no arbitrary apportionment of the cost to a unit or centre is necessary.
Variable or fixed	*Variable,* if total cost increases as production *or* sales volume increases.
Product or period	*Product,* if charged to cost units and finished stocks.
Functional or general	*Functional,* if arising exclusively from a management functional area such as marketing.
Revenue or capital	*Revenue,* if cost is wholly used up in one year or less either in production or services.
Notional or cash	*Notional,*if no immediate cash outflow is involved—exemplified by depreciation.
Avoidable or unavoidable	*Avoidable,* if accurate foresight would have prevented the cost from being incurred.
Controllable or uncontrollable	*Controllable,* if the head of the cost centre has the authority and means to affect the size of the cost.
Discretionary or committed	*Discretionary,* if cost can be varied by management decision. Examples: advertising, consultancy fees.

Special contexts
Next are listed those costs that apply only to specific contexts. Table XXIV gives the context, the pairs of opposites and the criteria for deciding to which class a given cost belongs.

TABLE XXIV. SPECIAL COST CONTEXTS

Context	Class 1 or 2	Criteria
Decision accounting	Sunk or relevant	*Sunk,* if cost already occurred at the time a decision is to be made.
Repair or replace	User or replacement	*User cost* is the full cost of retaining the asset.
Optimisation	Marginal or average	*Marginal* is total cost of x units less total cost of x minus 1 units.

TABLE XXIV. SPECIAL COST CONTEXTS

Context	Class 1 or 2	Criteria
Process costing	Common or post separation	*Common,* if cost occurs before separate end-products can be recognised.
Control accounting	Allowed or actual	*Allowed,* if cost equals budget adjusted for actual volume, or if it equals standard cost.
CVP analysis	Incremental or marginal	*Incremental,* if directly attributable fixed costs arise from the units, project or centre under review.
Decision accounting	Differential or total	*Differential* costs are the results of subtracting costs of one project from costs of its competitor for funds.
Optimisation and decision accounting	Opportunity	*Opportunity* costs are *both* the incremental costs arising from a projector product *and* the contribution lost by not undertaking a given alternative project or product.

Costing methods and techniques

Listed below are the types of costing methods and techniques appropriate for various types of product or service, by way of reviewing the material covered in Chapter 3.

SUMMARY OF COSTING METHODS

Costing method	Appropriate context
Job costing	No two cost units alike.
Batch costing	Products made to customer order.
Uniform costing	One product made in a single process.
Operating costing	Uniform service offered, with no variation in service unit permitted.
Contract costing	Large jobs subjected to written contracts and often lasting more than a year.
Process costing	A sequence of manufacturing processes irrespective of the number of end-products.

Marginal costing	When fixed cost apportionment to cost units is considered too arbitrary or too constraining in its effects on pricing.
Absorption costing	When it is important to price so as to ensure overheads are fully recovered from units sold.
Standard costing	When cost units or activities are sufficiently uniform to enable a standard to be evolved for control purposes.
Differential costing	When a comparison is required of two alternative uses of a set of resources.
Opportunity costing	Ideally, in all decision accounting contexts.

Costing rules

Here we shall review briefly the costing rules first stipulated in Chapter 3.

The Causative Rule (CR)

Costs should be charged against their causes. Thus externally invoiced expenses such as telephones and electricity should be analysed then debited against the cost centres incurring them in so far as this is possible. The CR provides a justification for marginal rather than absorption costing in as much as general overheads, especially office overheads, are argued not to be caused by the production of the cost unit. The opposite view holds that only overheads necessary to produce and sell products are incurred by rational management, so that it is right to charge cost units with a portion of general overheads. In a multidivisional group the CR offers an argument against divisions being charged with head office "management fees", so casts doubt on the validity of the capital charge used to obtain the value of residual divisional income.

The Rule Against Anticipating (RAA)

Costs should be charged only once they have been incurred. This rule applies to the books of account. It really means only that the books should reflect transactions that have actually happened, not those that only might do so. Thus bad debt write-offs should *reflect* the irrecoverability of debt but *not anticipate* it. The RAA has no application to project appraisal where anticipation is of the essence, nor to any other area where decisions have to be made about future resource allocations.

The Rule Against Deferrals (RAD)

Costs should be charged in the period in which they are incurred. The RAD, like the RAA, applies primarily to the books of account. It means costs should not be carried over from one year to the next *except* through the medium of period-end stocks and work-in-progress. Marginal costing follows the spirit of the RAD better than absorption costing, since the latter allows more costs to be deferred through closing stocks. In auditing terms, the RAD prevents window-dressing of final accounts.

The Rule Against Exceptional Items (RAE)

Cost units should be charged only with normal costs. This means abnormal costs become period costs not product costs. The RAE is especially important in process costing where abnormal losses take place. It also justifies using standard costs in product costing generally, with variances being treated as period costs—so long as the standards remain realistic.

The Realistic Value Rule (RVR)

Resources should be valued at their currently realistic value in planning, decision accounting and where practicable in monthly accounting for results as well. Realistic value is generally different from historic cost. For assets whose purchase is contemplated, the RVR means net present value. For assets currently in use, the RVR means replacement cost, as this is widely held to represent the assets' current "value to the business"—that is, its opportunity cost. More generally, strict application of the RVR would value all costs and assets at their opportunity cost in all contexts, but this is not a practical proposition. The RVR also underlies the choice of stock valuation method, as discussed in Chapter 4.

Core costing concepts

Cost

A cost is the sacrifice of resources, services or other benefits made in the course of undertaking an activity. In so far as the sacrifice cannot be measured in monetary quantities, it is excluded from the amount of the cost.

Value

Value usually means *exchange value;* the sum of money that can be realised in current market conditions when an item is sold. However, alternative meanings are more appropriate in specific contexts, as follows.

(*a*) *Use value*—the purposes fulfilled by something. For assets, use value is represented by, but not necessarily equal to, NPV.

(*b*) *Cost value*—historic cost.

(*c*) *Esteem value*—the prestige invested in, or associated with, an item that causes someone to be prepared more for it than is indicated by normal exchange value.

Profit
Increase in a firm's net assets during a trading period gives the value of *retained profit*. *Net profit* is sales less all costs; *gross profit* is sales less product costs.

Optimisation
Obtaining the best possible mix of resources—that is, the mix that maximises net profits or net present value of future cash flows.

Efficiency and productivity
Both relate the input of resources to the value of output. *Efficiency* is measured as *input per given quantum of output; productivity* as *output per given quantum of input* (often per direct labour-hour). Both concepts are related in the concept of added value, which is sales income less all externally invoiced resources (materials, services and expenses). Added value is increasingly used to represent the productivity of the whole firm.

Effectiveness
The extent to which intentions, plans or other specifications are realised in practice. Thus an effective accounting report is one that communicates clearly to the reader exactly what it is supposed to communicate.

Control
The process of ensuring that actual movements in volumes or values do not exceed specified maximum variations from a target amount.

System
Any ordered group of items, all of which have some specific purpose to fulfil. The purpose of a system is usually indicated by an epithet such as *control* system, *budgeting* system, etc. There is no implication in the concept of a system that it has to be associated with computers. A sentence, for example, is a linguistic system comprising ordered meaningful words.

Decision
A decision necessarily involves a choice between alternative courses of action. Decisions can be between two or more positive courses of action, such as producing either A or B; or they may be between either doing something or doing nothing, such as accepting a given project or not. Decision accounting is more concerned with the first type of decision and involves considering opportunity costs of alternative proposals. It can apply also to the second type of decision if doing nothing can sensibly be viewed as incurring the opportunity costs of doing the given something; for example, in decisions whether or not to use spare capacity to accept an order that does not cover its absorption cost but might well cover its incremental cost.

ADVANCED ASPECTS OF DECISION ACCOUNTING

Labour costs

We are used to treating labour costs as variable. This implies we can take on extra labour (through overtime and hiring casual labour) when volume is to be increased; but it implies also that we can shed labour when volume is to be cut. In practice, we may be unable to vary the amount of our direct labour resource hardly at all, especially in the short term. In these circumstances labour is a fixed cost and has to be paid irrespective of the decisions we make about its use. Labour costs, in this event, are sunk costs and should be excluded from computations of the opportunity costs of undertaking alternative courses of action. However, if labour is scarce, we perform our decision accounting calculations with a view to maximising the profit per labour-hour. In this event we evaluate alternatives on the assumption that *we use all the labour available on each project* we evaluate. If each project uses all the labour we have, *each project has the same labour cost,* which means that cost is general rather than differential, so here again it is excluded from our decision accounting calculations. In summary, we take only direct labour costs into account in making decisions if, in the given situation, they are in fact variable.

Discretionary costs

Discretionary costs such as marketing and advertising involve optimisation decisions. In theory, there is a size of advertising cost just large enough to maximise the net profits from expanding sales. Beyond this point marginal revenue (from extra sales induced by extra advertising) falls short of the marginal cost of the necessary extra advertising. The optimum is where marginal discretionary costs just equal the marginal revenues resulting from the costs in question having been incurred.

In practice, however, it is difficult to link discretionary costs with exact amounts of revenue. Less theoretically sound but more practically useful techniques are used. Advertising is quite widely budgeted as a fixed percentage of forecast sales. CVP analysis can be used to compute required sales volumes in order to yield a required profit, given the advertising cost provisionally agreed. If the required volume is right out of line with forecast sales, gap analysis is required, possibly involving market research into advertising cost effectiveness. Such research is itself a discretionary cost, but under existing accounting standards it is still possible to treat it as a capital cost to be written off over several years. Such treatment is against the spirit rather than the letter of current accounting standards and is not really in accordance with the RAD.

Order acceptance and user cost

Principles

Under-cost is depreciation plus repairs and maintenance *directly attrib-*

utable to holding and using the asset in question. It is relevant to deciding whether or not to accept an order at a given price and also to deciding what the minimum price for such an order should be. Depreciation and maintenance that would be incurred whether the order was accepted or not are irrelevant and excluded from the calculation of user cost attributable to the order.

Example

A machine which cost £24,000 originally is a depreciated straight line at 10 per cent a year. The current realisable value of the machine is £16,000, but the net book value is £16,800. Routine servicing runs at £80 a month. The machine has not been used for several months, as a result of which its net realisable value would decline to £15,000 and its servicing costs per month rise to £120.

The relevant costs are the incremental costs of accepting the order. These are twofold.

(*a*) Incremental decline in realisable value (£16,000 − £15,000) = £1,000
(*b*) Extra costs of servicing: 3 × (£120 − £80) ___= 120__
Total incremental user costs £1,120

The sum of £1,120 is the user cost of the order and represents the absolute minimum price at which it could be accepted. However, the decline in realisable value has an implicit opportunity cost. If the machine were sold now for £16,000, the firm could invest the proceeds at say 15 per cent. The realisable value is only £15,000 at the end of the order, so there is an opportunity cost of acceptance equal to the return forgone on the £1,000 realisable values sacrificed in taking on the order. This cost is of course £150 (15 per cent of £1,000). The true incremental cost of the order is thus £150 + £1,120 = £1,270. However, pricing the order at this minimum cost would make no contribution whatever to overheads in general, and to the committed costs of servicing and depreciation of the machine in particular.

Timing decisions

Contract extensions

Usually, contracts carry penalty clauses for late completion. This means a contract cannot be extended profitably beyond the contract period. Within that period, however, the incidence of overtime payments might be such as to discourage the firm from *minimising* completion time. For example, a phase of a contract lies on the critical path of the whole contract and must be completed in four months. The time could be halved from four months (1,200 man-hours) to two months (600 man-hours), but only by incurring 600 man-hours of overtime at 15 per cent of the basic hour by rate. Since 1,200 man-hours must be incurred anyway, there is no reason to incur them with overtime premiums unless there are compensating savings elsewhere, or unless the men involved can be employed on a more profitable contract in the second two months.

Timing of orders

Timing decisions may be disguised as order acceptance decisions, as in the example below.

A firm produces 10,000 product units a month. Each unit requires 2 kg of X at £1 per kilogram, 1 tonne of Y at £6 and component Z at £2. These prices are all fixed by contract with the firm. To terminate the supply contracts, the firm must give two months' notice to supplier X, three months to supplier Y and one month to supplier Z. Materials supplied could be sold onward on the following terms.

	Unit sales price	Unit variable selling costs	Unit contribution
X per kilogram	£1	£1.20	(20p)
Y per tonne	£4.80	£3.20	£1.60
Z	£1.90	£1.50	40p

The firm must pay its suppliers during the notice periods, but need not take delivery of the materials if it chooses not to.

Variable conversion costs to the firm are £25 an hour for 100 hours a month on the product in question. Among the fixed overheads are machines on hire at £20,000 a month on a hire contract subject to three months' notice of termination. The product could be supplied in a finished condition by M Ltd, which indicated a price of £8 a unit would be charged for 10,000 units a month.

Should the firm continue to make the product or buy, appears to be the question; but it involves also consideraion of the best time to give notice to suppliers and the best time to switch from making to buying. Preliminary considerations are as affirmed below.

Material X has a negative contribution on resale, so during the notice period it makes sense to refuse delivery of X even though payment would still have to be made. The monthly cost of X is $10,000 \times 2 \times £1 = £20,000$, which would be saved if M Ltd took over the supply of the finished product but would have to be paid during the notice period.

Material Y has a unit contribution on resale of £1.60. It makes sense to accept delivery during the three months' notice period and to realise per month $10,000 \times £1.60 = £16,000$. The cost of Y per month (saved if M takes over product manufacture) is $10,000 \times £6 = £60,000$, and this has to be paid during the three months' notice period.

Material Z has a unit contribution on resale of 40p, so it makes sense to accept delivery during the one-month notice period, thereby realising

10,000 × 40p = £4,000. The cost of Z per month is 10,000 × £2 = £20,000.

Machine hire costs of £20,000 a month would be saved after the three months' notice period, and variable conversion costs of £25 × 100 = £2,500 a month would be saved immediately on switching from making to buying.

We can now tabulate the costs and savings that would arise from an immediate decision to accept M Ltd's offer. This is done in the table below.

MONTHS

	1	2	3	4 (and each month thereafter)
	£	£	£	£
Savings in X	–	–	20,000	20,000
Contribution from Y	16,000	16,000	16,000	
Savings in Y	–	–	–	60,000
Contribution from Z	4,000	–	–	–
Savings in Z	–	20,000	20,000	20,000
Savings in hire costs	–	–	–	20,000
Savings conversion costs	2,500	2,500	2,500	2,500
Total benefits	22,500	38,500	58,500	122,500
Buy costs from M Ltd	(80,000)	(80,000)	(80,000)	(80,000)
Net benefit/(cost)	(57,500)	(41,500)	(21,500)	42,500

Since benefits exceed costs only from month 4, that is the month from which the firm should buy rather than make. Notice to cancel the machine hire and material Y can be given now; notice to cancel material X should be given at the end of month 1, and to cancel material Z at the end of month 2.

The value of information

The value of perfect information

If management knew which of several alternative outcomes would actually happen, decisions would be relieved of their uncertainty. It is possible to calculate the value of removing such uncertainty, as shown in the following example.

F Ltd is considering three projects, each with a different NPV depending on the state of the market. Thus:

	MARKET STATES		
	1	2	3
Probability	0.5	0.2	0.3
Project NPVs (£000s)			
Project K	80	10	5
L	40	90	60
M	70	60	50

On the information given we can calculate project expected values of NPV's with the following results.

$$\text{Project K} \quad (0.5 \times 80) + (0.2 \times 10) + (0.3 \times 5) \quad = 43.5$$
$$\text{L} \quad (0.5 \times 40) + (0.2 \times 90) + (0.3 \times 60) = 56$$
$$\text{M} \quad (0.5 \times 70) + (0.2 \times 60) + (0.3 \times 50) = 62$$

On the above basis M has the highest expected value of NPV and we select that. However, no matter which outcome actually occurs, M is not the most attractive alternative. If state 1 occurs, K is more attractive at 80; if state 2 occurs, L is more attractive at 90; and if state 3 occurs, L is again more attractive at 60. It is only the presence of uncertainty that is causing M to be chosen (and the minimax regret criteria would give the same result). Given perfect information the expected values of NPVs would be as follows.

Market state	Best project	NPV	Probability	Exp value
1	K	80	0.5	40
2	L	90	0.2	18
3	L	60	0.3	18
		Total exp value of NPVs		76

Perfect information gives us an expected value of NPVs at £76,000, which contrasts with the £62,000 obtained from selecting M in conditions of uncertainty. The difference between these two amounts is the value of perfect information to F Ltd—£14,000.

Perfect information is not available in the real world, but we need to understand its value as above, before we can evaluate how much we should be prepared to pay for *market research which does not give perfect information but does give improved information*. This is covered below.

The value of imperfect information

If we have some idea how close to perfect accuracy a market research report will be, we can deduce the value to the firm of such a report.

Suppose H Ltd is contemplating a new product launch and has ascribed prior probabilities of 0.3, 0.5 and 0.2 respectively to bad, normal and good market conditions. Product loss in bad conditions would be £30,000, profit in normal conditions £10,000 and in good conditions £40,000. This gives an overall expected value of profit of £4,000. The record of a market research firm, MRS Ltd, is shown in the following.

When MRS indicates the market will be:		*Bad*	*Normal*	*Good*
The chances of its being any of these are:				
	Bad	80%	20%	—
	Normal	20%	60%	20%
	Good	—	30%	70%

We next calculate the joint probabilities of the market research forecasts and the prior probabilities already ascribed, thus:

State of market	Prior probability	MRS prediction	Probability	Joint probability
Bad	0.3	Bad	0.8	0.24
Bad	0.3	Normal	0.2	0.06
Normal	0.5	Bad	0.2	0.10
Normal	0.5	Normal	0.6	0.30
Normal	0.5	Good	0.2	0.10
Good	0.2	Normal	0.3	0.06
Good	0.2	Good	0.7	0.14
			Total	1.00

Grouping the above results by MRS prediction headings; MRS will forecast bad:

	Probability
When actual market is bad	0.24
When actual market is normal	0.10
Total	0.34

MRS will forcast normal:

	Probability
When actual market is bad	0.06
When actual market is normal	0.30
When actual market is good	0.06
Total	0.42

MRS will forecast good:

	Probability
When actual market is normal	0.10
When actual market is good	0.14
Total	0.24

Assuming that if MRS forecasts a bad market, H Ltd will not launch the product, we can calculate the expected value of profits after the market research has been undertaken, thus:

MRS forecast	Actual state	Decision	Probability	Profit (£)	EV of profit (£)
Bad	Bad or normal	No launch	0.34	–	(1,800)
Normal	Bad	Launch	0.06	(30,000)	(1,800)
Normal	Normal	Launch	0.30	10,000	3,000
Normal	Good	Launch	0.06	40,000	2,400
Good	Normal	Launch	0.10	10,000	1,000
Good	Good	Launch	0.14	40,000	5,600

Total of EV of profit	10,200
EV of profit before research	4,000
Value of the imperfect information in the research	6,200

ADVANCED ASPECTS OF CONTROL ACCOUNTING

Zero base budgeting (ZBB)

Introduction
ZBB was introduced at Texas Instruments in the United States in 1969 by Peter Pyrrh, and was briefly in the public eye in 1976 when President Carter announced that they wished to introduce ZBB to the administration of the White House. It is a technique designed to help management allocate non-productive resources more efficiently—in other words, to cut overheads. The central facet of ZBB is its approach that *all* budgeted expenditure must be justified, as opposed to the widespread practice of sanctioning expenditure held at the actual level of the previous year.

Implementation
Each activity that takes place in the firm, outside of production, is described in a report called a "decision package". Management then evaluates every decision package by examining the costs and benefits of the activity concerned. This leads to priority ranking of the packages, and funds can then be allocated to activities in descending order of priority. In practice, high priority is given to activities essential to fulfilling legal requirements (e.g. accounting, maintenance for safety legislation, company secretarial activities) and to activities essential to business survival (buying, sales, strike-free industrial relations). It is thus the discretionary costs to which managerial scrutiny will be particulary directed, and savings on those costs are to be expected.

Advantages and limitations of ZBB
The advantages are:

    (*a*) provision of an impetus to avoid wasteful expenditure;
    (*b*) facilitated identification of inefficient and unnecessary activities;
    (*c*) obligation to examine closely cost behaviour patterns; and
    (*d*) provision of a channel for responding to changes in the business
environment that render an activity obsolete.

The disadvantages are:

    (*a*) danger of emphasising short-term gains at the expense of long-term
ones;
    (*b*) high cost of preparing and updating decision packages every year;
    (*c*) tendency to regard any activity not foreseen and sanctioned in the
most recent ZBB exercise as illegitimate reduces organisational respon-
siveness to unforeseen conditions; and
    (*d*) high volume of paperwork required.

Alternatives to ZBB
Change justification budgeting (CJB) allows cost centre managers to
obtain sanction for budgeted expenditure at current actual levels in real
(post-inflation) terms. Any *incremental* expenditure must be justified by
the same procedure as ZBB applies to *total* expenditure. CJB focuses on
new discretionary costs, is cheaper than ZBB, but does not make any
inroads on the wastage concealed in current levels of expenditure.

A synthesis of CJB and ZBB is provided by review period budgeting
(RPB). RPB goes through full ZBB procedures every three to five years
(matching well with the corporate plan horizon) and in the intervening
years uses CJB to keep down costs of the budgeting exercise itself. The
advantages of ZBB are largely retained in RPB so long as the review is
sufficiently thorough.

Aspects of performance evaluation

Non-monetary ratio analysis
Evaluation ratios need not be confined to those directly arising from the
final accounts. In particular circumstances ratios selected from among the
following might be more useful than traditional ratios, because of their
being more directly relevant to the concerns of divisional or profit centre
management.

    (*a*) The activity, efficiency and capacity ratios show how fully and
effectively available labour capacity has been used.
    (*b*) Machine capacity ratio (machine-hours available relative to max-
imum machine-hour capacity) and machine usage ratio (machine-hours

used relative to machine-hours available) show how machine capacity has been used or wasted.

(c) Value added per employee shows the average productivity of the firm in financial terms.

(d) Sales per m^3 of shelf space or per m^2 of floor space show the return in sales to each unit of scarce storage space resource.

(e) Sales, cost and contribution per call made by salesmen show the effectiveness of the selling effort.

(f) Generally, any relevant measure of output per unit of constrained or expensive input resource.

Multiple measures of performance

Goals, at corporate and profit centre levels, can be divided between result areas and success factors. Result areas identify those goals such as ROCE that cannot readily be regarded as subsidiary to, or included in, any other goal. Result areas common in business today are as follows.

(a) Obtain a good return for shareholders—measured by ROI.

(b) Enhance reputation as an employer of labour—measured indirectly by a range of things from annual increase in real net pay, via labour turnover, to net expenditure on employee welfare facilities.

(c) Enhance reputation for social responsibility—involves public relations investment, sponsoring sporting events, etc., and avoiding being associated with pollutants, but cannot be even indirectly measured.

(d) Independent growth. This goal overlaps with goal (a) but is not included in it, since a firm's ROI could be improved by being taken over, which involves loss of independence.

The above result areas depend on the achievement of subsidiary goals known as "success factors". For goal (a) success factors include increased market share, improved labour productivity and stability of earnings. For goal (b) success factors include good relations with trade-union officers, operating at adequate levels of profit (to maintain employment) and keeping out of the industrial relations tribunals. For goal (c) success factors include medium to high profile sports sponsorships, the obtaining of goodwill from key political and journalistic people and the cultivation of a caring image. For goal (d) success factors include low gearing ratios, high levels of retained profits (may conflict with goal (a)) and operating in non-contracting product markets (reinforces goal (a)).

Control in not-for-profit organisations

Fund accounting

A fund is a sum of assets set aside for specific uses. For charities and friendly societies there exists a general fund which is the equivalent of share capital and reserves for commercial companies. Charities raise funds in various ways from bazaars to direct requests for donations. Each of the fund-raising activities should be separately accounted for, so their comparative effectiveness can be easily gauged. Income and expenditure associated with specific funds should be recorded and controlled against those funds as if the fund were a continuing job cost centre.

Cost benefit analysis

In any not-for-profit organisation goals are, by definition, not profit or its surrogates such as ROCE. Government departments have policy goals, charities and clubs have goals specified in their constitution, while pressure groups have explicit goals, such as advancing the interests of consumers. Cost benefit analysis tries to quantify benefits in terms of goal attainment and match such benefits against costs, both private and social. Intangible costs and benefits are difficult to measure but estimates can be obtained using surrogate prices, shadow social prices or differential prices. A surrogate price is an estimate of an item's exchange value if a market existed for the item. Figures can sometimes be obtained for items traded in markets in order to obtain surrogate prices. Shadow social prices attempt to gauge "true" social cost (e.g. a fall in property values of houses near a proposed new airport) and true social benefit (e.g. a reduction in electricity costs for houses agreeing to try solar heating panels in a pilot scheme). A differential price is the difference between two costs. For example, a college might now cost £10 million a year to run and offers a staff student ratio of 12. At £9 million a year the staff student ratio would rise to 16 as a result of staff redundancies. County council educational authorities would have to decide if the £1 million differential price equated with the differential value of a change in staff student ratios of $33\frac{1}{3}\%$.

Cost benefit analysis does not depend for its usefulness on all items being transformable into monetary measures. Benefits are often easier to measure in non-monetary terms and costs can be attributed to units of benefit by way of highlighting the cost effectiveness of various proposals.

THE FRONTIERS OF MANAGEMENT ACCOUNTANCY

Operations research

Several techniques that originated in the field of operations research are now accepted as topics in management accountancy. Of these, perhaps the most important are optimisation techniques, exemplified by linear programming. At some teaching institutions, programming techniques are taught to the same diet of students three times: once in first-year quantitative studies; again in second-year management science (a near-synonym for operations research); and finally, in third-year management accounting courses. This reflects not only the importance of optimisation techniques in business but the nebulosity of the subject boundaries concerned.

Management accountancy also shares with operations research the study of stock control. However, extensions of stock- control techniques into queuing theory remain on the operations research side of the boundary.

Network analysis is an operations research technique that management accountancy has not yet wholly appropriated. Examination questions can be found in management accountancy that demand a familiarity with critical path analysis but they are still rather rare. Since network analysis is concerned with resource planning and control, its focus on time rather than on monetary cost seems insufficient reason to exclude it from the purview of management accountancy. In business generally, and the contract building business in particular, time is money. Control of the former necessarily involves control of the latter. It seems reasonable to expect, therefore, that in the near future both textbooks and examinations will treat network analysis as lying in the area of overlap between operations research and management accountancy. Any future editions of the present book will reflect such a shift of boundary and include a new section on this topic, should the time be ripe to do so.

It can be seen that management accountancy has borrowed quite considerably from operations research and that some topics critical to both areas are taught in both subjects. In an essentially practical arena like accounting, it is quite legitimate to appropriate techniques from other subject areas if it helps to give management tighter control over operations or make more effective decisions about resource allocation. Fuzzy subject boundaries are of no concern to the business manager.

Applied statistics

All the management accounting techniques that involve the manipulation of probabilities derive from statistics. Normal distribution tables, expected values and decision trees all originate in the branch of statistics concerned with probability theory. The vast bulk of accounting research depends on statistics for its methodology and on formal mathematics, especially algebra, for its expression. Practical accounting has become far more amenable to the application of statistical method since computers became general. Multi-outcome forecasting, simulation and the production of pay-off matrices appropriate for specific situations all become potentially cost effective with computers in a way and to an extent that were rarely possible before.

The division between statistics and management accountancy is more readily apparent than the division between operations research and management accountancy. Statistics overlaps accounting only in the use of probabilities, and we may with some validity consider that statistics applied to accounting problems is an exercise in the latter art as well as exemplifying the former science.

Economics

In many ways management accountancy is applied economics. Economics generates normative theories to optimise resource allocation, while management accountancy applies techniques to enhance the efficiency and effectiveness of all the responsibility centres in a firm. Managerial economics is a designation increasingly being given to that part of economics that deals with resource allocation within the firm. However it tends to be expressed at a higher level of abstraction and in more algebraic language than is readily understood by non-academic readers. Management accountancy acts as a bridge between the formal world of the managerial economist and the everyday realities and pressures of the uncertain and multifaceted world of the business manager.

One particular branch of managerial economics has received an increasing amount of attention from academic accountants in recent years: agency theory. Agency theory sees co-operative behaviour between people in organisations in terms of the formation and execution of what it calls "contracts" between parties with divergent interests. The costs associated with such contracts are studied in agency theory with a view to their minimisation (while at the same time contract benefits are maximised). Firms, divisions and cost centres are all viewed as examples of agency contracts. So far, agency theory has not produced anything directly applicable by the practising management accountant, and it may be some time before it does so. However, it does hold the promise of refining our ability to assess the value of information to contracting parties—an ability currently limited to the rather crude techniques outlined earlier in this chapter.

Behavioural science

Behavioural aspects of budgets

The interface between accounting and behavioural science has been principally studied in relation to budgeting. At the worst, budgets are seen as a device to put pressure on the labour force, with the role of budgetary police being attributed to the firm's accountants. At best, budgets are seen as a means of achieving goal congruence between employee and firm, as a result of maintaining a delicate balance between adequate employee participation and firm managerial direction.

Cost centre heads tend to pad out budget submissions by way of securing a safety margin against unforeseen adversity and of increasing the chances of future variances being favourable rather than adverse. Such padding is believed to be widely practised and constitutes a good reason for introducing ZBB. A budgetary target with a 50 per cent chance of attainment is seen by some writers as motivating better performance than a target figure perceived as too easy or too difficult to be worth trying for.

Expectancy theory has a useful contribution to make to optimising the motivational impact of budgets, since it focuses our attention on the two prime determinants of motivation: perceived realism of the target set and the valency of achieving the target (the net rewards, both objective and subjective).

Budgetary participation
Not all writers agree that employee participation in target setting is an unmixed blessing for the firm. Hopwood (1974), in particular, draws a distinction between morale effects (generally good) and productivity effects (which could be negligible). The latter will be significant, he believes, only if the social atmosphere within the firm is conducive to participation, if the employees do not actually prefer management to be authoritarian and if all those involved in the participation exercise are equally well informed on the main factors influencing their deliberations.

Other behavioural aspects of accounting
Hopwood relates behavioural studies to decision accounting and provides anecdotal evidence that figures tend to be manipulated in order to provide justification for those decisions managers would prefer to make rather than those that are implied by an unmanipulated set of figures. Ethics rather than further behavioural studies could be thought to offer the most effective solutions to this and similar problems. Behavioural accounting is none the less a growing field which is rapidly becoming seen as a branch of accounting separate from management accountancy. Behavioural studies will nevertheless remain of high relevance to the actual practice of management accountancy, since they address important questions on the mutual impact of accounting procedures and personnel.

THE QUINTESSENCE OF MANAGEMENT ACCOUNTANCY

Reporting

Introduction
The most important part of a management accountant's job is the preparation and presentation of reports. Costing, control accounting and decision accounting all need reports. Reports are also the principal means of judging the performance of the management accountant.

Report format
Format is concerned with the length, appearance and clarity of a report. It is the means by which the management accountant markets his work. An initial impact must be made on the reader to arouse his interest, so the report format should be visually attractive. Overcrowding of data should

be avoided and spacing should be used creatively to focus visual attention on those areas where it is desired to direct mental attention. The reader should be immediately aware from the cover of the report of its nature, its source and its various destinations. The report should begin with an abstract or synopsis of its main findings. Detail should be relegated to appendixes, as should any necessary evidencing documents. Diagrams or graphs should always be used to illustrate the patterns shown by the figures, and a sparing use of colour is often helpful.

Routine reports should be done according to a standardised format, while *ad hoc* reports should be styled somewhat differently to increase their impact.

Report content
Content must be timely and topical even if this has to be achieved at the expense of complete accuracy. It should be clearly relevant to the problems of the reader and not go off at a tangent at any point. Causes of problems should be identified and related to their symptoms logically, rigorously and in a well-evidenced fashion. Accounting and business jargon must be minimised; but where their use is unavoidable, terms used must be fully explained. Alternative solutions to problems should be briefly analysed and recommendations made as to which solution appears preferable.

Control

Control systems
In Chapter 6 we discussed the dangers of having a planning system, a budget, a standard costing system and an incentive system all pointing in different directions. A critical task of the management accountant is to reconcile and integrate these systems so that each one becomes optimally effective.

Responsibility accounting
Control systems will be subverted if cost centre managers consider they are being penalised for charges they could not reasonably have been expected to control. As far as possible, cost centres should be charged only with controllable costs. When it is necessary to charge them with uncontrollable costs, however, the reporting system should try to segregate them so that managers can see that their performance may be evaluated with due weighting being given to the burden of uncontrollable costs.

Variance analysis
Variance analysis reports should always give verbal comments on the probable causes of each variance. The method of calculating each variance should be briefly explained on a separate sheet to enable managers to form

their own independent judgments as to the relative significance of factors such as volume and efficiency underlying the variances. Under standard absorption costing, it is helpful to clarify the causes and effects of volume variances in particular.

Contingency theory applications

In the design and review of control systems, the management accountant should be sensitive to the nature of the different environments faced by different cost centre managers. Such sensitivity will be reflected in his classification of planned costs as between controllable, partly controllable and uncontrollable. A cost such as direct labour may be fully controllable in maintenance but much less so in the processing sections of the production line, where labour-hours are a function of work available to the section. In service cost centres labour is virtually a fixed cost and should be so reported. Contingency theory holds that the effectiveness of a control system is contingent on its environment. The law of requisite variety demands that variations in the environment be matched by appropriate counter-variations in the responses of the control system.

Decision accounting

Applied economics

Economic theories are either positive or normative. Positive theories attempt to explain how resource allocation decisions are actually made. Normative ones attempt to find the optimum decisions that *should* be made. Normative economics tends to assume a prime business goal of profit maximisation, subject to the constraining impact of risk aversion. In practice, other goals may be equally important, so optimisation rules derived from economics must be used with care. The management accountant should not presume to preach a goal of profit maximisation to a management that has previously and consciously adopted wider and more sensitive horizons.

Cost benefit analysis

All decision accounting involves cost benefit analysis. The evaluation of benefits depends on the priority given to various goals by management as well as their collective risk aversion. A good management accountant is aware of his management's goals and he reports benefits of proposed courses of action accordingly. Benefits that cannot be quantified should none the less be identified in preparing reports for management decision. The report should highlight not only short-term opportunity costs, but draw the reader's attention to long-term costs that may be affected by the decision, even if the effects cannot be quantified. The cost benefit approach to reporting for decisions is perhaps the quintessence of management accountancy. This approach aims to identify the changes in welfare and utility consequent upon taking decisions.

The greatest challenge to management accountancy, both in theory and in practice, lies in developing cost benefit analysis, so that it becomes sensitive enough for the handling of all types of decision in all types of context, especially those whose costs and benefits are not measurable with currently available techniques.

THE IMPLIED GOALS OF ACCOUNTANCY

Cost reduction

Accountants are expected to play a leading role in minimising costs within a firm. Accountancy, however, has surprisingly little to say about this task. The main technique in cost reduction programmes, value analysis, derives from engineering rather than the more familiar sources of management accounting tools. Value analysis examines all aspects of the provision of a product or service in order to find possible savings without sacrifice of quality. It includes work study, O and M analysis and a study of comparative material and conversion costs. The material components of a product are examined with a view to using cheaper but not inferior substitutes. Value analysis should cut down the incidence of planning variances and dovetails well with the approach taken in a ZBB review. Value analysis surveys existing products and services, while value engineering applies identical procedures to proposed products and services. Both value analysis and ZBB are likely to become increasingly important parts of the management accounting syllabus as the professional accounting bodies become more and more conscious of the accountant's implied duty with regard to cost reduction.

Organisational analysis

Contingency theory tells us *what* should be taken into account in designing a management information system founded on the books of account, but it offers little help in telling us *how* this can be achieved. The accounting system is to the firm what the central nervous system is to the human body. However, the nervous system is the product of millions of years of adaptive evolution, while the accounting system is apt to be imposed by head offices or external auditors with little regard to organisational environment, goals or structure. Even when due regard is given to these factors, precious little accounting theory yet exists to help translate organisational factors into accounting system designs. The "Rochester School" of American accounting academics is working on this problem. Its chief spokesman, M.C. Jensen, holds that an important goal of accounting is the integration of organisational analysis with information systems theory. If the Rochester School or anyone else produces such an integration, it would significantly change our current approach to management accountancy, as we would then have a conceptual framework for integrating the rather disparate topics that presently constitute the subject.

Evaluation

All accounting concerns evaluation. Indeed, we might even go so far as to assert that the art of accountancy is that of ascribing to things a true and fair value. Too many accountants duck the challenge of evaluation by taking refuge in historical costs and accounting standards. In this connection it may be apposite to mention Oscar Wilde's famous dictum that a cynic is a man who knows the price of everything and the value of nothing. The accountant has currently a rather poor image in many business quarters as the cost-cutting enemy of creative enterprise. A well-known after-dinner quote defines the accountant as the man who goes in after a battle and bayonets the wounded. This may well be an unfair distortion, but accountants are likely to continue evolving such an unfortunate image until more of them take seriously all that is implied by the notion of evaluation. The conventions of prudence and conservatism do not have to be used as a cloak for scepticism and the suppression of innovation. The realistic value rule of costing need not always mean the pessimistic value rule. Management accountancy evaluates a wide variety of items including costs, present values of future expected cash flows, decision net benefits and comparative performance. It has a wider purview than financial accounting, which evaluates profit to date, net assets and funds according to well-established and regulation-bound procedures. The evaluation of net benefits, present values and profit centre performance in a multigoal environment according to consistent rules is an implied goal of accounting that has yet to be realised. Only when we possess the tools to do these things within an integrated conceptual framework can accountancy in general and management accountancy in particular be said to have reached maturity as a discipline.

QUESTIONS

1. What arguments can be presented against the view that evaluation is the essence of accounting?

2. Why might control accounting be considered as simply a special branch of decision accounting?

3. When does historic cost constitute realistic value?

4. How far is it valid to suppose that the implied goals of accounting outlined above will remain unfulfilled unless it ever becomes possible to measure utility objectively?

5. In what circumstances are (a) normally variable costs fixed, and (b) normally discretionary costs committed?

6. How would you recognise a relevant cost for decision-making purposes?

7. What are the practical difficulties likely to be encountered in applying to discretionary expenditures the normative economics rule that marginal cost and marginal revenue should be made equal?

8. What is meant by the term "the value of imperfect information", and how may it be measured?

9. What relevance has behavioural accounting to the design of a budgetary control system?

10. How far is management accountancy:

(*a*) a reflection of what practising accountants in industry do; and

(*b*) merely a group of ill-related techniques in a futile search for a unifying theory?

For quantitative questions on this chapter, see numbers 39 to 43 in Appendix V.

Normal curve areas

$$Z = \frac{\text{Value} - \text{Mean}}{\text{Standard deviation}}$$

If a value is less than its associated mean, Z will be negative. However, in using the table below, the minus sign before the Z value is ignored.

Z	Area	Z	Area	Z	Area
0.0	0.0000	1.0	0.3413	2.0	0.4772
0.1	0.0398	1.1	0.3643	2.1	0.4821
0.2	0.0793	1.2	0.3849	2.2	0.4861
0.3	0.1179	1.3	0.4032	2.3	0.4893
0.4	0.1554	1.4	0.4192	2.4	0.4918
0.5	0.1915	1.5	0.4332	2.5	0.4938
0.6	0.2257	1.6	0.4452	2.6	0.4953
0.7	0.2580	1.7	0.4554	2.7	0.4965
0.8	0.2881	1.8	0.4641	2.8	0.4974
0.9	0.3159	1.9	0.4713	2.9	0.4981
				3.0	0.4987

For examples on the use of these tables, read pages 227–30.

Present Value Factors

The table gives the present value of a single payment received *n* years in the future, discounted at *x* per cent per year. For example, with a discount rate of 7 per cent a single payment of £1 in six years' time has a present value of £0.6663 or 66.63p.

PRESENT VALUE FACTORS: TO DETERMINE THE PRESENT VALUE OF SINGLE PAYMENT
RECEIVED *n* YEARS FROM THE PRESENT (OR VICE VERSA)

Years	1%	2%	3%	4%	5%	6%	7%	8%	9%	10%
1	0.9901	0.9804	0.9709	0.9615	0.9524	0.9434	0.9346	0.9259	0.9174	0.9091
2	0.9803	0.9612	0.9426	0.9426	0.9070	0.8900	0.8734	0.8573	0.8417	0.8264
3	0.9706	0.9423	0.9151	0.8890	0.8638	0.8396	0.8163	0.7938	0.7722	0.7513
4	0.9610	0.9238	0.8885	0.8548	0.8227	0.7921	0.7629	0.7350	0.7084	0.6830
5	0.9515	0.9057	0.8626	0.8219	0.7835	0.7473	0.7130	0.6806	0.6499	0.6209
6	0.9420	0.8880	0.8375	0.7903	0.7462	0.7050	0.6663	0.6302	0.5963	0.5645
7	0.9327	0.8706	0.8131	0.7599	0.7107	0.6651	0.6227	0.5835	0.5470	0.5132
8	0.9235	0.8535	0.7894	0.7307	0.6768	0.6274	0.5820	0.5403	0.5019	0.4665
9	0.9143	0.8368	0.7664	0.7026	0.6446	0.5919	0.5439	0.5002	0.4604	0.4241
10	0.9053	0.8203	0.7441	0.6756	0.6139	0.5584	0.5083	0.4632	0.4224	0.3855
11	0.8963	0.8043	0.7224	0.6496	0.5847	0.5268	0.4751	0.4289	0.3875	0.3505
12	0.8874	0.7885	0.7014	0.6246	0.5568	0.4970	0.4440	0.3971	0.3555	0.3186
13	0.8787	0.7730	0.6810	0.6006	0.5303	0.4688	0.4150	0.3677	0.3262	0.2897
14	0.8700	0.7579	0.6611	0.5775	0.5051	0.4423	0.3878	0.3405	0.2992	0.2633
15	0.8613	0.7430	0.6419	0.5553	0.4810	0.4173	0.3624	0.3152	0.2745	0.2394
16	0.8528	0.7284	0.6232	0.5339	0.4581	0.3936	0.3387	0.2919	0.2519	0.2176
17	0.8444	0.7142	0.6050	0.5134	0.4363	0.3714	0.3166	0.2703	0.2311	0.1978
18	0.8360	0.7002	0.5874	0.4936	0.4155	0.3503	0.2959	0.2502	0.2120	0.1799
19	0.8277	0.6864	0.5703	0.4746	0.3957	0.3305	0.2765	0.2317	0.1945	0.1635
20	0.8195	0.6730	0.5537	0.4564	0.3769	0.3118	0.2584	0.2145	0.1784	0.1486
21	0.8114	0.6598	0.5375	0.4388	0.3589	0.2942	0.2415	0.1987	0.1637	0.1351
22	0.8034	0.6468	0.5219	0.4220	0.3418	0.2775	0.2257	0.1839	0.1502	0.1228
23	0.7954	0.6342	0.5067	0.4057	0.3256	0.2618	0.2109	0.1703	0.1378	0.1117
24	0.7876	0.6217	0.4919	0.3901	0.3101	0.2470	0.1971	0.1577	0.1264	0.1015
25	0.7798	0.6095	0.4776	0.3751	0.2953	0.2330	0.1842	0.1460	0.1160	0.0923
26	0.7720	0.5976	0.4637	0.3607	0.2812	0.2198	0.1722	0.1352	0.1064	0.0839
27	0.7644	0.5859	0.4502	0.3468	0.2678	0.2074	0.1609	0.1252	0.0976	0.0763
28	0.7568	0.5744	0.4371	0.3335	0.2551	0.1956	0.1504	0.1159	0.0895	0.0693
29	0.7493	0.5631	0.4243	0.3207	0.2429	0.1846	0.1406	0.1073	0.0822	0.0630
30	0.7419	0.5521	0.4120	0.3083	0.2314	0.1741	0.1314	0.0994	0.0754	0.0573
31	0.7346	0.5412	0.4000	0.2965	0.2204	0.1643	0.1228	0.0920	0.0691	0.0521
32	0.7273	0.5306	0.3883	0.2851	0.2099	0.1550	0.1147	0.0852	0.0634	0.0474
33	0.7201	0.5202	0.3770	0.2741	0.1999	0.1462	0.1072	0.0789	0.0582	0.0431
34	0.7130	0.5100	0.3660	0.2636	0.1904	0.1379	0.1002	0.0730	0.0534	0.0391
35	0.7059	0.5000	0.3554	0.2534	0.1813	0.1301	0.0937	0.0676	0.0490	0.0356
36	0.6989	0.4902	0.3450	0.2437	0.1727	0.1227	0.0875	0.0626	0.0449	0.0323
37	0.6920	0.4806	0.3350	0.2343	0.1644	0.1158	0.0818	0.0580	0.0412	0.0294
38	0.6852	0.4712	0.3252	0.2253	0.1566	0.1092	0.0765	0.0537	0.0378	0.0267
39	0.6784	0.4619	0.3158	0.2166	0.1491	0.1031	0.0715	0.0497	0.0347	0.0243
40	0.6717	0.4529	0.3066	0.2083	0.1420	0.0972	0.0668	0.0460	0.0318	0.0221
41	0.6650	0.4440	0.2976	0.2003	0.1353	0.0917	0.0624	0.0426	0.0292	0.0201
42	0.6584	0.4353	0.2890	0.1926	0.1288	0.0865	0.0583	0.0395	0.0268	0.0183
43	0.6519	0.4268	0.2805	0.1852	0.1227	0.0816	0.0545	0.0365	0.0246	0.0166
44	0.6454	0.4184	0.2724	0.1780	0.1169	0.0770	0.0509	0.0338	0.0226	0.0151
45	0.6391	0.4102	0.2644	0.1712	0.1113	0.0727	0.0476	0.0313	0.0207	0.0137
46	0.6327	0.4022	0.2567	0.1646	0.1060	0.0685	0.0445	0.0290	0.0190	0.0125
47	0.6265	0.3943	0.2493	0.1583	0.1009	0.0647	0.0416	0.0269	0.0174	0.0113
48	0.6203	0.3865	0.2420	0.1522	0.0961	0.0610	0.0389	0.0249	0.0160	0.0103
49	0.6141	0.3790	0.2350	0.1463	0.0916	0.0575	0.0363	0.0230	0.0147	0.0094
50	0.6080	0.3715	0.2281	0.1407	0.0872	0.0543	0.0339	0.0213	0.0134	0.0085

11%	12%	13%	14%	15%	16%	17%	18%	19%	20%	Years
0.9009	0.8929	0.8850	0.8772	0.8696	0.8621	0.8547	0.8475	0.8403	0.8333	1
0.8116	0.7972	0.7831	0.7695	0.7561	0.7432	0.7305	0.7182	0.7062	0.6944	2
0.7312	0.7118	0.6931	0.6750	0.6575	0.6407	0.6244	0.6086	0.5934	0.5787	3
0.6587	0.6355	0.6133	0.5921	0.5718	0.5523	0.5337	0.5158	0.4987	0.4823	4
0.5935	0.5674	0.5428	0.5194	0.4972	0.4761	0.4561	0.4371	0.4190	0.4019	5
0.5346	0.5066	0.4803	0.4556	0.4323	0.4104	0.3898	0.3704	0.3521	0.3349	6
0.4817	0.4523	0.4251	0.3996	0.3759	0.3538	0.3332	0.3139	0.2959	0.2791	7
0.4339	0.4039	0.3762	0.3506	0.3269	0.3050	0.2848	0.2660	0.2487	0.2326	8
0.3909	0.3606	0.3329	0.3075	0.2843	0.2630	0.2434	0.2255	0.2090	0.1938	9
0.3522	0.3220	0.2946	0.2697	0.2472	0.2267	0.2080	0.1911	0.1756	0.1615	10
0.3173	0.2875	0.2607	0.2366	0.2149	0.1954	0.1778	0.1619	0.1476	0.1346	11
0.2858	0.2567	0.2307	0.2076	0.1869	0.1685	0.1520	0.1372	0.1240	0.1122	12
0.2575	0.2292	0.2042	0.1821	0.1625	0.1452	0.1299	0.1163	0.1042	0.0935	13
0.2320	0.2046	0.1807	0.1597	0.1413	0.1252	0.1110	0.0985	0.0876	0.0779	14
0.2090	0.1827	0.1599	0.1401	0.1229	0.1079	0.0949	0.0835	0.0736	0.0649	15
0.1883	0.1631	0.1415	0.1229	0.1069	0.0930	0.0811	0.0708	0.0618	0.0541	16
0.1696	0.1456	0.1252	0.1078	0.0929	0.0802	0.0693	0.0600	0.0520	0.0451	17
0.1528	0.1300	0.1108	0.0946	0.0808	0.0691	0.0592	0.0508	0.0437	0.0376	18
0.1377	0.1161	0.0981	0.0829	0.0703	0.0596	0.0506	0.0431	0.0367	0.0313	19
0.1240	0.1037	0.0868	0.0728	0.0611	0.0514	0.0433	0.0365	0.0308	0.0261	20
0.1117	0.0926	0.0768	0.0638	0.0531	0.0443	0.0370	0.0309	0.0259	0.0217	21
0.1007	0.0826	0.0680	0.0560	0.0462	0.0382	0.0316	0.0262	0.0218	0.0181	22
0.0907	0.0738	0.0601	0.0491	0.0402	0.0329	0.0270	0.0222	0.0183	0.0151	23
0.0817	0.0659	0.0532	0.0431	0.0349	0.0284	0.0231	0.0188	0.0154	0.0126	24
0.0736	0.0588	0.0471	0.0378	0.0304	0.0245	0.0197	0.0160	0.0129	0.0105	25
0.0663	0.0525	0.0417	0.0331	0.0264	0.0211	0.0169	0.0135	0.0109	0.0087	26
0.0597	0.0469	0.0369	0.0291	0.0230	0.0182	0.0144	0.0115	0.0091	0.0073	27
0.0538	0.0419	0.0326	0.0255	0.0200	0.0157	0.0123	0.0097	0.0077	0.0061	28
0.0485	0.0374	0.0289	0.0224	0.0174	0.0135	0.0105	0.0082	0.0064	0.0051	29
0.0437	0.0334	0.0256	0.0196	0.0151	0.0116	0.0090	0.0070	0.0054	0.0042	30
0.0394	0.0298	0.0226	0.0172	0.0131	0.0100	0.0077	0.0059	0.0046	0.0035	31
0.0355	0.0266	0.0200	0.0151	0.0114	0.0087	0.0066	0.0050	0.0038	0.0029	32
0.0319	0.0238	0.0177	0.0132	0.0099	0.0075	0.0056	0.0042	0.0032	0.0024	33
0.0288	0.0212	0.0157	0.0116	0.0086	0.0064	0.0048	0.0036	0.0027	0.0020	34
0.0259	0.0189	0.0139	0.0102	0.0075	0.0055	0.0041	0.0030	0.0023	0.0017	35
0.0234	0.0169	0.0123	0.0089	0.0065	0.0048	0.0035	0.0026	0.0019	0.0014	36
0.0210	0.0151	0.0109	0.0078	0.0057	0.0041	0.0030	0.0022	0.0016	0.0012	37
0.0190	0.0135	0.0096	0.0069	0.0049	0.0036	0.0026	0.0019	0.0013	0.0010	38
0.0171	0.0120	0.0085	0.0060	0.0043	0.0031	0.0022	0.0016	0.0011	0.0008	39
0.0154	0.0107	0.0075	0.0053	0.0037	0.0026	0.0019	0.0013	0.0010	0.0007	40
0.0139	0.0096	0.0067	0.0046	0.0032	0.0023	0.0016	0.0011	0.0008	0.0006	41
0.0125	0.0086	0.0059	0.0041	0.0028	0.0020	0.0014	0.0010	0.0007	0.0005	42
0.0112	0.0076	0.0052	0.0036	0.0025	0.0017	0.0012	0.0008	0.0006	0.0004	43
0.0101	0.0068	0.0046	0.0031	0.0021	0.0015	0.0010	0.0007	0.0005	0.0003	44
0.0091	0.0061	0.0041	0.0027	0.0019	0.0013	0.0009	0.0006	0.0004	0.0003	45
0.0082	0.0054	0.0036	0.0024	0.0016	0.0011	0.0007	0.0005	0.0003	0.0002	46
0.0074	0.0049	0.0032	0.0021	0.0014	0.0009	0.0006	0.0004	0.0003	0.0002	47
0.0067	0.0043	0.0028	0.0019	0.0012	0.0008	0.0005	0.0004	0.0002	0.0002	48
0.0060	0.0039	0.0025	0.0016	0.0011	0.0007	0.0005	0.0003	0.0002	0.0001	49
0.0054	0.0035	0.0022	0.0014	0.0009	0.0006	0.0004	0.0003	0.0002	0.0001	50

Cumulative Present Value Factors

The table gives the present value of n annual payments of £1 received for the next n years with a constant discount of x per cent per year. For example, with a discount rate of 7 per cent and with six annual payments of £1, the present value is £4.767.

CUMULATIVE PRESENT VALUE FACTORS

Years 0 to:	1%	2%	3%	4%	5%	6%	7%	8%	9%	10%
1	0.990	0.980	0.971	0.962	0.952	0.943	0.935	0.926	0.917	0.909
2	1.970	1.942	1.913	1.886	1.859	1.833	1.808	1.783	1.759	1.736
3	2.941	2.884	2.829	2.775	2.723	2.673	2.624	2.577	2.531	2.487
4	3.902	3.808	3.717	3.630	3.546	3.465	3.387	3.312	3.240	3.170
5	4.853	4.713	4.580	4.452	4.329	4.212	4.100	3.993	3.890	3.791
6	5.795	5.601	5.417	5.242	5.076	4.917	4.767	4.623	4.486	4.355
7	6.728	6.472	6.230	6.002	5.786	5.582	5.389	5.206	5.033	4.868
8	7.652	7.325	7.020	6.733	6.463	6.210	5.971	5.747	5.535	5.335
9	8.566	8.162	7.786	7.435	7.108	6.802	6.515	6.247	5.995	5.759
10	9.471	8.983	8.530	8.111	7.722	7.360	7.024	6.710	6.418	6.145
11	10.368	9.787	9.253	8.760	8.306	7.887	7.499	7.139	6.805	6.495
12	11.255	10.575	9.954	9.385	8.863	8.384	7.943	7.536	7.161	6.814
13	12.134	11.348	10.635	9.986	9.394	8.853	8.358	7.904	7.487	7.103
14	13.004	12.106	11.296	10.563	9.899	9.295	8.745	8.244	7.786	7.367
15	13.865	12.849	11.938	11.118	10.380	9.712	9.108	8.559	8.061	7.606
16	14.718	13.578	12.561	11.652	10.838	10.106	9.447	8.851	8.313	7.824
17	15.562	14.292	13.166	12.166	11.274	10.477	9.763	9.122	8.544	8.022
18	16.398	14.992	13.754	12.659	11.690	10.828	10.059	9.372	8.756	8.201
19	17.226	15.678	14.324	13.134	12.085	11.158	10.336	9.604	8.950	8.365
20	18.046	16.351	14.877	13.590	12.462	11.470	10.594	9.818	9.129	8.514
21	18.857	17.011	15.415	14.029	12.821	11.764	10.836	10.017	9.292	8.649
22	19.660	17.658	15.937	14.451	13.163	12.042	11.061	10.201	9.442	8.772
23	20.456	18.292	16.444	14.857	13.489	12.303	11.272	10.371	9.580	8.883
24	21.243	18.914	16.936	15.247	13.799	12.550	11.469	10.529	9.707	8.985
25	22.023	19.523	17.413	15.622	14.094	12.783	11.654	10.675	9.823	9.077
26	22.795	20.121	17.877	15.983	14.375	13.003	11.826	10.810	9.929	9.161
27	23.560	20.707	18.327	16.330	14.643	13.211	11.987	10.935	10.027	9.237
28	24.316	21.281	18.764	16.663	14.898	13.406	12.137	11.051	10.116	9.307
29	25.066	21.844	19.188	16.984	15.141	13.591	12.278	11.158	10.198	9.370
30	25.808	22.396	19.600	17.292	15.372	13.765	12.409	11.258	10.274	9.427
31	26.542	22.938	20.000	17.588	15.593	13.929	12.532	11.350	10.343	9.479
32	27.270	23.468	20.389	17.874	15.803	14.084	12.647	11.435	10.406	9.526
33	27.990	23.989	20.766	18.148	16.003	14.230	12.754	11.514	10.464	9.569
34	28.703	24.499	21.132	18.411	16.193	14.368	12.854	11.587	10.518	9.609
35	29.409	24.999	21.487	18.665	16.374	14.498	12.948	11.655	10.567	9.644
36	30.108	25.489	21.832	18.908	16.547	14.621	13.035	11.717	10.612	9.677
37	30.800	25.969	22.167	19.143	16.711	14.737	13.117	11.775	10.653	9.706
38	31.485	26.441	22.492	19.368	16.868	14.846	13.193	11.829	10.691	9.733
39	32.163	26.903	22.808	19.584	17.017	14.949	13.265	11.879	10.726	9.757
40	32.835	27.355	23.115	19.793	17.159	15.046	13.332	11.925	10.757	9.779
41	33.500	27.799	23.412	19.993	17.294	15.138	13.394	11.967	10.787	9.799
42	34.158	28.235	23.701	20.186	17.423	15.225	13.452	12.007	10.813	9.817
43	34.810	28.662	23.982	20.371	17.546	15.306	13.507	12.043	10.838	9.834
43	35.455	29.080	24.254	20.549	17.663	15.383	13.558	12.077	10.861	9.849
45	36.095	29.490	24.519	20.720	17.774	15.456	13.606	12.108	10.881	9.863
46	36.727	29.892	24.775	20.885	17.880	15.524	13.650	12.137	10.900	9.875
47	37.354	30.287	25.025	21.043	17.981	15.589	13.692	12.164	10.918	9.887
48	37.974	30.673	25.267	21.195	18.077	15.650	13.730	12.189	10.934	9.897
49	38.588	31.052	25.502	21.341	18.169	15.708	13.767	12.212	10.948	9.906
50	39.196	31.424	25.730	21.482	18.256	15.762	13.801	12.233	10.962	9.915

11%	12%	13%	14%	15%	16%	17%	18%	19%	20%	Years 0 to:
0.901	0.893	0.885	0.877	0.870	0.862	0.855	0.847	0.840	0.833	1
1.713	1.690	1.668	1.647	1.626	1.605	1.585	1.566	1.547	1.528	2
2.444	2.402	2.361	2.322	2.283	2.246	2.210	2.174	2.140	2.106	3
3.102	3.037	2.974	2.914	2.855	2.798	2.743	2.690	2.639	2.589	4
3.696	3.605	3.517	3.433	3.352	3.274	3.199	3.127	3.058	2.991	5
4.231	4.111	3.998	3.889	3.784	3.685	3.589	3.498	3.410	3.326	6
4.712	4.564	4.423	4.288	4.160	4.039	3.922	3.812	3.706	3.605	7
5.146	4.968	4.799	4.639	4.487	4.344	4.207	4.078	3.954	3.837	8
5.537	5.328	5.132	4.946	4.772	4.607	4.451	4.303	4.163	4.031	9
5.889	5.650	5.425	5.216	5.019	4.833	4.659	4.494	4.339	4.192	10
6.207	5.938	5.687	5.453	5.234	5.029	4.836	4.656	4.486	4.327	11
6.492	6.194	5.918	5.660	5.421	5.197	4.988	4.793	4.611	4.439	12
6.750	6.424	6.122	5.842	5.583	5.342	5.118	4.910	4.715	4.533	13
6.982	6.628	6.302	6.002	5.724	5.468	5.229	5.008	4.802	4.611	14
7.191	6.811	6.462	6.142	5.847	5.575	5.324	5.092	4.876	4.675	15
7.379	6.974	6.604	6.265	5.954	5.668	5.405	5.162	4.938	4.730	16
7.549	7.120	6.729	6.373	6.047	5.749	5.475	5.222	4.990	4.775	17
7.702	7.250	6.840	6.467	6.128	5.818	5.534	5.273	5.033	4.812	18
7.839	7.366	6.938	6.550	6.198	5.877	5.584	5.316	5.070	4.843	19
7.963	7.469	7.025	6.623	6.259	5.929	5.628	5.353	5.101	4.870	20
8.075	7.562	7.102	6.687	6.312	5.973	5.665	5.384	5.127	4.891	21
8.176	7.645	7.170	6.743	6.359	6.011	5.696	5.410	5.149	4.909	22
8.266	7.718	7.230	6.792	6.399	6.044	5.723	5.432	5.167	4.925	23
8.348	7.784	7.283	6.835	6.434	6.073	5.746	5.451	5.182	4.937	24
8.422	7.843	7.330	6.873	6.464	6.097	5.766	5.467	5.195	4.948	25
8.488	7.896	7.372	6.906	6.491	6.118	5.783	5.480	5.206	4.956	26
8.548	7.943	7.409	6.935	6.514	6.136	5.798	5.492	5.215	4.964	27
8.602	7.984	7.441	6.961	6.534	6.152	5.810	5.502	5.223	4.970	28
8.650	8.022	7.470	6.983	6.551	6.166	5.820	5.510	5.229	4.975	29
8.694	8.055	7.496	7.003	6.566	6.177	5.829	5.517	5.235	4.979	30
8.733	8.085	7.518	7.020	6.579	6.187	5.837	5.523	5.239	4.982	31
8.769	8.112	7.538	7.035	6.591	6.196	5.844	5.528	5.243	4.985	32
8.801	8.135	7.556	7.048	6.600	6.203	5.849	5.532	5.246	4.988	33
8.829	8.157	7.572	7.060	6.609	6.210	5.854	5.536	5.249	4.990	34
8.855	8.176	7.586	7.070	6.617	6.215	5.858	5.539	5.251	4.992	35
8.879	8.192	7.598	7.079	6.623	6.220	5.862	5.541	5.253	4.993	36
8.900	8.208	7.609	7.087	6.629	6.224	5.865	5.543	5.255	4.994	37
8.919	8.221	7.618	7.094	6.634	6.228	5.867	5.545	5.256	4.995	38
8.936	8.233	7.627	7.100	6.638	6.231	5.869	5.547	5.257	4.996	39
8.951	8.244	7.634	7.105	6.642	6.233	5.871	5.548	5.258	4.997	40
8.965	8.253	7.641	7.110	6.645	6.236	5.873	5.549	5.259	4.997	41
8.977	8.262	7.647	7.114	6.648	6.238	5.874	5.550	5.260	4.998	42
8.989	8.270	7.652	7.117	6.650	6.239	5.875	5.551	5.260	4.998	43
8.999	8.276	7.657	7.120	6.652	6.241	5.876	5.552	5.261	4.998	44
9.008	8.283	7.661	7.123	6.654	6.242	5.877	5.552	5.261	4.999	45
9.016	8.288	7.664	7.126	6.656	6.243	5.878	5.553	5.261	4.999	46
9.024	8.293	7.668	7.128	6.657	6.244	5.879	5.553	5.262	4.999	47
9.030	8.297	7.671	7.130	6.659	6.245	5.879	5.554	5.262	4.999	48
9.036	8.301	7.673	7.131	6.660	6.246	5.880	5.554	5.262	4.999	49
9.042	8.304	7.675	7.133	6.661	6.246	5.880	5.554	5.262	4.999	50

Essay Questions

1. Explain briefly the rationale behind economic order quantity (EOQ) models and discuss the extent to which the principles on which they are based can be used by a management accountant to help an organisation decide the most appropriate levels of service that it should offer its customers. (*ICMA*)

2. You have recently been appointed the assistant management accountant of an organisation having middle management employees with various line and functional responsibilities. A considerable number of management accounting reports are issued but few of these are widely used by executives. The first task you have been asked to undertake, in your new position, is a review of these reports. To assist in your review, you are required initially to prepare two lists indicating ways in which generally:

(*a*) a report *format* might be designed to have maximum impact; and

(*b*) a report's *content* might be presented to motivate the recipient to take effective action.

3. A long-established, highly centralised company has grown to the extent that its chief executive, despite having a good support team, is finding difficulty in keeping up with the many decisions of importance in the company. Consideration is therefore being given to reorganising the company into profit centres. These would be product divisions headed by a divisional managing director who would be responsible for all the division's activities relating to its products. You are required to explain, in outline:

(*a*) the types of decision areas that should be transferred to the new divisional managing directors, if such a reorganisation is to achieve its objectives;

(*b*) the types of decision areas that might reasonably be retained at head office; and

(*c*) the management accounting problems that might be expected to arise in introducing effective profit centre control. (*ICMA*)

4. Describe the capital asset pricing model and explain how it may assist in the determination of the discount rate used in the appraisal of capital projects. Discuss the major difficulties inherent in its practical application and use. (*ACCA*)

5. Write a report to your factory manager explaining why techniques applicable to the problems of joint product costing should not be used for

managerial decisions regarding whether a product should be sold as it stands or be processed further before sale.   (*ACCA*)

6. A company has been formed to provide a repair service for domestic appliances. It is a labour intensive organisation employing 200 maintenance engineers but involving a minimum of capital expenditure. As management accountant, you are requested to explain:

(*a*) what you consider to be the key areas for financial control; and

(*b*) the procedures you would adopt to measure corporate effectiveness.   (*ICMA*)

7. The effective use of the control information provided by an organisation's accounting department might be reduced by the behaviour of its operating managers.

(*a*) Explain briefly six motivations or attitudes that would result in less effective use of the control information.

(*b*) Indicate very briefly what actions the accounting department might take to improve the situation.   (*ICMA*)

8. (*a*) Outline and discuss the main objectives of a transfer pricing system.

(*b*) Consider the advantages and disadvantages of:

(*i*) market-based transfer prices;

(*ii*) cost based transfer prices.

Outline the main variants that exist under each heading.

(*c*) Discuss the relevance of linear programming to the setting of transfer prices.   (*ACCA*)

9. (*a*) Discuss the proposition that joint cost allocation procedures provide little useful information and none at all for decision-making purposes. Is there any justification for claiming further that they are not only useless but positively harmful?

(*b*) "Advice that a firm's budget should concentrate resources on the activity which yields the highest contribution per unit of limiting factor is of doubtful value, since usually there are multiple constraints and multiple goals. In practice budget preparation is a satisficing rather than an optimising process." Discuss.   (*ACCA*)

10. (*a*) Discuss the conditions that should apply if linear regression analysis is to be used to analyse cost behaviour.

(*b*) Outline the main features of a responsibility accounting system.

(*c*) Discuss the effect of a significant rate of inflation on the control function of a budgetary planning and control system.   (*ACCA*)

11. (*a*) Why can methods of control of research and development expenditure in an industrial company be expected to differ from the control of expenditure of other functions such as manufacturing, selling and administration?

(*b*) What are the main features that you would expect to find in a system for control of research and development expenditure in a large industrial company?   (*ICMA*)

12. (*a*) Explain the "learning curve" and discuss its relevance to setting standards.

(*b*) Discuss the problems which may arise in an organisation through the use of its budget as a key feature of both financial planning and control procedures.

(*c*) Explain the conventional calculation of material mix and yield variances and discuss their usefulness.   (*ACCA*)

13. The accountant's approach to cost volume profit analysis has been criticised in that, among other matters, it does not deal with the following:

(*a*) situations where sales volume differs radically from production volume;

(*b*) situations where the sales revenue and total cost functions are markedly non-linear;

(*c*) changes in product mix;

(*d*) risk and uncertainty.

Explain these objections to the accountant's conventional cost-volume-profit model and suggest how they can be overcome or ameliorated.

(*ACCA*)

14. Divisionalisation is a common form of organisational arrangement, but there is some diversity of opinion as to the best measure of divisional performance. Discuss this topic and describe and compare the main performance measures that have been suggested.   (*ACCA*)

15. Specify and comment on the objectives of budgeting. Describe the differences and similarities between budgets for planning and budgets for control.   (*ACCA*)

16. "The diverse use of routinely recorded cost data gives rise to a fundamental danger: information prepared for one purpose can be grossly misleading in another context" (from L.R. Amey and D.A. Eggington, *Management Accounting: A Conceptual Approach*).

REQUIRED:

(*a*) Discuss the extent to which the above statement is valid and explain your conclusions.

(*b*) (*i*) Provide illustrations of two management accounting reports containing routinely recorded data, specify the primary purpose of the reports and give examples of other specific contexts in which the information they contain might be grossly misleading.

(*ii*) Briefly give reasons why the information is valid for the primary purpose but grossly misleading in the alternative stated context.

17. One of the major difficulties of applying a financial reporting and control system based on flexible budgeting to a service or overhead department is identifying and measuring an appropriate unit of activity with which to flex the budget.

REQUIRED:

(*a*) Describe and comment on the desirable attributes of such a measure in the context of a valid application of flexible budgeting to a service centre or to a cost centre where standard costing is not applicable.

(b) Explain the difficulties in obtaining such a measure.

(c) List three suitable measures of activity, indicating the circumstances in which each would be suitable and the circumstances in which each of them would be misleading or unsuitable. (ACCA)

18. In product costing the costs attributed to each unit of production may be calculated by using either (i) absorption costing or (ii) marginal (or direct or variable) costing.

Similarly, in departmental cost or profit reports the fixed costs of overhead or service departments may be allocated to production departments as an integral part of the production departments' costs or else segregated in some form.

REQUIRED:

(a) Describe absorption and marginal (or direct or variable) costing and outline the strengths and weaknesses of each method.

(b) For any three of the following, explain why and to what extent each of the costing techniques is useful in providing relevant cost information for:

(i)   control purposes;
(ii) decision-making;
(iii) planning;
(iv) pricing;
(v)   stock valuation (ACCA)

19. In the context of cost reduction programmes explain the possible roles of (a) zero base budgeting, and (b) value analysis.

(ICMA adapted)

20. You are appointed as the management accountant of a large charitable organisation undertaking a wide range of social welfare activities on an international basis.

You are required to explain:

(a) how its financial features will differ from those of a commercial company; and

(b) how any three of the following systems might be used to advantage in this type of organisation.

(i)   Fund accounting.
(ii) Performance budgeting.
(iii) Cost benefit analysis.
(iv) Management audits.
(v)   Cash forecasting. (ICMA)

Quantitative Questions

1. From the information given below relating to a manufacturing company, you are required to:

(a) write up the cost ledger and prepare a costing profit & loss account showing the appropriate variances for the year ended 30th April 1984;

(b) ascertain the profit stated in the financial accounts for the year ended 30th April 1984 and reconcile this with the profit shown in your answers to (a) above;

(c) prepare a summary balance sheet as at 30th April 1984; and

(d) state in a short descriptive note a suitable alternative method of keeping the accounts of the company.

The summary balance sheet as at 30th April 1983 was as follows:

	£	£
Fixed assets		
Freehold land and buildings	495,000	
Plant and machinery	585,000	1,080,000
Current assets		
Stocks (at actual cost):		
Raw materials	210,000	
Work-in-progress	365,000	
Finished goods	125,000	
Debtors	1,290,000	
Short-term loans, cash and bank balance	620,000	
	2,610,000	
Current liabilities		
Trade creditors, dividends due,		
current taxation, etc.	690,000	1,920,000
		3,000,000
Financed by:		
Issued capital—ordinary shares		2,000,000
Capital and revenue reserves		600,000
9% debentures		400,000
		3,000,000

In addition to the normal financial accounts, from which the above balance sheet was compiled, the company kept cost control accounts. The balances of these accounts at 30 April 1983 were as follows:

	At standard cost	
	£	£
Cost ledger control		690,000
Raw materials	205,000	
Work-in-progress	368,000	
Finished goods	117,000	
	690,000	690,000

The following is a summary of transactions during the year ended 30th April 1984.

	£
Payments received from debtors	3,392,000
Payments received from borrowers, interest on loans	7,000
Total payments made	3,174,000
Purchases of raw materials on credit	809,000
Material price variance, calculated at time of purchase (adverse)	19,000
Material usage variance (adverse)	5,000
Direct wages: Actual (1,300,000 hours)	678,000
Standard @£0.5 per hour	655,000
Indirect wages	231,000
Depreciation	105,000
Indirect materials and expenses	193,000
Administration, selling and distribution expenses	585,000
Purchase of new plant and equipment	225,000
Debenture interest	36,000
Subscription to "A Political Party"	2,000
Grant to staff benevolent fund	25,000
Materials issued to production, at standard prices	800,000
Factory overhead absorbed to production at £0.4 per standard direct labour-hour	
Sales on credit	3,147,000
Recommended dividend on ordinary shares 15%	
Closing stock values, based on physical stock:	

	At standard cost	At actual cost
	£	£
Raw materials	180,000	179,000
Work-in-progress	345,000	351,000
Finished goods	119,000	120,000

(*ICMA*)

2. A foundry with 200 direct employees, each earning an average wage of £250 per week, produces 10,000 rough castings each four-week period. The castings have a direct material cost of £45 each and an average sales value of £120 each. Details of the overhead are:

Production:	Variable—	75% of direct wages
	Fixed —	£1,440,000 per annum
Selling and distribution:	Variable—	2½% of sales value
	Fixed —	£480,000 per annum

It is now proposed to machine the castings and this will increase the sales value by 50 per cent. To do this, both the direct wages and fixed production overhead will be increased by 75 per cent, while variable production overhead will be 80 per cent of the increased wages Variable selling and distribution overhead will increase to 5 per cent of sales value, while the fixed remains unchanged. Prepare two comparative statements showing the present and the future proposed cost and profit position as:

(a) a marginal cost and profit statement for the operation of a year of fifty-two working weeks;

(b) a cost and profit per unit by absorption cost method.

(calculations to nearest pound)

(ICMA)

3. The following overhead costs were both budgeted and incurred in a manufacturing company during October.

		Indirect wages (£)	Indirect materials (£)	Indirect expenses (£)
Production department:	1	15,000	3,000	—
	2	10,000	6,000	—
	3	20,000	4,000	—
Service department:	A	5,000	2,000	—
	B	10,000	3,000	—
Not allocated		22,000	3,000	55,000

Costs are apportioned to departments on the following bases:

Departments	Production (%) 1	2	3	Service (%) A	B	Total (%)
Overhead cost, not allocated	35	20	30	5	10	100
Service department costs: A	25	20	40	—	15	100
B	15	35	30	20	—	100

Service department costs are apportioned to production and service departments on the "repeated distribution" or "continuous allotment" method.

The company uses predetermined departmental direct labour hour rates for absorption of overhead into its product costs. Direct labour-hours for October were.

	Production department		
	1	*2*	*3*
Budgeted	20,000	40,000	30,000
Actual	21,200	38,600	28,100

You are required to prepare for October:

(*a*) an overhead distribution sheet for the production departments;

(*b*) a production overhead control account for the whole company; and

(*c*) an overhead account for each production department.   (*ICMA*)

4. At a recent conference on "Cost Control in a Period of Reduction in Demand", your managing director was impressed by the remarks of one of the speakers who advocated a marginal costing system of management reporting. The managing director has now asked you to compare the present absorption costing system with an alternative marginal costing system. You are required to.

(*a*) Tabulate merits of:

(*i*) a marginal costing system; and

(*ii*) an absorption costing system.

(*b*) Prepare for presentation to your board of directors two statements showing the budgeted results for the year in:

(*i*) an absorption costing form;

(*ii*) a marginal costing form.

Pay particular attention to the layout of your presentation, which should be based on the data shown below.

(*c*) Present ratios with each statement which will show the relative profitability of each product and comment briefly on these ratios.

The company produces two products; the standard cost data for each are as follows (one unit).

Product	*A*	*B*
Direct materials:		
Unit required	20	5
Price per unit	£0.50	£1.00
Direct labour		
Hours allowed	5	10
Rate per hour	£2.00	£1.50

Budgeted data for the year are as follows.

Direct labour-hours		55,000
Production overhead		£220,000
Administration, selling and distribution		£108,000
Product	A	B
Sales (£000s)	375	300
Sales price, each	£75	£100
Profit as a percentage of selling price	20	10

(*ICMA*)

5. A foundry with eight different departments produces four types of casting. Each department's costs are allocated to products on a net weight basis of casting handled. Data concerning each type of casting is given below.

Type of casting	Net output for one month (tonnes)	Departments processing castings
A	180	1, 2, 3, 5 and 7
B	200	1, 2, 3 and 4
C	60	1, 2, 4, 6 and 7
D	120	1, 3, 4, 5 and 8

The costs for one month are as follows.

Department	Total labour £	Material cost per tonne of casting £	Overhead as % of labour cost
1	2,800	14,00	10
2	3,960	10.50	15
3	1,500	—	20
4	4,180	—	10
5	6,930	12.50	10
6	240	—	25
7	3,600	1.20	20
8	480	—	10

You are required to prepare a monthly cost statement to show for each type of casting the cost per tonne and the total cost. (*ICMA*)

6. The data given below relate to period nos 5 and 6 in a department of a factory manufacturing a product by a continuous process. You are required to calculate for the department the following.

(*a*) For each period, using the present basis of average costs:

    (*i*) the profit made; and

    (*ii*) the value of closing work-in-progress.

(*b*) For period no 5 only, using the proposed first-in-first-out basis for charging out the finished products:

(*i*) the profit made; and

(*ii*) the value of work-in-progress at end of period 5.

Data:

Period no 5

Opening work-in-progress:	Units	
	400	
	Degree of completion	£
Direct materials	100%	462.80
Conversion cost	40%	186.20

Input:	Units	£
Direct material	2,800	4,253.20
Conversion cost		5,485.80
Output passed by inspection	2,690	
Closing work-in-progress	440	
	Degree of completion	
Direct materials	100%	
Conversion cost	30%	

Period no 6

Input:	Units	
Direct materials	3,100	4,904.80
Conversion cost		6,760.60
Output passed by inspection	3,110	
Closing work-in-progress:	380	
	Degree of completion	
Direct materials	100%'	
Conversion cost	25%	

Normal wastage is budgeted at 2 per cent of the physical input of materials and is regarded as comprising units on which both direct labour and full conversion costs have been expended. The costs of the department are calculated at present on an average cost basis, but the management is proposing to change to a first-in-first-out basis. The department is credited at £4 per unit with output passed by the inspection department.

A foundry produces brass castings consisting of 70 per cent copper, costing £450 per tonne, and 30 per cent zinc, costing £120 per tonne. Of the metal charged, 10 per cent is lost in melting—that is before pouring. Melting costs, other than materials, amount to £50 per tonne of metal poured.

Good castings produced vary, according to product type, from 50 per cent to 70 per cent of metal poured. The balance, consisting of runners, heads and scrap, is returned to stock for subsequent use, being valued at cost of metal content only.

Prepare costs of metal and melting for products with (a) 50 per cent, (b) 60 per cent, and (c) 70 per cent yields.

(*ICMA*)

7. Equinox is the main product of the Solstice Chemical Corporation. The product is manufactured in two processes, with all the output from process 1 (chemical C) being transferred to process 2. Additional raw material (chemical D) is added at the start of processing in process 2, and the finished product is packed in standardised containers and despatched to the finished goods store. A standard costing system is used and this is integrated with the company's financial accounting system. The following standards apply:

Process 1 (standard specification for 1,000 kg of C)		Process 2 (standard specification for 1,000 kg of Equinox)	
Direct material:		Direct material:	
400 kg of A at £0.36	£144	1,050 kg of C at £0.70	£735
700 kg of B at £0.08	56	50 kg of D at £0.50	25
Direct labour:		Direct labour:	
25 hours at £4.00 per hour	100	5 hours at £4.00 per hour	20
Variable overhead:		Variable overhead:	
25 direct labour-hours at £8.00	200	5 direct labour-hours at £9.20	46
Fixed overhead:		Fixed overhead:	
25 direct labour-hours at £8.00	200	5 direct labour-hours at £14.00	70
		Packing material:	4
	£700		£900

The standards allow for a normal loss in volume of 10 per cent of the good output in each process. This loss occurs evenly throughout the processing.

The following details apply for the operations of a particular week.

Purchases of raw materials	£
8,000 kg of A at 0.39 per kg	3,120
16,000 kg of B at £0.05 per kg	800
1,500 kg of D at £0.54 per kg	810

	Process 1		Process 2	
Direct material issued to Production				
	A	8,000 kg	C	22,000 kg (transferred from process 1)
	B	17,000 kg	D	930 kg
Direct labour	530 hrs at £4.10 £2,173		110 hrs at £3.80 £418	
Variable overhead	£4,134		£912	
Fixed overhead	£4,900 (actual) £5,000 (budgeted)		£1,510 (actual) £1,660 (budgeted)	
Packing material			£95	
Production and work-in-process	Kg	Degree of completion (%)	Kg	Degree of completion (%)
Opening work-in progress	2,100	50	1,050	50
Output (completed production)	22,000	100	17,000	100
Closing work-in progress	2,675	30	3,225	25

Direct material price variances are calculated when the material is purchased. Raw material stocks are, therefore, recorded at standard cost and issued to production at standard cost. All other production expenses are charged at "actual" from the expense accounts to the process accounts, and any variances are transferred from the process accounts to appropriate variance accounts. Such transfers are made weekly. Output transferred from process 1 to process 2 is transferred at standard cost and work-in-progress is valued on this basic.

You are required to:

(a) write up the process accounts for process 1 and process 2;

(b) comment on the mix of raw materials used in process 1 during the week; and

(c) comment on the profitability of process 2 if chemical C can be sold at £0.90 per kilogram and the market price of Equinox is £1.05 per kilogram.   (ACCA)

8. Stover Chemicals operates four manufacturing processes. Process 1 yields three joint products (X, Y and Z) in fixed proportions. Although each of these products could be sold at the split-off point (and there exists a ready market for each in this state), they are normally processed further—X in process 2, Y in process 3 and Z in process 4. This additional processing enhances their saleable values as follows.

Selling prices per litre			
	X	Y	Z
Product sold at split-off point	£0.80	£0.30	£1.30
Product sold after further processing	£1.20	£0.70	£1.75

The process accounts for the last operating period, when the plant was operating at full capacity, can be summarised as follows:

Process 1

	Litres	£		Litres	£
Opening work-in-progress	4,000	1,200	Production transferred		
Direct material	99,000	9,900	X to process 2	50,000	25,000
Processing expense		39,500	Y to process 3	30,000	15,000
			Z to process 4	20,000	10,000
			Closing work-in-progress	3,000	600
	103,000	50,600		103,000	50,600

Process 2

	Litres	£		Litres	£
Opening work-in-progress	2,000	1,267	Sales revenue	50,000	60,000
Input from process 1	50,000	25,000	Closing work-in-progress	2,000	1,267
Processing expense		13,333			
Profit to profit & loss account		21,667			
	52,000	61,267		52,000	61,267

Process 3

	Litres	£		Litres	£
Opening work-in-progress	1,000	650	Sales revenue	30,000	21,000
Input from process 1	30,000	15,000	Loss to profit and loss account		3,000
Processing expense		9,000	Closing work-in-progress	1,000	650
	31,000	24,650		31,000	24,650

			Process 4			
	Litres	£			Litres	£
Opening work-in-progress	2,000	1,700	Sales revenue		20,000	35,000
Input from process 1	20,000	10,000	Closing work-in-progress		2,000	1,700
Processing expense		14,000				
Profit to profit & loss account		11,000				
	22,000	36,700			22,000	36,700

The costs incurred, and the processing efficiency for the period to which the above accounts relate, can be assumed to be representative of current conditions. The joint costs in process 1 have been apportioned on the basis of the output (in litres) of X, Y and Z. All work-in-progress is complete as far as material content is concerned and (except for the closing work-in-progress in process 1) it is half-processed. The closing work-in-progress in process 1 is one-quarter processed.

You are required to:

(a) comment on the relative profitability of the products, in particular consider the loss arising on product Y in process 3;

(b) comment on the company's policy of processing all three products beyond the split-off point;

(c) restate the process accounts for processes 3 and 4 using sales values (at the split-off point) as the basis for the joint cost allocation;

(d) restate the process accounts for processes 1 and 4 using the sales values at the split-off point as transfer prices in transferring production from process 1 to the other processes; and

(e) discuss the utility of each version of the process accounts (one version in the question and two in your solution) and to comment on the joint cost allocation problem. (ACCA)

9. The Spot-on Company manufactures "dotties". The bin card for this product states that the maximum stockholding for it is 15,000 and the minimum 5,000. Four materials are used in the manufacture of dotties and information currently available about these materials is as follows.

	Number of kg required to produce one dottie	Information on bin card (in kg)		
Material		on hand	maximum	minimum
Doh	2	3,000	7,000	2,000
Ray	3	3,000	12,000	3,000
Mee	1	5,000	7,000	2,000
Fah	5	20,000	20,000	5,000

Information from various departments within the Spot-on Company about dotties is as below.

Raw material store
2,000 kg of Doh and 1,000 kg of·Fah in the store have been reserved for work-in-progress.

Finished goods store
The stock of dotties is 5,000, but 1,000 are on order and still have to be withdrawn from the store and sent to the warehouse for despatch.

Production control
2,000 dotties are in the process of manufacture and all the materials necessary to produce these have been either reserved or issued.

Sales department
Orders have just been received for 10,000 dotties which are to be delivered as quickly as possible, but so far the orders concerned have been processed no further than the sales department.

REQUIRED:
(a) Prepare statements for management which clearly show workings for:
   (i) the size of the production order to be placed, to bring stocks to a maximum;
   (ii) details of the quantities of materials which need to be issued with the production order; and
   (iii) information of the purchase order which will have to be placed to bring the stock of raw materials up to the maximum holdings required for each of them.
(b) In the table showing information on raw materials it can be seen that although twice as much Doh is required in the production of dotties than Mee, the maximum and minimum stockholdings shown on the bin card for these materials is the same. State briefly the factors that the firm would have taken into consideration when arriving at the maximum and minimum levels of stockholdings shown, and with reference to Doh and Mee explain how these factors may have caused the maximum and minimum stock levels to be the same.   (ACCA)

10. While three eccentric sisters, Alice, Betty and Clair, were on holiday in France they obtained the distribution rights for the UK market of a ready-mix flour which was packed in 1 kg bags for sale to housewives to use for baking a French bread. On 1st January 1984 the sisters put £1,000 from their savings into a bank account under the name of the Eccentric Sisters' Partnership, which they had formed for the purpose of distributing the flour. Initially they commenced operations from the

rambling old house in which they lived and, after discussion, decided not to charge overheads or to pay themselves a salary but rather to share any profits that the partnership might make equally between them on a six-monthly basis.

Once their capital was in the bank the sisters immediately made a purchase of 10,000 bags of the mix, which exactly exhausted their initial capital. They understood from the supplier that the price they would have to pay for the flour was likely to fluctuate considerably, but as they wanted to be able to offer their own customers a stable price on a six-monthly basis, they set their sales price at 15p per bag for their launch period.

During the following six months of the partnership's trading the following transactions took place.

January	Sold	5,000 bags
February	Bought Sold	5,000 bags @ 12p 5,000 bags
March	Bought	10,000 bags @ 10p
April	Sold	10,000 bags
May	Bought Sold	5,000 bags @ 12½p 5,000 bags
June	Bought Sold	5,000 bags @ 11p 5,000 bags

Early in July 1976 each of the sisters independently prepared her own version of the partnership's first half-year performance. On 10th July 1976 the sisters held a meeting to decide upon the amount to be distributed as their first profit shares. Alice was more than happy about the situation, saying that each would get more than they originally hoped, and with her share of £450 would take a trip to North America. Betty said that Alice must have made some mistakes in her calculations because she would only get £408.33 as her third share. Clair could not hold back her growing exasperation over what she considered to be the ineptitude of her sisters at calculating profit, and she jumped in to say that neither of them would ever make accountants—because, according to her, the correct distribution would be £421.43.

An argument started about who was right. When the sisters compared their statements they found also that, as well as their income calculations being different, the valuation they had obtained for closing stock on 30th June 1976 also varied in each case.

REQUIRED:

(a) Showing the calculations to support your answer, provide information of which methods the sisters had used to price out stocks in their various assessments of the partnership's performance. Present your results in tabular form to show the total income for the partnership and the value of the closing stock for each of the methods.

(b) Discuss the major conceptual difficulties associated with pricing out stock as far as the measurement of income and value is concerned. Refer to the sisters' calculations where appropriate.

(c) Do any of the methods used by the sisters overcome the difficulties that you have discussed, and can you make additional suggestions which might prove to be even more helpful to management who are trying to measure the performance of an organisation? Give reasons for your answer.   (ACCA)

11. A manufacturing company, in addition to its work for outside customers, has an internal requirement for 200 units a day for a specialty product it manufactures and markets itself. At present several operations are performed manually in meeting this requirement. Mechanised batch production is contemplated. This will involve a set-up cost of £700 for each batch put into production. The largest single batch size is 12,000 units. After each batch has been made, the set-up cost, which includes maintenance and cleaning, must be incurred before a new batch can be started. The variable cost of each unit is £10. The annual storage cost is £1 per unit, and the cost of financing the inventory is 8 per cent per annum. The specialty products are required for 240 working days a year, and the average inventory is one half of the number of units made in each batch.

(a) Selecting 4, 6, 8, 12, 24 and 48 as the number of batches per year upon which to base the calculations, determine the annual cost for the required quantity of the specialty product for the selected number of batches.

(b) Draw a graph, plotting three curves to illustrate:
    (i)   the annual total costs;
    (ii) the set-up cost; and
    (iii) the inventory carrying costs.

As determined in (a), ascertain from the graph the optimum number of batches to produce each year in order to minimise the total cost of setting up and carrying the inventory.   (ACMA)

12. Optimum Ltd makes a single product, the Opt. Opts sell for £30 each and demand is running at 1,000 units per annum, evenly distributed over the year. Technical features in production necessitate batch production methods to supply the expected demand. Currently the company produces in batches of 200 units, although this quantity is not determined by the technology. The cost card for the production of one Opt provides the following information.

		£	£
Material cost			6.00
Labour costs:			
Machining 2 hours	@ £1.75	3.50	
Assembly 1 hour	@ £1.25	1.25	
Packing ½ hour	@ £0.50	0.25	
			5.00
Other direct costs:			
2 machine hours	@ £4.00		8.00
Overheads			3.00
			22.00

On investigation you find that the overheads are comprised of elements for:

(*a*) the labour costs associated with the preparation time required for each batch of Opts of four hours, which is carried out by the packing staff;

(*b*) machine set-up costs of £40 per batch. This sevice is provided by an outside firm; and

(*c*) the absorption of other fixed overheads.

Opts are stacked three high on pallets which require storage space 1 metre square and are stored in a warehouse. The rent of the warehouse was negotiated many years ago at the favourable price of £10 per square metre. However, as demand for Opts has been dropping, the firm has been increasingly able to sublet its surplus warehouse space for £24 per square metre. Recently Optimum Ltd's labour force has been reduced. However, there is still plenty of spare capacity in the organisation as far as all classes of its labour are concerned. Nevertheless, the management has no intention of causing further redundancies. You may assume that the opportunity cost of interest on stockholdings is negligible.

REQUIRED:

(*a*) Compute the optimum batch size of Opts to be produced, explaining the formula you have used, commenting briefly on any assumptions you have made and relevant costs you have introduced.

(*b*) Comment briefly on the size of the average stock of Opts held, in the light of your answer to (*a*) above.   (*ACCA*)

13. A company which manufactures industrial pumps has decided to computerise its stock control system. In doing so it is proposed to change the accounting procedures. The current system is to:

(*a*) value all stock on a first-in-first-out basis;

(*b*) identify separately the cost of rejected material;

(*c*) charge the cost of rejects to a scrap account and credit this account with the value of scrap sold; and

(*d*) debit the balance on the scrap account to the finished goods account.

The proposed new system is to:

(*a*) value all stock on an average cost basis;

(*b*) average out the cost of defective material over the good production in each department; and

(*c*) credit the value of the scrap material to the department in which the rejection occurs.

The following data are given for component X.

Component X is machined from a bought-out casting. There are three operations in the machining department with direct wages in the proportion of 3:2:5. Direct expense is incurred equally by each operation.

Inventory at 1st October 1983:

		£
Costs:	Direct material	16,200
	Direct wages	1,300
	Direct expense	500
Units:	600 not started	
	100 completed operation 1	
	200 completed operation 2	

Inventory during October 1983:

		£
Costs incurred:	Direct material	108,000
	Direct wages	59,730
	Direct expense	16,500
Units:	5,400 purchased	
	4,800 transferred to finished goods	
	700 rejected from October castings	
	at the end of operation:	

1	200
2	200
3	300

Inventory at 31st October 1983:

Units:	500 completed operation 1
	300 completed operation 2

All scrapped material is sold and has a net value equivalent to 20 per cent of the original direct material cost.

First you are required for component X, from the data given for the month of October 1983, to calculate:

(*a*) the machining cost per unit of production during October, showing the individual operations separately;

(*b*) for the current system:

(*i*) the cost of material transferred from the machining department to the finished goods stores; and

(*ii*) the value of machining department inventory at 31st October.

(c) for the proposed new system:

    (i) the cost of material transferred from the machining department to the finished goods stores; and

    (ii) the value of machining department inventory at 31st October.

Unit costs should be calculated in £s to two decimal places, and any rounding differences should be included in the cost of materials transferred out.

Second, you are required to write brief notes on the effect of introducing the new system.   (ICMA)

14. Textiles Ltd operates a subsidiary, the Sunny Textile Company Ltd, which manufactures ladies' swimwear. Following the success of this subsidiary it has been decided to expand it by diversifying into the production of swimwear for all the family. An extension to the Sunny Textile Company Ltd's factory is now being built for this purpose. The contract for this extension is for £100,000. Ten per cent of the contract price had to be paid on signing the contract in December 1983. Another £50,000 has to be paid on 30th March 1984, with the balance due by 30th May 1984 or on completion.

The financial year of the Sunny Textile Company Ltd runs from 1st April and budgeted figures for the 1984 calender year have been produced as follows.

Month	Sales (before discounts allowed) (£)	Purchase of raw materials (before discounts received) (£)	Wages (£)	Fixed overheads (including depreciaiton of £1,000 per month (£)
Jan	6,000	10,000	5,000	2,000
Feb	6,000	10,000	5,000	2,000
Mar	24,000	10,000	5,000	2,000
Apr	48,000	10,000	5,000	2,000
May	48,000	10,000	5,000	2,000
June	48,000	10,000	5,000	7,000
July	24,000	10,000	5,000	2,000
Aug	12,000	—	4,000	2,000
Sept	2,000	10,000	5,000	2,000
Oct	4,000	10,000	5,000	2,000
Nov	4,000	10,000	5,000	2,000
Dec	2,000	10,000	6,000	7,000
Total	228,000	110,000	60,000	34,000

In budgeting cash at bank on 1st April 1984 at £50,000 the company has overlooked the contract payment for the factory extension due on 30th March 1984.

Although the Sunny Textile Company Ltd requires payment for its sales in the month following that in which the sale is made, and offers a settlement discount of 5 per cent for accounts settled within this period, experience has taught it to expect only half the payments when due. One-quarter of the payments follow during the second month after sale and the balance comes in the third month. Bad debts average $2\frac{1}{2}$ per cent of sales.

It is the company's policy to pay for supplies during the month in which they are delivered in order to take advantage of a 10 per cent prompt settlement discount offered by all its suppliers.

The level of stocks at the end of December 1984 are expected to remain unchanged from those prevailing in January. These are valued on a variable cost basis. The architect issued a final certificate for the factory extension on 19th April.

REQUIRED:
(a) Prepare for the Sunny Textile Company Ltd:
   (i) a budgeted profit & loss account; and
   (ii) a cash budget on a monthly basis,
both for the six months commencing 1st April 1984, stating clearly any assumptions that you need to make.

(b) Discuss the value of cash budgets to management, illustrating the points that you make by reference to any implications that you can derive from the cash budget that you have prepared.   (ACCA)

15. You are the cost accountant of a company making three different items of office furniture. You are required, using the information given, to:

(a) prepare an estimated profit for each item for the three months ending 31st March 1984;

(b) provide a forecast of cash receipts and payments for the month of March 1984; and

(c) state briefly the most important point revealed by the results reported in answer to (a) and (b) above.

The following relevant information is given.

Sales in units:

1984	Products		
	X	Y	Z
January	5,000	4,000	7,000
Febuary	6,000	3,000	7,000
March	7,000	4,000	6,000
April	6,000	6,000	6,000
May	4,000	6,000	8,000
June	3,000	5,000	12,000
Selling price per unit	£42	£47	£53

Direct material standards:

	Price per square yard (£)	Square yards per unit		
		X	Y	Z
DM1	4.00	3	5	–
DM2	2.50	2	–	3
DM3	3.20	1	2	7

Direct labour standards:

	Rate per hour (£)	Hours per unit		
		X	Y	Z
DL1	1.00	4	6	4
DL2	1.20	2	–	3
Direct expense per unit		£5.40	£7.60	£7.50
Overhead as % of direct cost		12½%	5%	20%

Products are made in the month prior to the month of sale. There are no inventories of part finished items. Labour is paid in the month of manufacture.

Materials are purchased in the month prior to manufacture, 50 per cent being paid for in the month of purchase and the balance in the following month.

Of the direct expense, £120,000 per year is an internal charge for depreciation. The remainder is for outside charges paid in the month after production.

Overhead costs are paid 20 per cent in the month prior to sale, 40 per cent in the month of sale and 20 per cent in each of the two months following.

Customers' remittances in respect of sales are received as follows:

60 per cent in month of sale, less 2½ per cent discount
30 per cent in month after sale
10 per cent in second month after sale

Taxation is to be ignored.   (*ICMA*)

16. Although Earlham Ltd currently has a fairly wide range of products, the overall mix of products closely conforms to the following breakdown of sales price.

		%
Sales price		100
Cost of goods sold (all variable):		
Direct materials	35	
Direct labour	20	
Variable overheads	25	
	—	80
Contribution towards profit and fixed overheads		20

There are no seasonal fluctuations and activity levels have been roughly constant for several years. The current working capital position is typical:

	(*£000s*)	(*£000s*)
Stocks—Raw materials	240	
Work-in-progress	120	
Finished goods	150	510
Debtors		210
Creditors		90

The activity for the past year can be summarised thus:

	(*£000s*)
Sales	1,200
Purchases of raw materials	420
Cost of goods sold	960

There is the opportunity for Earlham Ltd to increase immediately its level of activity from a sales turnover figure of £1.2 million per year to £2 million per year. The managing director suggests that such an increase in activity level will be profitable, as he says, "the contribution of 20 per cent on the extra sales of £800,000 is £160,000—this will be all additional profit as our fixed costs are unaltered. As there is no capital expenditure involved, we need not worry about availability of cash—in my experience in this firm, profit generates its own level of cash".

The production and marketing directors make the following points.

(*a*) Expansion is into a new type of product and market, and existing activities will be largely unaffected.

(*b*) Credit allowed to customers of the new products will, on average, be about thirty days more than is currently allowed. This increase in the period of credit given is for sales of the expansion products only.

(*c*) The number of days for which raw materials are on average held in stock will be increased by 10 per cent again for the expansion only.

(*d*) The length of time stocks are in w-i-p will be unaltered.

(*e*) The average length of time finished goods of the new products will remain in stock will be 20 per cent greater than the current average.

(*f*) Material costs for the expansion will average out at about 40 per cent of sales rather than the 35 per cent for existing products. Other variable costs will be unaffected, the overall effect being that contribution will be lower.

(*g*) Payments to suppliers will need to be made more promptly. This will affect *all* suppliers, and the number of days credit taken will fall for all creditors to only forty-five days.

(*h*) The cost of money is currently 14 per cent per annum. Therefore the proposed expansion needs to be carefully analysed to ensure that if additional cash has to be found to finance it, the expansion will be still profitable after the obtaining of cash.

The managing director considers there is little evidence that the expansion will be any different in (financial) operational terms from the organisation's existing activities. He suggests: "The expansion is merely scale expansion of our existing activities and there is no reason why, for example, credit allowed should increase".

REQUIRED:

(*a*) Prepare two statements which will show whether extra cash is required in order to facilitate the budgeted expansion. The statements should be based on:

(*i*) the scale expansion assumptions of the managing director—that is, assuming no change from the operating characteristics that the current activities display; and

(*ii*) the points raised by the production and marketing directors but excluding point *h*.

(*b*) Calculate the additional profit generated per year by the expansion after considering points *a*–*h* raised by the two directors.

Assume that there are 360 days in a year.

Note: Marks will not be lost for reasonable rounding or approximation of figures.   (*ICMA*)

17. XY Ltd, is examining its credit terms and their effect on profit. You are required, using the information given below, to calculate the effect on XY Ltd's profits that would result from a move to any of the three other credit term arrangements, A, B or C, that the company is considering.

Sales are currently 233,000 units per annum. Basing its conclusion on market studies, XY Ltd expects its sales to vary if it changes its credit terms to customers. The credit terms that it is considering, and for each set of terms, the likely demand in units, the proportion of sales expected to be made at net price, and the bad debts expenses, are shown below.

| Credit terms being considered | | | Probability of demand at level of sales (in thousands of units) | | | | | | |
Cash discount	Net		200	210	220	230	240	250	Total
A Nil	30 days		0.9	0.1	–	–	–	–	1.0
B 2% 10 days	30 days		0.1	0.3	0.4	0.2	–	–	1.0
C 5% 30 days	60 days		–	–	0.1	0.3	0.4	0.2	1.0

| Credit terms being considered | | Percentage of sales | | Bad debts expenses as % of sales before cash discount |
Cash discount	Net	with discount	without discount	
A Nil	30 days	–	100	1.0
B 2% 10 days	30 days	20	80	0.8
C 5% 30 days	60 days	40	60	0.8
Current position 5% 10 days	60 days	30	70	1.0

The selling price of the company's product is £10 per unit and the variable cost per unit is £6.5.

The company pays 11 per cent per annum for its bank overdraft.

The level of stocks held by the company increases at a rate of 20 per cent of the increase in unit sales, and decreases at a rate of 20 per cent of the decrease in unit sales.

The company obtains a cash discount of 2 per cent from its major supplier for payment within one month. Purchases from this supplier represent £2.5 per unit of the finished product.

Calculations are to be made to the nearest £100. Taxation is to be ignored. (ICMA)

18. In the third week of April the accountant of the SW division of Jackson Brothers plc* is reviewing the division's cash budget up to the end of the company's financial year (31st August). Each of the company's divisions has its own bank account, but arrangements are made centrally for transfers among these as a need or opportunity arises. Interest is

---

*In Great Britain, the Companies Act 1980 requires public limited companies to use Public Limited Company, or the abbreviation plc, as part of their names.

charged (or allowed) on such intracompany transfers at a market-related rate.

The three months of May, June and July are the SW division's busiest months, providing two-thirds of its annual profit, but there is always a cash-flow problem in this period. In anticipation of a cash shortage, arrangements have been made to borrow (internally) £100,000 over the busy period at an annual interest rate of 15 per cent (chargeable monthly). The agreed borrowing and repayment schedule is as follows.

> 1st May borrowing of £30,000
> 1st June borrowing of £70,000
> 1st July repayment of £20,000
> 1st August repayment of £60,000
> 1st September repayment of £20,000

The accountant has in front of him the budgeted divisional profit & loss account figures for the four months to 31st August and the profit & loss accounts for March and April—the latter being an estimated statement. These documents can be summarised as follows.

	March £	April £	May £	June £	July £	August £
Sales revenue	120,000	120,000	230,000	250,000	300,000	160,000
Factory cost of goods sold	100,000	100,000	182,500	197,500	235,000	130,000
Selling and distribution costs	4,200	4,200	6,400	6,800	7,800	5,000
Administrative costs and interest charges	7,000	7,000	7,375	8,250	8,000	7,250
	111,200	111,200	196,275	212,550	250,800	142,250
Divisional profit	8,800	8,800	33,725	37,450	49,200	17,750
	120,000	120,000	230,000	250,000	300,000	160,000

The accountant is using the following assumptions.

First, each factory cost of goods sold figure includes a fixed cost element of £10,000, of which £2,000 is depreciation. The remaining fixed factory cost can reasonably be assumed to be paid as it is charged.

Second, direct material cost is approximately 75 per cent of the variable factory cost of the firm's products. The suppliers of this direct material are paid in the month following its purchase. Other variable factory costs of production are paid in the month that the production takes place.

Third, half of the fixed selling and distribution cost is a depreciation charge for motor vehicles. The remaining cost under this heading is paid in the month in which it is charged.

Fourth, a monthly central administration charge of £1,000 and interest on any borrowings are charged to administrative costs and interest charges and credited to a head office current account. Other administrative costs approximately £6,000 per month are paid monthly.

Fifth, the undermentioned policies are followed by the division.

(a) The target month end stock level for finished goods is £10,000 plus 25 per cent of the variable cost of next month's budgeted sales. Finished goods are valued at variable cost for accounting purposes.

(b) The target month end stock level for direct materials is £10,000 plus 25 per cent of the material required for next month's budgeted production.

Sixth, all sales are on credit terms. Twenty per cent of the cash from customers is received in the month following that in which the sales were made. The remainder is received in the next month.

Finally, the cash at the bank and in hand at the end of April is expected to be approximately £10,000.

(a) You are required to prepare the division's cash budget for the months of May and June. Each cash figure should be rounded to the nearest £1,000. (*Note*: Do not use the formula in (b) below.)

(b) The accountant has been experimenting with the use of the following formula for predicting month end cash holdings:

$$CB = OB + 0.8S_{i-2} - 0.12S_{i-1} - 0.37S_i - 0.08S_{i-1} - 15$$

where CB is the predicted closing cash balance in £000s for month i.

OB is the (estimated) opening cash balance in £000s for month i

and S_i is the sales figure for month i in £000s actual or budgeted as appropriate.

Assuming that this formula is appropriate, comment on the effect on the division's cash holding at the end of May, of deviations of ± 10% in the May sales figure from the budgeted figure.

(c) Consider the possibility of introducing a discount scheme to encourage customers to pay promptly. How would you judge the worth of such a scheme?

(d) The finance director of Jackson Brothers plc is considering a change in the procedures for evaluating divisional performance. Instead of merely charging interest on intracompany cash borrowing, he is considering the charging of interest on the company's total investment in each division. Comment on this proposal and discuss the difficulties and advantages of such a system.   (*ACCA*)

19. From the data given below you are required to prepare for the year ending 30th June 1984.

(a) A production budget in quantities only.

(b) A purchasing budget giving quantities and values.

(c) The budgeted unit cost for each product.

(d) A budgeted statement of sales, cost and profit or loss for each of the products A, B, C and D.

Data:

Product	A	B	C	D
Sales, in units	20,000	10,000	5,000	40,000
Selling price, per unit	£60	£55	£50	£45

Direct material requirements per unit of product:

	A	B	C	D	Price (£)
Plastic (in feet)	12	12	–	10	1.00 ft
Metal strip (in feet)	6	8	20	–	0.50 ft
Wire (in lb)	–	4	6	10	0.80 lb
Paint (in litres)	1	1	$1\frac{1}{2}$	1	1.40 litres

Direct labour requirements per unit of product, in hours:

	A	B	C	D	Rate per hr (£)
Skilled	10	8	6	–	1.50
Semi-skilled	6	6	–	6	1.10
Unskilled	12	–	8	2	0.70

Factory overhead:

Indirect material plus warehousing and handling costs are absorbed by adding 50% to direct material costs.
Indirect wages and expenses are absorbed at a rate of £0.30 per direct labour-hour.

Inventories:	Held at 1st July 1983		Required at 30th June 1984
Finished goods		value	
product	Units	£000s	Units
A	5,000	290	2,500
B	1,000	55	1,500
C	1,000	52	1,000
D	12,000	480	15,000
Direct materials			
Plastic (in feet)	40,000	40	34,000
Metal strip (in feet)	50,000	40	11,000
Wire (in lb)	60,000	60	98,000
Paint (in litres)	10,000	10	21,500

The finished goods inventory is maintained on a FIFO basis. Direct materials are priced on a yearly average basis. Stocks are assumed to be issued proportionately to each product based on annual requirements.

20. In cases where sales is the principal budgeting factor, the sales forecast is a crucial part of the budgeting process. Frequently firms base their forecast of future sales on some relationship of past sales, which at the simplest level is mere extrapolation. However, attempts are often made

to refine any such extrapolation by considering the factors which affect the sales of an organisation.

The marketing director of the Four Casts Fishing Tackle Company has found that the sales of his firm can be predicted with some accuracy from:

$$S_{(t+1)} = K[S_t + S_{(t-1)} + S_{(t-2)}]$$

where S is the sales figure for a period; t the period just completed; $(t-1)$, etc., the previous period; and $(t+1)$ the next period, the one for which the forecast is required. K is some constant which is used to combine the effect of the major variables which affect the company's sales and is itself a function of five variables (v)—that is:

$$K = f(v_1, v_2, v_3, v_4, v_5)$$

Thus, in simple terms, the next year's sales forecast for the Four Casts Fishing Tackle Company is found from the sum of the last three years' sales multiplied by some constant. The only disadvantage found from this approach is that the constant has to be revised every three or four years.

Sales for the company over the past ten years have been increasing as follows: 24; 25; 27; 33; 40; 52; 65; 81; 116; 150.

REQUIRED:

(*a*) Calculate three values for K (working to one decimal place), each of which gives a reasonable forecast of the company's sales for a period during years 4 to 10. Use these values of K to prepare three sets of sales forecasts for years 4 to 10.

(*b*) What sort of factors do you think would go to make up the five variables (v) in the functional relationship which provides the company with its constant K?

(*c*) Comment briefly upon this method of sales forecasting. (*ACCA*)

21. Synchrodot Ltd manufactures two standard products: product 1, selling at £15; and product 2, selling at £18. A standard absorption costing system is in operation and details of the unit cost standards are summarised as follows.

Standard cost data—summary

	Product 1	Product 2
	£	£
Direct material cost	2	3
Direct labour cost	1	2
Overhead (fixed and variable)	7	9
	10	14

The budgeted fixed factory overhead for Synchrodot Ltd is £180,000 (per quarter) for product 1, and £480,000 (per quarter) for product 2. This apportionment to product lines is achieved by using a variety of "appropriate" bases for individual expense categories—for example, floor space for rates, number of work-staff for supervisory salaries, etc. The fixed overhead is absorbed into production using practical capacity as the basis, and any volume variance is written off (or credited) to the Profit & Loss Account in the quarter in which it occurs. Any planned volume variance in the quarterly budgets is dealt with similarly. The practical capacity per quarter is 30,000 units for product 1 and 60,000 units for product 2.

At the March board meeting the draft budgeted income statement for the April/May/June quarter is presented for consideration. This shows the following:

BUDGETED INCOME STATEMENT FOR APRIL, MAY AND JUNE 1984

	Product 1		Product 2	
Budgeted sales quantity		30,000 units		57,000 units
Budgeted production quantity		24,000 units		60,000 units
Budgeted sales revenue		£450,000		£1,026,000
Budgeted production costs				
Direct material		48,000		180,000
Direct labour		24,000		120,000
Factory overhead		204,000		540,000
		£276,000		£840,000
Add:				
Budgeted finished goods Stock at 1st April 1981	(8,000 units)	80,000	(3,000 units)	42,000
		£356,000		£882,000
Less:				
Budgeted finished goods Stock at 30th June 1981	(2,000 units)	20,000	(6,000 units)	84,000

	Product 1	Product 2
Budgeted manufacturing cost of budgeted sales	£336,000	£798,000
Budgeted manufacturing profit	£114,000	£228,000
Budgeted administrative and selling costs (fixed)	30,000	48,000
Budgeted profit	£84,000	£180,000

The statement causes consternation at the board meeting because it seems to show that product 2 contributes much more profit than product 1, and yet this has not previously been apparent.

The sales director is perplexed and he points out that the budgeted sales programme for the forthcoming quarter is identical with that accepted for the current quarter (January/Febuary/March), and yet the budget for the current quarter shows a budgeted profit of £120,000 for each product line and the actual results seem to be in line with the budget.

The production director emphasises that identical assumptions, as to unit variable costs, selling prices and manufacturing efficiency, underly both budgets, but that there has been a change in the budgeted production pattern. He produces the following table:

Budgeted production	Product 1	Product 2
January/February/March	30,000 units	52,500 units
April/May/June	24,000 units	60,000 units

He urges that the company's budgeting procedures be overhauled, as he can see no reason why the quarter's profit should be £24,000 up on the previous quarter and why the net profit for product 1 should fall from £4.00 to £2.80 per unit sold, whereas for product 2 it should rise from £2.11 to £3.16.

You are required to:

(a) reconstruct the company's budget for the January/Febuary/March quarter.

(b) restate the budgets (for both quarters), using standard marginal cost as the stock valuation basis.

(c) comment on the queries raised by the sales director and the production director and on the varying profit figures disclosed by the alternative budgets.   (ACCA)

22. (a) Prepare a flexible budget for a month at activity levels of 70, 80, 90, 100 and 110 per cent for a purchasing department having the undernoted cost characteristics.

(b) Calculate the average cost for processing a purchase order at each of the above levels.

The following information is given.

Staff and salaries:	
department head	£5,400 per annum
2 senior buyers	£3,000 each per annum
2 junior buyers	£2,100 each per annum
1 secretary	£1,800 per annum
2 typists	£20 each per week
Employee benefits	20% of salary payments
Space occupied	800 square feet
Rent	£5 per square foot per year
Heat and light	£840 fixed cost per year and £360 variable cost per year at 50% activity, but thereafter proportionately variable
Office services	20% of total rent, light and heat
Purchase orders issued at 100% activity	2,100 per month
Average number of lines per purchase order	15
Average typing speed	90 lines per hour

Purchase orders cost	£0.15 per set and wastage amounts to 5% of completed orders
Other typing and office supplies average	50% of purchase order cost

When not fully employed the typists have a fall-back job typing employee training records. Cost allotted to the fall-back job is confined to salaries only. When extra typing is needed the first thirty-five hours are covered by overtime at time and a half. Thereafter agency typists are employed at an inclusive charge of £1.50 per hour. The agency typists only have a 70 per cent efficiency compared with the regular staff.

All staff work overtime proportionate to activity level above 100 per cent.

The senior salaried staff are not paid overtime, but the junior buyers and the secretary get plain time for the additional hours worked.

You are to assume a month to be one-twelfth of a calendar year and to be comprised of four weeks of thirty-five hours each. (Work to nearest £1 in total cost and to two decimals of £1 for unit costs.)   (*ICMA*)

23. From the information given below in respect of a company which manufactures and sells a single product you are required to:

(*a*) calculate the standard cost of the product and the budgeted sales for week no 40; and

(*b*) prepare a suitable management accounting statement in respect of week no 40, clearly setting out budgeted and actual sales, standard and actual costs and variances.

WEEK NO 40

(1) *Variances* Note: Adverse variances are indicated by (A) and favourable variances by (F).

Direct materials price:	A	£440 (A)
	B	700 (A)
	C	300 (F)
Direct materials usage:	A	80 (A)
	B	280 (A)
	C	50 (A)
Direct wages rate		700 (A)
Direct labour efficiency		1,000 (F)
Variable production overhead		200 (F)
Fixed production overhead:	Expenditure	600 (A)
	Capacity	75 (A)
	Productivity	375 (F)
Operating profit variance:		
Due to selling price		3,200 (A)
Due to sales volume		3,500 (F)

(2) *Transactions Recorded*
Direct materials purchased:

	lb	Price per lb
A	11,000	£0.84
B	35,000	1.42
C	15,000	0.48
Direct wages paid 39,800 hours		£40,500
Overhead: Variable		10,000
Fixed		15,600

	Units	Price each (£)
Sales: Home	4,500	35
Export	1,600	33
Production: Actual	5,100	
Budget	5,000	

(3) *Other Information*
You may assume that there is no opening or closing stock of work-in-progress and that raw material and finished product stock accounts are kept at standard cost.

The standard quantities of raw material used in making one unit of the product are:

A	2 lb
B	6 lb
C	4 lb

Eight budgeted direct labour-hours are required to make each unit of product.   (*ICMA*)

24. As the management accountant of a retailing group you have been asked to evaluate the performance of one of the stores. The store has three departments:

A. Garden furniture
B. Sports equipment
C. Home decorations

You are required to:
(*a*) prepare a statement for the year ended 30th April 1984 showing the departmental contributions and the total profit for the store;
(*b*) comment on the current relative effectiveness of the departments; and

(c) recommend any changes you feel would improve total profitability. For this purpose you are to assume that the sales of each department can be expanded but are largely interdependent, as customers usually buy at two or more departments on each visit.

The information given below relates to the year ended 30th April, 1984.

Department	A	B	C
Sales (£000s)	290	120	300
Gross profit margin added to cost of goods sold (%)	45	100	50
Floor area occupied (square feet)	4,000	3,000	5,000

Staff: One supervisor is employed in each department at an inclusive cost of £3,000 per year.

One assistant is employed for each 500 square feet of floor space at an inclusive cost of £2,000 per year.

	£	Bases of apportionment
Rent and rates	36,000	floor space
Heat and light	19,000	floor space with a weighting of: Department A: 1.5 B: 1.0 C: 2.0
Advertising	20,000	% Department A: 45 B. 25 C: 30

Other expenses, not allocated departmentally, amount to £56,000 per annum. (*ICMA*)

25. The Miozip Company operates an absorption costing system which incorporates a factory-wide overhead absorption rate per direct labour-hour. For 1980 and 1981 this rate was £2.10 per hour. The fixed factory overhead for 1981 was £600,000 and this would have been fully absorbed if the company had operated at full capacity, which is estimated at 400,000 direct labour-hours. Unfortunately, only 200,000 hours were worked in that year, so that the overhead was seriously under-absorbed. Fixed factory overheads are expected to be unchanged in 1982 and 1983.

The outcome for 1981 was a loss of £70,000, and the management believed that a major cause of this loss was the low overhead absorption rate that had led the company to quote selling prices which were uneconomic.

For 1982 the overhead absorption rate was increased to £3.60 per direct labour-hour, and selling prices were raised in line with the established pricing procedures which involve adding a profit mark-up of 50 per cent on to the full factory cost of the company's products. The new selling prices were also charged on the stock of finished goods held at the beginning of 1982.

In December 1982 the company's accountant prepares an estimated profit & loss account for 1982 and a budgeted profit & loss account for 1983. Although sales were considered to be depressed in 1981, they were even lower in 1982 but, nevertheless, it seems that the company will make a profit for that year. A worrying feature of the estimated accounts is the high level of finished goods stock held, and the 1983 budget provides for a reduction in the stock level at 31st December 1983 to the (physical) level which obtained at the 1st January 1981. Budgeted sales for 1983 are set at the 1982 sales level.

The summarised profit statements for the three years to 31 December 1983 are as follows:

SUMMARISED PROFIT AND LOSS ACCOUNTS

	Actual 1981		Estimated 1982		Budgeted 1983	
	£	£	£	£	£	£
Sales revenue		1,350,000		1,316,250		1,316,250
Opening stock of finished goods	100,000		200,000		357,500	
Factory cost of production	1,000,000		975,000		650,000	
	1,100,000		1,175,000		1,007,500	
Less: Closing stock of finished goods	200,000		357,500		130,000	
Factory cost of goods sold		900,000		817,500		877,500
		450,000		498,750		438,750
Less: Factory overhead under-absorbed		300,000		150,000		300,000
		150,000		348,750		138,750
Administrative and financial costs		220,000		220,000		220,000
	Loss	(70,000)		128,750	Loss	(81,250)

(a) You are required to write a short report to the board of Miozip explaining why the budgeted outcome for 1983 is so different from that of 1982 when the sales revenue is the same for both years.

(b) Restate the Profit & Loss Account for 1981, the estimated Profit & Loss Account for 1982 and the budgeted Profit & Loss Account for 1983, using marginal factory cost for stock valuation purposes.

(c) Comment on the problems which *may* follow from a decision to increase the overhead absorption rate in conditions when cost plus pricing is used and overhead is currently under-absorbed.

(d) Explain why the majority of businesses use full costing systems, whilst most management accounting theorists favour marginal costing.

Note: Assume in your answers to this question that the value of the £ and the efficiency of the company have been constant over the period under review. (*ACCA*)

26. Before entering the market for the manufacture and sale of shower cubicle units the managing director and major shareholder of Home Showers Ltd, Roy Simpson, had carried out forecasting carefully to arrive at the following figures.

	£	£
Expected selling price (per cubicle)		140
Expected costs (per cubicle)		
Direct labour (10 hours at £3 per hour)	30	
Direct materials (20 kg at £1.25)	25	
Variable overheads (at £1.50 per direct labour-hour)	15	
Variable selling and delivery costs (per cubicle sold)	20	
Total variable costs (per cubicle)		£90
	£	
Expected fixed costs (per month)		
Manufacturing overheads	40,000	
Selling and delivery	5,000	
Administration	5,000	
		£50,000

"Normal production and sales levels once the company is established", states Roy Simpson, "will be 2,000 units per month. But for the first few months the company will obviously have to plan to produce and sell fewer units. With a contribution of £50 per unit it will need only 1,000 units to break even. Therefore the company shall never operate at a loss, as even the planned production and sales of the first month is exactly 1,000 units—and it is planned to increase production and sales monthly until the normal 2,000 units figure is reached."

After the firm had completed its first month's activities the part-time accountant produced statements reporting on those activities. The statements were as below:

Statement of manufacturing costs—month 1

	£
Direct labour (15,500 hours)	45,500
Direct materials (28,400 kg)	35,200
Variable overheads	21,400
Fixed manufacturing overheads	40,000
Total manufacturing costs	142,100
No of units produced	1,400
Cost per unit	101.50

Profit statement—month 1

	£	£
Sales 900 units at £150		135,000
Less: Manufacturing costs of		
sales 900 at £101.50		91,350
Gross profit		43,650
Selling and delivery costs	25,500	
Administration	5,500	
		31,000
Profit		12,650

Roy Simpson was extremely pleased by the figures and stated: "I thought that the company would make a loss, as sales were below our budget of 1,000 and this was, of course, the break-even expectation. But with a profit of more than £12,000 I am not complaining. I think the reasons for the company's success are the increase in sales price and the fact that labour standards are tight and known to be tight. The men know that ten hours per cubicle will be difficult to achieve. This motivates them and obviously they have achieved it. However, it would be interesting to see the exact causes of the profit being higher than expected".

REQUIRED:

(*a*) Prepare a budgeted profit statement, based on long-term standard costs, which use Mr Simpson's prior estimates of the first month's activity.

(*b*) Prepare a statement based on the first month's results which will be useful to Mr Simpson in highlighting deviations from the prior plan and which displays the reasons for any variances from the plan.

(*c*) Show how the results for the first month's activities derived in (*b*) above can be reconciled with the profit of £12,650 produced by the part-time accountant.

(*d*) List the three most important points to which you would draw Mr Simpson's attention concerning standards and variances in (*b*) above. Very briefly, producing no more than one short sentence each, give the reasons why each item is deserving of his attention.   (*ICMA*)

27. Stafford Ltd, a member of the Terrier Group, manufactures and markets a single product. The company operates a standard costing system and prepares its operating statements on a four-week period basis. The results of weeks 9–12—referred to as period 3—of the current financial year for Stafford Ltd are shown below.

	Budget		Actual	
	£	£	£	£
Sales		80,000		60,000
Manufacturing costs				
Direct materials	32,000		26,000	
Direct labour	16,000		12,600	
Overheads	20,000	68,000	19,500	58,100
Manufacturing profit		12,000		1,900
Selling and distribution expenses		4,000		4,300
Net profit/(loss)		8,000		(2,400)

The following additional information is available.

(a) Group policy is that no stocks of finished goods should be maintained, a requirement to which Stafford Ltd always conforms. Stocks of materials and work-in-progress were also unchanged over the period.

(b) The budget was prepared on the basis of producing 1,000 units each week. All production produced in any week is also sold during that week. Unit standards for selling price were £20, to show a net profit of £2.

(c) All sales and purchases were made at the standard prices used in the preparation of the budget.

(d) The standard labour time for each unit is four hours. The direct labour-hours worked, and paid, in period 3 were 12,000.

(e) Following an industrial dispute, all direct labour employees were on strike for the whole of week 12. The dispute was settled in time for work to be resumed at the commencement of the following week. The employees who participated in the strike were not paid for this time. However, it was agreed that overtime should be worked in the next period, to be paid at time and a half, to make up for the time lost. Previous experience of overtime working is that labour efficiency has been 90 per cent of standard and therefore management does not consider it will be possible to recover fully the production which has been lost during the period of dispute.

(f) All manufacturing overheads are fixed. Selling expenses are also fixed. Distribution costs amount to 3 per cent of sales revenue.

REQUIRED:

The preparation of an operating statement for period 3. This is to be presented to show the financial effects of the events of that period. Your statement should be in the form you consider to be most informative to management and should include a narrative in which you state the principles that have guided your analysis and presentation.   (ACCA)

28. W Ltd manufactured and sold during the past year 300,000 units of product A and 150,000 units of product B. The accounts for the year were as follows.

	£
Sales	1,650,000
Direct materials	300,000
Direct wages	400,000
Factory overhead: Variable	200,000
Fixed	150,000
Other overhead: Variable	100,000
Fixed	100,000

The following details for the year are given concerning the two products.

Product	A	B
Per unit:	£	£
Selling price	3.0	5.0
Direct materials	0.5	1.0
Direct wages	0.6	1.3 (recurring)
Other overhead, half-variable and half-fixed	0.5	0.3 (recurring)

Factory overhead, variable, is absorbed as a percentage of direct wages.

During the year it is expected that, owing to a fall in demand, the production and sales of Product A will be reduced by 20 per cent and of product B by 40 per cent. It is therefore decided to manufacture a further product, C, based on the following information.

Production and sales	100,000 units
Per unit:	£
Selling price	3.5
Direct materials	0.7
Direct wages	1.2

Other overhead, variable, will be the same as for product A.

Total fixed overhead, factory and other, will remain the same, and variable overhead, factory and other, will continue to be incurred at the same rates as in the past year.

Present to management the following information.

(a) A budget showing the anticipated results for the coming year.

(b) A profit-volume graph to compare the results of the past year with those anticipated for the coming year.

(c) Conclusions that can be drawn from information prepared in answer to (a) and (b) above, together with any recommendations you may wish to make.   (ICMA)

29. A company manufactures plastic-covered steel fencing in two qualities: standard and heavy gauge. Both products pass through the same processes involving steel-forming and plastic-bonding. The standard gauge sells at £15 a roll and the heavy gauge at £20 a roll. There is an unlimited market for the standard gauge, but outlets for the heavy gauge are limited to 13,000 rolls per year. However, the factory operations of each process are limited to 2,400 hours each per year.

Other relevant data are given below.

Variable costs per roll:

Gauge	Direct material	Direct wages	Direct expense
	£	£	£
Standard	5	7	1
Heavy	7	8	2

Processing hours per 100 rolls:

Gauge	Steel-forming	Plastic-bonding
Standard	6	4
Heavy	8	12

Agreement has been reached on revised working methods that will increase output of all processes by 10 per cent. This could be achieved without additional manpower or longer working hours.

You are required to calculate:

(*a*) the production mix which will maximise total contribution:

    (*i*) at present output levels; and

    (*ii*) assuming the 10 per cent production improvement is achieved.

(*b*) the total amount of productivity bonus which will be paid to employees under (*a*) (*ii*) on the basis of their receiving 40 per cent of the additional contribution. (*ICMA*)

30. A company is asked to quote for a special order to be delivered ex-works.

Direct material costs per unit of output are as below.

    For a total of 100: £18 each
                200: £18 less 10% discount each
                400: £18 less 20% discount each

The work would be done in two departments.

Department F employs highly skilled operators paid at £2.50 per hour. Each unit of output requires 6 direct labour-hours of work for

the first 100 units. However, experience has shown that an 80%
learning curve can be expected to operate.

Department G employs skilled operators paid at £2.00 per hour.
Each unit of output requires 3 direct labour-hours of work for the
first 100 units. Here, too, an 80% learning curve is expected.

Overtime in either department is paid at time and a half. No premium
for overtime is included in standard manufacturing overhead.

Standard manufacturing overhead per direct labour-hour is as follows.

	Department F	Department G
	£	£
Variable	1.00	1.00
Fixed	3.50[1]	2.00[2]

[1] Based on a budgeted level of 3,000 direct labour-hours per period.
[2] Based on a budgeted level of 2,000 direct labour-hours per period.

The special order will require special tooling of £300 which is chargeable
to the customer.

If the order received is for 100 or 200 units, the work will have to be
done in period no 8 which, for department F, is already loaded with 2,200
direct labour-hours of work. Department G, however, will be working at
only around 55 per cent of capacity.

On special orders of this type, it is the company's practice to add the
following margins on cost in arriving at selling prices.

Department F	20%
Department G	10%
Direct materials	2%
Subcontractor's work	2%
(when used)	

An outside subcontractor has offered, irrespective of the size of the
order, to do the work of department G on this order for a price of £8 per
unit, including collection from and delivery to the works.

You are required to calculate:

(a) the price per unit for an order of 100 units if made entirely in the
company;

(b) the price per unit for an order of 200 units if made entirely in the
company;

(c) a separate price per unit for an extra 200 units subsequent to the
order for 200 in (b) above, thus bringing the total order to 400 units;
(N.B. You are to assume that:

(i)   this additional order for the extra 200 units could be done
when there are no capacity limitations in either department; and

    (*ii*) the materials supplier would give the full discount for the 400 units.)

    (*d*) the change in unit selling price that would result from using the outside subcontractor instead of department G for an order of:

      (*i*)   100 units;

      (*ii*) 200 units; and

      (*iii*) 400 units.　　　　　　　　　　　　　　　　(*ICMA*)

    31. (*a*) Allegro Finishes Ltd is about to launch an improved version of its major product—a pocket-size chess computer—on to the market. Sales of the original model (at £65 per unit) have been at the rate of 50,000 per annum, but it is planned to withdraw this model and the company is now deciding on its production plans and pricing policy. The standard variable cost of the new model will be £50, which is the same as that of the old, but the company intends to increase the selling price "to recover the research and development expenditure that has been incurred". The research and development costs of the improved model are estimated at £750,000, and the intention is that these should be written off over three years. Additionally there are annual fixed overheads of approximately £800,000 allocated to this product line. The sales director has estimated the maximum annual demand figures that would obtain at three alternative selling prices. These are as follows.

Selling price £	Estimated maximum annual demand (physical units)
70	75,000
80	60,000
90	40,000

You are required to prepare a cost-volume profit chart that would assist the management to choose a selling price and the level of output at which to operate. Identify the best price and the best level of output. Outline briefly any reservations that you have with this approach.

    (*b*) With the facts as stated in (*a*) above, now assume that the sales director is considering a more sophisticated approach to the problem. He has estimated, for each selling price, an optimistic, a pessimistic and a most likely demand figure and associated probabilities for each of these. for the £90 price the estimates are as below.

	Annual demand	Probability of demand
Pessimistic	20,000	0.2
Most likely	35,000	0.7
Optimistic	40,000	0.1
		1.0

On the cost side, it is clear that the standard unit variable cost of £50 is an "ideal" which has rarely been achieved in practice. An analysis of the past twenty months shows that the following pattern of variable cost variances (per unit of output) has arisen.

(*i*)   An adverse variance of around £10 arose on 4 occasions.

(*ii*) An adverse variance of around £5 arose on 14 occasions.

(*iii*) A variance of around 0 arose on 2 occasions.

There is no reason to think that the pattern for the improved model will differ significantly from this one or that these variances are dependent upon the actual demand level. From the above, calculate the expected annual profit for a selling price of £90.

(*c*) A tabular summary of the result of an analysis of the data for the other two selling prices (£70 and £80) is as follows.

	£70	£80
Probability of a loss of £500,000 or more	0.02	0
Probability of a loss of £300,000 or more	0.07	0.05
Probability of a loss of £100,000 or more	0.61	0.08
Probability of break-even or worse	0.61	0.10
Probability of break-even or better	0.39	0.91
Probability of a profit of £100,000 or more	0.33	0.52
Probability of a profit of £300,000 or more	0.03	0.04
Probability of a profit of £500,000 or more	0	0.01
Expected value of profit (loss)	(£55,750)	£68,500

You are required to compare your calculations in (*b*) with the above figures and to write a short memo to the sales director outlining your advice and commenting on the use of subjective discrete probability distributions in problems of this type.

(*d*) Assume that there is a 10 per cent increase in the fixed overheads allocated to this product line and a decision to write off the research and development costs in one year instead of over three years. Indicate the general effect that this would have on your analysis of the problem.

(*ACCA*)

32. An engineering company has been offered a one-year contract to supply a motor-car component XY at a fixed price of £8 per unit. Its normal capacity for this type of component is 25,000 units a year. The estimated costs to manufacture are shown below. These costs are considered to be firm except for the direct material price.

Cost data:

Variable costs per unit:

	£
Direct wages	1.50
Direct material	2.25
Direct expenses	0.65

Semi-variable costs per annum:

	Output levels		
	80%	100%	120%
	£	£	£
Indirect wages	15,400	16,000	23,000
Indirect materials	8,600	9,000	9,900
Indirect expenses	2,000	2,500	3,000

Fixed costs per annum:

	£
Supervisory salaries	10,000
Depreciation	4,000
Other overheads	16,000

REQUIRED:
(a) Calculate the cost and profit per unit and total annual profit, assuming that the customer's orders in the year total:
   (i)   20,000 components; or
   (ii) 25,000 components; or
   (iii) 30,000 components;
and that direct material is £2.25 per unit.

(b) Calculate the estimated profit for the year if it is assumed that the probability of the total order is:
   (i)   0.3 for 20,000 components;
   (ii) 0.6 for 25,000 components; and
   (iii) 0.1 for 30,000 components;
and that for direct material is:
   (i)   0.5 for £2.25 per unit;
   (ii) 0.3 for £2.50 per unit; and
   (iii) 0.2 for £2.75 per unit.

(c) State whether you would recommend the contract be accepted, giving brief reasons for your decision.   (ACCA)

33. Inglestone Ltd can purchase the patent and the manufacturing rights of any one of three products. The costs of the rights are:

Product A	£130,000
Product B	£190,000
Product C	£200,000

At a meeting with three of Inglestone's directors, the management accountant stated: "We are all agreed on the facts. Each venture is a very short-term project. The fixed manufacturing and advertising costs of each venture will be:

	A £000s	B £000s	C £000s
Fixed manufacturing cost	120	20	20
Advertising costs	50	30	20

Sales and production will, once known, dovetail and there will therefore be no stock build-up. The sales prices and variable costs per unit are:

	A	B	C
Sales price per unit	£340	£190	£130
Variable cost per unit	£140	£110	£70

However, the sales volume is the crunch question. We do not know what the sales level will be but we do know the various possibilities. Product A could be a complete flop, it could sell well, or it might sell very well. B is also quite variable, whereas with C the range of outcomes is quite small. The various possible sales volumes and their associated probabilities are:

	Product					
	A		B		C	
Sales volume units	Probability	Sales volume units	Probability	Sales volume units	Probability
---	---	---	---	---	---
zero	0.1	3,000	0.1	7,000	0.8
2,500	0.4	4,000	0.3	8,000	0.1
4,000	0.5	6,000	0.3	9,000	0.1
		8,000	0.3		

Based on the assumption that the above facts are all completely accurate, and we agree with this, all we need do is make the decisions as to which one product to undertake. What are your views, gentlemen?"

REQUIRED:

(a) Calculate the expected money value of each product, and on the basis of this advise Inglestone of the best course of action.

(b) List and comment briefly on three other factors which may be relevant in a practical situation to the final choice between the three available courses of action.

(c) (Consider only product A). The marketing manager agrees that the subjective probabilities assigned to sales levels given are as accurate as it is practical to assess. However, he suggests that if a market research study were undertaken, it would be possible to ascertain with complete accuracy exactly which of the sales levels specified would be effective—that is, it would indicate whether the sales would be zero, 2,500 or 4,000 units. This market research would cost £20,000 and could be undertaken before deciding whether to purchase the patent and manufacturing rights. Assuming the fixed manufacturing costs are all avoidable if no production takes place, is it worth while to undertake the market research?

Ignore tax and the cost of capital. (*ICMA*)

34. Owing to the financial failure of an overseas competitor, a company sees the opportunity of taking up immediately a market for its product of 325,000 tonnes per annum, which is forecast to rise at 9 per cent per annum. Sales revenue is expected to be £8 per tonne ex plant.

The company proposes to go into this market immediately and considers methods of supply involving the import from elsewhere, the hiring of plant locally, and the construction of new plant.

Details are as follows:

(*a*) *Import from elsewhere.* It could import up to a maximum of 500,000 tonnes per annum of the product at an average cost of £7.5 per tonne at the plant.

(*b*) *Hire of plant locally.* It could hire plant capacity of 500,000 tonnes per annum at a nearby site. This is available immediately. The terms of the hiring are £1.2 per tonne of capacity for a minimum of twelve years, the plant owner being responsible for any variable operating costs. Direct material costs of £6 per tonne would be payable by the company.

(*c*) *Construction of new plant.* It could build a plant with an effective capacity of 500,000 tonnes per annum which will be completed in three years. In the meantime, requirements may be imported. Capital expenditure will be £1.75 million, spent at the end of each year, as follows.

June 1984	£0.30 million
1985	£0.45 million
1986	£1.00 million

The expected life of the plant is twelve years and its salvage value is expected to be £0.3 million. Direct material costs are expected to be £6 per tonne, variable operating costs £0.3 per tonne, and fixed operating costs £100,000 per annum. The company requires a cut-off rate of 20 per cent DCF for projects involving capital expenditure.

You are required to recommend what action the company should take to achieve its objective. Support your recommendation with relevant calculations.

Ignore taxation and inflation considerations. (*ICMA*)

35. A company wishes to decide when to replace the vehicles that it operates in its transport fleet.

Data:

The capital cost of a vehicle is £6,000
Its estimated trade-in value is:
  If replaced after 3 years   £1,000
  If replaced after 4 years   £700
  If replaced after 5 years   £300

Assume that corporation tax is 50 per cent and that there are taxable profits to absorb capital allowances.

Tax allowance is 100 per cent in the first year, and there is one year's delay in payment of tax and allowances.

The purchase and trade-in of vehicles is made at the beginning of a year.

The company's cost of capital for investment purposes is 15 per cent.

| | *Operating costs (excluding depreciation)* | | |
Year	Annual repairs and maintenance (£)	Tyres (£)	Fixed costs (£)
1	280	—	900
2	840	250	900
3	1,120	–	900
4	1,340	250	900
5	1,260	–	900

Fuel costs are estimated at £0.10 per mile. Expected annual mileage is 25,000 miles.

You are required to calculate which is the most economic option for the company: to replace its vehicles on a cycle of three, four or five years.

The table below shows the value today of £1 to be received or paid after a given number of years.

Present value of £1 After n years	15%
1	0.87
2	0.76
3	0.66
4	0.57
5	0.50
6	0.43
7	0.38
8	0.33
9	0.28
10	0.25
11	0.21
12	0.19
13	0.16
14	0.14
15	0.12
16	0.11
17	0.09
18	0.08
19	0.07
20	0.06

36. Miles plc has the opportunity to produce a new product. Expected total sales volumes together with per unit sales prices and basic variable production costs of the new product are as follows.

Year	Sales quantities (000s)	Per unit Sales price (£)	Basic variable production costs* (£)
1	20	10	5
2	30	10	6
3	50	14	6
4	50	14	6

*Basic variable production costs exclude operating costs.

There are two alternative machines which Miles could purchase in order to manufacture the new product: machine A and machine B. Some details of each machine are given below.

	Timing of cash flows (year)	Machine A (£000s)	B (£000s)
Purchase price of machine	0	300	400
Salvage value of machine	4	60	40
Cost of machine housing	0	50	30
Salvage value of machine housing	—	Nil	Nil
Fixed annual operating costs*	1–4	40	30

*Annual operating costs relate only to fixed cash expenses and therefore exclude depreciation of the machine and its housing. Miles depreciates on a straight line basis.

Machine A will require the installation of additional air-conditioning and an existing air-conditioning unit would be used for this purpose at an annual operating cash cost of £10,000. This air-conditioning unit has a book value of £60,000 and, if not utilised, will be sold now for £25,000. Installation costs will amount to £15,000 and the salvage value of the unit at year 4 will be £10,000. The unit has previously been subject to 100 per cent first-year allowances.

Machine B utilises some advanced technology and uses fewer raw materials, thereby reducing basic variable production costs by £1 per unit. A single routine overhaul of machine B will take place at the end of year 2 at a cost of £80,000. At this overhaul it will become apparent whether further repairs or modifications are needed. The cost of each possible level of repair or modification, together with their associated probabilities, are given below.

Level of further repair or modification	Cost, at year 2, of further repair or modification (£000s)	Probability
Nil	Nil	0.5
Minor	50	0.3
Major	140	0.2

The "major" level of repair and modification will entail reverting to traditional technology for the remainder of the product's life with a consequent loss of the saving on future variable production costs as well as a reduction of the year 4 salvage value to only £20,000. The "minor" level of repair or modification will not entail reverting to traditional technology and will not alter the salvage value of machine B. None of the repairs will alter other operating costs. It is expected that no further overhaul or repairs will be required after year 2.

For each machine all cash-operating expenses will be paid for at the end of the year to which they relate. However, sales revenues will be received as cash flows in the following manner.

> 70 per cent of each year's sales received at the end of that year
> 30 per cent of each year's sales received one year later

The corporation tax rate is 50 per cent and there is a one-year tax delay. All capital expenditure and installation costs, except those relating to machine housing, are eligible for 100 per cent first-year allowances, and all salvage values are subject to tax. Expenditure on the type of machine housing to be used is not eligible for any tax relief. All other costs are tax deductible expenses. Miles can take full advantage of any tax allowances at the earliest opportunity. An appropriate after tax discount rate is 14 per cent per annum.

REQUIRED:

(a) Ascertain the expected net present value of producing the new product by each of the two alternative methods. On the basis of expected net present value, advise Miles on which, if any, of the two alternative machines should be purchased.

(b) By paying a single lump sum now, Miles could obtain the services of a credit consultant who would ensure that all sales revenues were received in cash in the year of sale. Ascertain the maximum amount it would be worth paying to obtain the services of the credit consultant if such a payment were not a tax deductible expense.

(c) The managing director, who has recently read about the capital asset pricing model, suggests that as machine B appears riskier than machine A the discount rate used in its appraisal should be higher than that used for the appraisal of machine A. Comment on the managing director's suggestion. (ACCA)

37. XY Ltd has been operating a standard costing system for several years and wishes now to reconsider whether or not it is worthwhile investigating variances that are disclosed in its monthly management accounts. The management accountant examines the company's well-documented variance data relating to the past several years and obtains the following information.

First, variances can be condensed into three relevant classes.

(a) Class A. Those that continue over a period of time as a result of such inefficiencies as slow workmanship or bad materials.

(b) Class B. Those that arise from similar causes as in class A, but which do not continue, as they are either random or easily recognised and quickly corrected by the relevant manager.

(*c*) Class C. Those that continue over a period of time because the process has some inherent inadequacy which would be too expensive to correct in the short term, or where the original budget was incorrect.

Second, in the past, the frequency of occurrence of these variances has been; class A, 28 per cent; class B, 58 per cent; and class C, 14 per cent.

Third, past investigations disclosing a class B or class C variance have yielded no benefit to the company. Of those disclosing a class A variance, 75 per cent of the cases responded to treatment to eliminate the fault, but the remaining 25 per cent of cases did not do so.

Fourth, the average continuing cost of a variance that is not corrected is £78 per month, and the company considers that this can be capitalised at a net present value of 2 per cent per month for six months.

Finally, the average cost of carrying out an investigation is £65.

REQUIRED:

(*a*) Prepare two decision trees showing the position:

   (*i*) if an investigation of a variance is *not* undertaken; and

   (*ii*) if an investigation of a variance is undertaken.

(*b*) Using the above decision trees, calculate whether or not it is profitable for the company to investigate variances as a matter of routine.

38. An organisation currently owns twenty cars for business use by employees. At the end of December they will be due for replacement in accordance with the present policy. This policy is to trade in old cars for new after four years' service. As the management accountant, you are required from the data given below to do the following.

(*a*) Prepare a report on the merits of the present ownership/replacement policy, comparing this with the alternative of:

   (*i*) renting the cars; or

   (*ii*) reimbursing the employees for the use of their own cars.

(*b*) Recommend to management any change in policy you feel would be advantageous to the organisation, giving reasons for your proposal.

Data:

	For each car
Miles operated per annum	50,000
Petrol: miles per gallon	20
cost per gallon	£0.80
Regular servicing: average cost per annum	£200
Tyres: miles before replacement	25,000
	£
average cost per set	100
Major maintenance at an outside	
local garage: average cost for year 1	250
2	400
3	900
4	1,100

Car ownership

Original cost	4,000
Resale value, end of year 1	2,800
2	2,000
3	1,500
4	1,000
Insurance per annum	150
Road tax per annum	50
Capital costs are met from bank loans, average interest per annum	15%

Rental

The hire charge would be £140 per car per calendar month plus one penny for each mile run. The charge would include the cost of insurance, road tax, servicing and maintenance. A new car would be supplied initially and replaced every third year.

Reimbursement

Employees would be responsible for all costs incurred in using their cars and would be paid 9p per mile for all business miles run.

Taxation, cost of capital (other than bank loans) and inflation should be disregarded in all calculations.   (*ICMA*)

39. Your Uncle Peter operates a small engineering business which produces locks. One day when you visit him you find him discussing a problem with his accountant about the next three months' orders. It now looks certain that the firm will have spare capacity both as far as its plant and its skilled labour force are concerned. The accountant has produced some figures concerning the manufacture of a special consignment of Sure-Loks for a large building contractor. This builder has enquired about these and is prepared to purchase 2,000 of the locks at a price of £5 each. The two men are considering this enquiry.

The figures show that if the locks were made and sold at this price, the firm would be able to maintain its normal profit margin of 20 per cent on revenues. They agree to offer to make the locks for £5. The accountant leaves the office and your uncle pushes the piece of paper with the figures on over to you. He comments that a profitable job like this always seems to turn up just at the right time.

Looking at the information and computations, you find that the 2,000 Sure-Loks would take three months to produce and consume the following resources.

First, a special steel which will be required to produce the locks is already in stock. When it was purchased a few months back for another job, for which it was subsequently found to be unsuitable, it cost £1,000. However, today it can be replaced only by special order at a cost of £2,000. If the steel is not used to produce this special batch of Sure-Loks it could be used on another job in substitution for another type of metal which would currently cost £1,600 for the same volume.

Second, all the other materials required in the production of the Sure-Loks would have to be purchased, and their total cost would be £600.

Third, supervisors, who will not be working at full capacity during the next period, currently have an effective cost to the firm of £2 for every hour they work. The production of the 2,000 Sure-Loks would require 200 hours of supervision.

Fourth, the Sure-Loks will be produced during normal working hours using 1,000 hours of the organisation's skilled labour force which is paid £1.50 per hour. In addition 300 hours of casual labour paid at £1 per hour will be required for the job. The firm employs casual labour on an *ad hoc* basis.

Fifth, a special cutting machine will have to be hired for three months for the production. Hire charges for this machine are £75 per month, with a minimum hire charge of £300.

Sixth, all other machinery required in the production of Sure-Loks is already being purchased by the organisation on hire-purchase terms. The monthly hire-purchase payments for this machinery are £500. This consists of £450 for capital repayment and £50 as an interest charge. The last hire-purchase payment is to be made in two months' time. The cash price of this machinery was £9,000 two years ago and it has no current or future scrap value. It is depreciating on a straight-line basis at the rate of £300 per month. However, it still has a useful life which will enable it to be operated for another thirty-six months. The machinery is highly specialised and is unlikely to be required for other, more profitable jobs over the period during which the Sure-Loks are to be produced.

Finally, the firm's general overheads (excepting supervision and depreciation of machinery) are absorbed into product costs on the basis of 60 per cent of direct costs.

REQUIRED:

(a) A conventional cost accounting statement showing confirmation of the 20 per cent profit on revenues arrived at by the accountant.

(b) Your reasoned views as to whether the figures provided by the accountant were the ones that should have been used and as to whether it was the correct decision to offer to supply the locks.   (ACCA)

40. AB Ltd has just completed production of an item of special equipment for a customer, ST Ltd, only to be notified that the customer has gone into liquidation. After much effort, the sales manager has managed to locate one potential buyer, VW Ltd, which has indicated that it might be prepared to buy the machine if certain conversion work could be carried out.

The selling price of the machine to the original buyer had been fixed at £25,300 and had included an estimated normal profit mark-up of 10 per cent on total costs. The costs incurred in the manufacture of the machine were as follows.

	£
Direct materials	9,500
Direct wages	6,000
Overhead: Variable	1,500
Fixed, production	5,000
Fixed, selling and administration	1,000
	23,000

If the machine is converted, production management assesses that the following extra work would be needed.

> Direct materials, at cost   £1,600
> Direct wages:
>   department L: 3 men for 4 weeks at £75 per man/week
>   department M: 1 man for 4 weeks at £60 per man/week
> Variable overhead:
>   20% of direct wages
> Fixed production overhead:
>   department L: $83\frac{1}{3}$% of direct wages
>   department M: 25% of direct wages

The following additional information is available.

First, in the original machine there are three types of basic materials.
(a) Type P, which could now be sold to a scrap merchant for £1,500.
(b) Type Q, which could be sold to the scrap merchant for £1,000, but it would take 120 hours of labour paid at £0.75 per hour to put it into a suitable condition for sale.
(c) Type R, which would need to be scrapped at a cost to AB Ltd of £300.

Second, the materials for the conversion are at present in stock. If not needed for the conversion, they could be used in the production of another machine in place of materials that would currently cost £1,900.

Third, the conversion would be carried out in two departments. Department L is currently extremely busy and it is estimated that its contribution to overhead and profits is £2.50 per £1 of labour. Department M is very short of work. For organisational reasons its labour force cannot be reduced below its present level of four employees, all of whom are paid at the standard wage of £60 per week. The load of work on these employees is, however, only 40 per cent of their standard capacity.

Fourth, the designs and specifications of the original machine could be sold overseas for a sum of £750 if the machine is scrapped.

Fifth, an additional temporary supervisor would have to be engaged for the conversion work at a cost of £450. It is the company's normal practice to charge supervision to fixed overhead.

Finally, customer ST Ltd paid a non-returnable deposit to the company of 12 per cent of the selling price.

You are required to:

(a) calculate the minimum price that AB Ltd should accept from VW Ltd for the converted machine, explaining clearly how you have arrived at your figure; and

(b) state briefly any assumptions that you have made in arriving at your conclusions.   (ACCA)

41. The Aldergrove Co Ltd has in stock some material of type W which had cost £50,000 but are now obsolete and have a scrap value of only £14,000. Apart from selling the materials for scrap there are only two alternative uses for them.

Alternative I

Conversion and sale as specialist electronic equipment for the "Do It Yourself" market. Details of the extra work and materials needed are as follows.

Material X	400 units
Material Y	1,000 units
Direct labour	10,000 hours
Extra selling and delivery expenses	£18,000
Extra magazine advertising	£12,000

Conversion would produce 900 units of the saleable product and these would then be sold for £200 per unit.

Material X is already in stock and is widely used within the firm. Although present stocks, together with orders already planned, will be sufficient to facilitate normal activity, any extra usage by this alternative will require an immediate order for replacement of the materials used.

Material Y is also currently in stock, but it is no longer possible to obtain any further supplies. Material Y is highly sought after, and at present it is used in an extremely popular combined cassette deck/tuner/amplifier made by Aldergrove, which has a sales price of £260 per unit and total variable costs (excluding material Y) of £140 per unit. Each model of the cassette deck/tuner/amplifier produced uses 4 units of material Y. Current stocks of Y are insufficient to meet in full the demand for the tuning device. The shortage of material Y is the only effective constraint on supplying the demand for the amplifier.

The various market and book values per unit of X and Y are given below.

	X	Y
	£	£
Book value—per unit	100	10
Realisable value—per unit	85	18
Replacement cost—per unit	90	–

Alternative II

Adaptation for use as a substitute for sub-assembly 149B which is regularly used within the firm. Details of the extra work and materials needed are as follows.

Material Z	1,000 units
Direct labour	8,000 hours

Normally, 1,200 units of sub-assembly 149B are used per quarter at a price of £600 each. The adaptation of material W would reduce the quantity of 149B purchased outside the firm to 900 units for the next quarter only. However, owing to the reduction in volume of the quantity purchased, some discount would be lost and the price of those purchased from outside would increase to £700 per unit for that quarter.

Material Z is not available externally but is manufactured within Aldergrove Ltd. The 1,000 units required would be produced as extra production and are not available from stocks. The standard cost and normal book value of Z is as below.

Material Z—standard cost

	Per unit
	£
Direct labour—3 hours	9.00
Raw materials	7.00
Variable overhead 3 hours at £2	6.00
Fixed overhead 3 hours at £3	9.00
	31.00

The standard cost excludes the overtime premium for labour and if produced in overtime the actual labour cost would therefore be £3 per unit higher.

Aldergrove Ltd have entered into a long-term contract and the raw material cost of £7.00 is the actual figure which would be paid for the materials required to produce one unit of Z.

In all cases the work required in Alternatives I and II would take place as additional work and hence will cause overtime to be worked. The usual overhead recovery rates for production are as under.

| Variable overhead | £2 per direct labour-hour |
| Fixed overhead | £3 per direct labour-hour |

These recovery rates are accurate and based on full normal capacity.

Labour costs are normally £3 per hour, but the overtime premium is a further £1 per hour.

REQUIRED:

(a) Prepare suitable statements which indicate to Aldergrove Ltd whether the stocks of material W should be:

    (*i*)   sold;

    (*ii*) converted—alternative I; or

    (*iii*) adapted—alternative II.

State clearly which alternative is preferable.

(b) The production manager is confused by the figures of "cost" attributed to materials X, Y and Z in the statements you have produced in (a) above. Explain briefly why, for the purposes of the current decision, you have measured the cost or "value " of X, Y and Z in the manner you have.

(*ICMA*)

42. A group of companies is divided into ten operating divisions, each of which is autonomous. The cost of capital for the group is 12 per cent per annum and it is currently earning 15 per cent on its capital employed.

In the ROCE calculation, return is equated with net profit and capital employed is the figure at the beginning of the financial year. All fixed assets are depreciated on a straight-line basis. Investments in new projects include incremental working capital. Projects sold or withdrawn from operation are treated as consisting of fixed assets only.

If no new capital expenditure transactions take place the position of four of the divisions would be as given below.

Division	Capital employed as at 1st January 1984 (£000s)	Budgeted for 1984; Net profit (£000s)	Sales (£000s)
P	320	80	800
Q	450	150	1,400
R	280	84	700
S	200	26	200

The following transactions are proposed.

Division P: Investment of £100,000 to yield sales of £150,000 per annum and net profit of £20,000 per annum.

Division Q: Sale for £75,000 of a project that is budgeted to yield a net profit of £15,000 in 1984. The original equipment cost £600,000 seven years ago with an expected life of eight years.

Division R: (a) Sale of product line at book value. The original equipment cost £60,000 two years ago with an expected life of three years. This line is budgeted to yield a net profit of £20,000 in 1984; combined with (b) replacement of (a) above by investing £100,000 in a new product to yield £30,000 per annum.

Divison S: Investment of £80,000 in a project to yield sales of £36,000 per annum and a net profit of £11,200 per annum.

N.B. In connection with each of the above transactions, you are to assume that the sale and/or investment would be completed by 1st January 1984 so as to be included in the relevant ROCE calculations for the year 1984. Ignore taxation and inflation considerations and assume that actual results are as budgeted.

REQUIRED:

(*a*) On the assumption that each transaction goes ahead:

   (*i*)   calculate the new ROCE for each division for the year ending 31 December 1984.

   (*ii*) identify those divisional managers whose bonuses will be higher if they receive annual bonuses directly related to the level of their respective ROCE; and

   (*iii*) state, in respect of each division, whether the group's interests will be favourably or adversely affected by the proposed transactions. Explain briefly why in each case.

(*b*) Identify, with brief reasons, which proposals the group would approve if its new capital expenditure were limited to £200,000 for the four divisions.

(*c*) Compare the old results of division P and division S, both of which are in the same type of business, and advise briefly the divisional manager of division S how he might improve his performance based on the data concerning division P.

(*d*) Comment briefly on how the new project for division S fits in with the advice given in (*c*) above.

(*e*) Calculate the lowest price at which the equipment should be sold by division Q if the transaction proposed is to break even financially for the group.

(*f*) Explain briefly the concept of "residual income" in the context of performance evaluation.

(*g*) Calculate the residual income for each division for 1984 on the assumption that each transaction goes ahead.   (*ICMA*)

43. Amalgamated Processors plc is a divisionalised organisation that operates a standard costing and budgetary planning and control system in which the preparation of detailed operating budgets is undertaken by the divisions themselves after centrally determined profit targets have been communicated to them.

The Penbrock division of the company produces and sells a standardised component which is sold externally at £10 per unit and internally, to other divisions, at a transfer price of £9 per unit. The standard specification for this product is as follows.

Standard specification	£
2 m^2 of material A at £0.20 per m^2	0.40
5 units of component B at £0.37 per unit	1.85
15 minutes of labour at £2.00 per hour	0.50
Variable manufacturing overhead—	
150% of direct labour cost	0.75
Fixed manufacturing overhead	1.50
Standard unit manufacturing cost	5.00
Central office charge	1.00
Selling and distributive overhead	1.00
Standard unit cost	7.00

The fixed manufacturing overhead is absorbed on the basis of the "normal" monthly output of 15,000 units. The selling and distributive overhead relates solely to external sales, the monthly divisional budget for which comprises a fixed element of £9,600 and a variable element of £0.20 for each unit of budgeted external sales. The fixed selling and distributive overhead has been unitised assuming a "normal" monthly external sales level of 12,000 units. The "central office charge" element of the standard specification relates to a charge made by the "head office" for central services provided—this has also been unitised assuming the normal monthly activity level of 15,000 units. Unsold stock is carried at standard manufacturing cost.

The following details apply to the Penbrock division for April 1984.

PROFIT AND LOSS ACCOUNT APRIL 1984

	Actual		Budget	
	Units	£	Units	£
Sales—External	10,000	100,000	12,000	120,000
—Internal	4,000	36,000	3,000	27,000
	14,000	136,000	15,000	147,000

	Actual		Budget	
	Units	*£*	*Units*	*£*
Cost of goods manufactured	16,000	85,000	15,000	75,000
Less: Stock adjustment	2,000	10,000	—	—
	14,000	75,000	15,000	75,000
Selling and distributive overhead		13,000		12,000
Central office charges		15,000		15,000
Profit		33,000		45,000
		136,000		147,000

The "actual" cost of goods manufactured can be analysed as follows.

	£
Material A	6,500
Component B	31,745
4,250 labour-hours at £2.10	8.925
Variable manufacturing overhead	12,325
Fixed manufacturing overhead	25,505
	85,000

The stores records of the Penbrock division are kept at standard cost so that the material cost figures include both the cost of the actual direct materials used (priced at their standard cost) and the price variance on materials purchased during April. The details of usage and purchases are as follows.

Material A:	Usage	$34,000 \text{ m}^2$
	Purchases	$30,000 \text{ m}^2$ at £0.19 per m^2
Component B:	Usage	78,500 units
	Purchases	90,000 units at £0.40 per unit

The workstaff have complained that the quality of the most recently purchased batch of material A is inferior to the regular grade, that it gives rise to more waste and that it requires more time to process.

You are required to:

(*a*) prepare a statement for the general manager of the Penbrock division, analysing the reasons for the profit shortfall of £12,000 and to provide a commentary on this statement;

(*b*) comment on the practice of isolating material price variances at the time of the material's purchase; and

(*c*) comment on the transfer pricing method used by the Penbrock division. (*ACCA*)

Further Reading

BOOKS

Amey, L. R., and Eggington, D. A. *Management Accounting: A Conceptual Approach*. London: Longman, 1974.

Bromwich, M. *The Economics of Capital Budgeting*. Harmondsworth, Middx: Penguin, 1976.

Firth, M. *The Management of Working Capital*. London: Macmillan, 1976.

Flamholtz, E. *Human Resource Accounting*. Belmont, Calif: Dickenson, 1974.

Hopwood, A. *Accounting and Human Behavior*. Englewood Cliffs, NJ: Prentice-Hall, 1974.

Kaplan, R. S. *Advanced Management Accounting*. Englewood Cliffs, NJ: Prentice-Hall, 1982.

Mepham, M. J. *Accounting Models*. Stockport, Cheshire: Polytech, 1980.

Pyrrh, P. A. *Zero Base Budgeting: A Practical Management Tool for Evaluating Expenses*. New York: John Wiley, 1973.

KEY ARTICLES

Bromwich, M. "Standard costing for planning and control." *The Accountant*, 19/26 Apr and 23 May 1969.

Coase, R. "The problem of social cost." *Journal of Law and Economics*, Oct 1960.

Demski, J. S., and Kreps, D. M. "Models in managerial accounting." Supplement to the *Journal of Accounting Research*, 1982.

Hayes, D. C. "The contingency theory of managerial accounting." *Accounting Review*, Jan 1977.

Jacobs, F. H. "An evaluation of the effectiveness of some cost variance investigation models." *Journal of Accounting Research*, spring 1978.

Jensen, M. C. "Organisation theory and methodology." *Accounting Review*, Apr 1983.

Kenis, I. "Effects of budgeting goal characteristics on managerial attitudes and performance." *Accounting Review*, Oct 1979.

Ronen, J. and Livingstone, J. L. "An expectancy theory approach to the motivation impacts of budgets." *Accounting Review*, Oct 1975.

Ross, S. A. "The economic theory of agency: The principles problem." *American Economic Review*, May 1973.

Scapens, R. W., Ryan, R. J., and Fletcher, L. "Explaining corporate failure: A catastrophe theory approach." *Journal of Business Finance and Accounting*, spring 1981.

Weick, K. E. "Stress in accounting systems." *Accounting Review,* Apr 1983.

Index

Details of some other Macdonald & Evans
books on related subjects can be found on
the following pages.
For a full list of titles and prices write for the
FREE Macdonald & Evans Business catalogue
available from: Department BP1, Macdonald &
Evans Ltd., Estover, Plymouth PL6 7PZ

Accountants Guide to the European Communities

DENNIS EVANS

This book provides a much needed guide to the political, economic and financial institutions of the EEC and its member states (including Greece). It covers the organisation and function of the accountancy profession in the different countries, and the statutory and other requirements, including EEC directives, relating to the preparation of accounting information. Designed primarily for students preparing for the SCCA's postgraduate Diploma in European Studies, it will also be most useful to all university and professional students of accountancy and business studies, as well as practising executives, requiring a knowledge of the EEC and its workings. Foreword by Roy Jenkins. ". . . there is certainly more than enough in the book to give the reader a good idea of the rich complexity of the EEC and a better understanding of its policies and institutions." *British Book News*

Bigg's Cost Accounts

J. WALD

First published in 1932, this book has for many years been regarded as a standard work recommended by leading examining bodies throughout the world. However, over the past few years the growing complexity and sophistication of industry and commerce has increased the need for information. This important new edition seeks to reflect such developments and also incorporates the changes in interpretation and definition embodied in the revised ICMA publication *Management Accountancy — Official Terminology*.

Every aspect of cost accountancy, including budgetary control, standard costing, relevant costs and the entry system, are dealt with from the basic principles involved through to the application to the specific field in which the cost accountant is employed.

Throughout the book there are worked examples of the methods and principles studied, together with self-study tests at the ends of chapters which are designed to reflect the trend of recent professional examinations. Outline solutions are given as an appendix to help students check their own progress. Recommended by the Association of Accounting Technicians, The Association of Cost and Executive Accountants and the Institute of Administrative Accountants.

J. Wald is an accountancy lecturer and consultant, and secretary of the Association of Independent Tutors in Accountancy.

"Over the years this cost accounting students' 'Bible' has retained its clarity, and the reader preparing for examinations will obtain from it the necessary basic principles." *The Accountant's Magazine*

Company Accounts

J.O. MAGEE

During recent years company accounting has become more complex in its operations, and the legal requirements of the subject are ever more demanding. The need therefore for a clear yet detailed introduction to the subject is self-evident. This HANDBOOK aims to show the basic principles underlying the main aspects of accountancy in relation to limited companies.

For this third edition the text has been thoroughly revised to cover the requirements of legislation such as the Companies Act 1981 and the latest SSAP issued by the leading accounting bodies, and includes a completely new chapter dealing with inflation accounting. Contents include limited company accounts, profit and reserves, sinking funds, redemption of debentures, redeemable preference shares, accounting requirements of the Companies Act 1981, purchase of a business, company reconstructions, reduction of capital for internal reconstructions, amalgamations and absorptions, sources and applications of funds, consolidated balance sheets, consolidated profit and loss accounts, valuation of shares, inflation accounting. Recommended by the Institute of Administrative Accountants.

Company Secretarial Practice

L. HALL, revised by G.M. THOM

This HANDBOOK has been specifically written to meet the requirements of students preparing for the final examinations of the Institute of Chartered Secretaries and Administrators. It also covers the corresponding syllabus of Polytechnic Diplomas by which students may earn exemption from certain of the Institute's examinations. In addition, students preparing for the Higher Stage Company Secretarial Practice examination of the London Chamber of Commerce and Industry will find it useful supplementary reading.

This revision takes full account of the latest company legislation and much of the material formerly contained in the appendixes is now included in the main body of the text.

Cost Accounting and Budgeting

DAVID C. ASCH

Written to meet the requirements of the BEC National Accounting Technicians Option Module 11, this textbook is designed to provide a thorough understanding of the principles and methods on which cost accounting is based. Giving detailed coverage of the techniques, principles and methods involved in the field of cost accountancy and budgeting, it is also suitable for first-year BEC Higher National Certificate and Diploma courses and will also serve as an introductory text for foundation degree and general business studies courses.

The book begins with a comprehensive description of the aims, techniques and methods of cost accounting in relation to the collection, analysis and ascertainment of costs, and goes on to cover the use of cost information for budgeting, control and decision-making together with the impact of inflation on costs. Each chapter ends with a number of self-assessment questions — many of which have answers provided in an appendix — drawn largely from past professional papers. These serve not only to test the practical knowledge gained from the text but also to extend the student's understanding of the topic under study. One of the BECBOOK series.

Financial and Cost Accounting for Management

A.H. TAYLOR & H. SHEARING

This well established book provides a comprehensive and up-to-date treatment of all those aspects of accounting which business managers need to understand. It is directed not only to established managers seeking comprehensive guidance on these matters but also to those who are studying for the postgraduate Diploma in Management Studies, degrees in business administration, accountancy and other professional qualifications as well as to those on shorter courses in management accountancy.

The authors have assumed no prior knowledge of the subject and in a straightforward practical style examine critically the validity of traditional techniques. The text deals realistically with the topics of financial control techniques and data processing, as well as partnership, company and group accounting, the interpretation of financial data and its use for decision-making. The validity of established accounting practices also comes under critical examination. A number of appendixes include a brief computer glossary and notes on the provision of capital, taxation and inflation accounting.

This latest edition reflects modern developments within the field and takes full account of changes in the business environment such as the world recession, inflation and progress in international trade which have affected accounting techniques. The computerisation of accounting data, changes in UK accounting practice for company mergers and the UK current cost accounting standard are also dealt with, as are developments in accounting legislation, in particular with regard to company law and taxation. Special attention has also been given to small businesses in view of the recent substantial encouragement they have received.

Both authors are Principal Lecturers in Accounting at Ealing College of Higher Education and have wide experience in teaching at undergraduate and postgraduate levels. Their combined professional experience embraces accountancy and senior positions in industry.

Financial Accounting

R. BROCKINGTON

Part of the M&E Higher Business Education series this book aims to bring the student to an appropriate level of practical competence in financial accounting whilst at the same time developing the subject as an academic discipline. It will therefore serve as a basic text, in particular for first and second year students on courses leading to a degree in business studies, accountancy or management, as well as to students of the higher BEC Diploma. It will also be useful to third year students and to those taking professional accounting examinations.

Assuming no previous knowledge, the author approaches the subject through a consideration of the theoretical basis of modern practice, balanced by a detailed analysis of what an accountant does and why he does it. By examining the implicit frame of reference within which accounting operates and exploring the possibilities and consequences of adopting quite different frames, it is hoped that the conflict between theory and practice will provide a gateway to understanding the subject rather than a barrier to progress.

The format of the book is intended to give logical progression to study, although many chapters may be taken out of order.

Management Accountancy
J. BATTY

It is difficult to give an exact definition to the subject of management accountancy — there is still disagreement as to exactly what topics should fall within its scope — but basically it is the blending together into a coherent whole of financial accounting, cost accounting and all aspects of financial management. For this reason the author has, for the purposes of this book, interpreted the subject in its widest sense, including those procedures for raising capital as well as those for reporting to shareholders.

In endeavouring to give adequate coverage to the various subjects which comprise management accountancy, Dr Batty has referred to the syllabuses of the various professional bodies, and past examination questions are included at the end of each chapter.

The student's attention is also drawn to the fact that in questions on management accountancy, the definitive answer does not exist. The accountant strives for objectivity, but facts can be interpreted in many ways, and his task often amounts to reducing the number of interpretations to the minimum, and to put these forward in a way which will assist management to the greatest possible extent.

The book is primarily intended for students preparing for the final examinations of the various accountancy bodies. It will also be useful for students of management and final-year university students studying accountancy as a special subject. The book's practical slant will also assist practising managers and accountants in their planning, control and decision making. ". . . established as the standard textbook for students of the subject." ". . . impressively comprehensive . . . " *Accountancy Age* Recommended by numerous professional bodies, including the Association of Certified Accountants and the Institute of Chartered Secretaries and Administrators.

Managerial Accounting and Finance
J. LEWIS BROWN & LESLIE R. HOWARD

The role of the accountant has changed dramatically in recent years. The strict definitions of his task have been removed, and not only have established areas of operations been greatly developed, but the subjects in which the accountant is expected to perform his duties have expanded.

The concept of accounting information being widely used by management is no longer a revolutionary one, but the extension in the duties undertaken by the managerial accountant has now necessitated a separate specialisation in finance. This is a term used to denote the sphere of company financing operations affecting the stock company's shares and related dealings on the money market. In addition to this, current cost accounting has been formulated in order to cope with the effects of inflation. This allied to the advent of a more sophisticated mathematical analysis in the form of operational research, and the computer revolution, has been reflected in the greater specialisation and wider proficiency demanded of students.

Suitable for students of all the major accounting bodies.

Quantitative Approaches in Business Studies

CLARE MORRIS

Part of the M&E Higher Business Education series this new book aims to provide the student with confidence and proficiency in the use of numerical information as a basis for communication, planning and decision-making in business situations in the same way and with the same ease as they would use verbal information.

The author has in view the needs of students at the higher levels of business studies courses, in particular at BEC HNC/HND level, and first year courses at universities and polytechnics, as well as those working towards professional examinations such as those for the Chartered Insurance Institute, the Institute of Personnel Management, the accountancy bodies and students on post-graduate courses such as the Diploma in Management Studies.

Throughout the book the author has presented each topic simply as a way of utilising numbers to solve business problems. The text is wholly "problem-oriented", each chapter beginning with a realistic business problem the solution of which motivates the development of the content of the chapter. The problem is then re-examined and the usefulness and limitations of the solution are discussed. No previous knowledge is assumed and an introductory "remedial" chapter covers essential basic requirements. Each chapter is then provided with a list of what the reader needs to know so that he can refer back when necessary before proceeding. Throughout exercises are provided not simply as routine calculations to test the knowledge acquired but rather as suggestions for practical student-centred activities, and are followed by further questions providing a basis for more involved assignment-type work. "Businessmen will never have a better opportunity to understand averages, standard deviation, correlation, probability and sampling." *Business Review*

Wheldon's Cost Accounting

L.W.J. OWLER & J.L. BROWN

Previously published as *"Wheldon's Cost Accounting and Costing Methods"*, this textbook — highly successful throughout the world — is recommended by the main professional bodies concerned with cost accounting. Although primarily covering the needs of examinees, it will also be of interest to the practising accountant wishing to expand his knowledge of cost accounting and to the manager wishing to gain an appreciation of cost accounting techniques. This new edition introduces a number of new topics, such as the planning and operational variances approach to the analysis of variances, the investigation of variances and the use of transfer prices in process costing, so as to reflect the change of emphasis in the examinations set by the professional accounting bodies. Bibliographies have been included in appropriate chapters to enable the reader to develop further his knowledge of particular subjects. Extensive use has been made, where relevant, of the latest revision of the ICMA's *Management Accounting Official Terminology*, particularly in the sections on standard costing.

Leonard Owler has had a wide variety of experience both in industry and as a lecturer in cost and management accountancy, management, production methods and statistics.

Lewis Brown has also had a varied experience in industry, and has lectured extensively in the UK and Middle East, specialising in cost and management accounting, business finance and corporate planning. He is currently Lecturer in Management Accounting at the City University Business School, London.

". . . one of the recognised classics on cost accounting." *Management Accounting*

". . . highly recommended for any management accounting paper set by the main accountancy bodies." *The Accountant*